Moral Philosophy at
Seventeenth-Century Harvard

The Institute of
Early American History and Culture
is sponsored jointly by
The College of William and Mary
and The Colonial Williamsburg Foundation.

Norman Fiering

Moral Philosophy at
Seventeenth-Century Harvard
A Discipline in Transition

PUBLISHED FOR THE INSTITUTE OF

EARLY AMERICAN HISTORY AND CULTURE

WILLIAMSBURG, VIRGINIA

BY THE UNIVERSITY OF NORTH CAROLINA PRESS

CHAPEL HILL

For Renée and our children

© 1981 The University of North Carolina Press

Manufactured in the United States of America

Library of Congress Cataloging in Publication Data

Fiering, Norman.
Moral philosophy at seventeenth-century Harvard.

Includes bibliographical references and index.
1. Ethics—United States—History—17th century.
2. Harvard University—Curricula. I. Institute of
Early American History and Culture, Williamsburg, Va.
II. Title.
BJ352.F53   170'.0974   80-18282
ISBN 0-8078-1459-8

Preface

My interest in philosophical ethics was first awakened by Professor Maurice Mandelbaum in an undergraduate lecture course at Dartmouth College some twenty-five years ago. As a graduate student at Columbia University in the early 1960s, my first inclination was to write a thesis on the influence in America of Francis Hutcheson and some other Scottish philosophers of his school. That topic was not abandoned but rather broadened, and the dissertation I eventually completed in 1969 was entitled "Moral Philosophy in America, 1700 to 1750, and Its British Context." This dissertation did contain long chapters on the third earl of Shaftesbury and on Hutcheson, as well as chapters on Henry More and John Locke, but it was also generally concerned with the teaching and study of moral philosophy in America independently of the question of specific influences from overseas.

The origins of the present work, which borrows only in minor ways from my dissertation, cannot be dated precisely, for it is founded on a realization that came to me gradually, namely that I would not be able to write satisfactorily on the history of eighteenth-century ethics without first gaining some mastery of the development of seventeenth-century ethics. The need to study the seventeenth century seemed particularly urgent for the history of moral philosophy in New England, given the enormous influence of the Puritan fathers throughout the colonial period.

The chance to extend my research back into the seventeenth century was given to me by way of a three-year postdoctoral fellowship at the Institute of Early American History and Culture. Most of this book was written between 1969 and 1972 at the Institute. It was revised and supplemented during a year's leave in 1978–1979 at the National Humanities Center in Research Triangle Park, North Carolina. It will perhaps be evident to some of the learned that the book does not take systematic account of related work published by others since 1978 and, in some cases, of work published since 1972. I draw consolation, however, from the thought that the history of American philosophy of the seventeenth century has not been a field buzzingly alive with research activity during the past decade.

By the time I began my year's leave in 1978 I had given up my original grand intention of publishing a continuous history of moral philosophy in colonial America, from the beginnings to the Revolution. The hundreds of pages of manuscript and notes I had collected had become unmanageable when organized as a single work spanning two centuries of thought. I decided therefore to publish two, discrete volumes, each made up of materials excerpted, as it were, from the larger project. The first of these is the present volume. The second, *Jonathan Edwards's Moral Thought and Its British Context*, will appear in the fall of 1981. This book on moral philosophy at seventeenth-century Harvard provides necessary background and support for many of my arguments in the work on Edwards. It is hoped that the two books will be read and used as companion volumes, but they are not in exact sequence and the Edwards book is not a direct continuation of this book.

I have been so generously helped and encouraged by so many people and institutions since my academic career began that it is a pleasure at last to be able publicly to acknowledge some of these debts. It is essential that I mention first the late Professor Eugen Rosenstock-Huessy, whose spiritual and intellectual influence and legacy has been the dominant one in my life since I was first privileged to hear him speak in 1954. There is also much in this book that is a direct outgrowth of what I learned from Harold Steinberg and Leida Berg over a period of years. My mentors in American history at Columbia were Professors Eric McKitrick and Robert Cross, who have been unfailing friends and supporters since those days. During a five-year stint teaching at Stanford University, David Levin and Lewis Spitz were more senior faculty who often gave encouragement, and Jacques Kornberg was a friend with whom I could share my work.

The Institute of Early American History and Culture has been "home" since 1969 and to its professional staff, my colleagues, I am indebted for a multitude of favors—criticism and editing of written work, encouragement, financial aid for research materials and travel, recommendations and introductions, and more. My first Director at the Institute was Stephen G. Kurtz, who was succeeded by Thad W. Tate. One could not ask for more helpful and sympathetic administrators. Lester Cappon in retirement has continued to be a beneficent friend. My fellow editors John E. Selby and Michael McGiffert have been advisors as well as companions.

The manuscript of this book has been read and criticized in whole or part by Murray Murphey, Robert Middlekauff, Bruce Kuklick, John E. Selby, Michael McGiffert, and Walter J. Ong. Chapter 3, which appeared in part as an article in the *William and Mary Quarterly* in 1972, was given particular attention by Thomas P. McTighe and Sacvan Bercovitch. Virtually all of the Latin translations in the book, including the translations of sources not quoted, were done by John Mazaitis. Richard Limburg and Carol Esler also provided

help with translations. Final editing of the manuscript was performed by
David L. Ammerman and, with marvelously scrupulous care, Doris M. Leisch
of the Institute staff. In the course of my research the staff of the Harvard
University Archives, particularly Harley Holden, was consistently helpful.
For all this assistance I am profoundly grateful.

I cannot conclude without acknowledging the constant supportiveness of
my wife Renée over the many years when "my work" in the seventeenth and
eighteenth centuries has taken precedence over the exigencies of life in the
twentieth century.

Contents

Illustrations

Moral Philosophy at
Seventeenth-Century Harvard

The utility of moral and civil philosophy is to be estimated, not so much by the commodities we have by knowing these sciences, as by the calamities we receive from not knowing them.

THOMAS HOBBES

There is no science that stands in so near a relation to us, as Moral Philosophy: which teaches us our *Duties to God* and our King, our Kindred and Friends, and in general to all about us. Besides it points out the way we must follow to become *externally* happy: So that all Men are under an Essential Obligation, or rather an Indispensable Necessity, of resigning themselves to the study of it. Notwithstanding Generations of Men have successively continued for six thousand years, and yet this Science is still very imperfect.

NICOLAS MALEBRANCHE

The study of moral philosophy, how exceedingly beneficial may it be to us, suggesting to us the dictates of reason, concerning the nature and faculties of our soul, the chief good and end of our life, the ways and means of attaining happiness, the best rules and methods of practice; the distinctions between good and evil, the nature of each virtue, and motives to embrace it; the rank wherein we stand in the world, and the duties proper to our relations: by rightly understanding and estimating which things we may know how to behave ourselves decently and soberly toward ourselves, justly and prudently toward our neighbours; we may learn to correct our inclinations, to regulate our appetites, to moderate our passions, to govern our actions, to conduct and wield all our practice well in prosecution of our end; so as to enjoy our being and conveniences of life in constant quiet and peace, with tranquility and satisfaction of mind.

ISAAC BARROW

Introduction

The attention of the eighteenth century to problems in moral philosophy is well known. In both Britain and America questions pertaining to the nature of man, the proper basis of human relations, and the means of acquiring virtue and happiness were central preoccupations of the age. The object of this book is to examine some aspects of the background of this remarkable flourishing of moral philosophy in the eighteenth century. It was apparent to me from the start that very little philosophy was indigenously generated in America, especially during the seventeenth century, but it is possible nevertheless to investigate profitably the study and teaching, and to some extent the writing, of the subject on these shores, however derivative it was.

In the course of my research three themes emerged that clearly deserved and required close treatment. The first theme is predominantly formal and is addressed most directly in the first chapter. It concerns not the internal evolution of the content of academic moral philosophy, but rather the history of the subject as part of the history of the university curriculum in general, with the primary focus being Harvard College in the seventeenth century. What were the origins of the moral philosophy course? What was its relation to Reformed Christianity? What were the justifications for its teaching? Such are the main questions addressed in this first part. Every course in the university curriculum, whether in the seventeenth century or the twentieth century, has a formal history. Disciplines go through phases of expansion and contraction. Some disappear altogether by way of absorption into another discipline that is believed to be more solidly grounded in "reality." Formerly independent and stable courses of study may disintegrate through a process of fission into several other disciplines that as a group supplant their original bearer. Most important, disciplines may retain their old names but be entirely changed in substance. In the case of the formal history of moral philosophy, almost all the kinds of developments that can occur in the history of a discipline may be observed. I will return to this point in more detail later.

The second theme is one that is forced upon any student of seventeenth-century thought. During this period, after a century or more of grumbling dissatisfaction by Humanists, the Scholastic inheritance was decisively rejected, and the mind of the West entered a new era. In logic, in natural philosophy, in metaphysics, and in ethics intellectual changes more profound than any that had occurred before were underway, for it was in the seventeenth century above all that the transition from medievalism to modernism took place. Given that moral philosophy was inextricably intertwined with theological notions, with assumptions about man, with prevailing ideas about nature, and indirectly with the conditions of society and politics, the subject was bound to undergo great upheaval in the seventeenth century, and so it did. To tell the story in all its fullness was, however, beyond my capacities, especially with regard to the bearing of social and cultural change on moral philosophy. My treatment is confined principally to a recounting of the steps by which the Scholastic-Aristotelian approach to ethics was abandoned in favor of newer modes of thought, influenced above all by the Cartesian revolution, broadly conceived. It is a manifest fact that the moral philosophy texts in use at Harvard in 1650 were vastly different from those in use in 1710. Taking that difference as a beginning, I have asked: what precisely were the changes, what was their nature, and, more tentatively, why did they occur?

Before previewing here the third theme, an important caution must be introduced concerning the work as a whole. This is a study above all in the history of philosophy. It is not about the evolution of morality, which is a topic belonging to social and cultural history, and the reader will find here little direct speculation even on the relationship between high-level ethical analysis, which is my primary concern, and practical effects or causes. That a relationship exists I do not doubt. Changes in mores, customs, social attitudes, economic behavior, and political structures unquestionably affect philosophical ethics and in turn are altered to some degree by philosophy, but the subject is simply too large to be treated in the context of the task I have set for myself. It will be seen that the one area of interrelation between thought and behavior that I have addressed is that between ethics and practical psychology. But I have not attempted to move from my conclusions about changes in human psychology to related conclusions about society. And although I take it as a matter of faith that the ideas of, let us say, Descartes may be grounded in broader contexts of change than the history of ideas itself, and that the favorable reception of Descartes's ideas may be explained in part by reference to pre-existing cultural conditions involving society, politics, and economics, I have shrunk from the labor of trying to make these relationships concrete.

Philosophical ethics may be defined as the systematic and critical study of moral experience. It is concerned with questions of definition, meaning, epistemology, psychology, causes, origins, and so on. It is not concerned with specific opinions about behavior or with unanalyzed moral conventions. All of the moralists or ethicists treated in this book were also exhorters to virtue, as were Socrates and Aristotle, for example, but it is not their thought as preachers that I am interested in. My attention is directed to the abstract questions and to critical thought: How may a moral opinion be justified? What are the criteria for moral judgments? What are the foundations in theology, in nature, or in psychology for a system of morals? How is moral knowledge gained or improved? What is the relation in the individual between moral knowledge and conduct? What is the nature of moral knowledge itself?

The third theme addressed in this work is the most specific. It arises from a consideration of the particular developments within the field of moral philosophy in the seventeenth century. I have had an interest for many years in the origins of the so-called sentimentalist school of eighteenth-century British ethics, typified by the philosophical theories of the Scottish moralist Francis Hutcheson. The sentimentalists argued that the source of moral judgments and of moral conduct is in special feelings or affections, rather than in reason or intellect, which at best play a complementary role, and that man is naturally endowed with such moral affections. Hutcheson's work was extremely popular in some circles in America, and it seemed to me that this popularity was based on an inner affinity between sentimentalism and Puritan religious thought. The obvious parallels between Jonathan Edwards's moral philosophy and Hutcheson's, assuming they were developed independently of each other, suggested such an affinity. The problem then became one of searching seventeenth-century moral thought for evidence of inchoate sentimentalism, looking in particular at the theory of the passions in this period and at psychological theories in general. Such evidence was not hard to find, and many pages in this book are devoted to discussions of psychological theory in the context of moral philosophy and to the remarkable transformation in attitudes toward feelings that occurred in the seventeenth century. The repudiation of Classical ethics, Stoic and Aristotelian, was based partly on the failure of those systems to find a positive role for the affections in the life of virtue. The third theme examined then, particularly in chapters 3 and 4, is that of the changing ideas about the role of passions in moral experience.

My assumption is that the rise of sentimentalist ethical theory was the most significant development in the history of ethics between 1675 and 1725. It was not, however, the only development, and the emphasis this subject receives here should not obscure that point. For although Aristotelianism and Stoicism were sharply depreciated in the course of the seventeenth-century revolution in psychology and ethics, important new forms of intellectualist and rationalist ethics were formulated in the same period, with widespread influence on moral thought.[1]

1. In a sequel to the present work I have treated at some length the impact of the new intellectualism. See Fiering, *Jonathan Edwards's Moral Thought and Its British Context* (Chapel Hill, N.C., 1981).

Although this book focuses solely on developments in ethics visible in America, the geographical limitation has not turned out to be a serious impediment to a relatively broad consideration of seventeenth-century thought. For the fact is, little happened in British and Continental intellectual history that did not also have ramifications for American intellectual life. There were, of course, specific circumstances in America (to which I hope I have given adequate attention), but it has been possible, nonetheless, to tell a representative story, a story with implications for the history of Western philosophy in general, not just for American thought. As Samuel Eliot Morison has written, Harvard in the seventeenth century was a "narrow gorge through which a stream of learning, the Arts and Sciences, Philosophies, and Humane Letters, poured from the Old World into New England."[2] One of my chief aims in this book has been to describe and define the emergence of what I call the "new moral philosophy," which was the new discipline that at the end of the seventeenth century supplanted the traditional commentary on Aristotle's *Nicomachean Ethics*. The new moral philosophy was not at all a peculiarly American product, and I believe that the conception presented here of this post-Aristotelian, post-theological discipline is useful for understanding and periodizing the history of British ethics no less than American. The new moral philosophy was an amalgam of elements from Protestant divinity, Augustinian and Cartesian psychology, and Neoplatonism, as well as from traditional Classical and Scholastic ethics. It was a subject broader and richer in scope and depth than that which had been taught since the Middle Ages as moral philosophy, and the new moral philosophy had a fruitful history until its eventual dissolution in the nineteenth century into a variety of separate components.

It is possible, then, to speak of three main stages in the trajectory of Western moral philosophy: the medieval or formative stage, when the subject was closely tied to its Classical origins and also limited by church restraints, both Catholic and Protestant; the stage of the new moral philosophy, beginning in the late seventeenth century and continuing into the nineteenth century, when the subject became autonomous and soared far beyond Classical speculation, absorbing also many ideas that had originated in religious and theological discourse; and finally, the disintegrative stage, when the new moral philosophy broke down into several individual fields of study, mainly the nineteenth-century social sciences and the technical ethics of academic philosophy, which were quite different from the elements that had gone into the formation of the middle stage. In this book I deal only with the first two phases, and particularly with the transition to the second stage.

A few of the distinguishing characteristics of the new moral philosophy can

---

2. Samuel Eliot Morison, *The Founding of Harvard College* (Cambridge, Mass., 1935), v.

be mentioned here in anticipation of discussions later in the book. The new subject was naturalistic in method, as compared to Christian philosophical anthropology, and much more psychologically oriented than Classical ethics. It was both normative and descriptive in complex interplay because one of the prevailing ideas of the time was that the empirical and introspective study of human nature and human relations would itself lead to absolute standards or norms for moral conduct. It was generally theistic in outlook and took for granted that immutable divine law was as discoverable in ethics as it was in physics. It was engaged with practical life almost as a matter of faith, because nearly everyone fervently believed that nothing in life could be more important than conduct in accordance with virtue. It was democratic and universalist in the sense that exclusive forms of moral achievement, whether aristocratic or religious, were eschewed as being hardly worth comment. Finally, it was extraordinarily comprehensive in its interests, radiating outward from the intensive study of man to concern with religion, society, politics, and economics.

One of the main implications of this book is that eighteenth-century moral philosophy is not properly regarded as merely a revival of Classical ethics, but should be seen as a new development that incorporated, sometimes rather subtly, a Christian heritage. Yet at the same time there is no doubt that the study of the ancients went on intensively. Indeed, it would be fair to say that relatively few philosophical arguments introduced in seventeenth- and eighteenth-century British ethics did not have parallels in Classical discussions of ethics two thousand years before. "So fully and clearly are all the principles and doctrines of morality explained in the writings of the ancient moralists," the Scottish moral philosopher George Turnbull wrote in 1740, "that there is no conclusion, and almost no reasoning, in any of the best modern writers upon morality and natural religion, that is not to be found in some ancient philosopher, if not in all of them."[3] And William Guthrie wrote in the preface to his 1755 translation of Cicero's *De Officiis*, that "it is to Cicero that we owe what is most valuable in Grotius, in Puffendorf, in Cumberland, in Wollaston, and Hundreds of other Writers."[4] But such opinions did not go unchallenged in the seventeenth and eighteenth centuries, and I believe that they are only partly valid. Eighteenth-century moralists did not themselves always know where their ideas had come from, and there were reasons in an "enlightened" age for blindly ignoring the influences of Christian anthropology. In any case, "the defects of heathen morality" is a topic

---

3. George Turnbull, *The Principles of Moral Philosophy: An Enquiry into the Wise and Good Government of the Moral World* (London, 1740), 431.

4. M. T. Cicero, *His Offices* . . . , trans. William Guthrie (London, 1755), preface.

treated below at length with regard to seventeenth-century thought, and in general the confrontation of pagan and Christian moral thought will be frequently adverted to in the ensuing chapters.

I have had the good fortune in writing this book of being able to rely for much information on two masterpieces of American historiography: Samuel Eliot Morison's three volumes on Harvard College in the seventeenth century and Perry Miller's two volumes on the New England mind.[5] But neither of these works anticipates to any degree the contents of the present book. In the course of his superb reconstruction of Harvard in all of its aspects in this early period, Morison necessarily could devote only a few pages to the study of moral philosophy. For obvious reasons, he did not attempt to look at any of the disciplines in detail, and yet for each of them a separate, full story might be told.

Perry Miller's great work, on the other hand, was deficient for my purposes on broader grounds. Miller's interests lay more with the religious mind than with the philosophical (if we define the latter rather strictly). To some extent, because New England intellectual culture was highly religious, the distinction is inoperative, yet the difference I am referring to may be illustrated by a single, large example. It makes sense in Miller's terms to speak of the decline of Puritanism, meaning a decline in the New England "way," a breakup of the unity of clergy and society, a drift toward secularism, the fracturing of the comparatively unified social and political point of view that was behind the Great Migration of the 1630s. In the history of philosophy, however, it is not usual to speak of "declines," because the historian of philosophy is interested in following the path of a single thread, or several threads, rather than the transformation of an entire culture. In this work I pay considerable attention to the "decline," or the transformation, of Scholasticism and the Aristotelian inheritance in ethics, a focus that may give the appearance of being comparable to Miller's. But instead of looking at this process in connection with the dissolution of the Puritan frame of mind, I am interested in the Aristotelian tradition in ethics, as it was expressed at Harvard, as a chapter in the history of ethics. Moreover, knowing as we do that the investigation of ethics or moral philosophy has had a more or less continuous history in the West since the time of Socrates, it would be absurd to characterize the decline of Aristotelianism as some sort of demise when in the next century, the age of Hume and Kant, the study of ethics reached unprecedented heights. My goal, then, contrary to

5. Morison, *Founding of Harvard*; Morison, *Harvard College in the Seventeenth Century*, 2 vols. (Cambridge, Mass., 1936), hereafter cited as Morison, *Seventeenth-Century Harvard*; Perry Miller, *The New England Mind: The Seventeenth Century* (Cambridge, Mass., 1954), hereafter cited as Miller, *New England Mind*, I; and Miller, *The New England Mind: From Colony to Province*, 2d ed. (Cambridge, Mass., 1953), hereafter cited as Miller, *New England Mind*, II.

Miller's far more comprehensive scheme, is to trace the study of moral philosophy in the seventeenth century as a prelude to the next age, an age that can hardly be interpreted as a diminution from the preceding one from the point of view of moral philosophy itself.

Finally, it may not be out of place here to reflect on the question of the contemporary influence of the high-level ideas discussed in this book. It should be noted, first of all, that moral philosophy in the seventeenth and eighteenth centuries was not yet the technical academic subject it was to become in the later nineteenth century. Much of the writing of it was, in fact, done by clergymen and others outside colleges and universities.[6] However, it is true that a good deal of learning and acuteness was required before one could participate importantly in the ongoing debates, and there is no doubt that the history of the subject is the history of the ideas of an elite group. In addition, in seventeenth-century America virtually no philosophy at all was being taught or written (and hardly any read) outside the peripheries of Harvard College, which makes the subject still narrower. Yet it would be a mistake, I believe, to underestimate the indirect influence even on the popular mind of what was taught at the college. "A College in a new Country," William Livingston pointed out in 1753, will "more or less influence every Individual amongst us, and diffuse its Spirit thro' all Ranks, Parties and Denominations."[7] Certain of the intellectual assumptions gained at college remain with one for life and are passed on to others, who may not have gone to college, in innumerable ways. It is at least arguable, therefore, that to understand the academic discipline of moral philosophy in colonial America is to come close to understanding some of the primary elements of thought at all levels of society.

6. For example, both Benjamin Franklin and James Logan in 18th-century Philadelphia wrote fairly extensively on moral philosophy, although neither one had been to college.

7. Livingston, in *The Independent Reflector* . . . , ed. Milton M. Klein (Cambridge, Mass., 1963 [orig. publ. New York, 1753]), 421.

I

The Question of Autonomy
for Natural Ethics

There are some very unwise Things done,
about which I must watch for opportunities,
to bear public Testimonies.
One is, the Employing so much Time upon Ethicks,
in our Colledges. A vile Peece of Paganism.[1]

"Then there is [Aristotle's] 'Ethics,' " Martin Luther complained, "which is accounted one of the best, but no book is more directly contrary to God's will and the Christian virtues. Oh, that such books could be kept out of the reach of all Christians!"[2] There speaks an authentic Christian voice. It would make matters simple if we could take such a pronouncement as the sole authentic Christian expression. But the case is more complex. Luther's opinion was only one type of a wide variety of responses that pagan moral thought provoked from Church spokesmen. From the earliest centuries of Christianity until well into the nineteenth century the vexatious issue of the proper relation of Christian virtues and the Christian life to pagan moral ideals inspired debate, until finally Humanist classicism began to lose its force, leaving only post-Christian secular philosophies and moral indifference for the Church to contend with.

Everyone is familiar with the old notion, now recognized as erroneous, of a historical "war" between religion and science. The deficiencies of this notion lie in the inaccuracy of describing a complex relationship in terms of war alone, when sometimes there was peace, sometimes coexistence, sometimes harmony, and sometimes mere confusion. The "opposition" between Western religion and pagan ethics was similar. Attempts were made to annihilate pagan ethics in the name of Christian divinity and biblicism, but there were

---

1. June 28, 1716, *Diary of Cotton Mather*, II, *1709–1724* (Massachusetts Historical Society, *Collections*, 7th Ser., VIII [Boston, 1912]), 357, hereafter cited as *Diary of Cotton Mather*.

2. Luther, *To the Christian Nobility* (Wittenburg, 1520).

also attempts by avowed Christians to harmonize the two, attempts to evade the issue, and—long before the vogue of natural religion in the eighteenth century—even attempts to supplant Christian moral revelation with pagan, or what was thought to be pagan, wisdom.

Pagan Moral Thought and Christian Education

The specific problem of the place of ethics in college curricula through the centuries was necessarily inseparable from the more general question of how pagan ethics was fitted into the whole matrix of Christian teachings. The very existence of Classical moral philosophy as a subject for study depended largely upon various assumptions in Christian theology. What the limits of moral philosophy were to be, what it was to encompass in its investigations, was in inverse relation to the expansiveness of Christian teaching. When theology asserted the breadth and absolute exclusiveness of its doctrines over such concerns as the delineation of the foundations of right and wrong, the definition of the goals of life, the establishment of the true human ideal, and the best means of discovering or attaining these and other ends, and at the same time stifled speculation and critical examination, moral philosophy as such was largely excluded or nullified. When religious influence was lax, apathetic, constrained, or divided, moral philosophy was likely to flourish.

The most noticeable characteristic of the troubled history of the relationship of Christianity to pagan moral thought is its repetitiousness. Most of the basic possibilities and differences had already been enunciated by the church fathers and pagan apologists before the fifth century, and all were reiterated in various forms in the thirteenth century, in the fifteenth century, and in the eighteenth century. Distilled here into simple formulas, the recurrent questions were such as these: What is the best way of distinguishing Classical and Christian ethics? What are the uses, if any, of Classical ethics for Christians? What is the exact nature of the superiority of Christian ethics? To what extent do the ideas and sentiments of admittedly sublime figures like Pythagoras, Plato, Cicero, and Seneca anticipate Christian ethics? To what extent did the great pagan moralists borrow from Hebraic revelation? (This problem was actively studied until late in the eighteenth century.) How can the traditions be harmonized? In what ways are they utterly incompatible? Clearly, very great matters were at stake in the answers to these questions. Indeed, the whole significance and value of the Judaeo-Christian revelation rested on how they were answered.

From the beginning there was no serious possibility of ignoring Classical culture and pretending that the Church could be sufficient unto herself. Christianity began as a specific faith in the midst of Hellenistic culture, including the Hebraic. It had no intellectual culture of its own. Its increasingly self-conscious task was to forge a new civilization making use of the ingredients of the past plus its own vision. When Tertullian at the end of the second century uttered his famous dismissal of the pagan inheritance, "What has Athens to do with Jerusalem, the Academy with the Church!" he proposed a course of action not only undesirable but impossible.[3] Greco-Roman moral thought represented a shining and fascinating achievement that could not be ignored. As was repeatedly noted in later centuries, even St. Paul had recognized the impressive capacities of natural men in Romans 2:14–15: "When Gentiles who do not possess the law carry out its precepts by the light of nature, then, although they have no law, they are their own law, for they display the effect of the law inscribed on their hearts." The problem for Christian writers in later centuries was how to put natural moral knowledge into proper perspective.

Five broad solutions to the problem of the reconcilement of "natural" moral philosophy and Christian education are found most in evidence over the centuries. These five are not necessarily logically independent of one another, but they were often independently stated; nor is this an exhaustive list, although it is exemplary. For convenience we will label these solutions as follows: the arguments from (1) Christian hegemony; (2) common grace; (3) history; (4) disparity; and (5) practical morality.

1. The argument from Christian hegemony refers to the fruitful, pragmatic position adopted by St. Augustine, and used continuously after him, that justified exploitation of pagan cultural resources in the interest of higher purposes. Augustine declared that it was perfectly acceptable for Christians, like the ancient Hebrews, to "spoil the Egyptians," as in Exodus 3:22 and 12:35, that is, to carry off the cultural riches of the Classical world, provided only that it be done for the fulfillment of Christian ends.[4] The dramatic story of Augustine's own conversion, which took place with the aid of, not despite, Cicero and Plato, was eloquent validation of this approach. The argument was frequently used in the seventeenth century. The moderate Anglican clergyman Edward Reynolds, for example, preaching a sermon in 1657 on "The Use of Humane Learning," stated that "truth is God's where ever it is found. . . . As Israel took of the Egyptians Jewels of Silver, and Jewels of Gold; as David consecrated the Spoils of the Philistins, Moabites, Syrians, and all Nations whom he subdued to the Lord . . . , so the spoils of all secular Learning are to be dedicated to Christ, and the use of his Church."[5] To some extent this reasoning rested philosophically upon the idea that follows.

3. See Charles Norris Cochrane's masterpiece, *Christianity and Classical Culture: A Study of Thought and Action from Augustus to Augustine* (Oxford, 1940), especially chap. 6. H. Richard Niebuhr, *Christ and Culture* (New York, 1951) provides a general discussion of the problem.

4. Augustine, *On Christian Doctrine*, trans. D. W. Robertson, Jr. (Indianapolis, Ind., 1958), Bk. II, sec. xl.

5. In Reynolds, *The Works of . . . Edward Reynolds . . .* (London, 1678–1679), 884. To cite

2. The concept of common grace as a technical matter in theology is laden with difficulties. It refers generally to the universal blessings of God, as distinguished from special supernatural grace, which is bestowed more narrowly. Here we are using the term "common grace" only as a convenience to signify the wide spectrum of ideas in Christian thought that have attributed to the natural man certain primary moral capacities, which, divinely given in themselves, must be respected. John Calvin, who was a Humanist scholar before he became a theologian, believed that the knowledge of *all* that is "most excellent in human life," however secular or ostensibly natural, is communicated to us through "the Spirit of God." There is no reason for anyone to ask, Calvin said, "What have the impious, who are utterly estranged from God, to do with this Spirit?" God "fills, moves, and quickens all things by the power of the same Spirit, and does so according to the character that he bestowed upon each kind by the law of creation. . . . If the Lord has willed that we be helped in physics, dialectic, mathematics, and other like disciplines, by the work and ministry of the ungodly, let us use this assistance." The development of the arts of learning over the course of time testifies to "a universal apprehension of reason and understanding by nature implanted in men." The mind of man, "though fallen and perverted from its wholeness, is nevertheless clothed and ornamented with God's excellent gifts," Calvin continued, and to despise truth when found in secular writers is to "dishonor the Spirit of God." We cannot deny that the truth "shone upon the ancient jurists who established civic order and discipline with such great equity," no less than it shone upon natural scientists, mathematicians, physicians, and so on.[6]

The argument from common grace as I have used it here includes also the vast Natural Law tradition. Roman Catholic theologians in particular, led by St. Thomas Aquinas, had the greatest respect for natural human ability and accepted the possibility of discovery and development in moral knowledge as well as in other areas. The Lutheran Reformation reacted powerfully against this trend, but among some Calvinists and especially in the Anglican church, the essential Thomist structure was preserved.[7] Bishop Lancelot Andrewes,

one more example out of hundreds, the English translators of Peter de la Primaudaye's *The French Academie*, 2d ed. (London, 1598), in defense of La Primaudaye's use of pagan moral literature, quoted Augustine on Egyptian gold in their preface (p. 6).

6. Calvin, *Institutes of the Christian Religion*, ed. John T. McNeill, trans. Ford Lewis Battles (Philadelphia, 1960), Bk. II, chap. ii, secs. 12–17, hereafter cited as Calvin, *Institutes*, II, ii, 12–17. See also, Quirinus Breen, *John Calvin: A Study in French Humanism*, 2d ed. ([Hamden, Conn.], 1968), 150–179.

7. Olive M. Griffiths, *Religion and Learning: A Study in English Presbyterian Thought from the Bartholemew Ejections (1662) to the Foundation of the Unitarian Movement* (Cambridge, 1935), 94*ff*; Thomas Cuming Hall, *History of Ethics within Organized Christianity* (London and New York, 1910); H. R. McAdoo, *The Structure of Caroline Moral Theology* (London, 1949), 17; Eugene F. Rice, Jr., *The Renaissance Idea of Wisdom* (Cambridge, Mass., 1958), 124*ff*.

highly influential in early seventeenth-century England, typically argued that the Fall hurt, bruised, and soiled the soul, but it did not totally destroy natural moral understanding. Man is far gone from original righteousness, but he is not an outlaw. Even Luther's colleague, the Humanist Philip Melanchthon, made use of the old Scholastic defense of natural moral reason in his ethics textbook. Though he essentially agreed with Luther that "philosophy" and the Gospel must never be confused, Melanchthon also maintained that "the blurred impress of the law of God" survived as a remnant from before the Fall and is valuable in dealing with moral questions.[8] The modern church historian Ernst Troeltsch has described Melanchthon as the "Protestant doctor of Natural Law." Melanchthon strove so hard to reconcile "the Lutheran tension between the Law and Christianity, between Reason and Revelation," Troeltsch wrote, that the original enmity was ultimately merged in "the idea of a friendly harmony which has been divinely ordained."[9] Melanchthon's position regarding rationally derived moral knowledge was roughly similar to St. Thomas Aquinas's earlier and Richard Hooker's or Lancelot Andrewes's a little later. It should be noted, however, that explicitly incorporated in this theory was the reservation that *recta ratio*, or that "right reason" by which Natural Law is known, is inadequate, without the aid of scriptural revelation, to attain *complete* moral truth; nonetheless, no fundamental disharmony was assumed to exist between the best moral philosophy and Christian theology.[10]

It is important to emphasize that, practically speaking, the place reserved for natural reason in moral thought was largely occupied by Aristotle, with a little additional space made for Seneca and Cicero. The invocation of the doctrine of common grace (as we have interpreted it here) was not intended to be an invitation to original critical thought in ethics, to the blooming of a thousand different flowers. The purpose of the doctrine was rather to explain the achievement of the best pagan philosophy and to authorize its study.

3. The third defense of the study and use of pagan moral philosophy was quite different from both the notion of common grace and the principle of Christian hegemony. This argument rested on the widely held historical thesis that behind the best pagan writings was the influence of the "ancient theology" (*prisca theologia*) that originated with Moses.[11] The Greek father Origen was possibly the first to argue that Christians need feel no shame in

8. Hall, *History of Ethics*, 496–504. See also, J. T. McNeill, "Natural Law in the Teaching of the Reformers," *Journal of Religion*, XXVI (1946), 168–182.

9. Troeltsch, *The Social Teaching of the Christian Churches*, trans. Olive Wyon (London and New York, 1960 [orig. publ. Tübingen, 1912]), II, 467–477, 503–515, 523–540.

10. Vernon J. Bourke, *History of Ethics* (Garden City, N.Y., 1968), chap. 6, brings together excellently the "right reason" theories prominent between 1200 and 1500.

11. See D. P. Walker, "The *Prisca Theologia* in France," *Journal of the Warburg and Courtauld Institutes*, XVII (1954), 204–259.

borrowing from the Classical heathen authors because these writers were themselves direct or indirect imitators of the Bible! Christians were simply taking back from the pagans what was never truly theirs.[12] Others of the church fathers, including Augustine, also contributed to this tradition.[13] A millennium and a half later the American moral philosopher Samuel Johnson of Stratford, Connecticut, expressed this same belief in the influence of the "ancient theology" while reassuring a troubled correspondent that Johnson's own book on ethics had not strayed as far from revealed sources as might appear. The conviction that the great Greek philosophers were hardly more than plagiarists of Moses in some of their opinions was widely current in the seventeenth century, especially among the Cambridge Platonists. Many Americans who believed in the *prisca theologia* were no doubt influenced by Theophilus Gale's *Court of the Gentiles* (1669–1677), which was in part devoted to proving that thesis.[14]

The defense of pagan moral philosophy based on the tradition of the *prisca theologia* had one major advantage over the argument from common grace: it permitted one to continue to believe that the Fall of Man was deeply destructive to human moral ability. Pagan knowledge of fundamental ethical principles was explained not as a triumph of natural reason but as the result of the transmission of Mosaic revelation to the early Greek philosophers. Thus the dogma of innate depravity was preserved without dilution.

4. The theory of common grace, which found in all men at least the remnants of right reason and the spark of a natural inclination to the good, was based on the assumption that there are degrees of sacred knowledge. The model implies a vertical framework ascending upward from common understanding to the esoteric truths of divine revelation. The fourth form of accommodation between moral philosophy and Christian theology, while not excluding the belief in a hierarchy of knowledge, attempted rather to compartmentalize natural and supernatural sources of knowledge along horizontal lines of outer and inner. Natural knowledge was suitable for guiding the outer man, but for inner guidance and reformation supernatural revelation was a necessity. I have not found the original propounder of this scheme, but it is apparent that both Italian Renaissance concepts of civic virtue and responsibility and also, in a different way, Reformation pietism and sectarianism contributed to it. In the *Epitome Doctrinae Moralis* of Theophilus Golius

12. Philippe Delhaye, *Christian Philosophy in the Middle Ages* (London, 1960), 45. Origen may himself have been borrowing from the claims made by Josephus in the lst century.

13. See Augustine, *Christian Doctrine*, trans. Robertson, II, xxviii.

14. Johnson to Benjamin Colman, June 12, 1746, in Herbert Schneider and Carol Schneider, eds., *Samuel Johnson, President of King's College: His Career and Writings* (New York, 1929), II, 326. Johnson's contemporary Jonathan Edwards was also a convinced believer in the *prisca theologia*. On Gale in America, see chap. 6, below.

(1592), which was one of the Aristotelian ethics texts used at seventeenth-century Harvard, ethics is defined as "the doctrine or teaching concerning the establishment of *external* behavior and actions according to virtue," and Cicero's *De finibus* is cited.[15] Though natural ethics is imperfect by Christian standards, Golius wrote, it is useful for civil life (*civilis vita*). Bartholomaeus Keckermann (1571–1608), a popular authority on many subjects for early New England scholars, made a similar distinction: "Theology is concerned with the absolute, with virtues and the spiritual grace that lead to eternal felicity, while Ethics is concerned with practical civic and social virtues, which may exist even under an infidel government where the true Word is unknown. Civic virtues, although incomplete without divine grace, are none the less real virtues, as dawn is real light."[16]

Speaking as an apologist for secular learning, the great German theorist of Natural Law Samuel Pufendorf described the compartmentalization as follows: "The Law of Nature considered in itself is shut up within the bounds of this life, tending only to render man *sociable*; while the end of *Moral Theology* is to form the Christian, that is, a man who ought indeed to live here below honestly and peaceably, but who nevertheless expects the principal rewards of his Piety after this life."[17] This solution by division or disparity was doomed to be unstable, however, for it did justice neither to the vigor of Christian ideas in the outer realm of society and politics, nor to the potency of secular ethics in the service of personal reformation and inner fulfillment. In addition, the distinction between internal and external failed to recognize the long history of interpenetration between pagan and Christian thought in both spheres of life, which inevitably made any neatly drawn lines superficial. The temporary success of such a distinction depended in part upon keeping academic ethics as innocuous as possible by teaching an emasculated Aristotle and avoiding all areas of potential confrontation with Christian presuppositions. In other words, the potentiality of the two systems for real rivalry was necessarily minimized by this concept of the nice complementarity of pagan moral philosophy and Christian doctrine.

Notwithstanding these criticisms, this alleged disparity between pagan and Christian morals, based upon the difference between external duties and inner dispositions, captured a real difference in emphasis, for what was most origi-

15. In the original, "*de externis moribus & actionum.*" Golius, *Epitome doctrinae moralis, ex decem libris ethicorum Aristotelis* . . . (Cambridge, 1634 [orig. publ. Strasbourg, 1592]), 21. Italics added.

16. Quoted in Morison, *Seventeenth-Century Harvard*, 260. For another example from 1645, see A.S.P. Woodhouse, ed., *Puritanism and Liberty: Being the Army Debates (1647–9) from the Clarke Manuscripts* . . . (Chicago, 1951), 247–248.

17. Quoted in Henry Grove, *A System of Moral Philosophy*, ed. Thomas Amory (London, 1749), 56. This work was published posthumously.

nal and even unique in Judaeo-Christian ethics was its focus on the inner man and his development.[18] Aristotle, it might be said, was better at describing statesmen than saints. Although the Classical and civic Humanist concern with training citizens for duties in state and society survived healthily enough in the seventeenth and eighteenth centuries, the most arresting and novel trend in moral philosophy in this period encouraged the subordination of merely external rectitude to standards of inwardness derived from Christian "anthropology" and psychology. When the Scholastic walls between natural ethics and Reformed theology crumbled in the seventeenth century, under the impact of both evangelical pietism and scientific naturalism, the concept of a separate ethics for each the inner and the outer man was no longer tenable. The resulting amalgam at the end of the seventeenth century, which we have referred to in the introduction as the "new moral philosophy," was in part a blend of Christian anthropology and the Classical tradition in ethics.

5. The final rationale for the teaching of Classical ethics that must be mentioned was less a theory than a matter of academic expediency. Like the theory of compartmentalization or disparity just described, this rationale called for a tempered and restrained moral philosophy. The argument was simply that insofar as the teaching of moral philosophy slipped over into moral training it was beneficial and ought to be part of the curriculum. We get a taste of this reasoning in a statute from the University of Caen in 1495. Caen assured a heavy dose of moral philosophy through regular public lectures on the *Nicomachean Ethics*, and in order "that scholars in the future may have greater reason and occasion for proficiency in moral philosophy, *which is especially useful to youths*, their respective teachers [other than the public lecturer] shall be required to go over the same books of moral philosophy with their scholars in their own house . . . before it is lectured on publicly."[19] The reference to the usefulness of moral philosophy for youths—when both Plato and Aristotle had held on the contrary that it was a subject suitable primarily for mature men—suggests that when ethics was taught in universities up until almost the twentieth century, it invariably shaded into moral exhortation, and

18. See the early essay by Arthur O. Lovejoy, "The Origins of Ethical Inwardness in Jewish Thought," *American Journal of Theology*, XI (1907), 228–249. The substance of this article concerns the anticipation of Jesus's teaching by some passages in Hellenistic "Wisdom literature." Lovejoy takes it for granted, however, that in Judaeo-Christian moral thought there is "an appreciation of the inner springs of conduct, and a sense of subjective 'sin'—that the Greek mind scarcely ever attained." The emphasis on "motive as contrasted with act," and the conception of "the morally supreme thing in the experiences of life as consisting, not in the deeds done before men, but in the progressive purification of the inner life before the searching judgment of a Father 'which seeth in secret' " is a distinctive Judaeo-Christian contribution.

19. Lynn Thorndike, ed., *University Records and Life in the Middle Ages* (New York, 1944), 369–370. My italics.

moral exhortation not only was necessary for college students (until the nineteenth century generally several years younger than present-day college students), but satisfied also the concerns of administrators, parents, the church,
and society. The ethics course conveniently served the dual purpose of training
students in a particular philosophical art while offering excellent opportunity
for regular moral preaching. Yet, at the same time, moral philosophy was not
expected to be so aggressively presented as to pose an alternative system of
values to that enjoined by the Christian church.

We can give two brief examples (one English, the other American) of
seventeenth-century treatments of the relation of secular ethics to Christianity
that incorporate some of the arguments we have already seen and also tell us
something about early Harvard. Edward Reyner (b. 1600) was the founder
of a dissenting academy at Lincoln, England, shortly after the Restoration.
Reyner introduced three points in defense of secular moral science. It makes
plain, he said, "that the *Moral Law* of God is written naturally in the Heart,
seeing divers of the Heathen, who were amiably and laudably moral, were
never by grace elevated above Nature." Secondly, it shows "what *Dictates*
and *Doctrines* even *Nature* teacheth men." And, finally, pagan ethics can
"*shame Christians*, who enjoy Means of Grace, the light of the Gospel, yet
come very short of even Heathen men in Moral Virtues."[20] Reyner's first
point is evidently a commentary on Romans 2:14–15. The second refers to
the important problem of accurately distinguishing the gifts of nature and the
gifts of special grace. His last point significantly brings in the practical rather
than the theoretical benefits of the study of ethics and adds a fresh twist to the
motivation we observed behind the University of Caen statute of 1495.[21]

The dissenting academies, as Samuel Eliot Morison has demonstrated, in
some ways had more in common with seventeenth-century Harvard than did
Oxford and Cambridge, and arguments similar to Reyner's can be found in

20. Reyner, *A Treatise of the Necessity of Humane Learning* . . . (London, 1663), edited and
published posthumously by his son, John Reyner, who succeeded him at Lincoln Academy,
quoted by J. W. Ashley Smith, *The Birth of Modern Education: The Contribution of the Dissenting Academies, 1660–1800* (London, 1954), 27. A copy of Reyner's *Treatise* was in Increase
Mather's library in 1664. See Julius Herbert Tuttle, "The Libraries of the Mathers," American
Antiquarian Society, *Proceedings*, N.S., XX (1909–1910), 289. On the resemblances between
the dissenting academies and Harvard, see Morison, *Seventeenth-Century Harvard*, 166.

21. In the *Institutes*, II, ix, 5, Calvin remarked that Christians fearful of death should blush
with shame when they see the contempt of death that the pagan philosophers displayed. This
ironic slant, that corrupt Christians to their shame must be taught by the best of the heathens, was
commonly adopted. Roger L'Estrange defended his translation of Seneca (1678) as follows: "In
[the present] state of Corruption, who so fit as a good honest *Christian Pagan* for a Moderator
among *Pagan-Christians*?" Quoted in Meyer Reinhold, ed., *The Classick Pages: Classical
Reading of Eighteenth-Century Americans* (University Park, Pa., 1975), 73. Seneca in particular
was pointed to for the purpose of shaming.

America at about the same time. Perry Miller has noted that, in general, "the progression from classical morality to Christian ethics was a natural one for the Puritan, and the education which he insisted should be prerequisite to preaching the Christian gospel included Plato, Seneca, and Plutarch as well as Augustine and William Ames."[22]

The second example is from America, Harvard President Charles Chauncy's commencement sermon in 1655: *"God's Mercy, Shewed to His People in Giving Them a Faithful Ministry and Schooles of Learning for the Continual Supplyes Thereof."*[23] In this address Chauncy was responding to current sentiments even more radically anti-intellectual and anti-Classical than those expressed by Luther 125 years earlier, specifically to William Dell's *The Tryal of Spirits . . .* (London, 1653). Dell and several other antinomian sectarians in England called for an exclusively scriptural education for ministers, relying on the "mere motion of spirit" to accomplish the usual ends of learning. So serious was this onslaught that some observers feared the universities would be destroyed.[24] In his sermon, which was in effect a defense of the curriculum at Harvard, Chauncy noted first that even in Scripture there are "some testimonies out of humane writers, as *Tit*: 1.12. *Acts* 17.28. I *Cor*: 15.33.," which would not be there if God had intended the study of humane writers to be unlawful. Second, "there are certain principles of trueth written, even in corrupt nature, which heathen authors have delivered unto us, that doe not cross the holy writ," and "it cannot be denied that all trueth, whosoever it be that speakes it, comes from the God of truth." Who can deny, Chauncy asked, "but that there are found many excellent and divine morall truths in Plato, Aristotle, Plutarch, Seneca etc."[25]

Chauncy also took issue with the even more extreme view that anathematized not just pagan authors but the very organization of the disciplines. According to this position, theology or divinity should be the only academic art, and grammar, rhetoric, logic, and ethics should be thrown out. But this would include the very "grounds of languages," like Latin, Greek, and Hebrew, Chauncy rejoined, necessary among other things for the study of the Bible, and besides, Chauncy asked, does not Scripture itself teach us some

22. Miller, *New England Mind*, I, 98.

23. An excerpt, from which I am quoting, is printed in Perry Miller and Thomas H. Johnson, eds., *The Puritans*, rev. ed. (New York, 1963), 704–707.

24. Richard Schlatter, "The Higher Learning in Puritan England," *Historical Magazine of the Protestant Episcopal Church*, XXIII (1954), 167. See also, Miller, *New England Mind*, I, 74–77, and especially the bibliography of this controversy over higher learning in England on p. 508; and Barbara J. Shapiro, "The Universities and Science in Seventeenth Century England," *Journal of British Studies*, X (1970–1971), 65.

25. Morison, *Seventeenth-Century Harvard*, 326, describes Chauncy as "an enthusiast for humane letters," which, of course, does not imply that Chauncy lacked anything in his devotion to religion. Chauncy assumed the presidency of Harvard in 1654.

"natural Philosophy?" One could retain the Bible as the foundation of all truth, Chauncy believed, and find in it still the bases for the various disciplines. "Ethicall, Politicall, or Morall precepts . . . are to be found in holy Scriptures," Chauncy observed. In short, even within the admittedly pagan framework of the so-called liberal arts, the curriculum can still without difficulty be heavily weighted with Christian teaching.[26]

A similar balance of natural and supernatural, Classical and Christian, may be found in the student disputations of the time. Two Harvard commencement *quaestiones* from the seventeenth century taken together reveal the poles between which moral philosophy had to find its niche. In 1663 Simon Bradstreet responded affirmatively to the question, "Whether the distinction between good and evil is known by the Law of Nature?" (*An discrimen boni et mali a lege Naturae cognoscatur?*) But, as though to balance the issue, eleven years later in 1674 John Bowles argued the negative of the question, "Whether natural theology is sufficient for salvation?" (*An Datur Theologia Naturalis ad Salutem Sufficiens?*)[27]

To summarize thus far, moral philosophy figured prominently in the controversial relationship between pagan thought and Christian culture for several reasons: (1) it was a discipline with indisputably pagan origins; (2) Christianity was itself deeply concerned with moral attainments and moral knowledge, which made it a rival of moral philosophy; and, finally (3) unlike some other parts of the Classical inheritance, such as logic, grammar, and rhetoric, moral philosophy could not easily be regarded as merely a propaedeutic study. Christian leaders were thus faced with a complex problem, one which called for accommodation. As John Flavel, the English Puritan writer, summarized the issue in the 1680s, the contributions of philosophy "are too great to be despised, and too small to be admired."[28]

The historian of higher education must always be wary of confusing the *theory* behind the curriculum at any given time with actual pedagogical

26. Cf. Richard Bernard's *The Faithfull Shepheard* (London, 1607) from an earlier period: "What Art or Science is there, which a Divine shall not stand in need of. . . . Grammar, Rhetorick, Logicke, Physicks, Mathematicks, Metaphysicks, Ethicks, Politicks, Oeconomicks, History, and Military Discipline" were all useful in his task. Quoted by William Haller, *The Rise of Puritanism . . . , 1570–1643* (New York, 1938), 138.

27. The extant printed Harvard commencement *theses* and *quaestiones* (the former refer to bachelor's ceremonies, the latter to master's) up to 1708 are reprinted in Appendix B to Morison, *Seventeenth-Century Harvard*. See also, John Langdon Sibley, *Biographical Sketches of Graduates of Harvard University . . .* (Cambridge, Mass., 1873–1970), II, 54, 392, hereafter cited as Sibley, *Harvard Graduates*.

28. Flavel, *The Whole Works of . . . J. Flavel . . .* , 3d ed., I (Edinburgh, 1731), 276. Discussion of the place of moral philosophy in religious education still continues. See David A. Dillon and John A. Oesterle, "Moral Philosophy in the Catholic College," *Thomist*, XVI (1953),

practice. The theory of the curriculum has its own interesting history going back to Plato and is important because it may well represent the conventional intellectual ideals of an age much better than the academic actualities do. Conversely, the history of the existing, rather than the theoretical, curriculum in any given era or in any particular institution is most often shaped by all sorts of immediate problems and needs and can only be known through a survey of such things as textbooks, student notebooks, autobiographical reminiscences, and lecture notes.[29]

In the area of theory the Middle Ages inherited a strong tradition that made moral philosophy one of the basic components of the circle of learning. In *The City of God* Augustine reported favorably on the Platonic and Stoic schema that divided knowledge into moral, natural, and rational philosophy, or in more modern terms, into ethics, physical science, and logic. The somewhat different Aristotelian tradition, transmitted principally by Boethius, began with a fundamental distinction between theoretical and practical knowledge, and under the latter fell ethics and politics. Both of these arrangements left their mark on the medieval curriculum in theory and in practice, but they had to compete with basically monastic programs, like those of Cassiodorus and others, which deliberately excluded secular ethics.[30]

Until quite recently it was thought that moral philosophy was not taught at all in the medieval period until after Aristotle's *Ethics* was recovered in the thirteenth century. The familiar division of the arts into the *trivium* and *quadrivium* seemingly left no room for it, nor could it find a secure place in the higher faculties of law and theology. Nonetheless, the research of Philippe Delhaye has shown that ethical studies did go on in certain inconspicuous ways, even though the theoretical curriculum provided no formal place for them. Moral philosophy was taught primarily in the context of grammar, where the use of such authors as Plato, Horace, Virgil, and Seneca was heavily moralized. In fact, this emphasis on moral teaching provided one of the means by which these works could be redeemed for use in a Christian culture, since to master them for literary pleasure alone was hardly justifiable.

449–471. The question that the moral theologian asks of the moral philosopher is: "Since the coming of the Christian revelation, which provides us with all that is necessary to arrive at an ultimate end, what advantage—in fact, what need or use—is there for a science of human conduct based on reason alone?"

29. On the theory of the curriculum in relation to 18th-century moral philosophy, see Fiering, "President Samuel Johnson and the Circle of Knowledge," *William and Mary Quarterly*, 3d Ser., XXVIII (1971), 199–236.

30. *The City of God against the Pagans* (Cambridge, Mass., 1957–1972), III, *Books VIII–XI*, trans. David S. Wiesen, Bk. VIII, sec. iv; Bk. IX, sec. xxv; Jerome Taylor, ed. and trans., *The 'Didascalicon' of Hugh of St. Victor: A Medieval Guide to the Arts* (New York and London, 1961), *passim*.

Anonymous anthologies of maxims and short selections illustrating morals, known as *floralegia*, were also used. Corresponding to the practice were several classification-of-knowledge schemes, other than the famous *trivium* and *quadrivium*, that did reserve a definite theoretical place for "moral philosophy" as distinct from "moral theology." (The former was understood to begin with man; the latter with God.) Peter Abelard, for one, believed that moral philosophy was the most noble of the disciplines taught by the pagans and the very summit of the sciences.[31]

It is hard to say to what extent this indirect study of morals before the availability of Aristotle's great work included the critical examination of problems, but the teaching practice itself, such as it was, illustrates an important principle. Before a discipline is fully accepted or sometimes even recognized, it may exist dispersed throughout the visible curriculum if the need for it is felt. At the University of Geneva, for example, which was founded by Calvin in 1559, moral philosophy did not stand on its own feet, but it was taught by the professor of Greek, three hours a week, in the form of commentaries on Aristotle, Plato, Plutarch, and some Christian authors.[32] Any adequate history of a discipline must take into account such covert pre-formations.

Ethics and the Harvard Curriculum

The New England Puritans were true descendants of the Scholastics in their intense interest in the theory of the curriculum, which they generally called *technologia* or *technometria*, the study of the arts (*techne*) in general.[33]

31. Philippe Delhaye, " 'Grammatica' et 'Ethica' au XIIᵉ siècle," *Analecta Mediaevalia Namurcensia*, Hors Serie 2 (Louvain and Lille, n.d.), extrait des *Recherches de théologie ancienne et médiévale*, XXV (1958), 59–110. Also, Delhaye, "La Place de l'éthique parmi les disciplines scientifiques au XIIᵉ siècle," in *Miscellanea Moralia in Honorem Eximii Domini Arthur Janssen* (Gembloux, [1949?]), 29–44.

32. Charles Borgeaud, *Histoire de l' Université de Genève*, I: *l'Academie de Calvin, 1559–1798* (Geneva, 1900), 66. There is a tradition that when Theodore Beza was asked which book he preferred after the Bible, he answered, "Plutarch's Lives and Morals." The manuscript commonplace book of John Hancock (Harvard A.B., 1689, the grandfather of the famous signer) in Houghton Library, Harvard University, Cambridge, Massachusetts, records this anecdote as does Benjamin Wadsworth's (Harvard A.B., 1769) manuscript commonplace book, Harvard University Archives.

33. There were more complicated formulations. For example, Johann Heinrich Alsted's *"praecognita"* for the organization of the disciplines included *archelogia*, which provides the design, purposes, and final causes of the sciences; *hexilogia*, the relation of cognition to action; *technologia*, the nature and differences of the particular arts; and *didactica*, the method of teaching. These were described in the introduction to Alsted's great *Encyclopaedia . . .* (Herborn, 1630), a major resource for 17th-century New England scholars. See Leroy E. Loemker, "Leibniz and the Herborn Encyclopedists," *Journal of the History of Ideas*, XXII (1961), 323–338, and

Technologia included the careful definition of the individual arts so that each would have a distinct place and exact foundations; the rigorous systematization or methodizing of the internal matter of each of the arts; and the discussion of the logical relation of the arts to each other.[34] The goal of *technologia* was both pedagogical and philosophical. "Perhaps we have laid bare the innermost essence of the Puritan mind," Perry Miller observed, "when we find that its highest philosophical reach was a systematic delineation of the liberal arts."[35] In such a context of highly self-conscious concern about curricular organization it was inevitable that ethics would be carefully scrutinized.

The modern logician most deeply respected in early New England was the sixteenth-century philosophy professor at the Collège de France Peter Ramus, and one of Ramus's main interests in logic was *technologia*, though he did not use that word for it. Ramus worked intensively on the internal ordering of logic and rhetoric and their relation to each other and apparently never got to ethics, though according to his nineteenth-century biographer a manuscript entitled *Traité de Morale* once existed.[36] It is hard to say what might have been in this treatise, but we know in any case that on Christian religious grounds Ramus was an opponent of ethics as it was traditionally presented. In an address given in 1551 he expressed indignation that Aristotle's ethics was imposed on college students, who could learn from it only impieties, such as that the sources of happiness are found within oneself and that all the virtues

---

reprinted in Ivor Leclerc, ed., *The Philosophy of Leibniz and the Modern World* (Nashville, Tenn., 1973), 276–297. See also, Miller, *New England Mind*, I, 102–103.

34. On technologia in New England, see Miller, *New England Mind*, I, 158–180, and 105–108; Porter G. Perrin, "Possible Sources of *Technologia* at Early Harvard," *New England Quarterly*, VII (1934), 718–724; and Morison, *Seventeenth-Century Harvard*, 161–164. On Ramist technologia in general, see Walter J. Ong, S.J., *Ramus, Method, and the Decay of Dialogue: From the Art of Discourse to the Art of Reason* (Cambridge, Mass., 1958); Wilbur Samuel Howell, *Logic and Rhetoric in England, 1500–1700* (Princeton, N.J., 1956); Keith L. Sprunger, "Ames, Ramus, and the Method of Puritan Theology," *Harvard Theological Review*, LIX (1966), 133–151, and "Technometria: A Prologue to Puritan Theology," *Jour. Hist. Ideas*, XXIX (1968), 115–122; and Lee W. Gibbs, "William Ames's Technometry," *ibid.*, XXXIII (1972), 615–624. Gibbs's dissertation—"The Technometry of William Ames" (Th.D. diss., Harvard University Divinity School, 1967)—which consists primarily of a translation of, and a detailed commentary on, Ames's Latin work on technologia, is a particularly valuable source. It has recently been published as *William Ames: Technometry* (Philadelphia, 1979). On the larger history of encyclopedic schemes, see Fiering, "Samuel Johnson," *WMQ*, 3d Ser., XXVIII (1971), 199–236; Robert Flint, *Philosophy as Scientia Scientiarum and a History of Classifications of the Sciences* (Edinburgh, 1904); Taylor, ed. and trans., *'Didascalicon'*; and Joseph J. Schwab, "Structure of the Disciplines: Meanings and Significances," in G. W. Ford and Lawrence Pugno, eds., *The Structure of Knowledge and the Curriculum* (Chicago, 1964), 6–30.

35. Miller, *New England Mind*, I, 161.

36. Charles T. Waddington, *Ramus (Pierre de La Ramée) sa vie, ses écrits et ses opinions* (Paris, 1855), 473.

are in our power and may be acquired by natural means.[37] The petitionary circumstances under which Ramus made this speech, however, were such that he might not have stated in it his complete view of the matter.[38] Certainly in his other work Ramus frequently referred to pagan authors, such as Virgil and Cicero, in order to illustrate forms of reasoning and rhetoric.[39]

Whatever Ramus's ultimate position would have been, for New England his great authority was drawn totally into the camp of the enemies of moral philosophy by a passage in William Ames's *Marrow of Theology* (*Medulla Theologica*, 1623), which cited the same 1551 speech of Ramus's mentioned above. "The judgment and desire of that greatest master of the arts, Peter Ramus," on the subject of Aristotle's ethics, "was no less pious than prudent," Ames wrote.[40] There is no question about Ames's own attitude toward the teaching of ethics, for he descanted on the matter forcefully and influentially in several places:

> The sole rule in all matters which have to do with the direction of life is the revealed will of God. . . . What is called right reason . . . is nowhere else to be discovered than where it is—in the Scriptures. It does not differ from the will of God revealed for the direction of our life. . . . When the imperfect notions about honesty and dishonesty found in man's mind after the fall are truly understood, they will be seen to be incapable of shaping virtue. . . . Therefore, there can be no other teaching of the virtues than theology which brings the whole revealed will of God to the directing of our reason, will, and life.[41]

Although Ames was broadly learned in pre-Cartesian Catholic and Protestant literature and had particular respect for Thomas Aquinas, he detested the

37. *Ibid.*, 357.

38. See Walter J. Ong, S.J., *Ramus and Talon Inventory* . . . (Cambridge, Mass., 1958), 156. Ramus's co-worker and sometime coauthor Omer Talon did directly attack the first book of the *Nicomachean Ethics* in a written work. See *ibid.*, 472.

39. In 1584 Gosivino Mulhemius published *Logica ad P. Rami dialecticam conformata* (Frankfort), which substituted biblical verses for Ramus's Classical illustrations. See Miller, *New England Mind*, I, 156.

40. William Ames, *The Marrow of Theology*, 3d ed., trans. and ed. John E. Eusden (Boston, 1968 [orig. publ. London, 1629]), Bk. II, chap. ii, sec. 18, hereafter cited as Ames, *Marrow of Theology*, II, ii, 18.

41. *Ibid.*, 13, 15–16. Ames wrote "a treatise to show that, in the Christian dispensation, ethics is absorbed into theology," his *Adversus ethicam disputatio theologica*, printed in his *Philosophemata* (Leiden, 1643), 119–142. See Ong, *Ramus, Method, and the Decay of Dialogue*, 146. It is usually assumed that Ames was influenced in this regard by his teacher, William Perkins. Cf. the following from Perkins's *A Golden Chaine; or the Description of Theologie* (London, 1591): "The body of Scripture is a doctrine sufficient to live well. It comprehendeth many holy sciences, where-of one is principal, others are handmaids or retainers. The principal science is theology. Theology is the science of living blessedly for ever." Quoted by F. Ernest

influence of Aristotle, remarking that scarcely anyone can be named who "having previously professed the Peripatetic philosophy, later received the truth of the Christian faith." Plato, on the other hand, was acceptable, for a number of Christians, including Augustine, had once been Platonists.[42]

Ames dealt explicitly with the argument we noted earlier, that defended the legitimacy of ethics as an "external" study. It is an error, he said, to hold

> that the end of theology is the good of grace and the end of ethics is moral or civil good (as if no moral or civil good were in any way spiritual or the good of grace). This is to say that the proper good, blessedness, or end of man is not a single good, and that a man's virtue does not lead him to his end and chief good. They say that theology is concerned with the inward affections of men, and ethics with outward manners— as if ethics, which they consider the prudence which governs the will and appetite, had nothing to do with inward affections, and theology did not teach outward as well as inward obedience.[43]

Ames concluded that "there is no precept of universal truth relevant to living well" whether it be in economy, morals, politics, or law, "which does not rightly pertain to theology."[44]

In Ames's conception of "encyclopedia," that is, the circle of knowledge, or *technologia*, both ethics and metaphysics were absorbed into theology. In

Stoeffler, *The Rise of Evangelical Pietism* (Leiden, 1971 [orig. publ. 1965]), 53. Perkins is informatively discussed in Ian Breward's introduction to *The Work of William Perkins*, ed. Breward (Berkshire, Eng., 1970).

42. Quoted in Keith L. Sprunger, *The Learned Doctor William Ames: Dutch Backgrounds of English and American Puritanism* (Urbana, Ill., 1972), 141. Sprunger has a good discussion of Ames's ethics in relation to the Catholic Scholasticism of the preceding centuries on pp. 177– 182. See also, Eusden, trans. and ed., introduction to Ames, *Marrow of Theology*, 15. Paul Dibon, *La Philosophie néerlandaise au siècle d'or: l'enseignement philosophique dans les universités a l'époque précartésienne* (Paris, 1954), 152, has some interesting remarks on Ames; Ames is the subject of three separate studies in Matthew Nethenus, Hugo Visscher, and Karl Reuter, *William Ames*, ed. and trans. Douglas Horton (Cambridge, Mass., 1965). Reuter's study in particular (first published in German in 1940) is basic for understanding the academic and clerical mind in early America, though the author himself unfortunately shows no knowledge of the American scene.

43. Ames, *Marrow of Theology*, II, ii, 17. In his "Technometry" Ames attacked one by one nearly all of the common defenses of the teaching of secular ethics. The findings of so-called *natural* moral and civil philosophy are in fact derived from more than nature, Ames wrote, for they "flow from the vestiges of the integral state of man [Adam before the Fall] which remains in the human soul only through divine grace." To the claim that ethics was concerned only with external conduct in the world, Ames replied that "ethics no less than theology claims the ability to reform man according to the image of God by prescribing the precepts of virtue and calling men away from vice." See Gibbs, "Technometry of Ames," 188–191.

44. Ames, *Marrow of Theology*, I, i, 12.

what were almost his last written words, a revision made in the 1634 Latin edition of his *Medulla*, he reaffirmed this opinion:

> There are two parts of theology, faith and observance. . . . Out of the remnants of these two parts have sprouted among certain philosophers two new theologies—Metaphysics and Ethics. Metaphysics, in fact, is the faith of the Peripatetics and ethics is their observance. Hence, to each of these two disciplines they ascribe that which deals with the highest good of man. Everyone knows that this is the case with ethics. But it applies to metaphysics too, which they even call theology. . . . [But], when theology . . . is handed down correctly in these two parts of faith and observance, metaphysics and ethics vanish spontaneously.[45]

Ames proposed a revolutionary program intended to bring about the withering away of the pagan philosophical establishment and the dictatorship of a practical Christian theology. For this schema in diagrammatic form, see page 27.[46] All theology was divided into faith and observance, and what might be called ethics was identified with religious observance, "the submissive performance [by man] of the will of God for the glory of God."[47] Observance itself was divided into inner disposition and outward acts, both being necessary in a holy life.

A contemporary of Ames's, Bishop Joseph Hall of Norwich, had remarked that among the "old Heathens" moral philosophers took the place of "Divines," or clergy. These philosophers "received the *Acts* of an inbred law, in the *Sinai* of Nature," Hall wrote, "and delivered them with many expositions to the multitude."[48] Similarly, Ames's prescient fear was that the divines in his time would deteriorate into the moral philosophers of old, abandoning revelation and relying only on the inbred law and the Sinai of nature. Ames was no different from many other writers in the seventeenth century in believing that the science of living is the pre-eminent art, to which all other arts should be subordinate. But he maintained that this art is theology, which he defined as the teaching of "living to God," not moral philosophy.

It is significant that in Ames's organization of the divisions of learning, theology was treated as a formal part of the arts course. Such an arrangement was unheard of in medieval universities. The arts faculty normally had responsibility only up to the master's degree and was not permitted to teach

45. Quoted in Sprunger, "Technometria," *Jour. Hist. Ideas*, XXIX (1968), 122. See also, Gibbs, "Ames's Technometry," *ibid.*, XXXIII (1972), 615–624.

46. This chart is a compression of some charts and text in Sprunger, "Technometria," *ibid.*, XXIX (1968), 115–122.

47. Ames, *Marrow of Theology*, II, i, 1.

48. Hall, *Characters of Vertues and Vices* (London, 1608), in Rudolph Kirk, ed., *Heaven upon Earth and Characters of Vertues and Vices* . . . (New Brunswick, N.J., 1948), 143.

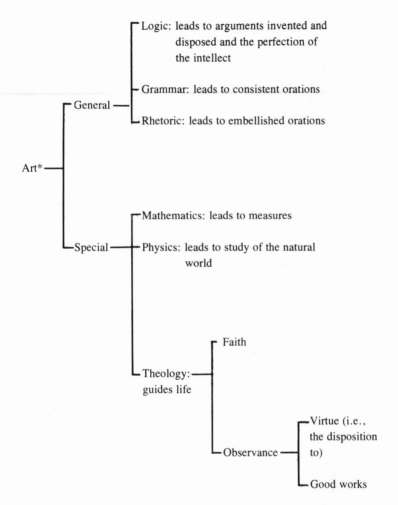

Art*
- General
  - Logic: leads to arguments invented and disposed and the perfection of the intellect
  - Grammar: leads to consistent orations
  - Rhetoric: leads to embellished orations
- Special
  - Mathematics: leads to measures
  - Physics: leads to study of the natural world
  - Theology: guides life
    - Faith
    - Observance
      - Virtue (i.e., the disposition to)
      - Good works

*Defined as: "the idea of *eupraxia* methodically delineated by universal rules"

theology, which required special training and competence. The historian John Eusden regards Ames's innovation as "a declaration" of the Puritan position that theology is an art "for every man, not reserved for the expert or the *perfectiones*."[49] It followed from Ames's reasoning that if theology is truly as much a practical as a theoretical science, ethics as well as metaphysics would be banished, and theology would take the place of both. Yet not even in the

49. Eusden's introduction to Ames, *Marrow of Theology*, 2.

Zion of New England was theology or divinity ever allowed to assume such an exclusive role. At Harvard and Yale theology was a vital and pervasive supplement to the students' academic diet during the four undergraduate years (supplied mainly through the required reading of Ames's *Medulla* and the inditing or copying of hundreds of sermons), but it became a subject of concentrated study only for those entering the ministry, and then not until after the B.A. had been earned.[50] In other words, despite Ames's wishes, the spirit of Christian piety and works was no more and no less a part of the undergraduate Harvard community than it was a part of the Massachusetts community at large.

Ames's influence in seventeenth-century New England was unparalleled, as is well known. Cotton Mather described him in the *Magnalia Christi Americana* as the "angelical doctor," elevating him, it would seem, to the position of Puritan counterpart to St. Thomas Aquinas.[51] If Ames had lived to come to America as planned, he would almost certainly have been appointed to the presidency of Harvard. And Morison claims that his influence over the curriculum at early Harvard "probably exceeded that of any other scholar."[52] But on the matter of ethics Ames's guidance was rejected. The fact is, Ames's ultra-purist position probably represented a minority view most of the time. Other powerful authorities, such as J. H. Alsted, continued to follow the preponderant Scholastic example of retaining an autonomous moral philosophy in the circle of knowledge, though as a lesser form of truth than that reached in theology.[53] Moreover, from what is known of the Cambridge

50. As William T. Costello, S.J., *The Scholastic Curriculum at Early Seventeenth-Century Cambridge* (Cambridge, Mass., 1958), 128, has noted, theology was "the primary frame of reference" for all learning, but this does not mean that theology displaced the traditional ordering of the curriculum. Costello's discussion of the role of divinity or theology at Cambridge University is excellent and generally applies to Harvard. See especially pp. 110–113.

51. Mather, *Magnalia Christi Americana: or, The Ecclesiastical History of New England . . .* (Hartford, Conn., 1820 [orig. publ. London, 1702]), I, 215.

52. Morison, *Founding of Harvard*, 143. See also, Miller, *New England Mind*, I, 196. If Ezra Stiles was not momentarily confused, Ames's *Marrow of Theology* was required reading for seniors at Yale until 1778! (*The Literary Diary of Ezra Stiles . . .* , ed. Franklin Bowditch Dexter, II [New York, 1901], 388.) Stiles was reporting on "Books recited by the several Classes at my Accession to the Presidency." See also, Thomas Clap, *A Brief History and Vindication of the Doctrines Received and Established in the Churches of New England . . .* (New Haven, Conn., 1755), 10–14. Reading of Ames at Harvard was mandated until at least as late as 1726, and probably for long after that. See C. K. Shipton, ed., "Benjamin Wadsworth's Book . . . Relating to College Affairs," *Harvard College Records* (Colonial Society of Massachusetts, *Collections*, XV, XVI, XXXI [Boston, 1925, 1935]), III, 456, hereafter cited as *Harvard College Recs*. These are the official records of Harvard in the colonial period.

53. The organization of Alsted's *Encyclopaedia* is printed in Henry Evelyn Bliss, *The Organization of Knowledge and the System of the Sciences* (New York, 1929), 334. On Alsted's great influence in New England, see Morison, *Seventeenth-Century Harvard*, 158. See also, Gibbs, "Ames's Technometry," *Jour. Hist. Ideas*, XXXIII (1972), 618, and n. 33 above.

University curriculum in the seventeenth century, particularly at Emmanuel College, which had the closest connections with Harvard's founding, some ethics (nearly all of it Aristotelian) was an integral part of the program, class time being devoted to it for all four years.[54] The pertinent official documents from Harvard in the seventeenth century suggest that there, too, despite Ames's strictures, ethics had a continuous, albeit shaky, career.

New England's First Fruits, published in London in 1643, the year after the first Harvard class had graduated, contains a well-known description of the college. This famous document indicates that during the second year of what was at first only a three-year course, about two hours a week of formal class time were spent on *"Ethicks* and *Politicks."*[55] This amounted to about one-third of the total lecture time of the second year, a respectable but minor part of the program as a whole. We need not take the reference to "Politics" very seriously. Traditionally moral philosophy was considered to have three parts, ethics, politics, and "economics," the first pertaining to the study of virtue in the individual, the second to virtue in the state and society, and the third to virtue in domestic or family relations. But Aristotle's *Politics* was rarely part of the curriculum anywhere, and what politics there was, was introduced through the study of justice as it was treated in the *Nicomachean Ethics*.

In addition to this bachelor's requirement, *First Fruits* specifies that among the requirements for the second or master's degree was the presentation of a written "System, or Synopsis, or summe of Logick Naturall and Morall Phylosophy, Arithmetick, Geometry and Astronomy." This task was undoubtedly less demanding than it sounds. The college laws of 1655, which also state the master's degree requirements, have "or" rather than "and" astronomy, suggesting that something less than the formidable *summa* mentioned in *First Fruits* was acceptable and that after the bachelor's degree specialization was permitted.[56]

54. See Morison, *Founding of Harvard*, 67–72, wherein is described Richard Holdsworth's "Directions for a Student in the Universitie," a manuscript in the Emmanuel College Library, Cambridge University, England. See also, Costello, *Curriculum at Cambridge*, chap. 2.

55. The entire document is printed in facsimile in Morison, *Founding of Harvard*, Appendix D, 432–437, and the curriculum is conveniently tabulated in Morison, *Seventeenth-Century Harvard*, 140–143.

56. According to the regulations, these synopses were to be kept in the college library, but almost none seem to have survived. The best example of one that includes all of the fields mentioned is Samuel Johnson's *"Technologia sive technometria or ars encyclopaidia manualis ceu philosophia"* (1714), which was done at Yale. It has been translated and printed in Schneider and Schneider, eds., *Samuel Johnson*, II, 56–186. The College Laws of 1655 are reprinted in *Harvard College Recs.*, III, 327–339. The laws of 1734 are even more explicit about allowing for specialization in preparation for the master's degree: "What Bachelour soever shall make a Common place, or Synopsis of any of the Arts, or Sciences . . . shall . . . be capable of a Second Degree." *Ibid.*, I, 147.

Included among these first fruits is a reprinting of the first Harvard commencement broadside, that of 1642, listing the bachelor's *theses*. The *theses* were printed on a single sheet, organized according to the discipline under which they were studied, and were a group product, drawn up by a committee of the graduating class under the supervision of the tutors and the president. They were intended to represent the proficiency of all the members of the graduating class in the whole circle of knowledge. The master's degree *quaestiones*, on the contrary, were specialized, single propositions, or rather questions, that the individual candidate selected and responded to, either negatively or affirmatively. On the printed commencement broadsides the candidate's name always appeared next to his *quaestio* (see fig. 1). The complete, printed bachelor's *theses* of only twelve commencements from seventeenth-century Harvard have survived. We have, however, from a manuscript booklet compiled in the middle of the eighteenth century by an unknown recorder, a few of the *theses* that were presented at twenty other commencements before 1700. We also know the *quaestiones* from thirty-seven commencements before 1700.[57] These commencement sheets are valuable sources of information about the form and content of colonial higher education. At this point it is not their substance that requires our attention so much as the formal characteristics of the curriculum that may be deduced from them.

In the 1642 commencement sheet under the general head of *"Theses Philosophicas,"* a subhead entitled *"Ethicas"* is clearly entered with eleven individual *theses* under it. Also under *Theses Philosophicas* are subsections for *"Physicas"* and *"Metaphisicas."* A second general head is *"Theses Philologicas"* under which appear the subsections grammar, rhetoric, and logic, with appropriate *theses* or propositions under each. This basic format of two broad categories, philosophy and philology, three arts as subheads, and appropriate *theses* under each subhead, continued until at least 1647 (see fig. 2). Thereafter, unfortunately, there are no surviving printed broadsides or manuscripts of *theses* until 1653, when the format was changed markedly, perhaps signifying an alteration in educational ideals.

On the broadside published for the commencement of August 9, 1653,

---

57. I am indebted to Mr. Kimball C. Elkins, former curator of the Harvard University Archives, for a list of the extant materials. Morison, *Seventeenth-Century Harvard*, Appendix B, does not print the theses and questions that have survived only in manuscript. These appear in two sewn booklets at the Harvard archives, both apparently drawn up by the same person. One lists the theses *"in Comitus Publicis defensa,"* that is, only those that were publicly defended, for 48 commencements between 1660 and 1753. Normally there was time during the commencement ceremonies for the public defense of only a few of the many bachelors' theses prepared by the graduating class. The other booklet lists the *quaestiones* in entirety from the commencements between 1660 and 1753.

there is for the first time evidence of profound disagreement over the curriculum at Harvard, for this sheet contains no sections of ethics and metaphysics whatsoever (see fig. 3). *"Physicae"* remained, as did logic, grammar, and rhetoric, but instead of ethics and metaphysics the arts from the old quadrivium, *"Arithmeticae"* and *"Geometricae,"* were added. The two main heads, philosophy and philology, were also eliminated, and another new entry

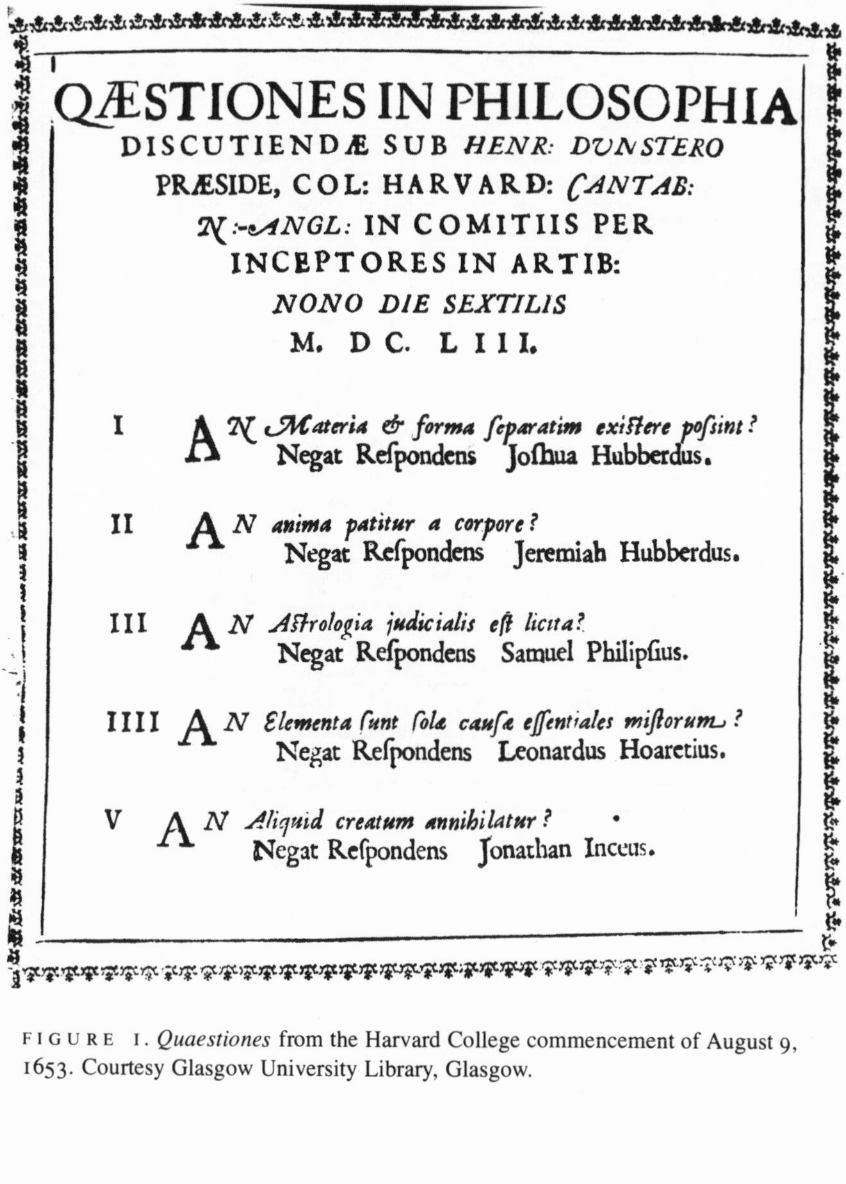

QÆSTIONES IN PHILOSOPHIA

DISCUTIENDÆ SUB *HENR: DUNSTERO*
PRÆSIDE, COL: HARVARD: *ÇANTAB:*
N:-ANGL: IN COMITIIS PER
INCEPTORES IN ARTIB:
NONO DIE SEXTILIS
M. D C. L I I I.

I   A*N Materia & forma separatim existere possint ?*
        Negat Respondens   Joshua Hubberdus.

II   A*N anima patitur a corpore ?*
        Negat Respondens   Jeremiah Hubberdus.

III   A*N Astrologia judicialis est licita ?*
        Negat Respondens   Samuel Philipsius.

IIII   A*N Elementa sunt sola causa essentiales mistorum ?*
        Negat Respondens   Leonardus Hoaretius.

V   A*N Aliquid creatum annihilatur ?*
        Negat Respondens   Jonathan Inceus.

FIGURE 1. *Quaestiones* from the Harvard College commencement of August 9, 1653. Courtesy Glasgow University Library, Glasgow.

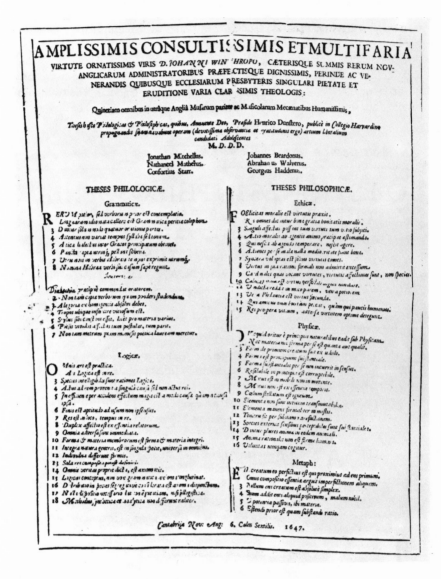

FIGURE 2. *Theses* presented at the Harvard College commencement of 1647. Courtesy Glasgow University Library, Glasgow.

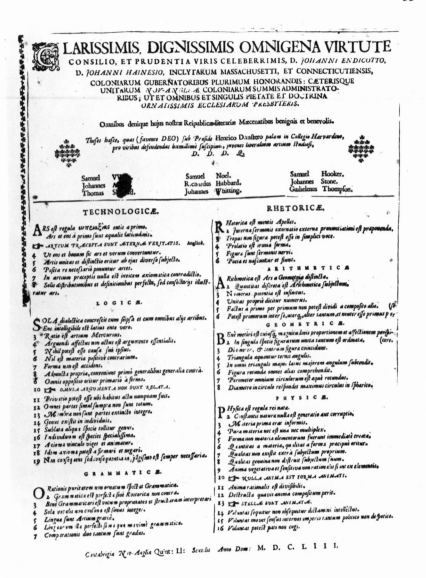

FIGURE 3. *Theses* presented at the Harvard College commencement of August 9, 1653. Courtesy Glasgow University Library, Glasgow.

on the sheet was *"Technologicae,"* with eight *theses* under it. Thus, whereas in 1642 and 1647 the picture, in outline, had looked like this:

THESES PHILOLOGICAS
Grammaticas
Rhetoricas
Logicas

THESES PHILOSOPHICAS
Ethicas
Physicas
Metaphysicas

for the August 9, 1653, commencement we have:

Technologicae
Logicae
Grammaticae
Rhetoricae
Arithmeticae
Geometricae
Physicae

It might be hoped that the content of the technologia theses would themselves explain the change, but none of them refers to ethics or to the abandonment of the general distinction between philosophic and philologic theses. The August 9, 1653, divisions of learning perhaps show the direct influence of William Ames. Theology is missing, but if *"Arithmeticae"* and *"Geometricae"* are reassembled as the one art of *"Mathematicae,"* it is a schema such as Ames proposed.

Any explanation of this change in curriculum organization is complicated by another strange circumstance. In 1653 Harvard held two commencements in two days, one on August 9, the other on August 10. This peculiarity grew out of the adjustment required when it was decided to extend the period of study necessary for the bachelor's degree from three to four years. The August 9 commencement broadside was as I have described. The August 10 broadside was organized identically except for two items. The first is insignificant: instead of *"Arithmeticae"* and *"Geometricae"* a single category of theses *"Mathematicae"* was substituted. But in addition to this there was included after *"Physicae"* a category of theses *"Ethicae"*! (See fig. 4.) One wonders if such inconsistency in the same year was the product of internal disagreement among classes or tutors or overseers or whomever. Since two different graduating classes were represented, the difference may be an indi-

cation of the relative freedom the graduating seniors had to organize the academic content of the commencement programs.

For the next thirty years after 1653 the standing of ethics was apparently quite precarious, if the organization of the commencement broadsides is any guide. Then in 1687, or slightly before, the opponents of the formal appearance of ethical theses won a decisive victory, for from that year to 1751 a separate category for ethics did not appear again on any Harvard commencement broadside. Looking at this sequence in somewhat more detail, we see that for the period between 1653 and 1669 there is little to go on, but in 1669, according to the manuscript report, the status of ethics is ludicrously paradoxical: under the very heading *"Ethica"* appeared the proposition, *"Ethica non est specie distincta a Theologia"* (Ethics is not distinct from theology). At the same time, under the heading of metaphysics was the proposition, *"Theses metaphysicae non dantur"* (There are no theses of metaphysics). This intolerable situation was dealt with at least temporarily in 1670, a year for which a printed broadside has survived. In 1670 the order on the broadside was the same as for August 10, 1653: *Technologicae, Logicae, Grammaticae, Rhetoricae, Mathematicae, Physicae,* and *Ethicae* (see fig. 5). And under the last was the thesis, singled out for public debate: *"Ethica est specie distincta a Theologia."* Again judging from the manuscript record, in 1671, 1673, and 1676, ethics probably took its place among the other arts and sciences. But in 1678, this time without paradox, though with dubious "method" (under theses *"Physicae,"* of all places), ethics was once more denied: *"Ethica non datur specie distincta a Theologia."* This, too, was marked for public debate. Metaphysics was also eliminated in the theses of 1678, but more sensibly in a proposition printed under *"Technologicae,"* which was the propaedeutic meta-discipline specifically concerned with determining the place of all the arts. In 1680, ethical theses were again listed. In 1683 the same paradoxical situation existed as in 1669: under theses *"Ethicae"* the statement is made that in fact ethics is not a subject distinct from theology. In 1684 there was once again an ethics division at the commencement. But the *theses technologicae* of 1687 proclaimed the final word until 1751: *"Ethica a theologia non realiter differt"* (Ethics does not really differ from theology), which was also publicly debated.

Between 1687 and 1751 the order remained as it had been in 1670 and on the August 10, 1653, broadside, except that ethics was dropped from the end of the list. There were simply technologia, logic, grammar, rhetoric, math, and physics, a victory for the Amesians, although theology was not listed. Finally, in 1751 the pattern that had stood fast for sixty years was shattered by the addition of not only ethics but metaphysics, too; and, as though even at this late date to offset these two pagan subjects, a category of *theses "The-*

FIGURE 5. *Theses* presented at the Harvard College commencement of 1670. Photograph by George M. Cushing. Courtesy Massachusetts Historical Society, Boston.

ologicae" was for the first time included.[58] It seems likely that by this date chaos reigned in the theory of the curriculum. The developments recorded here on the organization of the commencement broadsides may be rough indicators of social and intellectual change, though curricula are usually behind rather than ahead of the times. A separate category of *theses "Politicae,"* for example, was not added until 1778! Thereafter, at least until 1790, the last year for which I have seen a Harvard commencement sheet, the breakdown was: technologia, grammar, rhetoric, logic, metaphysics, ethics, politics, theology, mathematics, and physics.

It is notable that several of the post-1670 commencement broadsides that contained theses related to the autonomy of ethics also had those theses marked for public debate. Since on any commencement program there was time for only a few public disputations, that so many of the publicly debated theses concerned the place of ethics and metaphysics in the curriculum suggests extraordinary interest in the question that William Ames had posed so forcefully a generation before. As late as the 1720s the issue apparently still had life in it, for although there was to be no change in the organization of the commencement broadsides during that decade, in 1721 the defiant if vague proposition appeared: *"Ethica est Scientia."* But then in 1723, as though in reply, there is the thesis, *"In* Scriptura Sacra *omnes* Ethicae *Virtutes sunt Inveniendae"* (All the ethical virtues are found in Holy Scripture).[59]

We have seen thus far that the description of the Harvard curriculum that appears in *New England's First Fruits* of 1643 specified instruction in ethics, that master's degree candidates were expected to have some training in ethics, and that sporadically until 1684 the commencement broadsides indicate the formal and official acceptability of Classical ethics at Harvard. What other evidence is there pertaining to this matter? According to Morison the next official statement of Harvard studies following *First Fruits* dates from 1655, just after Charles Chauncy assumed the presidency, succeeding Henry Dunster, the first effective president. Part of the purpose of this 1655 statement was no doubt to spell out the order of studies under the new four-year program.

---

58. Of the extant printed sheets prior to 1709, those for the following years include an ethics category: 1642, 1643, 1646, 1647, Aug. 10, 1653, and 1670. The following do not include a separate ethics category: Aug. 9, 1653, 1678, 1687, 1689, 1691, 1693, and 1708. The manuscript booklet of theses publicly defended between 1660 and 1753 by its nature cannot tell us which commencements did not have *theses ethicae*, since it is a selective list. But it does reveal that ethical theses were disputed in 1669, 1670, 1671, 1673, 1676, 1680, 1683, and 1684.

59. In a master's *quaestio* in 1712 Benjamin Prescott affirmed that ethics is a field of learning distinct from theology, but the master's candidates were more independent in their assertions. On the other hand, in a 1697 *quaestio* Eliphalet Adams denied that the heathen virtues were real virtues, which was an indirect way of dispensing with moral philosophy. Adams was echoed in 1706 by Nathaniel Gookin, who argued the same, and in 1724 by John Wight, who asserted that "the nature of virtue [was] unknown to the pagan philosophers."

This program stated that students were to concentrate on elementary logic, Greek, and Hebrew in the first year; on logic more heavily in the second year; "and the third yeare in the principles of Ethickes." The fourth and final year would be devoted to metaphysics and mathematics, the students at the same time "carrying on their former studyes of the weeke for Rhetoricke, Oratory and Divinity." Divinity referred to regular Saturday morning exercises for all four years. It is perhaps significant that this 1655 announcement also stipulated "that in the teaching of all Arts such Authors bee read as doe best agree with the Scripture truths, wherein the speciall Care of the President and Fellows shall bee used and their direction therein attended."[60] Morison believed that more attention was given to ethics, physics, and metaphysics during Chauncy's administration, which lasted for seventeen years, than during Dunster's. This is possibly true, but the definition of ethics in Chauncy's day may also have been more superficial. The ethical propositions presented at the commencement of 1647, for example, probed rather deeply into the Classical disputes; whereas the ethical propositions of 1670 were more in the nature of commonplace maxims. Unfortunately there is no other official statement concerning the Harvard curriculum for the seventeenth century. The next announcement is from 1723.[61]

Concerning the master's degree requirements, the Laws of 1655 make clear that the candidate had the option of preparing a synopsis of moral philosophy among other subjects. But judging from the surviving seventeenth-century master's *quaestiones* sheets, comparatively few students concentrated on moral philosophy. Most of the *quaestiones* concern metaphysical topics until 1669, when they become heavily theological. The proximity of this date to the time when ethics was dropped from the subjects considered suitable for defense at commencement suggests that sometime in the 1670s there was a reaction, in the spirit of William Ames, against metaphysics and ethics as autonomous studies. This change in emphasis may have been an anticipation of New England's Reforming Synod of 1679, called in the wake of the devastation of King Philip's War to search out the causes of God's displeasure with New England. Although the report of that synod, written mainly by Increase Mather, specifically stressed the importance of the college for the spiritual welfare of the community and encouraged support for it, the whole tone of the synod was in the direction of Christian renewal based on fidelity to Scripture. It seems likely that some sort of purification of the curriculum would occur in association with the reforming movement in the 1670s, at least in the sense that the more obvious lapses from the standards of authorities like William

60. This Programme of 1655 is printed in part in Morison, *Seventeenth-Century Harvard*, 144–145; and in full in *Harvard College Recs.*, III, 327–339. See also, n. 54 above.
61. See Morison, *Seventeenth-Century Harvard*, 148–150, 160.

Ames would be corrected.[62] Though "moralism" was not yet seen as a danger to vital religion to the same degree that it would be in the eighteenth century, it was a standing truth that undue attention to ethics and not enough to the Gospel could lead to the delusion that "saving Grace and Morality were the same," as Increase Mather warned.[63]

The reform sentiment of the 1670s, however, is not sufficient to explain the absence of a category of *theses ethicae* from the commencement broadsides for the entire first half of the eighteenth century, since moral philosophy was without doubt continuously studied at Harvard during this period and was specifically required by college laws. Cotton Mather was troubled enough about the attention to moral philosophy in 1716 to resolve in his diary to make public testimony against "the employing of so much Time upon *Ethicks*, in our *Colledges* [he must have had in mind Yale, too]. A vile Peece of Paganism."[64] A decade later Mather was still complaining about the collegiate emphasis on ethics. In his *Manuductio ad Ministerium* (1726) he referred to ethics as *"That* whereon they employ the *Plough* so long in many Academies," calling it a *"Vile Thing*; and no other than what honest *Vockerodus* has justly called it; *Impietas in Artis formam redacta* [impiety put together in the form of an art]." Ethics is "a *Sham*," Mather insisted. "It presents you with a *Mock-Happiness*; It prescribes to you *Mock Vertues* for the coming at it: And it pretends to give you a Religion without a CHRIST, and a *Life* of PIETY without a *Living Principle*; a *Good Life* with no other than *Dead Works* filling of it. . . . Study no other *Ethics*, but what is in the *Bible*."[65]

---

62. The report of the synod is printed in Bk. V, Pt. iv, of Cotton Mather's *Magnalia*, and in Williston Walker, *The Creeds and Platforms of Congregationalism* (Philadelphia, 1960 [orig. publ. New York, 1893]), 409–439, with valuable related material. On the reforming spirit of the 1670s, see Miller, *New England Mind*, II, 30–39. Miller mentions the key sermons.

63. See Miller, *New England Mind*, II, 34.

64. *Diary of Cotton Mather*, 357.

65. Mather, *Manuductio ad Ministerium: Directions for a Candidate of the Ministry*, ed. Thomas J. Holmes and Kenneth B. Murdock (New York, 1938 [orig. publ. Boston, 1726]), 37–38, hereafter cited as Mather, *Manuductio*. Henry Grove, a prominent dissenting minister and moral philosopher in the early 18th century, and a teacher in one of the dissenting academies in England, considered Mather's strictures in the *Manuductio* far out of line: "Dr. Mather, a Divine of New England, is so severe in his censure of Moral Philosophy, as to call it by no better name than *Impietas in artis formam redacta*. . . . I know of none who have run the charge so high as this Gentleman." *Moral Philosophy*, ed. Amory, 11. Grove's writings were well known in America. He is sketched in Caroline Robbins, *The Eighteenth Century Commonwealthman: Studies in the Transmission, Development and Circumstance of English Liberal Thought from the Restoration of Charles II until the War with the Thirteen Colonies* (Cambridge, Mass., 1959), 251–254, and in Smith, *Birth of Modern Education*, 49, 97–101. Grove argued, contrary to Mather, that moral philosophy was essential to the work of a good minister. It may have been the publication of Grove's *System* that led to the reintroduction of an ethics section in the commencement broadsides after 1751.

Cotton Mather died in 1728, to the end a trustee of the old ways. In 1733 Yale, which had since its foundation (like Harvard after 1687) presented at commencement only *theses technologicae, logicae, grammaticae, rhetoricae, mathematicae,* and *physicae,* introduced for the first time a specific group of ethical theses. Is the force of accepted custom at Cambridge enough to explain the apparent paradox of liberal Harvard being eighteen years behind conservative Yale in this matter? Perhaps there was a living memory at Harvard of a bitter battle over the question, and it was not until mid-century that anyone wanted to take responsibility for reintroducing the controversial *theses ethicae.*[66]

There is no question that the general *organization* of the commencement broadsides was not an accurate reflection of the actual *content* of studies at seventeenth- and eighteenth-century Harvard. An examination of the individual theses themselves, as distinguished from the subject headings, reveals dozens of propositions in ethics, under physics (especially in matters pertaining to moral psychology), under logic, and sometimes under *technologicae.* The avoidance of the provocative heading, *theses ethicae,* while ethical disputations in fact went on, may have been a necessary compromise. One thing that seems clear is that it is probably too easy a solution to the discrepancies we have observed to dismiss the evidence of commencement theses as altogether insignificant. The graduating seniors themselves, through elected "collectors of theses," prepared these lists. And it was not unusual for the president or the tutors to disallow some of them. That it became the annual practice at both Harvard and Yale to print and publicly distribute the commencement theses was in itself a statement of the colleges' intimate relation to the surrounding community of learned men, since this had not been the practice in England when Harvard was founded. It is necessary to go to Edinburgh for a parallel. Moreover, as a number of diaries and other material attest, the community took note of this evidence of what the students were learning.[67] Throughout colonial New England it was understood that Harvard and Yale were the nurseries of each year's crop of ministers and other leaders and that what was

66. A Yale thesis in 1723 had stated: "There is no art of ethics." But the 1730s were a definite turning point. At Yale the study of ethics became explicit on the broadsides. At Harvard, though the organization of the commencement broadsides did not change, the content of the theses beginning in the 1730s showed an unmistakable increase in the study of ethics. By 1747 a Yale thesis could assert, *"Ethices scientia est omnium copiosissima"* (Ethics is the most fruitful of all the sciences).

67. Porter G. Perrin, "The Teaching of Rhetoric in the American Colleges before 1750" (Ph.D. diss., University of Chicago, 1936), has much valuable information on the compilation of the theses at both Harvard and Yale and also gives a number of examples of observers' comments on them. Samuel Sewall of Boston, for example, watched them closely. There is also basic information in the pioneering study by William Coolidge Lane, "Early Harvard Broadsides," Amer. Antiq. Soc., *Procs.,* N.S., XXIV (1914), 264–304.

happening in the colleges would inevitably affect the whole tone of religion in Calvinist America. There may indeed have been a tacit understanding at Harvard, dating back to the time of Increase Mather's presidency in the 1680s, that however much was actually taught of moral philosophy, the commencement broadsides would not show it too blatantly.

From *Eupraxia* to Ethics

The compelling influence of the idea of virtue on the eighteenth-century mind in both Britain and America is well known. The belief in virtue as the most worthy goal for mankind and as the essential ingredient in a good society united American and British educated men who in other areas could hold quite divergent views. Virtue could mean many different things, as is true of all abstract values, but the use of the term in the eighteenth century signified nevertheless a certain common spirit, despite differences in details. What must be understood, in any case, is that the widespread virtue-devotion of the eighteenth century is not properly interpreted when it is seen merely as evidence of a decline into contemptible "moralism" and "legalism" from former high standards of Christian piety. It is true that when New England Puritans, representing seventeenth-century values, witnessed a disenchantment with their own conceptions of piety and orthodoxy, this change appeared to them indicative of spiritual deterioration. But much eighteenth-century virtue-devotion was highly spiritual, even though it was less supernaturally oriented than seventeenth-century piety. Special revelation was a less important ingredient in the prevailing metaphysical outlook of the eighteenth century, but there was no less strength of conviction, zeal for rectitude, and attachment to transcendent standards of moral behavior.

One of the by-products of eighteenth-century virtue-devotion was the tendency, at least in America, to consecrate all of the curriculum to the goal of attaining virtue. And since moral philosophy was the specific art of virtue, for many years after about 1730 this discipline held first place as *ars artium* and *scientia scientiarum*, displacing theology.[68] On the one hand, this eighteenth-century development that gave so much importance to earthly virtue appears to have been utterly contrary to the highest religious values of Puritanism. Yet it is also true that many of the religious and moral commitments characteristic of Puritanism were quite compatible with such an outcome, especially when it

68. An exemplary instance of the process by which other disciplines were subordinated to moral philosophy can be traced in the various "encyclopedia" schemes of Samuel Johnson of Connecticut over a 50-year period. See Fiering, "Samuel Johnson," *WMQ*, 3d Ser., XXVIII (1971), 199–236.

is recognized that the eighteenth-century quest for virtue was no superficial moralism but a profound spiritual drive in its own right. Seventeenth-century American Puritanism and the mainstream of eighteenth-century virtue-devotion shared a number of traits. The two movements held in common a belief in the value of self-denial as an important indicator of moral worth and the conviction that sensualism vitiates spiritual development. The Puritans as a group and one wing, at least, of eighteenth-century moral philosophers were also alike in their emphasis on the quality of inward dispositions as a measure of virtue. Insistent self-scrutiny, which for the Puritan meant scrupulous searching of the soul for signs of grace or sin, was for the moral philosopher of a later time part of an effort to come to terms with "human nature" as one of God's creations. Puritanism and eighteenth-century moral philosophy had in common, too, a fondness for exhortation, and in general, the two groups shared a great seriousness about the conduct of life.

In addition to these continuities in certain goals and values, some similarities between seventeenth-century Puritans and eighteenth-century moral philosophers are also evident in their approach to higher learning and its uses. Thus, for example, just as the eighteenth-century moralist and educator John Witherspoon of Princeton could tell his students in 1770, "You may plainly perceive both how extensive and how important moral philosophy is. . . . Its importance is manifest from this circumstance, that it not only points out personal duty, but is related to the whole business of active life. The languages, and even mathematical and natural knowledge, are but hand maids to this superior science," so Cotton Mather, a half-century earlier, was already dreaming of the same end, only with Christian "piety" in the place of moral philosophy: "Oh! That I could find the Leisure to form an Enchiridion of the Liberal Sciences, which might enable Persons easily to attain them: and at the same time, consecrate the whole Erudition unto the Designs of Piety."[69] Mather's ambition hearkened back to Peter Ramus's program of curricular reform in the sixteenth century, and to Ramus's English successors in encyclopedics—William Ames, and the seventeenth-century Cambridge logician, Alexander Richardson, much admired in New England.[70]

69. John Witherspoon, *Lectures on Moral Philosophy*, ed. Varnum Lansing Collins (Princeton, N.J., 1912), 140; *Diary of Cotton Mather*, 570.

70. The philosophical succession of Ramus to Richardson to Ames was an established part of New England lore. Samuel Johnson of Connecticut introduced his *"Technologia sive technometria"* in 1714 with a kind of genealogical preface that ran as follows: "From Greece philosophy was introduced into Italy and thence into Germany, Holland, Spain, France, and England. In these countries not a few of the greatest men were found; for their doctrine was Christian. Among these innumerable men the principal sects were Platonists, Peripatetics, and Eclectics. The leader of the eclectic sect was that great man, Ramus, at whose feet, as it were, there followed Richardson, and then Ames, the greatest of them, followed him and we follow Ames." Schneider and Schneider, eds., *Samuel Johnson*, II, 56–186.

The philosophy of the curriculum that pervaded teaching at seventeenth-century Harvard perhaps owed more to the obscure figure of Alexander Richardson than to anyone else. The presuppositions of William Ames's technologia, for example, were in large part borrowed from Richardson's *The Logicians School-Master: or a Comment upon Ramus' Logicke*, a work that circulated in manuscript for a number of years before it was published posthumously in 1629 and again in 1657. Richardson himself was no mere parrot of Ramus, but an original thinker in his own right.[71] What is most significant about Richardson's thought for our purposes is its extraordinary emphasis on, and expansion of, the Aristotelian ethical concept of *eupraxia*, meaning "well-acting." The particular uses to which Richardson put *eupraxia* form an important link, I believe, between seventeenth-century piety and eighteenth-century virtue, or better, between seventeenth-century New England religious metaphysics and eighteenth-century moral philosophy.

"Eupraxia est objectum et finis artis" (Eupraxia is the object and end of the arts), an undergraduate thesis asserted in 1678, and in 1666 the master's candidate John Reyner responded in the affirmative to the *quaestio, "Utrum omnes Disciplinae tendant ad eupraxiam?"* (Whether all the disciplines tend toward *eupraxia?*) In *The First Principles of the Doctrine of Christ . . .* , a kind of catechism of theology published in Boston in 1679, James Fitch stated that *eupraxia* is the idea or pattern by which God rules Himself, an argument that gave the notion of *eupraxia* a theological foundation.[72] In Aristotle there is nothing like this breadth of meaning attached to *eupraxia*, but the term's origin in the *Nicomachean Ethics* reveals the persistence in New England of certain Classical notions of virtue even after Ames's purge.[73] It would not be too far from the truth to claim that Richardson, and even Ames himself, in attempting to dispense with naturalistic ethics in favor of a moral virtue grounded solely in revelation, succeeded rather in unwittingly providing a metaphysical basis for a much-expanded autonomous ethics. It is this paradoxical proposition that we must briefly explain here.

71. Very little is known about the sources of Richardson's ideas other than the Ramist influence, but it is evident that he was much affected by Neoplatonism, possibly from Italy. The New England divine Thomas Hooker, who had been Richardson's student, commented that God let Richardson die young "lest the English Nation should glory too much in their strength" (see Miller, *New England Mind*, I, 119). Another Puritan student of technologia, John Yates, author of *A Modell of Divinitie . . .* (London, 1622, 1623), also spoke "reverently" of Richardson. See Sprunger, *Learned Doctor Ames*, 112.

72. Fitch, *First Principles*, 14–15. *Theses Technologicae* in 1708 and 1711 also asserted that *eupraxia* is the object and goal of the arts.

73. In Book VI of the *Nicomachean Ethics eupraxia* refers to the unity in moral conduct of correct intellectual judgment with appetites or desires in perfect harmony with that judgment. Etymologically the word means "to do well," but at a high level in which both right thinking and good character are blended.

The Richardson-Ames theory of technologia taught at Harvard in the seventeenth century was in some respects a form of natural theology, for it assumed that the divine design of the universe was sufficiently manifest in the created world to be reliably deduced from natural evidence. The world was formed in accordance with intelligible patterns, vestiges of which are also in the human mind. The problem of the arts is to find the rules or axioms that went into the making of things, the artifacts of God. This task is greatly facilitated, according to the theory, by the exact correspondence that exists between the innate endowments of the human mind and the intelligible pattern of the material creation. A good statement of this theory and its connection to *eupraxia* appears in the "Synopsis Logicae" entered in a student notebook by Samuel Shepard (Harvard A.B., 1658), which deals specifically with the question, "Whether the arts are in things?"[74]

"Art is a rule of eupraxie, leading or guiding the creation in its operations towards its end," Shepard wrote or copied. The creation is not governed by "fortune and chance." The universe of "second beings," or the orders below men, are "guided by some hand . . . to which they yield obedience in subservience to the rule." By "rule" Shepard did not mean "any particular praecept or canon, as if all things were controuled by one singular word of command, in all their several orders, classes, comings and goings; or that rationall beings have the same individuall rule with naturall." Rule, he said, pertains to the "whole body of Laws given to the whole volume of second beings, and imprinted in the fabrick of the creature, contained in all catholicke axioms." These axioms or natural laws of the creation are derived by the method of analysis or resolution and constitute the elementary principles of the circle of the arts.[75]

The end or purpose of the arts is "the eupraxie" or "well acting of the creature," according to Shepard's notes, and he arrayed several arguments to establish this principle, which we need only summarize here. The main

74. Shepard's notes are in Abraham Pierson's "Notes of Lectures Attended at Harvard College," an unpaginated manuscript notebook in the Beinecke Library, Yale University, New Haven, Connecticut. Pierson graduated A.B. from Harvard in 1668. Although the notebook was eventually owned by Pierson, the material in it is from several different Harvard students. It includes several versions of Richardson's "*Prolegomena de arte in genere*," one of them by John Davis (Harvard A.B., 1651). A partial list of the contents of the notebook is given in Morison, *Seventeenth-Century Harvard*, 157n.

75. According to William Ames's "Technometry," contrary to what one would expect, analysis "begins with sense perception," moves to "observation, which carefully notes and retains those things which have been perceived," and is completed by induction. Ames expressly approved of the Baconian method. See Gibbs, "Technometry of Ames," 175. "Analysis" in 17th-century logics could refer to entirely different methods, forming general principles from concrete instances, as indicated here, or resolving general principles into components. Cf. Neal W. Gilbert, *Renaissance Concepts of Method* (New York, 1960).

points are as follows. All of nature, including man, can attain to "happiness" only through well-acting. "Naturall agents," that is, "second beings" or subrational creatures, "being voide of a discursive faculty" are unable to learn the rules of the arts "ab extra" or to receive "the precepts conducing to happiness by instruction from an external agent." The faculties of beings lower than man "are not soe exquisitely and purely tempered as to understand the dictates and suggestions of the learnedest schoolemaster." In animals, therefore, the rules of art are but the "impression and stampe of those great characters and statute laws upon their beings, whereby they are bent and inclined to make use and improvement of the most proper and requisite for the attaining of the end." But because of such instincts and natural traits, even the "inferior ranckes and classes of second beings have also a place in the Encyclopedia, and can lay title and claim to a share and portion in the rules of art." For creatures lower than man, as well as for man himself, "there is a naturall happinesse," which is related to their goodness in well-acting or *eupraxia*. "The highest happiness the creature [any creature] can attain to is well acting," but the "more noble [the creature is] the greater the beatitude." It is the "right acting of the [human] will" that comes "nearest to the action of the first being [God], which is the patterne of all noble acts," and there- fore the happiness of rational agents is greater and "more eminent than the faelicitie of naturall agents."

The end of the arts, then, is to lead "the creature to its happiness" via the path of *eupraxia*. Every particular rule of the arts "gives in its mite to the making up of this summe," Shepard wrote, and insofar as each rule "tends this way and gives its direction to this ultimately, soe far forth is it to be admitted a member of this corporation, and denominated a praecept of the arts. The whole body [of the arts together] is a compleat rule of happinesse." When well assembled, and when the end of *eupraxia* is kept constantly in view, art "doth as it were take the creature by the hand and lead through all the mazes of difficulty and meandrous turnings in which it is prone to loose itselfe and run aground. Directing it in the right course it ought to steere, it lays out the bounds of its acting, and workes or markes out the way it ought to walke in; it is [a] pilote through the narrow seas, to keep it from bulging upon the rocks of errour, or being swallowed in the quick sand of mistake."

It is important to note in all this, that rather than being simply the way of true happiness on earth, which was the Aristotelian connotation, *eupraxia* in New England meant thinking and acting in accordance with the principles inherent in the divine mind. All of the arts, all human knowledge, can only be a consolidation or an ingathering of the fragments of the archetypal "ideas" of God, who has implanted both in mankind (as ectype) and in nature (as entype) the eternal forms and rules of the arts. Copying from Richardson into his commonplace book in 1681, John Leverett, a future president of Harvard, wrote that "the cause and author of all true learning is God himself; and therefore of the Arts themselves[.] Though the observation of the Rules in Nature is attributed to Man, yet the Arts themselves [or] the Rules of them are from God. These Arts indeed being nothing but the Wisdome of God shineing in the things."[76]

In this context all scholarship, and higher education in general, becomes a sacred activity, since as a whole it is engaged in a kind of reconstitution of the splintered and refracted divine original. Although the meaning of the image "the circle of learning" (*enkuklios paideia*, encyclopedia) was subject to a variety of interpretations, one theory current in New England in the early period emphasized the archetypal flow from God in the Creation and the return to Him again, via the learned arts, of the original or pre-existing pattern. The end of learning, John Milton wrote, is "to repair the ruins of our first parents by regaining to know God aright." This concept of a cosmic circle of wisdom and goodness, emanation from God and remanation to Him, applied here specifically to learning, was also popular in Neoplatonist thought, which made the theory of technologia consistent with this influential body of metaphysical and theological teaching.[77]

76. Leverett's manuscript commonplace book is in the Massachusetts Historical Society, Boston. Rice, *Renaissance Idea of Wisdom*, ix, 28, has commented on the "moralization" of the idea of "wisdom," the term used by Leverett. "The secularization of the idea of wisdom is . . . a significant part of the effort of Renaissance thought to free philosophy and science from their traditional status of handmaidens to theology. Religion itself remained untouched; but several areas of human knowledge, of which ethics was the most important, achieved a new and preponderant importance." By the beginning of the 15th century, according to Rice, wisdom meant primarily moral philosophy or virtue (p. 40). In support of this assertion, one thinks of Pierre Charron's vastly influential *De la Sagesse* . . . (Bordeaux, 1601), a basic work in moral philosophy found in dozens of early American libraries, particularly in the South, in one or the other of two 17th-century English translations.

77. John H. Muirhead, *The Platonic Tradition in Anglo-Saxon Philosophy: Studies in the History of Idealism in England and America* (New York, 1931), 54, notes that Aristotle no less than Plato maintained that "that which knows and that which is known (reason and the world of reason) are really the same thing," yet it is obvious that the pre-eminent proponents of this concept in the 16th and 17th centuries were the Neoplatonists. No direct connection between Alexander Richardson and the Cambridge Platonists, who flourished somewhat later, has been established, but the affinity between New England Puritans and Cambridge Platonism is undeniable and became manifest toward the end of the 17th century when Henry More replaced Aristotle as the leading intellectual force in American philosophy. I discuss More's influence in chap. 6, below. Morison, *Founding of Harvard*, 99–100n, has observed that although no influence of the Cambridge Platonists "can be discerned in the writings of the early New England puritans" (a belief that in my opinion is open to question), there were a number of personal connections. Benjamin Whichcote, often considered the founder of the Platonist school, "married in 1643 the widow of Matthew Craddock, the first Governor of the Massachusetts Bay Company. . . . Ralph Cudworth was brought up by his stepfather, Dr. John Stoughton, brother of Israel Stoughton, an early Overseer of Harvard College. Ralph's brother James emigrated to New England, and became a friend to President Dunster."

All of the arts, William Ames had said, are subordinate to theology, a belief
that on the surface appears to be no different from the traditional medieval
idea that theology is the queen of the sciences to which all other areas of
knowledge are but handmaids. Ames's claim that theology is a practical and
not simply a speculative or contemplative discipline made a difference, however. It is a practical discipline, he said, "not only in the common respect that
all disciplines have εὐπραξία, good practice, as their end, but in a special and
peculiar manner compared with all others."[78] Reason itself, like all other
things, has a *eupraxia*, and necessarily the *eupraxia* of divine reason or
wisdom is the end and summation of the entire creation.[79] Theology is the
highest science not only because it pertains to the highest things, but also
because the "art of living" is the most "proper study" for man, and that form
of living that "approaches most closely the living and life-giving God" is the
best. Theology, which specifically teaches the art of living to God, is thus the
ultimate form of *eupraxia*.[80]

Yet the *eupraxia* of theology differed totally from the *eupraxia* of all the
other arts in that it was knowledge derived directly from revelation rather than
from "things," or nature. Ames emphatically distinguished theology from the
other five basic arts by the crucial reservation that its rules and principles are
uniquely neither found in things, through sense perception, observation, and
induction, nor impressed upon the human mind and waiting there for development and elaboration. Without this reservation Ames's *eupraxia* of theology
would have been indistinguishable from the naturalistic moral theology that he
outrightly rejected. "The basic principles of theology," Ames said, "though
they may be advanced by study and industry, are not in us by nature."[81] The
primary consequence of the Fall of Man was the loss of his ability to discern
reliably the goodness of things, that is, to recognize and choose what is truly
good. For the other arts, human reason does have sufficient capability to
arrive at truth without special revelation, but for the truth of well-acting or
well-living, the Holy Scriptures are indispensable.[82] So definite was Ames on

78. Ames, *Marrow of Theology*, I, i, 10.

79. The *eupraxia* of God is, of course, not discursive, but a single, simple, unique act.
"Insofar as it exists in God or the exercise of God, εὐπραξία is one unique and most simple act;
nevertheless, in the work exercised (namely, in created things which are all concrete and divis-
ible), it comes out manifold and various as it were from refraction of rays, and therefore is perceived by the eye of reason and exercised by man as manifold and divided." Quoted in Gibbs,
"Technometry of Ames," 160.

80. Ames, *Marrow of Theology*, I, i, 4–5.

81. *Ibid.*, 3.

82. Gibbs, "Technometry of Ames," 173–175. Ames explained ancient Greek and Roman
knowledge of the principles of honesty, justice, and equity, such as it was, by reference to the
influence of the ancient Hebrews.

this point that he left no room whatsoever for the development of a natural theology or a natural morality. Indeed, Ames took issue with those who, like Francis Bacon, assigned a category of human learning to that "knowledge or rudiment of knowledge concerning God, which may be obtained by the contemplation of His creatures." Such knowledge, Bacon argued, "may be truly termed *divine* in respect of the object, and *natural* in respect of the light [the light by which it is known]."[83]

The concept of *eupraxia*, then, can hardly be said to have neatly given rise to the moralizing of the curriculum found in the eighteenth century when we see that Ames was so careful to prevent exactly that possibility by reserving the determination of moral ends for theology alone, considered to be a revealed science only. Yet it seems undeniable that the resilient idea of *eupraxia* was inherently susceptible to springing back to its Aristotelian origins. The Yale College thesis of 1730, *"Omnes Artes & Scientiae, Arti vivendi subservire Debent"* (All the arts and sciences should be subordinate to the art of living), may seem on the surface to be very different from the seventeenth-century New England notion that all of the arts and sciences should be subordinate to the ultimate *eupraxia* of theology, the art of living *to God*, but by the second quarter of the eighteenth century Ames's original intent was lost. Only the skeletal ideal remained of subordinating potentially aimless learning to the doctrine of right living.

The new moral philosophers were as dedicated as the Puritan practical theologians to the task of reforming human conduct and human aspirations in the light of divine truth (albeit naturally discoverable truth) and to displacing Scholastic philosophy with the practical end of well-doing, which they called virtue. Missing from the views of the philosophers were convictions like Ames's about the exclusive role of scriptural revelation. "As for metaphysics," the brilliant moralist the third earl of Shaftesbury wrote in 1710, "and that which in the schools [i.e., among the Scholastics] is taught for logic or for ethics, I shall willingly allow it to pass for philosophy when by any real effects it is proved capable to refine our spirits, improve our understandings, or mend our manners." The goal of learning, Shaftesbury proposed, is not

83. Francis Bacon, *Of the Advancement of Learning*, ed. G. W. Kitchin, Everyman's Library (London and New York, 1915 [orig. publ. London, 1605]), 88. On Bacon's influence in 17th-century America, see Fiering, "Samuel Johnson," *WMQ*, 3d Ser., XXVIII (1971), 210–214. Among other criticisms of natural theology, Ames argued that "nothing can be known about God by natural light except what is known through effects or through argumentation from one attribute to another, and these conclusions may come into being also by supernatural light"; in addition, "everything of truth and certainty that is known about God by natural light has likewise been divinely revealed, i.e., is known also by supernatural light." Quoted in Gibbs, "Technometry of Ames," 187.

"defining material and immaterial substances, and distinguishing their properties and modes," but the "discovery of our own natures." The rest, he said,
is mere pretension.[84]

A hearty concern for moral philosophy was integral to the revolt against
Scholasticism. More than one thinker in the seventeenth and early eighteenth
centuries saw himself in the role of a new Socrates, bringing philosophy and
theology down to earth after a long period of fruitless wrangling in logic and
metaphysics.[85] Descartes and Gassendi both believed that "all philosophical
speculation should bear fruit in a doctrine of behaviour."[86] "By the science of
morals," Descartes wrote, "I understand the highest and most perfect which,
presupposing an entire knowledge of the other sciences, is the last degree of
wisdom."[87] A Cartesian disciple whose work was popular in England and
America, Antoine LeGrand, maintained in his *Body of Philosophy* that ethics
is the highest kind of philosophy, both "in Usefulness and the Worthiness of
its End. For whatsoever other Sciences prescribe, is only an Exercise and
Accomplishment of Human Wit: whereas the Rules of Ethicks are the Reme-
dies of the Soul." LeGrand put moral philosophy ahead of logic, natural
philosophy, and metaphysics, arguing, "Who is there amongst Men, that doth
not prefer the Love of Good before the Love of Truth, and that would not
rather embrace Vertue, than to please himself with the barren Knowledge of
it?" Moral philosophy, he said, is the "Mistress of Manners," the "Directrix
of Human Life," and the "Science of Life," in general. It is not so well
known that John Locke was similarly preoccupied with developing a science
of conduct. Not only in his *Thoughts on Education*, in which the problem of
attaining virtue is central, but even in the *Essay Concerning Human Understanding* this concern is evident. In the introduction to the *Essay* Locke wrote:
"Our business here is not to know all things, but those which concern our
conduct. If we can find out those measures, whereby a rational creature,

84. Anthony, earl of Shaftesbury, *Characteristics of Men, Manners, Opinions, Times*, ed.
John M. Robertson, 2 vols. bound as one (Indianapolis, Ind., 1964 [orig. publ. London, 1711]),
I, 188. The quotation is from Shaftesbury's *Soliloquy: or Advice to an Author*, which like most of
the other parts of the *Characteristics* was originally published separately, in 1710.

85. Ames himself used the example of Socrates in an address to theological students at the
University of Franeker in 1623. (See Nethenus, Visscher, and Reuter, *William Ames*, ed. and
trans. Horton, 173.) A few years later the famous Dutch theologian Gisbert Voet (or Voetius)
(1589–1676) used the same image: "Our theologians, like Socrates, may be said to have brought
theology from heaven down to earth, or, better, to have raised it to heaven from earth and
scholastic dust. On this point the English writers [like Ames] . . . are conspicuous." (*Selectae
disputationes theologicae . . .* , 5 vols. [Utrecht, 1648–1649], from the excerpt printed in
John W. Beardslee III, ed. and trans., *Reformed Dogmatics: J. Wollebius, G. Voetius, F. Turretin*
[New York, 1965], 268–269.)

86. Anthony Levi, S.J., *French Moralists: The Theory of the Passions, 1585–1649* (Oxford,
1964), 334.

87. Quoted by Flint, *Philosophy as Scientia Scientiarum*, 104.

put in that state in which man is in this world, may and ought to govern his opinions, and actions depending thereon, we need not to be troubled that some other things escape our knowledge."[88] What must be noted, in sum, about the seventeenth-century philosophy and theology that impinged on New England is the remarkable convergence among leading figures in both disciplines toward an emphasis on doctrines of living, the formulation of a synthetic practical faith in a world of cosmological and religious uncertainty. The pietistic movement in Reformed Protestantism, of which Ames was a great representative, with its stress on "practical theology," coincided with an existing trend in academic philosophy, a combination that gave great impetus to the growth of the new moral philosophy.

Programs like Shaftesbury's for infusing all learning with the goal of acquiring true virtue became an eighteenth-century creed, nowhere taken more seriously than among Puritan descendants in Scotland and America. Thus, for example, the Scottish moralist David Fordyce, whose ethics text was dominant at Harvard for the last half of the eighteenth century, affirmed that "every art and science is more or less valuable as it contributes more or less to our happiness. . . . Moral art or science, which unfolds our duty and happiness, must be a proper canon or standard, by which the dignity and importance of every other art and science are to be ascertained. It is therefore pre-eminent above all others; it is that master-art, that master-science, which weighs their respective merit, adjusts their rank in the scale of science, prescribes their measure, and superintends their efficacy and application in human life." Moral philosophy, Fordyce continued, is properly the "directress of life, the mistress of manners, the inventress of laws, and culture, the guide to virtue and happiness, without some degree of which man were a savage, and his life a scene of barbarity and wretchedness."[89] It is a near certainty that Fordyce was completely unaware that the pre-eminent role he assigned to moral philosophy was identical in most respects to that assigned by William Ames to technologia and the *eupraxia* of theology more than a hundred years earlier. Moreover, there could hardly have existed at Harvard in the mid-eighteenth century the same awareness that we have today from a distant perspective of the gradual absorption of seventeenth-century pietism into a philosophical movement, namely moral enthusiasm, or virtue-devotion.[90] Yet even without

88. Antoine LeGrand, *An Entire Body of Philosophy According to . . . Descartes, Written Originally in Latin*, trans. R[ichard] Blome (London, 1694), 346–347. See Lord Peter King, *The Life of John Locke . . .* , 2d ed., I (London, 1830), 198.

89. [David Fordyce], "The Elements of Moral Philosophy," Pt. ix in Robert Dodsley's *The Preceptor . . .* , 8th ed., II (London, 1793 [orig. publ. 1748]), 243. Fordyce's *Elements* was published separately for the first time in 1754, and there was a 4th ed. by 1769. It also appeared in all eight editions of *The Preceptor* published in the 18th century.

90. For the relationship of Jonathan Edwards to this development, see Fiering, *Jonathan Edwards's Moral Thought*.

such contemporary understanding of how New England—indeed, Britain as well—had gotten from there to here, the small coterie of learned men at Harvard and vicinity did know instinctively that in a changed world full of dangers to religion and morals, a work such as Fordyce's *Elements of Moral Philosophy* "felt" right as the best that could be expected from the times, without reverting to suicidal reactionism.

Nature and Conscience

One irony of the Protestant movement is that for all its emphasis on Scripture as the sole and proper basis of Christian belief, the attention that the Reformers at the same time focused on conscience left open a convenient route away from any form of religious authority, even written revelation. The emphasis on conscience, however unintendedly, could all too easily be diverted into subjectivism and individualism. Similarly, for all of the stress in Calvinism on man's debased state after the Fall, the notion of conscience yet remained as a measure of the spark of natural moral understanding and goodness, in apparent contradiction to the orthodox teaching about reprobation. Philosophically and theologically conscience was an ambiguous attribute of humanity, at once central to religion and morals but also troublesome in its implications because of its susceptivity to interpretation in naturalistic and individualistic terms. Although the subject of conscience as such was not taught as part of the academic moral philosophy course—it did not fit into the Aristotelian format—it is necessary to review it here briefly, since certain ideas from the theory of conscience merged into the new moral philosophy that began to be taught in the late seventeenth century.

Most of the notions about conscience that were current in the seventeenth century had already been worked out in the Middle Ages. The Reformers added to the existing ideas not so much new theories as new emphases, and they tended generally to attribute to conscience greater authority, especially when compared to other sources of religious authority. The medieval theologians, notably Bonaventure and Thomas Aquinas, borrowed from Aristotle some psychological concepts, and from Stoic moral theory as expressed in Cicero and Seneca they took some substantive descriptions of conscience, but the developed theory, despite these Classical roots, was essentially a creation of Christianity, rooted in the writings of St. Paul and the early church fathers.[91]

The basic elements of the theory of conscience as it was derived from the

91. For medieval theories of conscience I am following mostly Odon Lottin, *Psychologie et morale aux XII*[e] *et XIII*[e] *siècles*, II (Louvain, 1948), 203–240.

thirteenth century are simple enough to describe, although all parts of the theory were subject to one sort of controversy or another. The term "conscience," a translation from the Greek "*syneidesis*," referred specifically to the judgment of the mind concerning the moral goodness or badness of a *particular act*. Experience with a retrospective bad conscience was primary in the formulation of the theory, and this experience was then later elaborated into a notion of conscience as a judgment antecedent to action, telling the agent beforehand about the moral value of a possible act. A distinction was also drawn between the satisfaction of good conscience and the remorse of bad conscience. But many Protestant writers in particular questioned whether an unregenerate person could have either a good conscience or a directive (that is, antecedent) conscience.

If the term "conscience" referred technically only to particular judgments, what was the basis of such judgments? The general moral knowledge that provided the principles or norms of conscience was called "*synteresis*" (also "*synderesis*"). Although this term was in nearly universal use, there remained, nevertheless, considerable debate about the exact nature of synteresis. Bonaventure believed that synteresis properly was the natural inclination to good located in the will, in effect, a natural human intention or disposition to do right. The more intellectual or gnomic function of conscience was subject to error, but individual conscience, which for Bonaventure included both general principles of action and particular judgments, would still always be guided by the general inclination to the good that was intrinsic to the will.[92]

St. Thomas, on the other hand, located synteresis in the intellect rather than in the will, calling it an innate habit, or a natural property of the mind, but not a special faculty as some others had designated it. He identified it as the source of the universal or general propositions that must come into play in any moral judgment. The model of the action of conscience for Thomas was the syllogism, with the major premise supplied intuitively by synteresis and the minor premise deduced rationally from the general rule to the individual case. Conscience, then, supplied the conclusion to the sequence of reasoning, in the form of a judgment on a particular act. Synteresis and conscience worked in complementary fashion, the one with the general, the other with the specific, and were related as habit to act.[93] The principles of Natural Law were

92. McAdoo, *Caroline Moral Theology*, 66, holds that "there is no trace in Caroline theology, nor for that matter among the reformed moralists, of that view of conscience as seated in the conative side of our nature, which has been identified with the Franciscan schoolmen. Everywhere the Thomist tradition predominates." Cf. the Harvard thesis of 1646: *Synteresis fundatur in intellectu* (Synteresis is grounded in intellect). Yet there is some evidence opposed to McAdoo's categorical statement.

93. Cf. Thomas Aquinas, *Summa Theologica*, trans. Fathers of the English Dominican Province, 3d ed. (London, 1938), Pt. I, Q. 79, art. 12, hereafter cited as Aquinas, *Summa Theologica*.

assumed to correspond with synteresis, the only difference being that the latter is concerned specifically with moral conduct, giving the directives that individuals ought to follow and thus serving as the foundation for conscience, whereas Natural Law is less practically oriented toward individual behavior.

This sketch of the functioning of conscience as understood in the Scholastic tradition is rudimentary but will suffice as background to the analyses characteristic of seventeenth-century Puritanism. The inherited body of ideas about conscience, it should be noted, whether voluntarist as in Bonaventure's theory, or intellectualist as in Thomas's, imparted in a general way certain basic principles about the nature of man, even after the Fall: Human beings are innately moral, in the sense that they necessarily see things in moral terms; morality is naturally important to humankind, indeed a matter of urgent concern; intuitive reason provides mankind with some basic tenets of morality, such as equity, justice, and honesty (there was some controversy, however, about how specific the content of synteresis is); conscience not only brings judgment but in combination with synteresis may also serve as an inducement or incitement to good conduct; and in a theory like Bonaventure's, there was also the assumption that man is naturally inclined to goodness in his will. In short, the very tradition of discourse concerning conscience included certain principles that were not easily reconciled in all cases with other theological notions characteristic of Calvinist Protestantism.

The primary difference between the Protestant and Catholic theories of conscience, as is well known, concerned the degree to which each group believed that external authority is binding upon conscience. Both accepted that only the word of God could bind the conscience, that is, could supply the authoritative and obligatory general rules by which individual judgments were to be made. But the question remained of determining when, in fact, God has spoken and beyond that, of determining what, in fact, He has said. Reliance on Scripture, as interpreted with the assistance of God's grace, as opposed to reliance on the authority of an earthly hierarchy, was the original Protestant solution to the problems posed by the inherent vagueness of the theory of conscience. But despite this biblical standard, Protestants found it virtually impossible to stabilize the moral authority presumed to govern conscience. From the point of view of religious solidarity the difficulties raised by this

---

Synteresis is a habit of the soul of certain practical principles bestowed on us by nature, by which we are incited to good and which "murmurs" at evil. *Conscientia* is not a habit but an act, or the application of moral knowledge to individual cases. "But since habit is a principle of act [i.e., comes before "act" logically, habit being a facility in acting], sometimes the name conscience is given to the first natural habit—namely *synderesis*: thus Jerome calls *synderesis* conscience" (*ibid.*, art. 13). On the complicated relationship between habits and acts, see the summary of theories and the bibliography in Fiering, "Benjamin Franklin and the Way to Virtue," *American Quarterly*, XXX (1978), 199–223.

absence of fixed authority were tremendous. Subjectivism and individualism could run rampant. From the point of view of common morality, however, the moral consensus in the West was such that with the exception of occasional fringe groups, the breakdown of clear authority over conscience made little practical difference in the seventeenth and eighteenth centuries. Even materialists and atheists could be good citizens, it was discovered.

A second significant difference between Protestants and Catholics concerned their contrary assumptions about the effects of the Fall, both on man's knowledge of moral principles and on his disposition toward right conduct. The Protestants tried to assign only the barest minimum of moral powers to the natural man, reserving the glories of conscience mainly for the regenerate. But the very meaning of conscience required that one describe it in universal terms, or else it would no longer be conscience.[94] To refuse to recognize the universality of conscience was to demote part of mankind to the level of beasts, which even the severest Calvinists were not prepared to do. So in this case, too, it was difficult to confine conscience within orthodox limits of meaning.

Two texts on conscience were particularly influential in early New England, William Perkins's *Discourse of Conscience* (1596) and William Ames's *Conscience with the Power and Cases thereof* (English, 1643; Latin, 1630). A summary of each, viewed from the perspective of subsequent developments in moral philosophy, will suggest the eminent suitability of the Puritan theory of conscience for adaptation to the uses of secular moral philosophy.

In reading William Perkins's theory of conscience one is immediately impressed by his determined construction of a sacrosanct personal inner space, separating the individual from earthly context and leaving only the privacy of the individual's relationship with God. Perkins defined conscience nominally as part of the faculty of understanding, but he described it as highly specialized in its purpose and different from any other activity of the mind. He called conscience a "naturall power, facultie, or created qualitie," although he did not intend to elevate it to the status of an entirely independent faculty. Conscience is found only in rational beings, namely angels and men, not in beasts, and also not in God, who is perfectly righteous and therefore does not need a conscience. In its functions of bearing witness, giving sentence, and judging what one has done or may do, conscience differs from all other "gifts of the mind," such as intelligence, opinion, knowledge, faith, and prudence.[95]

94. In a letter to John Endicott written in Aug. or Sept. 1651, Roger Williams defined conscience as a "persuasion fixed in the mind and heart of a man which enforceth him to judge . . . and to do so and so with respect to God." This conscience, Williams said, "is found in all mankind, more or less, in Jews, Turks, Papists, Protestants, pagans, etc." Bradford Swan typescript of Williams's letters in the Rhode Island Historical Society, Providence.

95. Perkins, *A Discourse of Conscience* . . . , in Thomas F. Merrill, ed., *William Perkins,*

One limitation of conscience that distinguished it from the eighteenth-century notion of a moral sense, it should be noted, was its application only to the actions of the possessor. It was not a judge of the actions of others, although, presumably, synteresis could serve as a general criterion for judging the deeds of others.

For the religious mind the most important attribute of conscience, indeed its raison d'être, was its "divine nature." Conscience, according to Perkins, is "placed of God in the middest betweene him and man, as an arbitratour to give sentence and to pronounce either with man or against man unto God." In both the Catholic and Protestant traditions, the divine nature of conscience is integral to its meaning. It is the divinity of conscience that differentiates it from any mere subjective self-constraint or urging and removes it from the category of a merely cultural construct, such as the superego purports to be. Perkins's etymological interpretation of the word "conscience" indicated its holy nature as he understood it. "*Scire*, to know, is of one man alone by himselfe: and *conscire* is, when two at least knows some secret thing." Conscience, like the eye of God, knows what the mind thinks. Sinful thoughts cannot be hidden from it. Therefore, through conscience man and God know together; they are "partners in the knowledge of one and the same secret." This partnership can only be with God, for only He "knows perfectly all the doings of man, though they be never so hid and concealed: and by a gift given him of God, man knowes together with God, the same things of himselfe." This gift of self-awareness or of reflection upon our thoughts and deeds is the essence of conscience.[96] In Perkins's thinking, the terms "conscience" and "conscious" are hardly differentiated, as they are not in Latin and some other European languages. Conscience is God's sharing in man's consciousness of himself.

In earlier Scholastic treatments of conscience one does not find to the same degree as in Perkins either the personalizing of the relationship between man and God via conscience or the stress on interior scrutiny, that is, the intense concern with conscience as the light that illuminates the hidden recesses of sin in the inner man. The strong Puritan belief in the value of reflexivity in the moral and religious life, which is apparent in Perkins's writings, contributed

---

1558–1602, English Puritanist: His Pioneer Works on Casuistry . . . (Nieuwkoop, Netherlands, 1966 [orig. publ. Cambridge, 1596]), 5–6, hereafter cited as Perkins, *Discourse*. Breward, ed., *Work of Perkins*, notes in his excellent introduction that Perkins "did not entirely escape the danger of treating [conscience] as a separate faculty." Perkins rejected the Thomist notion that conscience "was equivalent to reason . . . because it failed to do justice to the inwardness of conscience and its capacity to go against reason. Perkins insisted that as the vicegerent of God it was superior to reason" (pp. 64–65).

96. Perkins, *Discourse*, 7.

generally, as we will see, to the increased psychological awareness of secular moral philosophy in the seventeenth and eighteenth centuries.

Conscience has two main functions, according to Perkins. It bears witness, and it gives judgment. Like "a Notarie, or a Register," it "hath alwaies the penne in his [its] hand, to note and record whatsoever is said or done." It observes and takes notice of all and reports on it inwardly and secretly. Conscience then gives judgment, which it does in the light of the binding power of God's commands. For only the word of God has the "prerogative to bridle, binde, and restraine the conscience." Human laws cannot bind the conscience morally or affect man's salvation.[97] Human laws cannot define sin or sanctity. Perkins did affirm that obedience to the magistracy is an ordinance of God, which therefore makes it incumbent upon men and women in conscience to fashion their outward behavior in accordance with order and peace. But there is a great difference, Perkins argued, between this principle and what he saw as the Roman Catholic practice, which enforced spiritual obedience of conscience to human law. Men are obliged in conscience to obey only God's word, which includes "the very law of nature written in all men's hearts . . . in the creation of man" as well as the commandments of Scripture.[98]

Perkins saw an inherent contradiction in any claim by mere men to exercise authority over the judgments of conscience, a contradiction based on confusion between the inner and the outer man. God is able to command conscience because His laws are spiritual and directed toward the spirit, which He has immediate access to. Divine law commands "bodie and spirit, with all the thoughts, will, affections, desires, and faculties, and requires obedience of them all according to their kind."[99] The laws of men, however, cannot command thoughts and affections and can "reach no further than the outward man, that is, to body and goods, with the speeches and deeds thereof." The end of human law is and should be only to maintain the "external and civil peace which is between man and man," not to maintain the "spiritual peace of conscience." Since men have no way of penetrating the inward lives of other men and are unable to discern the most private inclinations and judgments, it is not "meete," Perkins wrote, that magistrates or others should attempt to command conscience, of which they have no witness.[100]

In line with his tendency to personalize the exercise of conscience, which becomes in his conception not so much an involuntary process of reasoning—a moral syllogism linking individual acts to general rules—as an internal companion and counselor, Perkins emphasized the role of conscience in ante-

97. *Ibid.*, 22.
98. *Ibid.*, 10.
99. *Ibid.*, 31.
100. *Ibid.*, 31–32.

cedent judgments. Conscience gives judgment of things to come "by fore-telling and (as it were) saying inwardly in the heart, that this thing may bee well done. Of this kind of judgment, every man may have experience in him-selfe, when he is about to enterprise any business either good or bad." We are pilgrims in this world, Perkins wrote, and God "hath appointed our con-science to be our companion and guide, to shewe us what course we may take and what we may not."[101] Indeed, in Perkins's eyes conscience is the direct voice of God not only in guiding conduct but also in discovering spiritual truth. Conscience is the medium through which the most intimate relations with the Holy Spirit are sustained. It is through the *regenerate* conscience that the saved get "infallible certainty" of the pardon of sin and of life everlasting. Perkins guarded against the danger of such a notion dissolving into a mere "feeling" of assurance by arguing that this knowledge, which after all is communicated through a rational faculty, derives its certainty from a logical deductive process of understanding, not simply from a sense of "inward delight or peace." An "unfallible certentie of pardon or sinne and life ever-lasting is the propertie of everie renued conscience," Perkins held. The manner of "imprinting" is by the Holy Ghost "inlightening the minde and conscience with spiritual and divine light." Gradually a syllogism is formed by which one sees himself or herself in congruence with God's expectations of man, and a rational certainty follows:

> Every one that beleeves is the child of God:
> But I doe believe: Therefore, I am the child of God.[102]

In the state of regeneration conscience has a more active and positive role than it does for the natural man; it serves as a "solliciter to put [one] in mind of all his affaires and duties which he is to performe to God: yea it is the controller to see all thinges kept in order in the heart, which is the temple and habitation of the Holy Ghost."[103] As a unique spiritual principle and interior guide, Perkins's renewed or regenerate conscience is hardly a step away from the "candle of the lord" that Benjamin Whichcote and other Cambridge Platonists later in the seventeenth century made so much of. The difference, of course, is that for Whichcote and his colleagues, the concept of a special, exclusive regenerating grace was much de-emphasized, and the idea of a *universal* natural/divine light featured instead. In a later chapter we will see how similar Henry More's "boniform faculty" was to Perkins's conscience as

101. *Ibid.*, 41. Cf. Breward, ed., *Work of Perkins*, 65: "When Perkins spoke of good con-science never leading astray, it was not because he saw it as an autonomous guide in which modern subjectivism announced itself, but rather because a good conscience, regeneration, and obedience to the word were inseparable."

102. Perkins, *Discourse*, 61.

103. *Ibid.*, 65.

an inner representation of the spirit. Among the Cartesians also in the latter part of the seventeenth century conscience was expanded into a principle of moral and psychological optimism. "The Dictates of Reason are so evidently imprest upon [man's] Mind," Antoine LeGrand wrote, "that he readily follows what is Just and Right without any Matter, without any Written Law, without any compulsion of the Magistrates, and discerns betwixt that which is equal and unequal, by the Light of his Conscience only." LeGrand believed that the Ten Commandments were only cursorily stated in the Old Testament because God had already written them in human hearts.

> For a Ray of the Primordial Reason, appears in Man by a twofold preeminence: for being endued with Reason, the light which illuminates other Creatures outwardly and superficially only, is his property and part of his Essence. And in the second place, the Sense of Right and Truth and Affection for it, is most intimately present in his Heart, whereby he is directed both in his Speculation and Practice. The Minds of Men are stored with the Seeds of Vertue and Honesty, which are excited by the least admonition, like a spark of Fire, which being only assisted with a small Blast, displays it self into a great Flame.[104]

William Ames was in the same tradition as Perkins, but he was more of an academician, more influenced by Scholasticism (from which he tried to break free), and less of a popularizer. Perkins had avoided the term "*synteresis*," but it is explicit in Ames's work, and Ames in general was concerned about defining his opinions in relation to the Roman Catholic tradition. Conscience, Ames wrote, "stands in the place of God himselfe." Its operation may be divided into three parts. It is a law, a witness, and a judge to the sinner. The structure is strictly syllogistic. Synteresis supplies the general law or the major proposition; for example: "He that lives in sinne shall dye." Then comes the minor proposition or the particular application in the form of a witness: "I live in sinne." Ames called this action "*syneidesis*," the Greek equivalent of the word "conscience." Finally, there is the judgment, which Ames called the "*crisis*": "I shall dye."[105] Ames took particular care to point out that the proceedings of conscience are discursive and syllogistic rather

104. LeGrand, *Body of Philosophy*, trans. Blome, 357. This work by LeGrand was in the estate of a Boston bookseller by 1700. See Worthington Chauncey Ford, *The Boston Book Market, 1679–1700* (Boston, 1917), 168. LeGrand's logic, along with Antoine Arnauld's, was widely taught in New England beginning in the 1680s.

105. Ames, *Conscience with the Power and Cases thereof . . .* , in *The Works of . . . William Ames* (London, 1643), I, 3–6, hereafter cited as Ames, *Conscience*. Perkins, *Discourse*, 38, gives a slightly different example: "*Every murtherer is cursed*, saith the minde; *Thou art a murtherer*, saith conscience assisted by memorie; *Thou art cursed*, saith conscience, and so giveth her sentence."

than a matter of "simple apprehension" or intuition, for the primary function of conscience is to *convict* of sin, not to *know*. It is not a "contemplative judgement, whereby truth is simply discerned from falsehood; but a practical judgement," which directly moves with ineluctable force from general understanding of God's law to one's own spiritual or moral condition.[106]

The internal movement of conscience could be corrupted, however. On this everyone agreed. Satan may mislead a person, or the passions blind the judgment. Perkins had sketched out the course of a descent into personal hell, beginning with obstinacy and perversity, moving on to the gradual extinction of the light of nature, the emergence of a reprobate mind that calls evil good and good evil, the seared conscience that has lost all sensitivity and is incapable of remorse, and finally arriving at the ultimate degeneracy when a person is caught in "exceeding greedinesse to all manner of sinne."[107] The question of whether synteresis could be totally extinguished had been actively debated in the Middle Ages. An even more difficult problem for Protestants was determining its degree of efficacy when one lacked supernatural regeneration. Ames expressed the prevailing view, with all of its ambiguities. Knowledge of Natural Law is "still conserved" even after the Fall, yet "that Law which is written and ingraven in nature, containing the rules of honesty and naturall justice, is in a manner wholly buried by originall corruption, and almost totally overwhelmed by custome in sinning," so that "neither these rules of honesty, which are within the booke of the mind, are fully and perfectly legible, nor can our understanding read anything therein, distinctly and plainly." Thus, like the written law in the Old Testament, "conscience only deepens man's self-conviction of sin" without providing clear guidance.[108] Ames thought of conscience as *wholly buried* when it was proposed as a basis

---

106. Edward Reynolds, *A Treatise of the Passions and Faculties of the Soule of Man* . . . (London, 1640), in *Works*, 773, defined conscience similarly to Ames: It is "not any distinct Faculty of the soul, but only a compounded Act of Reason, consisting in Argumentation; or a *practick Syllogism*, inferring always some Applicative and Personal Conclusion, Accusing, or Executing." Cf. also Samuel Willard, *A Compleat Body of Divinity* . . . (Boston, 1726), 573: "Conscience properly belongs to the practical Understanding and is therefore fitted to Conduct a Man in acting according to Rule. Whether Conscience be an Habit, or only an Act I dispute not; but that it is not a Faculty or Power distinct from the Understanding, I think may be made good, if we consider the Nature of the Understanding and Usefulness of it in Man, which is not only to inform him in the Theory of Things, but also to guide him in practice." Willard wrote this description in *ca.* 1701.

107. Perkins, *Discourse*, 68.

108. Ames, *Conscience*, II, 2; see also, *Marrow of Theology*, II, ii, 15. That conscience was a negative, restraining faculty rather than a basis for doing positive good was also the view of Ames's contemporary Francis Bacon. Although the "light of nature" is "imprinted upon the spirit of man by an inward instinct, according to the law of conscience," Bacon wrote, it is sufficient only "to check the vice, but not to inform the duty." *Advancement of Learning*, ed. Kitchin, 210.

for autonomous ethics, but only as *indistinct* when it was needed to make men aware of their moral inadequacy. The position taken by the New England minister Samuel Willard at the end of the seventeenth century seems to have been the common one and more or less represents both Perkins's and Ames's views: "Since the Fall, there are some remains of the Law on the Conscience of Men, enough to leave them without excuse, yet not sufficient to direct them in the way of Holiness or Righteousness."[109]

The typical Calvinist or Puritan demeaning of the natural man, although highly conspicuous when the necessity of salvation was discussed, did not preclude considerable recognition of human goodness in other contexts. Like many Scholastics and Humanists before him, Ames accepted that all created things have a natural tendency toward God from whom they came; that in all creation, including man, there is a "natural inclination or principle" leading to obedience to the law of nature, and "a peculiar stirring up of living creatures to higher activities."[110] A belief in the synteresis of the will, such as posited by Bonaventure, is evident in Ames's thinking. Ames's own voluntarism led him at one point to describe synteresis as *habitus*, that is, a disposition in the heart, heart and will being virtually synonymous in his writing.[111] Even under the condition of "spiritual death" that follows from sin, "God imparts a certain moderation," which takes the form of "vestiges of God's image," and these vestiges appear both in the understanding and in the will. Because of these vestiges all men retain "a certain inclination to dimly known good," and the "shadows of virtue are approved and cultivated by all." Somewhat unusual, perhaps, was Ames's assertion that even the sensitive appetite "possesses some dispositions which make it possible for the will commanding rightly to be more easily obeyed; and so these dispositions partly resemble virtue."[112]

Yet we also find all of the expected reservations and contradictions to these optimistic comments. If there is in man a faint natural inclination to good, Ames also held that Original Sin has established a "habitual deviation . . . or a turning aside from the law of God." Not only is the whole man corrupted in terms of his general moral capacities, but each of his parts—intellect, conscience, will, "affections of every kind," and "the body and all its members" —is also depraved. Sin brings with it "a certain ineptness and perversity of

---

109. Willard, *Compleat Body*, 577.

110. Ames, *Marrow of Theology*, I, viii, 21, ix, 23.

111. Ames located virtue in the will, not in the practical intellect. Virtue is "a condition or habit [*habitus*] by which the will is inclined to do well" (*ibid.*, II, ii, 4). The will is also "the proper and prime subject" of the grace by which man is called and saved, and the conversion of the will "is the effectual principle in the conversion of the whole man" (*ibid.*, I, xvii, 23). For discussion of theories of will in 17th-century New England, see chap. 3, below.

112. Ames, *Marrow of Theology*, I, xiv, 22–28; II, ii, 7; see also, I, x, 26.

all bodily faculties, which in their way are in conflict with the right way of doing things approved by God." And in "any moral situation," the "very inclination is morally evil."[113]

All of the evidence we have adduced here about the place of naturalistic ethics in relation to Christian teaching, from the ancient world through the seventeenth century, leads to the same inconclusiveness. On the one hand there was the Hebraic inheritance of revealed law, which some hoped and believed would be a sufficient foundation for both academic teaching and practical life. This law was manifested in both Scripture and conscience. On the other hand there was the Classical inheritance of moral philosophy, running from Socrates to Plutarch, a collective achievement of such magnitude and diversity that educated men could not ignore it. Clergy and scholars in the tiny outpost of Western culture that was Harvard in the seventeenth century, like learned men elsewhere in Europe and Britain, did their best to balance these influences, in some cases by overt syncretism and in others by advancing the unrealistic hope of a purified and purged Christian ethics, free of pagan contamination. There were advocates, too, of a revived paganism, continuing a tendency that had originated in Italian Humanism. The new moral philosophy that emerged in the course of the seventeenth and early eighteenth centuries necessarily contained elements from many sources, both Christian and pagan, and the exact nature of the amalgam could not have been predicted by anybody. It was both profoundly Judaeo-Christian in some essentials and also deeply indebted to Plato, Aristotle, and Cicero. The basis of moral authority shifted slowly to "reason" and "nature" from Scripture and revelation, and at the same time the traditions of orthodoxy represented by the institutional clergy counted for much less. But it was a Christianized reason and a Christianized nature that came to the foreground, albeit well camouflaged. Certain Christian assumptions about transcendence and grace were implicit in the moral philosophy enterprise of the eighteenth century. Nearly all of these issues and changes were reflected in the study and teaching of moral philosophy at Harvard prior to *ca.* 1700.

113. *Ibid.*, I, xiii, 2, 4, xvii, 7; see also, I, xiv, 8.

2

Scholastic Ethics

*The end of moral philosophy is
human happiness, i.e., the sort of state
as perfect as possible for man,
prescribed by correct natural reason
for his life on earth among men.*[1]

The controversy at Harvard over whether ethics might be taught independently of theology, or more precisely, whether it could rest on intellectual foundations that were independent of theology, was in most respects an idle quarrel. By the time Harvard was founded some form of study of Aristotle's ethics was a deeply ingrained, if always precarious, component of university education. To have ignored this tradition would have exposed Harvard graduates to the risk of exclusion from the republic of learned men. For a newly founded, provincial institution such a risk was all the greater. The Puritan clergy who dominated the college were men who hoped to have the best of both worlds: the freedom to exercise discrimination in what they accepted of the old ways, and, at the same time, the satisfaction of being full-fledged participants in a culture grander than their own. This kind of balancing act is typified in church polity by the concept of nonseparating Congregationalism within the Anglican church. The ambiguity of the Puritans' relationship to moral philosophy is another small example. The New England way had a distinctive contribution to make, but it was not intended to be a revolutionary one. The modest defense recorded by a Harvard student in the late 1660s to the charge that New Englanders put too much stock in William Ames, who was after all a "nobody" and "unheard of," captured exactly the prevailing spirit of compromise: Every new thought must have its time, the student copied, and "'Tis noe disparagement" to the "antient philosophers that something was obscured from them."[2]

---

1. Franco Burgersdyck, *Idea Philosophiae, Tum Moralis, Tum Naturalis* . . . 2d ed. (Oxford, 1637), 6.
2. This answer to Ames's denigrators appears in Abraham Pierson's "Notes of Lectures Attended at Harvard College," MS, Beinecke Lib., Yale Univ.

Direct evidence of the nature of ethical studies at seventeenth-century Harvard in the form of student notebooks is skimpy, but there is fairly solid knowledge of the "textbooks" that were in use. A review of some of these and the available commencement theses, together with the bit that can be gotten from manuscript notebooks kept by students, makes up a clear enough picture. Our immediate concern is with ethical studies prior to about 1690. For in the closing years of the century events combined to bring about a break with the past order. The arrival of Charles Morton fresh from association with the dissenting academies in England, the de facto leadership of the college by John Leverett and William Brattle, and perhaps related to these two events, the adoption in the 1680s of Henry More's *Enchiridion Ethicum* (1667) as the principal text for moral philosophy definitely extracted Harvard from the Scholastic pattern in ethics. These important changes leading out of the seventeenth century we will consider in the fifth and sixth chapters.

To speak of a book as a "text" at a seventeenth-century university can mean several different things. We must always keep in mind, first of all, that college work in this period was still preponderantly oral. Students read books for the purpose of developing their forensic skills. For many different philosophical questions there were a limited number of arguments on both sides that had to be committed to memory, ready to be drawn upon in debate, and these traditional arguments could be found in a variety of works. Since mastery of the traditional arguments was one of the goals of education in philosophy, what we would today call the "point of view" of the author was relatively unimportant, and a text by a fourteenth-century Roman Catholic might do as well as one by a seventeenth-century Protestant. That books were expensive in general and relatively scarce in Massachusetts compelled such latitude.

Students were certainly not given long syllabuses of required reading to do on their own. Many young scholars went through college owning only a few volumes, including a Bible.[3] The college library was usually not open to the first three classes, and only the exceptional senior would turn to it frequently in any case.[4] To say that a book was "used as a text" in early America does

3. The earliest record of a student's library at Harvard College, as far as I know, is the list that Solomon Stoddard made in his commonplace book in 1664, when he was at the college preparing for his master's degree in divinity. The manuscript notebook is owned by Union Theological Seminary in New York City and is not mentioned by Morison in his history of Harvard in the 17th century. Stoddard owned about 85 titles in 1664, but a library that large was unusual for a student. He may have collected a substantial number of his books after earning his baccalaureate degree when he set about to read in earnest for the ministry. See Fiering, "Solomon Stoddard's Library at Harvard in 1664," *Harvard Library Bulletin*, XX (1972), 255–269.

4. The rules governing the use of the library as of 1667 are in *Harvard College Recs.*, I, 194–196. See also, Samuel Eliot Morison, *Three Centuries of Harvard, 1636–1936* (Cambridge, Mass., 1936), 32.

not mean, then, that every student owned a copy. It primarily means that at the least such a book is known to have been a resource used by students in preparing for their disputations. It may also mean that a tutor lectured from the book and that students took notes from these lectures and thus had a personal précis, such as it was, of the work. Many students must have recited in class or disputed on the basis of their notes alone, or on the basis of the notes of a student predecessor at the college which one might have reason to feel were more reliable than one's own. Both books and lecture notes were widely shared and passed on from student to student.

All of the ethics texts in use at Harvard prior to Henry More's were unmistakably in the Peripatetic tradition, not excluding its various Scholastic accretions. Even works that expressed discontent with such subservience to Aristotle failed to escape the Aristotelian and the Thomist impress. The science itself had been given a certain form by Aristotle and his commentators, and to break that mold it was necessary to found a new discipline, as it were, the "new moral philosophy." This step was not so much a matter of finding an area of concern entirely outside of Aristotle's ken as of shifting the emphasis and enlarging the scope of the subject.

It will be our goal here to convey an impression of what the college student learned, or at least heard, in his encounter with academic moral philosophy in seventeenth-century New England prior to about 1690, and to isolate some of the areas of controversy and special significance. The result will be consciously biased by my interest in bringing to the foreground mainly those questions and issues that will help to reveal the lines of development leading into the eighteenth century, an interest that obviously did not concern Harvard students in the seventeenth century.

Our knowledge of Harvard textbooks in the seventeenth century largely depends upon the remarkable work of Arthur O. Norton. For twenty years Norton searched for surviving copies of books that contained autograph signatures of early Harvard students. Often volumes were found with a succession of student names, making clear the book's repeated formal or informal use for decades.[5] Samuel Eliot Morison's investigation of the curriculum at seventeenth-century Harvard and Perry Miller's *New England Mind* confirmed

5. Arthur O. Norton, "Harvard Text-Books and Reference Books of the Seventeenth Century," Col. Soc. Mass., *Transactions*, XXVIII (1935), 361–438. This same volume of *Transactions* contains two other useful articles on 17th-century libraries and reading: Charles F. Robinson and Robin Robinson, "Three Early Massachusetts Libraries," 107–175, and [Samuel Eliot] Morison, "[Note on] the Library of George Alcock, Medical Student, 1676," 350–357. Other standard studies are: Tuttle, "Libraries of the Mathers," Am. Antiq. Soc., *Procs.*, N.S., XX (1909–1910), 269–356; Alfred C. Potter, "Catalogue of John Harvard's Library," Col. Soc. Mass., *Trans.*, XXI (1919), 190–230; and the supplement to Potter, Henry J. Cadbury, "John Harvard's Library," *ibid.*, XXXIV (1943), 353–377.

and also drew heavily from Norton's data. From the work of these scholars and other sources as well, a small, selective list of available ethics texts may be culled. I intend to review here four of these books, chosen first of all because of their prominence, and secondly because together they illustrate several stages of development.[6]

It is essential to remember, however, that these few works were part of a vast Latin literature now largely ignored or forgotten, especially the Protestant contributions to it. (Roman Catholic scholars have made greater efforts to study the late sixteenth-century and seventeenth-century Scholasticism representative of their faith.) Because of the hiatus in basic historical research encountered here, there are great dangers that discussions will be inadvertently wrested from their proper context and particular ideas given a significance they do not deserve when set in proper relation to the whole. The "immense accumulation of scholastic thought" lay before the Puritans "like an Aztec city before the plunderer," Perry Miller once noted.[7] My only criticism of this apt image is that it suggests far too much independence of the plunder than actually existed. The Puritans were not somehow historically exempted from the weight of the philosophical past. In the area of moral philosophy, at least, there is almost no better reference work to which one can turn for enlightenment on seventeenth-century Puritan thinking than the *Summa Theologica* of Thomas Aquinas.[8] We must begin, then, with some account of the long Christian dialogue with Aristotle's *Nicomachean Ethics* as it manifested itself in Cambridge, Massachusetts, from 1640 to 1690.

6. A more complete survey of the reading of ethics in 17th-century New England would have to include, in addition to the four works discussed in this chapter, the following titles: Lambert Daneau (Daneus), *Ethices Christianae* . . . (Geneva, 1577); William Pemble, *A Summe of Moral Philosophy* . . . (Oxford, 1632); Alsted, *Encyclopaedia*, Part IV, *"Philosophie practica"*; Joannis Magirus (or Koch), *Corona virtutum moralium, universam Aristotelis summi philosophi ethicen exacte enucleans* . . . , rev. ed. (Frankfort, 1628); Bartholomaeus Keckermann, *Operum Omnium . . . Tomus secundus in quo speciatim methodice & uberrime de ethica, oeconomica, politica disciplina* . . . (Geneva, 1614); Francesco Pavone, *Summa ethicae: sive, introductio in Aristotelis* (Mainz, 1621), and there were still others.

7. Miller, *New England Mind*, I, 90.

8. To Perry Miller's credit it must be pointed out that in practice he definitely did not make the mistake of underestimating the full depth of 17th-century Harvard's immersion in neo-Latin Scholastic literature. Costello, *Curriculum at Cambridge*, has less bearing on Harvard than might be thought because Costello's interests are primarily concentrated on the period before 1650. However, Costello's comment that "the presence of the standard Catholic commentators throughout the [student] notebooks, not only in ethics and the other branches of philosophy, but especially in theology, will come as no surprise to those who have studied either [Oxford or Cambridge] in the seventeenth century," can be expanded to include Harvard as well. Costello continues correctly: "The break with Continental scholastic thought came only with the breakup of scholasticism itself" (p. 183, n. 108).

Golius

Theophilus (or Gottlieb) Golius's *Epitome Doctrinae Moralis, Ex decem libris Ethicorum Aristotelis ad Nicomachum collecta* (1592) was one of the earliest published of the moral philosophy texts commonly used at Harvard. Golius was a professor at the newly founded Protestant University of Strasbourg. One measure of the impressive longevity of his exposition of Aristotle is that as late as 1726 Cotton Mather could still recommend it to students as a good source for the minimal understanding of pagan moral thought that Mather was willing to tolerate.[9] The *Epitome* was in Increase Mather's library in 1664, and Arthur O. Norton found a copy of the 1634 Cambridge edition that contained the names of four successive Harvard students from 1685/1686 to 1706. John Harvard owned a copy, which was probably the 1621 Argentorati (Strasbourg) edition that passed into the Harvard Library and is listed in the 1723 catalog. A student notebook of Jonathan Mitchell's (Harvard A.B., 1647) includes extracts from Golius.[10] Golius's ethics was probably used intensively from the founding of Harvard until as late as the 1690s. It is the work most representative of ethical study in seventeenth-century America based on the "textual" rather than the systematic method.[11] Generally speaking, a textual approach, which purported simply to examine what Aristotle said, was less liable to encounter hostility from the theologians.

Whatever the circumstances, the teaching of moral philosophy in a Christian culture almost always required some defense, at least until the eighteenth century, when the contrary rather suddenly became the case. Golius indicated in his dedication that the academic senate of his institution required the study of Aristotle's ethics, a mandate with which he had no quarrel. The merits of the work are many, he said, for "what Aristotle did not invent he brought to perfection."[12] But Golius also pointed out immediately that ethics as found in

9. Mather, *Manuductio*, 38.

10. Tuttle, "Libraries of the Mathers," Am. Antiq. Soc., *Procs.*, XX (1909–1910), 288; Norton, "Harvard Text-Books," Col. Soc. Mass., *Trans.*, XXVIII (1935), 386; Potter, "John Harvard's Library," *ibid.*, XXI (1919), 209; *Catalogus Librorum Bibliothecae Collegij Harvardini . . .* (Boston, 1723). Morison discusses Mitchell's notebook in *Seventeenth-Century Harvard*, 159–160, 261. Morison is incorrect, however, in referring to Theophilus Golius as a professor at Leiden and as a personal friend of John Winthrop, Jr. (see *Founding of Harvard*, 143). Theophilus Golius died in 1600, before Winthrop was born. Winthrop's friend was Jacob Golius, a famous orientalist at the University of Leiden in the 17th century.

11. On the controversy in Holland and elsewhere over whether Aristotle should be taught through textual analysis and commentary or through systematic presentation, see Dibon, *Philosophie néerlandaise*, 15, 61. Costello, *Curriculum at Cambridge*, 13–14, observes that as books became more available, there was a progression from the lecture commentary on the text, which was in effect a way of supplying the text to the student, to the lecture commentary upon "the *cursus* or manual."

12. References to pages in the *Epitome* are all to the Cambridge 1634 edition and will appear

Aristotle is properly concerned only with "external" behavior and actions, or civil life, thus distinguishing it from Christian goals (2). Yet the pursuit of mundane happiness, which is the specific end that ethics may serve, is a reasonable goal, Golius believed, even though it is imperfect by Christian standards. Pagan ethics may be useful in three ways, he said. It can help men to know their own natural excellence, such as it is; it can lead them to be more virtuous in their dealings with others; and it may serve as a resource for the better understanding of related matters, such as jurisprudence or even the second table of the Decalogue.[13] Therefore, to the question, "Whether it is proper for Christians to study moral philosophy?" (the presentation throughout is catechetical), Golius gave an emphatic yes, provided moral philosophy is kept secondary to Christian teaching and is confined to the illumination of domestic and public duties alone (3).

There were objections to the teaching of moral philosophy on other than religious grounds, however. The teacher of moral philosophy to college boys had to answer to Aristotle himself, who held that young men in general are not properly equipped for the study of ethics and politics, for they tend to be guided by emotions rather than reason and, in addition, lack the wisdom that comes from worldly experience. To impose the study of ethics upon youth is therefore pointless and unprofitable (I. iii. 1095a).[14] Golius sympathized with Aristotle's low estimation of youth but ultimately maintained in the face of Aristotle that young men are equal to the task of studying ethics (10).[15]

There was a third objection, one that Aristotle himself had also considered seriously and that in fact paralleled in some respects the radical Christian position of William Ames and others. The question was whether ethics, as an art of living virtuously rather than a theoretical science, can be formally taught at all. In other words, what is the precise value of the academic moral philoso-

---

in parentheses in the text. I am indebted to John Mazaitis for translations of the relevant sections of all the texts considered in this chapter.

13. The Ten Commandments were traditionally divided into 2 tables. Commandments one through four, pertaining to the worship of God and duties toward Him, were the first table; commandments five through ten, pertaining to duties toward other men, were the second table.

14. All quotations or paraphrases from Aristotle's *Nicomachean Ethics* are from the translation of Martin Ostwald (Indianapolis, Ind., 1962). For purposes of comparison, the use of an index, and other conveniences, I have occasionally referred to the Loeb Library translation by H. Rackham, rev. ed. (Cambridge, Mass., 1934). References to Aristotle's *Ethics* are in parentheses in the text, giving both the number of the "Book," the section, and the location in the Bekker edition.

15. See Hector's rebuke to Paris and Troilus in Shakespeare's *Troilus and Cressida*, II, ii, 164–171: "And on the cause and question now in hand / [you] Have gloz'd, but superficially; not much / Unlike young men, whom Aristotle thought / Unfit to hear moral philosophy: / The reasons you allege do more conduce / To the hot passion of distemp'red blood / Than to make up a free determination / 'Twixt right and wrong. . . ."

phy lecture course for the practical life of virtue, and beyond that, how indeed is virtue attained or learned? Aristotle's answers to these questions, although highly complex, had an immense influence on subsequent centuries, and Golius's *Epitome* for the most part merely repeated Aristotle's analysis. So fundamental was this analysis to Western ethical thought until the eighteenth century that it is necessary to give at least a sketch of it here.

Aristotle distinguished first of all between two general kinds of virtues, corresponding to two characteristics of the rational soul: intellectual virtues, which are exemplified in mastery of theoretical knowledge, and moral virtues, which are expressed in practical action. The former may unquestionably be developed by teaching in the ordinary sense. But the moral virtues, on the contrary, Aristotle said, require practical training, or doing, for their cultivation and can never be acquired through words or thought alone. The moral virtues are acquired "habits" of action and in this way are analogous to the technical and creative arts, although in this case the results of the artistry are impressed on the agent himself, not on some external object (II. i. 1103a). Repeatedly in the *Nicomachean Ethics* Aristotle returned to this theme, that the moral virtues are mainly the product of habituation in practical action, for it was one of his most basic conclusions. Now if this is the case, where does the moral philosophy course, or what Golius called teaching "by doctrines," fit in? (40)

The prerequisite for the fruitful study of ethics, according to Aristotle, is that one be already on the road to virtue. Without this prerequisite, ethics is not teachable in the classroom. The full attainment of moral goodness or virtue is properly divided into two parts. There must first be the pre-formed "characteristic" or habit which has been developed by "actively engaging in particular actions" (III. v. 1114a).[16] In addition to this established personal character or habit of virtue, there must also be "practical wisdom," which is "the capacity for deliberating well about what contributes to the good life in general" and is also one of the intellectual virtues of the soul (VI. v. 1140a).[17] The relation between the personal characteristic (or habit) of virtuous action,

---

16. The Greek word for "characteristic" in this sense is *"hexis,"* which was traditionally translated into the Latin *"habitus"* and then into the English "habit." But the connotation of "habit" in modern English is so far removed from Aristotle's *hexis* that Ostwald has quite properly abandoned the term "habit" and substituted "characteristic." "Disposition" might also be equivalent to "habit" in Aristotle's sense. See Fiering, "Franklin and Virtue," *Am. Qtly.*, XXX (1978), 199–223.

17. Here, too, time has distorted the traditional terminology. The Greek for Ostwald's "practical wisdom" is *"phronesis,"* which was almost invariably translated into the Latin *"prudentia"* and then into the English "prudence." But "prudence" has lost almost all of its technical character and does not convey to the modern English-speaking student anything like what *"prudentia"* meant at Harvard in the 17th century. Hence, "practical wisdom" is today a more suitable translation.

and practical wisdom (or prudence), is a little like that between ends and means, except that in this case the means of attaining virtue, true practical wisdom, cannot itself exist independently of personal character, the end or goal. A man who deliberates well about the means of attaining his ends but at the same time lacks the preliminary characteristic of virtue can at most be "clever"; he will not be wise. He will not have true practical wisdom. Practical wisdom is an instrumental quality related specifically and exclusively to the goal of virtue.

The classroom teaching of ethics consists only of the study of practical wisdom as distinguished from the formation of the habit of virtue. Pre-existing virtue as an acquired, or habitual, characteristic of the personality determines the choice of ends, or points the soul the right way, and practical wisdom, which may in fact be developed through study, determines the steps that must be taken to implement the choices (VI. xii. 1144a). In sum, teaching by doctrines (as opposed to practice) does have some bearing on moral actions and certainly justifies the study of moral philosophy, although it makes up only a lesser and dependent part of the pursuit of moral virtue. The moral virtues should principally be understood as characteristics acquired through practical training and habituation, which is more the responsibility of the home than the school.

We should also note that Aristotle made a strong case for the intrinsic value of the classroom study of moral philosophy, or practical wisdom, on the grounds that it constituted the cultivation of one side of the rational soul. This activity would be "desirable" in itself even if it produced nothing; but, as we have seen, such teaching does definitely contribute to the fulfillment of man's proper function, which is living according to virtue (VI. xii. 1144a). Practical wisdom was then both an intellectual virtue of the soul and a practical one. Because ethics was a unique hybrid, involving both practical life and theory, problems sometimes arose in classifying it as a discipline.[18]

The three main objections to the teaching of ethics in college—that it is un-Christian, that it is unprofitable for youths, and that it cannot be "taught" at all—were thus dealt with. But the full significance of Aristotle's argument regarding the last objection cannot be understood without some consideration of alternative positions, positions that Aristotle himself entertained to some degree.

Aside from certain theological objections, there are two possible alternatives to the Aristotelian dictum that moral virtues, like other practical virtues, are necessarily first established through the practical activities that correspond

---

18. Whether ethics was an art, that is, directive, or a science, that is, objective, was a question occasionally under discussion. See Costello, *Curriculum at Cambridge*, 37–38, and nn. Thomas Aquinas considered it properly a science.

to the virtues. The first was the argument that virtue is primarily the result of natural inheritance. The obvious circularity of Aristotle's opinion that "we become just by the practice of just actions, self-controlled by exercising self-control, and courageous by performing acts of courage" seemed to allow for some beginning in nature or natural ability. Golius quickly dismissed this possibility, using Aristotle's own arguments against it, since it was antithetical to Christian dogma concerning sin and grace. But it is worth our time to linger with "natural ability" for a moment, even if no seventeenth-century Harvard student could seriously have entertained it for long as a basis for virtue.

Aristotle held that none of the virtues are actually implanted in us by nature, but neither, he said, are they contrary to nature. "We are by nature equipped with the ability to receive them, and habit brings this ability to completion and fulfillment" (II. i. 1103a). This is the first point. Nature is receptive but essentially neutral. Here Golius was compelled to introduce his one major qualification, even though he appears to have accepted Aristotle's general analysis: Aristotle's opinion is after all "mere philosophizing," he wrote, for sacred Scripture tells us rightly that "the heart of man is evil from youth" (51). That his qualification was simply dropped into the presentation with no real attempt at dialectical resolution of the problems it posed for the Aristotelian schema as a whole is typical of Golius's rather superficial exposition of Aristotle.

Aristotle himself diminished the importance of natural inheritance by his enormously influential teaching regarding the place of reason and volition in the practice of virtue. For an act to be truly virtuous, he argued, at least three criteria must be met: (1) the moral agent must *know* what he is doing; that is, he must deliberately choose to act the way he does; (2) he must choose the action for its own sake; and (3) the act must spring from a firm and unchangeable character (II. iv. 1105a). These are qualities that cannot accompany actions done from nature alone. Natural or primitive virtue, precisely because it lacks the process of deliberation and conscious choice, is not real virtue.[19] A habit was understood to be an adventitious modification of nature, and in that sense virtue was a habit and not just unmodified nature. Moreover, it is not certain that the products of nature will be firm and unchangeable. The relation between natural virtue and true virtue, or virtue in the full sense, is analogous to that between cleverness and practical wisdom. Merely natural virtue, like cleverness, is incomplete and ill founded.

It seems that the various kinds of character inhere in all of us, somehow or other, by nature. We tend to be just, capable of self-control, and to

19. In the 18th century an implicit distinction developed between "goodness," a spontaneous quality, and "virtue," which is the result of deliberation. The former was defended as a true moral quality to a degree that was never possible as long as Aristotelianism was dominant.

show all our other character traits from the time of our birth. Yet we still seek something more, the good in a fuller sense, and the possession of these traits in another way. . . . If a man acts blindly, i.e., using his natural virtue alone, he will fail; but once he acquires intelligence, it makes a great difference in his action. At that point, the natural characteristic will become that virtue in the full sense which it previously resembled (VI. xiii. 1144b).

Our capacities have been given to us by nature, but we do not by nature develop into good or bad men (II. v. 1106a).

Aristotle was convinced enough of this fact to give considerable support to the famous Socratic teaching that virtue is a form of knowledge or wisdom. It is because practical wisdom is indeed truly essential to virtue, according to Aristotle, that Socrates was misled into believing that the virtues were *only* forms of wisdom. Socrates was wrong in that belief, Aristotle held, but he was right in insisting that without wisdom there can be no virtue. For all virtue is necessarily "united with a rational principle" (VI. xiii. 1144b). This belief is the dominant note in the *Nicomachean Ethics*, and it has resounded through the ages, though Aristotle was never entirely consistent on the extent to which nature contributes to the end. (He never made clear, for example, how much of the "characteristic" of virtue depends upon natural gifts, such as "intelligence," which in his schema is a kind of primary intuition, and how much on practical training.) The Aristotelian position was reinforced both by the Stoic emphasis on right reason as the immanent ethical norm in man, and by the Thomist concept of reason as the criterion of moral good; so that in Western moral thought until the eighteenth century intellectualist ethics, or a moral psychology that made rational deliberation of some sort the foundation of virtue, was the prevailing dogma.

A few other points in Aristotle concern the natural virtues, which were cited to differentiate them from real or full virtues. All of these arguments appear condensed in Golius:

Natural virtues are found in infants and children and there are traces sometimes even in beasts. True virtues, on the other hand, are acquired by long practice. True virtues are good for *both* the possessor and others, whereas natural virtues may be harmful to others. Natural virtues may be separated from one another [so that a person may have one and not others]. But true virtues are chained together by *prudentia* [practical wisdom], so that whoever has one, seems to have them all. True virtues are never found without *prudentia*, because only *prudentia* can lead us to true virtue by its ability to arrive at the mean (174).

By the "mean" Golius meant, of course, the appropriate choice between the vicious extremes of action.

If the role of nature in ethics was easily dismissed at seventeenth-century Harvard, the other great alternative to the Aristotelian emphasis on training and intellect was not. This was the argument that the virtues have a divine origin. The fourth-century B.C. Greek mind did not distinguish between nature and grace as readily as did the medieval, but it is of some importance that there is found in Aristotle in several places an adumbration of the idea that true virtue is ultimately dependent upon God's assistance. Christian commentators like Golius made the most of it, for it obviously added to Aristotle's acceptability as a moral teacher. The Philosopher mentioned this possibility most directly at the beginning of the seventh book of the *Nicomachean Ethics*, where he discussed three types of vice and their opposites. There is the vicious character, the morally weak character, and the brutish character. The exact meanings of these types we need not consider here. In the discussion of the opposite of brutishness, however, we find the following:

> The most fitting description of the opposite of brutishness would be to say that it is superhuman virtue, a kind of heroic and divine excellence; just as Homer has Priam say about Hector that he was of surpassing excellence: "for he did not seem like one who was child of a mortal man, but of god." Therefore, if, as is said, an excess of virtue can change a man into a god, the characteristic opposed to brutishness must evidently be something of this sort. . . . The quality of gods is something more worthy of honor than human virtue or excellence. . . . If it is rare to find a man who is divine . . . it is just as rare that a brute is found among men (VII. i. 1145a).

It is evident that Aristotle did not intend to stress this rare superhuman virtue. And for the brief attention he gave to it, it received disproportionate attention among later Christian moralists. Golius's commentary on this so-called "heroic virtue" is typical insofar as he attempted to assimilate the passage to Christian theology. To Aristotle's example of Hector, Golius added several Roman examples, Regulus's fidelity, Scipio's self-control, and so on, and then continued, "from sacred history, Abraham's faith, Joseph's purity, Joshua's courage, Job's patience, Solomon's wisdom, and of all heroic virtues the most perfect example presented to us is Christ our saviour" (176). What is remarkable about this gloss is the absence of any break in the two lists and any acknowledgment of the entirely divergent presuppositions of the two great cultures represented in it. One hopes the Harvard tutors did not let such patchwork syncretism pass by without comment. There would be ample opportunity here for the astute teacher to remove the virtues of the saints altogether from the Aristotelian structure consisting of acquired character, practical wisdom, and the mean. In any case, early in the next century one Harvard master's candidate, John Wainwright, seems to have acutely perceived the difficulties Aristotle's concept of heroic virtue—or rather the Christian interpretation of heroic virtue—could raise for the Peripatetic ethical system as a whole. Wainwright argued the negative of the *quaestio*, "Whether heroic virtue consists in observing the mean?"[20]

A number of the early commencement theses are illustrative of some of the Aristotelian doctrines we have been examining. At the very first commencement in 1642, two of the ethical theses referred to practical wisdom, which was, they stated, both an intellectual and a moral virtue (*Prudentia est virtus intellectualis et moralis*), and the most difficult of the virtues (*Prudentia virtutum difficillima*). The first is true—we can imagine a young student arguing—because the study of moral philosophy has both intrinsic and practical value; it is a necessarily desirable intellectual activity in itself and is also essential to the attainment of moral goodness. And practical wisdom is the most difficult of virtues because it is the one that underlies all the others. A third thesis in 1642 posited that the act of a virtue precedes its habit (*Actio virtutis habitum antecellit*), in other words, that a virtuous character is formed through repeated practice. The next year two theses dealt with the nature of *"habitus,"* or the characteristic of virtue. A single act does not engender a habit, one thesis stated (*Per unum actum non generatur habitus*). The other asserted that a habit does not disappear through the mere cessation of the acts that formed it (*Habitus non pereunt sola actuum cessatione*).[21] A thesis at the 1646 commencement implied the distinction between a virtuous "habit" or characteristic and practical wisdom: An ethical end is not the subject of deliberation (*Finis non cadit en deliberationem*). In other words, in the psychology of the virtuous man, according to Aristotle, the predisposition to a virtuous end already exists as a habit, and it is only about the means to the end that deliberation takes place (VII. viii. 1151a).

Before leaving Golius, two other central Aristotelian ethical formulations should be mentioned, namely the doctrine of happiness and the doctrine of

20. *An virtus heroica consistat in mediocritate?* (1712). The nature of so-called "heroic" virtue was widely discussed in the 17th and 18th centuries. With regard to the doctrine of the mean itself, many Christian commentators attacked it sharply, including William Ames in the 17th century. But it was also defended in Harvard commencement theses in 1647, *Virtus in sua ratione formali non admittit excessum* (Virtue in its *ratio formalis* admits of no excess); in 1670, *Virtutis via, respectu extremorum, jacet inter Scyllam et Charabdin* (The path of virtue, with respect to extremes, lies between Scylla and Charybdis); and in 1680, *Virtus consistit in mediocritate*, indicating the strength of the Aristotelian influence on a key issue. In 1680, while the doctrine was supported by the undergraduates, it was challenged by the master's candidate Edward Payson, who argued the negative of the *quaestio, An virtus consistat in Mediocritate?*

21. See above, n. 16 and chap. 1, n. 93.

moral weakness. Several commencement theses reflected the Classical analysis of happiness. Moral happiness is the end or goal of ethics, one stated (*Foelicitas moralis est finis Ethices*, 1643), and another, Moral happiness lies in the practice of virtue (*Foelicitas moralis est virtutis praxis*, 1647). *Moral* happiness was presumably to be distinguished from *eternal* happiness, which could not be achieved by the practice of virtue alone. At the August 10, 1653, commencement it was affirmed that virtue is the royal road to happiness (*Ad beatitudinem via regia est virtus*). Such propositions on the identity of happiness and virtue were also repeatedly affirmed in eighteenth-century moral philosophy, but it would be a mistake to assume that the meanings of the key terms in the equation remained the same.

Happiness was one of the few subjects on which Golius spelled out a rather complete counter-Aristotelian position. Aristotle was unsatisfactory on the subject of happiness, Golius argued, for his famous definition—"an activity of the soul in conformity with the highest virtue"—did not point beyond this earth. The question of what true happiness is, has been much debated, Golius observed, with Cicero, Augustine, and Plato all having spoken on the subject (13). But Plato in this matter was superior to Aristotle, Golius believed, when he said that the highest happiness for man is found in the contemplation of the Good, if by the Good we mean the idea of God. For human happiness does consist above all in the contemplation of God. Plato, however, lacked the support of divine revelation with which to defend himself, whereas Christians know for certain that all happiness is from God and that He is the source of all good things (16). Golius then added one of the very few scriptural citations in his book: "And this is eternal life, that they know thee the only true God, and Jesus Christ whom thou hast sent" (John 17:3).

That all creatures seek the good and that the highest good for man is "happiness" almost everyone agreed. But in this most fundamental matter of what the ultimate end of human activity ought to be, that is, in what happiness consists, it was always necessary, as Golius illustrated, to qualify the conclusions of the ancient moralists. The word "happiness" is one of the most enduring in ethical thought, but its meanings were many. It was well understood at seventeenth-century Harvard that the pagan moralists were least acceptable when it came to their knowledge of the ultimate end. In 1663 one student copied into his commonplace book in Latin a condensed version of the great passages in Thomas Aquinas's *Summa Contra Gentiles* concerning happiness (Bk. III, Pt. i, chaps. xxv–xl). Human happiness, the student wrote, does not consist in carnal pleasures as the Epicureans believed. And the cerinthians were also in error, who pretended that after the resurrection Christ will reign over a thousand years of sensuality. Nor does happiness consist in honors, glory, worldly power, or even in acts of moral virtue, wherein the Academics, the Stoics, and the Cynics are all refuted. The ultimate happiness for man consists in the contemplation of God (*"Sed ultim*[ ] *hominis foelicitas consistit in contemplation Dei"*).[22] The practical theologians like Ames, who rejected secular philosophy, condemned the belief that happiness is the ultimate aim of man and especially opposed the notion that contemplation is the proper end of human endeavor. In his *Marrow of Theology* Ames protested that although it is possible "to live both happily and well, *euzoia*, living well [or rightly], is more excellent than *eudaimonia*, living happily." *Euzoia* was simply a variation of *eupraxia*. What should be striven for, Ames wrote, is that "goodness which looks to God's glory," not personal happiness. Some Puritans, not unexpectedly, tended to regard a life of activity, rather than of contemplation, as the highest good, and preferred to emphasize the duty of self-denying service to God's will over the promise of direct fulfillment in the intellectual love of God.

The nature and psychological basis of virtue and the end or goal of virtue have all been discussed. But what of the person who appears to fail in virtue? Aristotle's treatment of the subject of moral weakness in relation to knowledge (in Book VII of the *Nicomachean Ethics*) was necessarily of particular interest to Christians. The "morally weak man," according to Aristotle's psychology, is one whose rational moral calculations are correct in the beginning but who in the course of action tends to abandon this knowledge and gives in to lower appetites. In the seventeenth century this type of behavior was usually called incontinence. Aristotle distinguished it from the action of the morally strong or continent man who feels the tug of base appetites but successfully resists it, and from the self-indulgent, profligate, or incorrigible man who gives in to his lower appetites on principle and in whom there is no conflict. As Aristotle posed it the central problem is, How can a man be morally weak in his actions when his basic assumption about what he ought to do is correct? Socrates' well-known dictum, that true knowledge is sufficient for virtuous behavior if the right end is in view, was in the background of Aristotle's discussion.[23] "It would be strange," Aristotle observed, following Socrates, "if, when a man possesses knowledge, something else should overpower it and drag it about like a slave" (VII. ii. 1145b). To put the problem in another way, given Aristotle's belief that virtue is a "habit" guided by correct practical knowledge, in what sense, if any, may it be said that the incontinent man "knows" what he is doing?

In answering this question Golius followed Aristotle in the details, but he

22. John Holyoke (A.B., 1662), "Commonplace Book," 1662–1663, MS, a Harvard notebook given to the Houghton Lib., Harvard Univ., Cambridge, Mass., only in 1942. It was acquired after Morison's and Miller's major works on Harvard in this period were completed. Holyoke was the uncle of Edward Holyoke, a president of Harvard in the 18th century.

23. The entire subject is expertly treated in James Jerome Walsh, *Aristotle's Conception of Moral Weakness* (New York, 1963).

put a Christian stamp upon the whole theory. Golius quickly dismissed certain special cases that avoided the central issue, such as that of a person being caused to act against better knowledge by external coercion or disease, or the case of the impetuous man who is overcome by the effects of passions like love, hatred, or anger and does not deliberate at all at the critical moment. He concentrated on the person who, in Aristotle's words, "has" the knowledge but does not use it or apply it at the critical time. In such circumstances, a person introduces instead a kind of parallel but defective reasoning which, influenced by the appetites rather than right reason, in the end determines the action. The psychological picture is that of two tracks, each complete in itself, but the vicious track has been laid by sensory knowledge. For both Golius and Aristotle the existence of two independent tracks, each with its own set of reasons, keeps the analysis somewhat short of a full theory of what is today commonly called rationalization. Golius had in mind a lapse from correct reasoning rather than a concept of the subservience of reasoning in general to subrational desires. Both writers adhered to the intellectualist tenet that the full possession of correct understanding or right reason would natu-rally lead to virtuous action.[24] The morally weak man, Aristotle wrote, acts like a man asleep or drunk who mouths the correct knowledge but fails to exercise it when he should. He has temporarily slipped to a lower level of activity (VII. iii. 1147a, x. 1152a). Golius described this kind of moral weak-ness as being "*ex ipsa natura*," a disunion in human nature itself between the rational and the appetitive elements in the soul, thereby relating it to the dogma of Original Sin. These two elements, he said, are almost always at odds with each other, for the goods recommended to the soul by right reason entail pain and effort, while the goods recommended by the appetites, though by nature inferior, bring pleasure to the senses. The two shape the judgment in contrary ways and divide the soul of the weak man into two parts. In this con-dition a person may, in a sense, knowingly sin (182). Golius's conclusion was like Aristotle's: "Moral weakness does not occur in the presence of knowl-edge in the strict sense," and it is sensory knowledge, not true knowledge, that is dragged about by appetite (VII. iii. 1147b). But there is a categorical quality in Golius's description of the division of the personality that is not found in Aristotle and conforms instead to the standard description of the dis-ordering psychological effects of the Fall from paradise. "For Understanding rul'd not, and the Will / Heard not her lore, both in subjection now / To sensual Appetite, who from beneath / Usurping over Sovran Reason claimed / Superior sway," was the way John Milton described it.[25]

To illustrate his analysis Golius, like Aristotle, used syllogisms, but Golius

24. There will be further clarification of this point in chap. 3, below.
25. *Paradise Lost*, Bk. IX, ll. 1127–1131.

took as his example Adam and Eve. Two moral syllogisms competed in the minds of our first parents. The first is in accordance with right reason:

God commands obedience and to obey God is "pium" and
"honestum" (holy and righteous).
To abstain from the fruit of the tree is commanded by God.
Therefore, the fruit should be abstained from.

The second syllogism, which Adam and Eve in fact followed, is from "appetite or Satan." It is significant that Golius assumed that Satan works through appetite rather than will.

To be like God is "pulchrum" and "jucundum" (beautiful
and pleasant).
But if you eat this fruit you will be like God.
Therefore, you ought to do this.

The voice of Satan speaking through the appetites leads us to desire and choose what is immediately attractive rather than to follow the duty of obedience to God. In different terms, the conflict is between the self-will and vaunting pride of the concupiscent soul that wants to be equal to God and the rational obedience of the righteous soul.

Christian orthodoxy forbade any simple Manichean dualism of body and soul, and a good deal of uncertainty remained about the exact nature of moral weakness. Golius did not provide a full enough analysis to allow for a more detailed understanding of his meaning than can be gathered from the above. The sin could be in pride and ambition, in a failure of will to control momentary impulse, or in intellectual error. One seventeenth-century Protestant theologian, Leonard Riisen, suggested that the first sin was a "complication of actions," and that it is futile to worry about the first step. By "thoughtlessness man had ceased to consider God's interdict and his own truthfulness and goodness." (This idea is something like Aristotle's concept of oversight.) There followed "incredulity or distrust, by which man had not the faith in God's word which he should have had, but cast it out by hesitation, presently by denial, not believing that the fruit was seriously forbidden him or that he would die." (This describes a process similar to rationalization.) "Then we have the credulity with which he began to give ear to the devil's words and presently he made an error of judgment. From this, his longing (*appetitus*) in will and his inclination to concupiscence existed to eat the fruit; and lastly the overt action."[26] Calvin and Theodore Beza had earlier stressed that it was the

26. Quoted in Heinrich Heppe, *Reformed Dogmatics* . . . , ed. Ernst Bizer, trans. G. T. Thomson (London, 1950), 301–302.

deliberate and direct disobedience to God's command, rather than any form of greedy intemperance in the face of temptation, that was at the heart of the sin.

Eustache

The *Ethica* of Eustache de Saint-Paul was simply a separately published section of his *Summa Philosophiae quadripartita, de rebus Dialecticis, Ethicis, Physicis, et Mathematicis*, which first appeared in 1609.[27] Morison refers to the complete *Summa Philosophiae* as one of seventeenth-century Harvard's favorite books. "Many theses and quaestiones may be traced to this little compendium of Scholastic philosophy—which was mentioned favorably by no less a personage than Spinoza," Morison notes, and we may infer considerable student use of it.[28] John Harvard had a copy of the *Summa Philosophiae* in his library, and a Harvard student owned a copy of the *Ethica* in 1665. Solomon Stoddard in 1664 owned a copy of Eustache's two-volume work on divinity. Eustache also had some influence on Descartes, according to Étienne Gilson, though not notably in the area of ethics. At least two of the dissenting academies in England used Eustache in ethics, Matthew Warren's academy in Taunton, founded in 1679, and Sheriffhales Academy, founded in 1663.[29] Anthony Levi describes Eustache's *Summa Philosophiae*, after full recognition of its faults, as "a clear, competent, and compendious presentation of scholastic philosophy."[30]

As may be gathered from Eustache's distinguished if minor place in relation to Spinoza and Descartes, his work on ethics was considerably more sophisticated than Golius's. If Golius's *Epitome* with its catechetical organization was directed to undergraduates alone, Eustache's work would be

27. Eustache was a Cistercian who taught in the theology faculty at the Sorbonne. I am using an edition of the *Ethica* from London, 1658. Page citations are in parentheses in the text. There was at least one other London edition in 1693 and a Cambridge edition in 1654. Levi, *French Moralists*, 152, states that there were seven editions of the *Summa Philosophiae* before 1623.

28. Morison, *Seventeenth-Century Harvard*, 159.

29. Potter, "John Harvard's Library," Col. Soc. Mass., *Trans.*, XXI (1919), 207; Norton, "Harvard Text-Books," *ibid.*, XXVIII (1935), 405. Eustache's work on divinity was the *Summa Theologiae tripartita: de Deo, rebusque divinis ac supernaturalibus*, 2 vols. (Paris, 1613–1616); see Fiering, "Stoddard's Library at Harvard," *Harvard Lib. Bul.*, XX (1972), 225–269. On Descartes, see Gilson, *Index Scolastico-Cartésien* (Paris, 1912), and Levi, *French Moralists*, 152. See also, Smith, *Birth of Modern Education*, 48, and H. McLachlan, *English Education under the Test Acts, Being the History of the Non-Conformist Academies, 1662–1800* (Manchester, Eng., 1931), 46.

30. Levi, *French Moralists*, 158.

suitable for graduate bachelors also. Moreover, as a Roman Catholic he was not under the influence of the Reformation tendency to neutralize Aristotle's ethics through a limited kind of textual presentation only. Eustache was unmistakably working in the Scholastic tradition. His *Ethica* contains frequent allusions to Thomas Aquinas; there is some close and difficult analysis of problems, particularly regarding the nature of the will; and relatively little crude, undialectical contraposing of Christian dogma against Aristotelian teaching. On the contrary, Eustache's book is properly speaking a work in moral theology more than moral philosophy. He began with an already partially unified foundation. In addition, Eustache expressed some Neoplatonic ideas. Aristotle is the main platform of Eustache's ethical thought, but no more than that.

Most noticeable in Eustache's short book is the disproportionate amount of space the author gives to discussion of the will, an amount required in part by the somewhat uncommon position he took with regard to this faculty. Eustache was a proponent of the so-called liberty of indifference, or the sovereign freedom of the will in relation to intellectual judgment. The problem of free will was typically a Scholastic rather than a Classical problem, and a strict commentary on Aristotle would hardly have to attend to the subject at all.[31]

Besides the defense of the liberty of indifference, another peculiarity in Eustache's work on ethics is his treatment of angels and demons as influences on human choice. Golius had referred to the satanic voice of the appetites, but without elaboration. Eustache worked out this theory somewhat, though it was of course not original with him. The study of spirits other than the human soul was a major interest in the seventeenth century. In response to the threat of atheistic materialism, interest in spirits tended to increase rather than diminish as the century progressed.[32] According to Eustache, the will of man is moved by angels and demons as well as by God and by other men. God's effect on the will is a necessary cause and unique in its operation. Angels, demons, and other men, on the contrary, can only *incline* the will of man: angels toward the true good, demons toward the apparent good, and other men toward both true and apparent goods. Eustache listed a variety of ways in which demons can operate on human behavior: altering sense perceptions, working on the imagination, exciting animal spirits, and so on (50–60).

At the same time there is much traditional Aristotelianism in Eustache that duplicates Golius. On such matters as the relation of habit and act, and the nature of the specific virtues such as temperance, courage, and justice, for example, they were in rough agreement. Eustache, like Golius, discussed the three types of virtue and vice, one of the former being the heroic type of

---

31. The complex 17th-century debates concerning the will are treated in chap. 3, below.
32. This subject is given somewhat fuller treatment in chaps. 5 and 6, below.

virtue, already mentioned, which is the highest kind of virtue and depends upon divine gifts. Beneath the heroic man is the temperate man (the *sophron*), or better, the man of self-mastery, whose internal balance is such that he acts virtuously without evidence of strain or conflict. The man of self-mastery is distinguished from the continent or morally strong man (the *enkrates*) we have already referred to, who has a powerful appetitive nature that he must struggle to control and whose moral strength is evidenced by his victory over himself. On the relatively low level of virtue exemplified in the continent man, the virtues lack internal connection; individual virtues must be mastered one by one through restraint. But the *sophron*, the man of self-mastery and balance, possesses the practical wisdom or prudence that serves as the common foundation upon which all of the virtues rest and are joined (111).

A good example of Scholastic treatment of an issue in philosophical ethics is Eustache's handling of the question, Whether vice is contrary to nature? Vice is contrary to the nature of man as an essentially rational being, Eustache held, for man is properly a creature of right reason. However, vice may conform to our sensitive nature, which is inclined to the sensible or sensory good alone rather than to the true good distinguishable by reason, in which case it would seem vice is not contrary to nature. But even the sensitive appetite may be said to be inclined by nature to obey reason, since the opposition to which it is disposed is the product of *fallen* nature, rather than a prelapsarian condition. Therefore, strictly speaking, Eustache concluded, vice is contrary to human nature, for it opposes the nature of man as man, that is, as a rational animal (141–144). Such a view, characteristic of Thomism, treated human nature rather more optimistically than most Puritans would have done.[33]

In several places Eustache made use of the related Scholastic principle that the actions of all men, even when they do wrong, are governed by the choice of what appears to be good at the moment. Reason at its best points out what appears to be morally good, or good in general, and commands the will to incline toward it; the sensitive appetite, serving the passions, is also inclined toward good, but it is the good that appears good for the agent at the time. The sensitive appetite is never directed toward evil as such, but toward a partial good, namely the pleasurable good, which often happens to be contrary to the rational good and the law of God, although it may on occasion accidentally coincide with the rational good. A psychology such as this underlay Golius's analysis of Adam's sin—the choice of the lesser good dictated by sensitive

---

33. Cf. Costello, *Curriculum at Cambridge*, 114, on this point: Lutheranism and Calvinism "held that man is intrinsically and irreparably corrupt, original sin having infected our nature with an incurable moral disease. . . . Catholics, on the other hand, hold that man's nature is essentially uncorrupted, that is, that original sin, while depriving man of the supernatural and preternatural perfections (*dona superaddita*) of sanctifying grace, freedom from concupiscence, and immortality, leaves the natural faculties unimpaired and his nature good."

appetite. A Harvard commencement thesis from August 10, 1653, stated the point succinctly: *"Malum non appetitur formaliter"* (Evil is not [is never] formally sought).[34] The rational appetite, or the will, is never directed to evil as such. In a sermon in 1664, which Solomon Stoddard outlined in one of his notebooks, Jonathan Mitchell stated this commonplace in another way: "All that sin deliberately choose sin as good: that [which] is chose before another, is preferred under the notion of better." According to Eustache, God is the true end of all human actions and all men have the same end, though they may not know it or choose rightly in relation to their proper end. To buttress this point he cited the famous Augustinian maxim, "We were made for God and are restless until we find our end in Him" (14, 23, 64). Whether the deliberate choice of evil is a psychological possibility was a much debated question and one we will return to in the next chapter.[35]

We have noted that the problem of the will as a special faculty of the mind was characteristic of medieval and modern, but not of Classical, ethics. Similarly, a strict commentary on the *Nicomachean Ethics* would not require much attention to the theory of the passions. Aristotle addressed himself to the subject of the passions or affections to some extent in his psychology (*De Anima*) and in his rhetoric, but hardly at all in his ethics. Francis Bacon in the *Advancement of Learning* had called attention to this deficiency, and others in the seventeenth century remarked on it. "Here again I find it strange," Bacon commented, "that Aristotle should have written divers volumes of ethics, and never handled the affections, which is the principal subject thereof."[36] Bacon did not realize that in his time the affections were in the process of becoming a principal subject of ethics, but they had not been that in the Greco-Roman world.

The Stoics were more interested in the passions than Aristotle had been, but primarily as "diseases" of the soul that needed to be classified. The passions had no value in the attainment of virtue and, according to Stoic theory, were best studied in many of their aspects as part of physics or its branch, physiology. Indeed, the Stoics revived the extreme intellectualist doctrine of

34. Similarly in 1703 Robert Breck responded in the negative to the master's *quaestio, An homo possit velle malum, qua malum?* (Whether man can will evil, as evil?)

35. Eustache's defense of free will would seem to have committed him to accepting the possibility of gratuitous malice, as it did the great Spanish metaphysician Francisco Suarez. "In order for the will to perform an evil act, it is not necessary that there be a preceding error," Suarez held, "either in the speculative or the practical judgment." But this was an unusual opinion. Suarez, *Disputationes metaphysicae* (Salamanca, 1597), XIX, secs. 7, 10, quoted by Leon Mahieu, *François Suarez, sa philosophie et les rapports qu'elle a avec sa théologie* (Paris, 1921), 465. On Suarez's influence at Harvard, see chap. 3, below.

36. Bacon, *Advancement of Learning*, ed. Kitchin, 171.

Socrates that founded virtue on knowledge alone. Where the passions seemed to have an influence leading to vice, they were treated for the most part as a species of intellectual error or false judgment that had to be eliminated for the sake of virtue. The integration of the theory of the passions into moral philosophy began with Thomas Aquinas, whose *Summa Theologica* in the *Prima Secundae* (i.e., the first part of Part II) treated the passions systematically and at some length.[37] Saint Thomas adopted the moderate Peripatetic attitude toward the nonrational appetites (and the passions, which were assumed to be derivative from these appetites), that they were neither good nor bad in themselves but were to be judged on the basis of the degree to which they were subservient to, or in accordance with, right reason.

In Thomas's theory there are some echoes, too, of the Augustinian doctrine of the passions, which formed the groundwork of a tradition quite different from the intellectualist systems of the pagans. The passions "are evil if our love is evil, good if our love is good. . . . All these emotions are right in those whose love is rightly placed."[38] As a Harvard thesis from 1647 stated it, "Individual affections can be attributed now to virtue, now to vice" (*Singuli affectus possunt tum virtuti tum vitio subjici*). The important matter was what underlay the affections and what end they served. The influential sixteenth-century English Puritan William Perkins attacked the Aristotelian doctrine of the mean by arguing that "without renovation of affections," the "mediocritie of which they speake" is "nothing." "All vertues that are not joyned with a renovation and change of the affections, are no better than sinnes. This point the Philosophers never knew."[39]

Following Aquinas, Eustache's *Ethica* includes considerable commentary on the passions or the affections, most of which was quite typical of late Scholastic treatises on the subject. Eustache agreed with St. Thomas that the passions are motions in the sensitive appetite in respect to the assumed good or evil of what the senses apprehend, and they are always accompanied by bodily changes. In some sense, beasts may have them, too. In connection with Eustache's discussion there was perhaps more physiology brought in than was common earlier.

A perennial problem in defining the passions was the difficulty of categorizing emotions such as love and joy, which in the Scriptures are attributed to bodiless beings like God and angels, that is, beings without sensitive appetites,

37. Levi, *French Moralists*, 22: "The treatise on the passions derives as a genre from the Prima Secundae."

38. Quoted by Thomas from Augustine's *City of God*, in *Summa Theologica*, Pt. II (first part), Q. 24, arts. 1–4.

39. William Perkins, *The Whole Treatise of the Cases of Conscience* (London, 1614), in Merrill, ed., *William Perkins*, 163.

as well as to men. Thomas's response to this dilemma became the standard one:

> When love and joy and the like are ascribed to God or the angels, or to man in respect of his intellectual appetite, they signify simple acts of the will having like effects, but without passion. Hence Augustine says (*De Civ. Dei* ix. 5): "The holy angels feel no anger while they punish . . . , no fellow-feeling with misery while they relieve the unhappy: and yet ordinary human speech is wont to ascribe to them also these passions by name, because, although they have none of our weaknesses, their acts bear a certain resemblance to ours."[40]

One may see in this reply as much an avoidance of the problem as anything else. The question of the true nature of love and the problem of distinguishing its types, from sexual love to divine charity, either could be a fruitful source of psychological insight into man, offering the key to an integrated picture of his nature, or it could be used to emphasize a radical division in the human soul between the qualities of intellect and spirit and those of the body. Anthony Levi sees in Eustache a tendency toward the exaggeration of the "gulf between the sensitive and the rational appetites, the higher and lower parts of the soul."[41] This tendency was especially apparent in Eustache's linking of the passions (or the sensitive appetite) exclusively, it would seem, to material sense-data (to the phantasms, or "imagination" in the Renaissance meaning), and in his tying the will or rational appetite to intellectually apprehended goods alone.[42] One consequence of such a neat division is that the passions cannot then be conceived of as ever having a nonmaterial, or a non-sensory, abstract good as their object, and all the important ideals of life—such as honor, glory, virtue, and even God—must be made purely rational objects rather than ends desired by the whole man. (A similar presupposition was probably behind Golius's analysis of Adam's Fall.) This development in the theory of the passions was a deviation from Thomist teaching and early Scholastic doctrine in general, which had been largely under the influence of Proclus and the Pseudo-Dionysius, and which emphasized the unitary nature of love, binding together the lowest and the highest beings in the creation.[43] Eustache retained much of this background, but he was also affected by the Neostoic revival of the sixteenth century, which encouraged a divorce between the higher and the lower elements in the soul.

At the same time, Eustache was quite critical of the extreme Neostoic doc-

---

40. Aquinas, *Summa Theologica*, Pt. II (first part), Q. 22, arts. 1–3.
41. Levi, *French Moralists*, 164.
42. See Eustache, *Ethica*, 77ff.
43. This is the so-called "caritas synthesis" described in Anders Nygren's *Agape and Eros*, trans. Philip S. Watson (Philadelphia, 1953), 609–664.

trine that called for the eradication of the passions as vicious in themselves. To the question of whether the passions may be found in a wise man, Eustache answered that if by passions are meant "turbulent emotions that go beyond the limits of reason," the Stoics are correct in believing that wisdom requires the passionless state of "*apatheia.*" But, he said, not every passion is a vice or sin. "They may be used well or ill, but are not bad of themselves. Their goodness or evil depends upon the goodness of one's *willing (voluntate).*" This statement reflects the Augustinian view. The virtues have passions as their proper matter, Eustache continued, and, therefore, whoever lacks passions is going to lack virtues (82). And he followed Thomas in arguing that even those passions that exceed reason can be called wrong, but not sinful. For an act to be sinful, an act of will, or as Thomas said, the consent of the will, must intervene. Passions can incline to sin, but having them is not in itself a sin. As Levi has pointed out, it is a curious characteristic of this period in moral thought that the usual categories of Stoic, Augustinian, Scholastic, and Platonist became exceedingly intertwined and in different respects a moralist may have been associated with all of these together.

The influence of certain Neoplatonic ideas is unmistakable in Eustache.[44] This association is most apparent in his discussion of "intellectual love" (*amor intellectualis*), a subject that was ordinarily slighted in Scholastic treatises. Eustache defined intellectual love as "a delight in divine things," and a kind of "trance (*raptus*) of the rational appetite" (86). Thus it is located in the will and is not properly a passion. But it is significant that Eustache, following the Platonists, introduced "*pulchrum*" (beauty), which is perceived through the senses, along with "*bonum*" as a cause of this highest kind of love. Golius, it will be remembered, more or less identified *pulchrum* with the temptation of the sensual, as though the holy and righteous was not also lovable for its beauty and pleasingness. In the Platonic tradition, God represents not just duty but also beauty. One of the most often repeated commonplaces from Cicero was that the allurement of virtue, when it is truly seen, is the rival of any form of vice. Through the influence of the Cambridge Platonists and others in the seventeenth century, the idea of beauty as a positive factor in natural morality was to become a subject of increasing importance in British ethical philosophy. When the rigid distinction between rational and sensitive appetite broke down in the seventeenth century, through a redefinition of the faculty of will, the Platonic concept of intellectual love could serve as one model for a new, more integrated human psychology.[45] Whatever

44. Levi, *French Moralists*, 159: "If Eustache has not read Ficino himself, he is certainly acquainted with the derivatives." Eustache was thus one more conduit of Neoplatonic ideas to Massachusetts prior to the full blossoming of the Platonic school at Cambridge University.

45. The theory of the passions in the 17th century and its bearing on thought in America is treated at length in chap. 4, below.

Eustache's theoretical position, in his discussion of the causes of love he showed a practical appreciation of the resonance by which love is transmitted: "There is no greater impulse toward loving than being loved in the first place. He is a hard soul who wishes to receive love without returning it" (89).

Burgersdyck

With the *Idea Philosophiae Tum Moralis, Tum Naturalis* (1631) of Franco Burgersdyck (Burgersdicius) (1590–1635) a new spirit is evident.[46] Burgersdyck was a Protestant like Golius and hardly less dependent upon Scholastic predecessors than Eustache. But his religion carried into his exposition of Aristotle's ethics more noticeably than was the case with Golius, and though, like Eustache, he was building upon Scholastic foundations, he expressed much more impatience with the Schoolmen. Burgersdyck's intellectual style is a little less formal and his terminology less traditional than those of his predecessors that we have mentioned, yet there was nothing like the breakthrough in these qualities that would come with Descartes's work. It is also noteworthy that Burgersdyck incorporated more Neoplatonic ideas than are apparent even in Eustache. Burgersdyck's use of Neoplatonism was representative of a tendency during the century that culminated in the Platonist school in seventeenth-century England. But Aristotle remained the dominant and formative figure on ethical thought in Burgersdyck's work as he would be for Burgersdyck's disciple at the University of Leiden, Adrian Heereboord, whose moral philosophy was also studied at Harvard.[47] To establish the teaching of philosophical ethics at Leiden, Burgersdyck had to overcome the opposition of Ames and other theologians and also to respond positively to student dislike of literal commentaries on the Aristotelian text. His manual of moral philosophy was directed to both of these ends.[48]

46. The *Idea Philosophiae Moralis* first appeared in 1623, and in subsequent separate editions in 1629, 1635, 1640, 1644, all at Leiden. It was published with the *Idea Philosophiae Naturalis* first at Oxford in 1631 and subsequently in 1637 and 1654. My references are to the Oxford 1637 edition. Page citations are in parentheses in the text. There is a bibliography of Burgersdyck's work in Paul Dibon, *Philosophie néerlandaise*, 123–126. Note Dibon's comment: "The history of the teaching of philosophy at the University of Leyden from 1620 to 1640 is practically inseparable from the history of the publications of Burgersdijk" (p. 94).

47. The excellent dissertation by Thomas A. McGahagan, "Cartesianism in the Netherlands, 1639–1676: The New Science and the Calvinist Counter-Reformation" (Ph.D. diss., University of Pennsylvania, 1976), 43, describes Burgersdyck as representative of the new Humanistic Aristotelianism that grew up during the Renaissance, imbued with the goal of rescuing Aristotle from the Schoolmen.

48. Dibon, *Philosophie néerlandaise*, 89–119, has a good brief study of Burgersdyck. Burgersdyck and Ames were contemporaries, and the two men were certainly well aware of each

Some appreciation of Burgersdyck's fame as an author of academic texts may be gleaned from John Locke's reference to him in the context of a rather sharp condemnation of excessive school learning. Locke favored instead such essentials in the life of a gentleman as "good Breeding, Knowledge of the World, Vertue, Industry, and love of Reputation." Seneca had complained, Locke noted, of a similar pedanticism in his own time, but "the *Burgersdicius's* and the *Scheiblers* did not swarm in those Days, as they do now in these."[49] Copies of Burgersdyck's ethics text still survive with Harvard student ownership recorded in them from 1662 into the eighteenth century. If one adds the enormous popularity of his logic and his physics and metaphysics texts, Burgersdyck's books were without question among the most widely distributed academic works in the entire seventeenth century.[50]

Burgersdyck defended the autonomy of moral philosophy but was also careful to note that the subject had a limited usefulness. The end of moral philosophy is human happiness only, the most perfect possible state that a man may reach in life here on earth with the aid of natural reason alone (6). Yet he introduced no sharp division between the moral requirements for a happy life on earth and the requirements for salvation. The one is treated as preparatory for the other. Moral philosophy, concerned with earthly happiness, ideally works in tandem with theology, for it may "prepare the soul for divine wisdom, and that wisdom in turn increases the virtues" (46). The love of God leads men to carry out their duties "and all the prescriptions that virtue requires" more fully. In Burgersdyck the notion of heroic virtue takes on more substance than was usual and is even integrated with love. Heroic virtue, Burgersdyck wrote, "is nothing more than virtue joined with a certain excellence and splendor. . . . Its excellence consists in a certain outstanding great-

---

other while Ames was professor of theology at Franeker between 1622 and 1633. Burgersdyck's student and successor at Leiden, Adrian Heereboord, referred approvingly to the "most learned" William Ames's exposition in the *Medulla Theologica* of the Platonist position that all of the creation exists first as idea or image in the divine mind (*Meletemata Philosophica* . . . [Leiden, 1654], 332). On Heereboord, see below, pp. 96–102.

49. Locke continued, "What would he [Seneca] have thought, if he had lived now, when the *Tutors* think it their great Business to fill the Studies and Heads of their Pupils with such Authors as these? He would have had much more reason to say, as he does, *Non Vitae sed Scholae descimus*, we learn not to Live, but to Dispute; and our Education fits us rather for the University, than the World." *Some Thoughts Concerning Education* (London, 1693), in James L. Axtell, ed., *The Educational Writings of John Locke* (Cambridge, 1968), 199–200. Christoph Scheibler's texts were also known at 17th-century Harvard.

50. See Norton, "Harvard Text-Books," Col. Soc. Mass., *Trans.*, XXVIII (1935), 361–366, 395. Burgersdyck's logic is found widely in libraries not only in New England but also in Virginia. His logic was still being recited at Harvard in 1726. For Burgersdyck's logic at Yale, see Richard Warch, *School of the Prophets: Yale College, 1701–1740* (New Haven, Conn., 1973), 201–205. For the use of Burgersdyck's texts at Cambridge University, see Costello, *Curriculum at Cambridge, passim*.

ness of the soul and also a fearless ability to undertake the greatest tasks, to bear up under them steadfastly and to conclude them happily. The greatness of soul is due to a certain special love and desire (*peculiari quodam amore desiderio*) for the last end to which [heroes] lift up their minds more loftily than do the common run of men" (317). Nevertheless, Burgersdyck was unambiguous on the point that moral philosophy without divine aid cannot reach to even the lowest step of spiritual happiness, whatever its ancillary value. It is forever confined to its own nature and to those natural goods that can be attained without the aid of grace (15, 49). Men require the "illumination" of grace to help them cleave to God.

The rapprochement between moral philosophy and divinity that Burgersdyck hoped to effect hinged on the idea of wisdom. Burgersdyck's concept of wisdom was much like Luther's and that of others after the Reformation who identified "wisdom" with revealed theology. "No unbeliever is a wise man," was the central message of a sermon at the Harvard chapel in 1664.[51] But the Lutheran rule had been that moral philosophy was always useless and often dangerous because it drew men away from wisdom, that is, from the true road to eternal salvation. For Burgersdyck, however, ethics was rightly a preliminary to the higher knowledge, not a digression from it. His aim was nonetheless similar to Luther's and to William Ames's in that he wanted to overcome the deep separation in Aristotle between theoretical and practical wisdom. "Theoretical wisdom . . . will study none of the things that make a man happy," Aristotle wrote, "for it is not at all concerned with the sphere of coming-to-be (but only with unchanging realities)."[52] Clearly, Christians who equated theoretical wisdom and theology could not accept this kind of barren contemplation that did not issue in a life of charity. Theology must include not only faith but also practice. "Contemplation of God is not just some opinion about his nature," Burgersdyck wrote, "but it is a most firm and effective kind of *persuasione* whose power not only clings to the mind but also penetrates to the will" (44–45). Luther or Ames would have the source of virtue descending from above only, from faith by grace and revelation, whereas Burgersdyck allowed for a degree of reciprocity between moral philosophy below and revealed theology above. The study of natural virtue, Burgersdyck believed, can contribute to the purging and purification of the soul by encouraging a turning away from the senses and toward reason.

Burgersdyck also expressly departed from Aristotle in his discussion of the virtue of piety, or the proper relation of man to God. For practical natural knowledge about this virtue, he said, we must turn rather to the "Pythago-

51. Solomon Stoddard, "Commonplace Book," MS. See the excellent discussion in Rice, *Renaissance Idea of Wisdom*, chap. 5.
52. *Nicomachean Ethics*, VI. vii. 1141b, xii. 1143b.

reans" and the Platonists, or to others conversant with human wisdom.[53] The idea of God, he affirmed, is natural to men, and human nature itself spontaneously gives rise to piety in some form, though there are many false notions and practices. From the right Classical sources (he specifically mentioned Cicero), we may learn about piety *in general*. Specifically Christian piety, however, can be learned about only through sacred Scripture. The main implication for ethics in Burgersdyck's discussion of piety is his assertion that in its proper form piety, not "practical wisdom" (*prudentia*), is the first virtue and the source of all the others (162–172). It seems clear that Burgersdyck in this case was attempting to translate a fundamental Judaeo-Christian doctrine into the terms of moral philosophy. Neither Golius nor Eustache had gone so far toward synthesis.

The general tenor of Burgersdyck's work nonetheless remains in the Aristotelian school. This is true for the structure of the work as a whole, for the majority of problems Burgersdyck addressed, and for the many particular discussions that more than anything else are simply learned expositions of Aristotle. The three main parts or concerns of ethics presented by Burgersdyck are roughly parallel to those treated by Aristotle: (1) the definition and attainment of the end, namely happiness; (2) an analysis of moral actions, their differences and principles, including the affections and pleasure and pain and their objects; and (3) the types of virtue, the doctrine of the mean, and friendship. This pattern was also followed by Eustache. Occasionally Burgersdyck introduced elaborations that while confined within the old framework added relevant new material. There is a treatment of "punishment" that drew much from Cicero and Seneca (231–234) and a discussion of "truthfulness" that brought in Augustine and many others and went beyond any Classical precedent (240*ff*). There are also indications that Burgersdyck had absorbed some of the casuistic literature prominent in his time. And in the context of an examination of the virtues of "*urbanitas*" and "*comitas*" (corresponding to Aristotle's Book IV, part viii), Burgersdyck risked the ire of both the Dutch precisians, such as Gisbert Voet, and the English Puritans by defending stage plays insofar as they are free of impiety, obscenity, and brutality (256).

Like Eustache, Burgersdyck rejected as un-Christian the Neostoic vaunting of indifference to feeling (88). The passions or affections may be described as diseases or sicknesses of the soul in the Stoic manner only when they are not kept in line by reason. He gave the standard Scholastic definition of the

53. In the 17th century the term "Pythagorean" had almost nothing like its present meaning. To Burgersdyck it undoubtedly included much of the Hermetic tradition. His main source was probably the vastly popular *Golden Verses of the Pythagoreans* by Hierocles, from which he quotes on p. 45.

passions—motions of the sensitive appetite in response to goods or evils, with associated bodily changes—and because they are positive, appetitive motions, he preferred the term "affections" to the term "passions," which overly emphasized passivity and was too general.[54] The Stoics went wrong, Burgersdyck maintained, when they connected the passions or the affections with the faculty of judgment or apprehension rather than with appetites. It was on this point that the Peripatetics and Stoics principally disagreed. The affections do not consist in judgments of truth or falsity, rather they are tendencies (74–77). Nor do the affections depend entirely on bodily temperament, as the ancient physician Galen believed, because we exercise no control over our temperament, but we do have some control over our passions. "If Galen is right, doctors not philosophers would determine how to attain virtue" (86). A Harvard thesis from 1643 similarly rejected the well-known Galenic theory: *"Mores non sequuntur temperamentum corporis"* (Moral character is not determined by bodily temperament).

At one point Burgersdyck came very close to the Cartesian view of the passions and even to the advanced position that we will find in Henry More. "Is there anyone who becomes bad," he asked, "because he has been set on the path of evil by a natural power?" A power like the passions, which in themselves tend to the good and in animals tend to safety and preservation itself? Either nature has conferred sensitive appetites on man vainly or even perversely, or the motions of the sensitive appetite, that is the affections, must not be considered as altogether among the evils of this world. Furthermore, through the good offices of the passions we are more powerfully carried to desired ends, achieve them more perfectly, and indeed, enjoy them more. Without love and hate our life is not even lively, let alone can we possess happiness in this life (88). All of our worldly experience can be colored by our feelings in the same way that a jaundiced liver makes everything look yellow. And we can only be at peace with ourselves when the sensitive and the rational appetite agree, or when the response of reason is in agreement with the response of the sensitive appetite to the image (*phantasm*) received by the senses (84).

Since the passions are an inseparable part of the good life, we must attend to the virtues of the sensitive appetite as well as to those in the will, or rational

54. The terms "passion" and "affection" were often but not always used synonymously. In the 17th century "affections" sometimes referred specifically to the emotions of the will or the higher soul, e.g., love of virtue, whereas the term "passions" was confined to the emotions of the sensitive appetite in reference to material objects. Levi, *French Moralists*, 112–126, discusses the problems created by this distinction. In the 18th century it became common to describe affections as calm and implicitly "rational" passions. These two distinctions were related historically and also logically in that both grew out of the desire to bring feelings and emotions into the moral life in an effective way while yet retaining a barrier against turbulent and blind passion.

appetite. The followers of Duns Scotus were in error, Burgersdyck held, in making all virtue "*proairetic*" only, that is, dependent on free choice of the will without a necessary preceding act of intellect or influence from lower appetites. It is true that only the rational appetite (or the will) peculiar to man is concerned with the *bonum honestum* and the *turpe* (the true good and the genuine evil), and that the sensitive appetite is directed toward the pleasurable and the useful good. Yet in man the sensitive appetite is capable of joining with the rational appetite in desiring the praiseworthy good and rejecting the blameworthy evil. In this way the affections of men differ from those of beasts and infants, which can be concerned solely with pleasure and pain.

Human virtue depends upon the agreement of all the parts of the soul. Even Thomas Aquinas spoke contrary to reason, Burgersdyck maintained, when he described justice as the one cardinal virtue that existed without any relation to the passions.[55] The justice of the soul lies in the harmony of all the moral virtues together, including the temperance of the appetites (137*ff*). Burgersdyck was borrowing here from the Platonic view of the cardinal virtues: temperance controlled the appetites, prudence governed the intellect, fortitude strengthened the resolutions of the will, and the justice of the soul kept all of these virtues in proper balance. Ames argued similarly that the Classical cardinal virtues are not four kinds of virtues "as conceived by many who have done manifest violence to both virtue and reason by referring artificially all individual virtues to these heads." Rather, "they are four conditions necessarily required in the disposition that deserves the name of virtue." In other words, all of them must be present in any fully virtuous act.[56]

Burgersdyck's emphasis on the contributions to virtue of the workings of the sensitive appetite raised an old theological problem, which we have already noted in Eustache. God and the angels are possessed of the highest virtues, yet it is clear that He and they exist independently of body and the motions of sensitive appetite. Therefore it is necessary, Burgersdyck said, to confine these comments to the moral virtues understood as civil or ethical rather than as theological (140).

The growing force of Florentine Platonism, associated with the work of Marsiglio Ficino, greatly encouraged the belief in the perfect continuity from earthly love to heavenly charity. On the other hand, Neostoicism with its over-intellectualization of the will tended to promote opinion in favor of a radical separation between the desires of the sensitive appetite and the so-called affections of the mind. The easiest solution to the dilemma posed by these competing ideas was to skirt the question entirely, as Burgersdyck in fact did.

55. For Thomas's view, see *Summa Theologica*, Pt. II (first part), Q. 60, arts. 1–5.

56. Ames, *Marrow of Theology*, II, ii, 24–34, quotation in 25. A Harvard commencement thesis in 1647 stated, *Cardinales quas vocant virtutes, virtutis affectiones sunt, non species* (The so-called cardinal virtues are properties of virtue, not species of it).

Moreover no surviving *thesis* or *quaestio* from seventeenth-century Harvard seems to have dealt directly with the problematical nature of love.

In his discussion of the sources and causes of virtue Burgersdyck, like Golius, generally accepted the Aristotelian argument in favor of practice, or frequent repetition, which he called *"consuetudo,"* custom or habit (154). With Aristotle, he considered and rejected as inadequate the alternatives of temperament, nature, and theoretical learning. Virtues are good characteristics similar to "habits." But nature and temperament enter in as conditions in that the number of actions or repetitions required to develop the characteristic will vary with the pre-existing disposition. *"Consuetudo"* thus presupposes some contribution from nature and learning.

Burgersdyck went beyond Golius in his recognition of the problems raised by this point of view, particularly its circularity. For it is obvious that good actions are not only a cause of interior virtue but perhaps even more so the effects or signs of it. Therefore, to call good actions the cause of virtue is to cite as a cause what is to be explained. "The very supposition of a *disposition* to right *action* being first obtained by repeated right action," Jonathan Edwards wrote more than a century later, "is grossly inconsistent with itself: for it supposes a course of right action, *before* there is a disposition to perform any right action."[57] Burgersdyck responded to this difficulty more artfully than had Aristotle himself. The actions that precede the inherent virtuous character are good, he said, because of their outcome alone, or are good, we might say, on "utilitarian" grounds, to use a nineteenth-century term. But the actions that follow from the developed virtuous habit are good not only for the results that are obtained but also because they are an outgrowth of the soul, that is, of a good will (157). In other words, "good" is used in two different senses, and the less satisfactory utilitarian good may eventually be transformed into the more desirable integral good of the virtuous personality.

As I have suggested above when commenting on Golius, there is a more fundamental opposition between Christian anthropology and Aristotelianism than Burgersdyck cared to acknowledge, as a moment's digression will serve to demonstrate. Aristotle's conception of the development of virtue through right action is not unsubtle, yet from the Christian view his moral thought appeared most vulnerable on this point. His conception of human nature seemed to be naively external or mechanical. Missing was an appreciation of virtue as an unfolding from the inside of the gift of love, whether that gift be considered natural or supernatural. The first cause of virtue has to be some

---

57. Edwards, *The Great Christian Doctrine of Original Sin Defended . . .* (Boston, 1758). I have used the Yale edition, edited by Clyde Holbrook, in *The Works of Jonathan Edwards* (New Haven, Conn., 1957–), III, 229. Edwards was attempting to refute the essentially Aristotelian position taken by his opponent John Taylor.

redeeming transfer of the spirit from someone who is possessed of it before, or who is, as in the Puritan belief in the efficacy of the preached Word, a vehicle of the spirit. Aristotle relied implicitly on a magical transformation of acts into internal habits, really a transformation of quantity into quality; but without love such a habit or characteristic could be only superficial.[58] The problem of circularity was endemic in pagan philosophy as that philosophy was perceived in the seventeenth century and earlier. St. Augustine for one reacted to it quite consciously. "In order, indeed, that we might receive that love whereby we might love, we were loved while as yet we had no love ourselves."[59] Since it was undeniable that training and habituation were useful at least at a preliminary level, Burgersdyck attempted to moderate somewhat the rigor of the famous Reformation formula that good works do not make the good man, the good man does good works.

The Calvinist theologians in Holland and England, although not themselves free of Scholastic and Aristotelian influences, were more uncompromising than the philosophers on the question of the efficient cause of virtue. Virtue is a habit of the will, William Ames said, a proposition that has an Aristotelian ring but was in fact based on a profound redefinition of the meaning of habit.[60] In his *Cases of Conscience* Ames raised the question directly of "whether it be not enough for a man to doe that which is good, unlesse we labor also for an habit of vertue, whereby our hearts may be inclined to that which is good?" The very phrasing of the question anticipated the answer: "If the habit of vertue be absent, although we should doe some good works, yet we are not rooted and grounded in good, but are rashly carried away with evill, and that goodnesse soon vanisheth." That good which is done without "an honest and good heart" cannot be "pleasing unto God."[61] A habit of the will for Ames was an inward, permanent disposition, "a condition or habit [*habitus*] by which the will is inclined to do well," with the discernment of intellect serving only as a contributing factor. Such a habit can be the product only of regeneration by the Holy Spirit. For Ames, the principal source of virtue is a redeemed will, in effect an "infused habit," although he did not use this traditional

58. One might compare these words from John Winthrop's famous address, "A Modell of Christian Charitie" (1630): "The way to drawe men to the workes of mercy is not by force of Argument from the goodnes or necessity of the worke, for though this course may enforce a rationall minde to some present Act of mercy . . . yet it cannot worke such a habit in a Soule as shall make it prompt upon all occasions to produce the same effect but by frameing these affeccions of love in the hearte which will as natively bring forthe the other, as any cause doth produce the effect." Reprinted in Edmund S. Morgan, ed., *Puritan Political Ideas, 1558–1794* (Indianapolis, Ind., 1965), 84.

59. Quoted in Vernon J. Bourke, ed., *The Essential Augustine*, 2d ed. (New York, 1974), 178, from *On the Grace of Christ*, 26.27, trans. Marcus Dods.

60. Ames, *Marrow of Theology*, II, ii, 7.

61. Ames, *Conscience*, II, chap. 8.

term.[62] Daily use and exercise, Ames believed, can increase only those true virtues that already proceed from sanctifying grace. The will is the "first cause . . . of the goodnesse or sinfulnesse of any Act of man."[63]

Among the Protestant pietist theologians, as distinguished from the Protestant Scholastic theologians, habit came to mean specifically an *inner* tendency. An "act of virtue is either outward or inward," Ames wrote, "the inward act belongs to the will itself." The inward act is the will's tendency or inclination, and is essential to virtue. "The outward act without the inward is properly neither good nor evil. But the inward can be good or evil without the external, because the goodness of an act depends first and chiefly upon the will, and this is often acceptable to God, although the outward deed is lacking."[64] This conception of virtue, with its pronounced emphasis on the quality of the intention behind moral actions, had no counterpart in Aristotle, for whom "will" meant primarily "choice," not an interior condition constitutive of the whole man.

An ethics of intention was not new in Christian thought. Before the recovery of the *Nicomachean Ethics* Peter Abelard had attempted to construct a moral system on this basis. Closer to Ames were a number of remarks in Calvin's *Institutes* stressing the importance of intention.[65] And the idea was overwhelmingly present in all of Puritan thought where there was a concern to search the heart for signs of purity and sanctification. According to John Downame's *Christian Warfare* (1604), God "respecteth not so much our actions as our affections; nor our workes as our desires and indeavours; so that he who desires to be righteous, is righteous; he that would repent doth repent. . . . For the Lord accepteth the desire for the deede. . . . 2 Cor. 8:12." Similarly, Edward Reynolds wrote that "to do only outward works of duty, without the inward principle, is at best but to make ourselves like those mixt Beasts, Elephants and Camels, . . . which though they do the work of tame Beasts, yet have the nature of wild ones."[66] But, of course, intention was not the whole of ethics. If the good will is a necessary ingredient in the good act, it is not a sufficient one, for "goodnesse is a perfection, and doth arise from the perfection and integrity of all the causes."[67] Goodness is a

62. Ames, *Marrow of Theology*, II, ii, 4; I, xxvi, 23. Cf. Aquinas, *Summa Theologica*, Pt. II (first part), Q. 51, arts. 2–4: "Whether any habit is caused by acts? Whether a habit can be caused by one act? Whether any habits are infused in man by God?"

63. Ames, *Marrow of Theology*, II, ii, 42; *Conscience*, III, 91.

64. Ames, *Marrow of Theology*, II, ii, 21–26.

65. See, for example, Calvin, *Institutes*, III, vii, 7: "The outward work of love is not sufficient, but it is intention that counts!"

66. John Downame, *The Christian Warfare* . . . (London, 1604); Reynolds, *Israel's Prayer in Time of Trouble* . . . (London, 1678), in *Works*, 575.

67. Ames, *Conscience*, III, chap. 17.

correspondence between a man's redeemed will or intention and God's will, a harmony of subjective inclination (man's will) and objective law (God's will), which is unattainable without divine grace. Although a good intention is more virtuous than an outward act, neither is complete without the other.

The degree of importance or weight that was given to internal criteria for virtue may be taken as a rough test of the presence of specifically Judaeo-Christian ethics as opposed to pagan strains. Any complete ethical theory must to some extent include in its concept of meritorious action both intentions and results; yet in the Protestant Reformed tradition the purity and intention of the heart or will was the sine qua non of true virtue. The thrust of the original Protestant revolt, which was against elements of formalism in the Roman church, established inwardness as a fundamental tenet of Protestant moral theology. It is true that Aristotle had not ignored the criterion of disinterestedness in describing virtuous action, and disinterestedness may be seen as a form of inner purity. The moral person in the Aristotelian conception must not act with ulterior motives, although concern for reputation or for honor and fame was allowable. Nevertheless, Christian theologians perceived a lack of depth in the Classical accounts of ethical merit. The exact meaning of the word "habit" was itself troublesome in this regard, since it connoted both internal and behavioral modification of the soul, yet without clarity as to the proportion or the depth of the internal transformation. In Reformed Protestant writings the noble deeds of the heathens were, in comparison to Christian virtues, acknowledged to be good only in their material form. Insofar as they issued from an impure heart, which they necessarily did, they were radically bad. The actions of the unregenerate and the heathens lacked such essential motives as gratitude for God's redeeming grace, the goal of acting in the service of God's glory rather than one's own, and the desire to serve as an example to others of the efficacy of faith.[68] The growth of utilitarian and associationist ethics in the nineteenth century represented a further departure from a "Christian" moral psychology, for these systems almost completely neglected subjective criteria for determining merit and even departed from the Classical standard, which had never gone so far in valuing only external effects. On the other hand, a variation of the religious definition of virtue persisted and continues to persist in the romantic tradition, which places supreme value on inward dispositions such as a good heart, right affections, and sincerity.

In addition to the conundrum posed by Aristotle's theory that virtue had somehow to create itself, his Christian critics also condemned the *Nicomachean Ethics* for being irremediably relativist. Neither created "nature," nor God, nor any transcendent principle remained outside the circle of prac-

68. See the discussion in Heppe, *Reformed Dogmatics*, ed. Bizer, trans. Thomson, 576–579.

tical action by which to measure its worth.[69] For an ultimate standard (in effect a cultural standard) Aristotle fell back simply on the judgment of the "good man," or the man of high moral worth. For the criterion of good we have only to rely on those around us who are most good. William Ames criticized Aristotle for adhering to the "crooked law that the judgment of prudent men is the rule for virtue. . . . There are nowhere such wise men under whose judgment we might always stand and, even if there were, they could not always be known or consulted by the would-be virtuous."[70] Christians believed they had been granted the means of escaping from the pagan dilemma by the gift of scriptural revelation and by the discovery of the divine authority of conscience.

Heereboord

Adrian Heereboord (1613–1661) revered his predecessor in the chair of philosophy at Leiden University, Franco Burgersdyck, and the two men are often associated in historians' references. Heereboord wrote a synopsis of his teacher's logic (the two works were sometimes bound together), and he also prepared from manuscripts the posthumous edition of Burgersdyck's *Institutiones Metaphysicae* (1640).[71] Heereboord's principal treatise in ethics, *Collegium Ethicum*, first appeared in 1648. This work was later incorporated into his *Meletemata Philosophica* of 1654, the book through which Heereboord's general influence was mainly felt and which contains a good deal more ethical material than the *Collegium Ethicum* alone. A. O. Norton located three copies of the *Meletemata* with a total of thirteen autographs of Harvard students distributed among them, most from the eighteenth century. As early as 1664 Solomon Stoddard owned a copy of the *Meletemata* and several student notebooks contain references to or excerpts from this Dutch scholar.[72] Perhaps the earliest of these is in John Holyoke's commonplace book of 1663, pertaining to Heereboord's logic. Charles Morton seems to have used Heereboord as the focus of discussion in his teaching of moral philosophy at Harvard in the 1690s, and Heereboord was also used in the ethics courses at a number of dissenting academies, including Rathmell, Sheriffhales, and

69. See A. H. Armstrong, "The Greek Philosophical Background of the Psychology of St. Thomas," Aquinas Society of London, Paper no. 19 (London, 1952), 12.

70. Ames, *Marrow of Theology*, II, ii, 14.

71. See Morison, *Seventeenth-Century Harvard*, 191, 252; Dibon, *Philosophie néerlandaise*, 117–123; and McGahagan, "Cartesianism in the Netherlands," 218–243.

72. Norton, "Harvard Text-Books," Col. Soc. Mass., *Trans.*, XXVIII (1935), 361–431; Fiering, "Stoddard's Library at Harvard," *Harvard Lib. Bul.*, XX (1972), 255–269.

Bethnal Green.[73] The surviving official record of the curriculum at Harvard in the first quarter of the eighteenth century called for recitation from Heereboord's *Meletemata* during both the sophomore and junior years, and the book was probably in active use until the 1730s.

By the time Heereboord's *Meletemata Philosophica* was published in 1654 the intellectual climate in Europe had changed dramatically from what it had been when Burgersdyck began his career, and it is clear from the first pages of Heereboord's masterwork that a revolution was underway.[74] The preface to this massive and rather repetitious compendium of nearly a thousand pages contains a synopsis of the history of philosophy.[75] In it the Scholastics are denounced with a new vigor as benighted and frivolous, the perpetrators of terrible confusion between philosophy and theology, and the deformers of arguments. They bent religion to the opinion of the philosophers through the use of vain, turgid, and harmful subtleties and thereby contaminated theology. In the eyes of Thomas Aquinas, Heereboord wrote, Aristotle and God walked side by side, but in fact the Lord of Israel followed far behind the Lord of Aristotle. Only with Dante and Petrarch did the restoration of philosophy and learning begin. The major restorers of religion were Erasmus, Luther, and Melanchthon. "Let us wipe the dust finally from our eyes and let us not cling to Aristotle alone. . . . Let us open the book not just of Aristotle but of nature and turn the pages not just of him but most especially of it" (4–6). There is, predictably, much praise of the new learning, by which Heereboord meant the work of Ramus, Bacon, Campanella, and especially Descartes. Descartes is the true light who has opened not a few secrets of nature and exhibited the key to philosophy (10).

In general, Heereboord was well read and comprehensive in adducing authorities, ancient and modern. His brief against the Schoolmen found expression also in a Latin style and vocabulary closer to the Ciceronian. The

73. Smith, *Birth of Modern Education*, Appendix A. Many New England libraries had Heereboord's *Meletemata* in them. See, for example, *A Catalogue of Curious and Valuable Books, Belonging to the Late Reverend & Learned Mr. Ebenezer Pemberton* . . . (Boston, 1717).

74. I am using the Amsterdam 1680 edition. Page citations are in parentheses in the text. Besides the first edition in 1654 there were also editions in 1659 and 1665. Morison's translation of the full title of the *Meletemata*, which is in both Latin and Greek, is as follows: "Philosophical Exercises, in which the complete content of Metaphysics is set in motion, the whole of Ethics explained scholastically and antischolastically, the physical universe expounded by means of theorems and commentaries, and the principal matter of Logic propounded by thorough disputations, with a supplement containing [sixty-three Ethical as well as some miscellaneous disputations in] Natural Philosophy with new comments [and Pneumatica]." Morison omitted the phrases in brackets. See *Seventeenth-Century Harvard*, 233–234, and the illustration facing p. 234.

75. Dibon notes that Heereboord's thinking evolved in successive editions of the *Meletemata*, but I have not been able to compare editions. Therefore, it is not safe to assume that comments in the 1680 edition also appeared in 1654.

Meletemata was probably the meatiest modern work in ethics available to Harvard students before the publication in the late 1660s of Henry More's seminal *Enchiridion Ethicum*. Too much should not be made of Heereboord's Cartesianism, however, for it was an enthusiasm that manifested itself more in natural philosophy, or science, than in any other area.[76] Paul Dibon has called Heereboord a "Cartesian scholastic" in order to describe the spirit of synthesis and conciliation that characterized his and other academic philosophers' work in Holland after mid-century.

According to Heereboord natural ethics is possible only because men have retained from their Adamic state notions of good and evil in their minds and hearts. These moral principles are a certain "remaining witness of the divine image in man" (668).[77] The book of nature, the natural light in men, and Natural Law all refer to the same thing—a certain primeval wisdom, the relics of original justice. These principles are innate in that they are implanted in the soul from the beginning; nonetheless, they do not emerge until a person begins to exercise his reason, although they do not depend upon training in syllogisms and formal demonstrations (671).

Heereboord's treatment of the conventional Scholastic theory of the natural light is of some interest. Aristotle had divided the operations of the mind by which truth is sought and followed into five virtues or habits: "Science" is the study of the logical deductions that may be made from already existing knowledge of necessary and eternal things; "Art" has to do only with the production or making of things according to rational principles; "Practical Wisdom," or prudence, is the quality of reasoning well in the interest of the morally good

76. Samuel Sewall read Heereboord's Cartesian physics to his students when he was a teaching fellow at Harvard in 1673–1674; before that, in 1671, the students had refused to be taught from a discredited Aristotelian text (see Morison, *Seventeenth-Century Harvard*, 233). Descartes's works were in Solomon Stoddard's library early in the previous decade, and Cotton Mather was reading Descartes in the early 1680s, if not considerably earlier (see *Paterna: The Autobiography of Cotton Mather*, ed. Ronald A. Bosco [Delmar, N.Y., 1976], 64). The rage for Cartesianism that existed in Holland in the 1670s undoubtedly had repercussions at Harvard, which had more in common theologically with Holland than with any other place. A critic of the situation at Leiden University in the 1670s wrote: "Our youth scarcely promoted from the lower schools, even before they can turn a sentence or ten words into good Latin, or understand a single rule of logic, begin immediately to champion the Cartesian philosophy as if they had a great knowledge of it. No one speaks to them any more of Religion or of the Catechism. One begins and ends with a Cartesian seminar where one must doubt of all things, even of whether there is a God. If by chance the Bible is spoken of, this is greeted with a laugh, as a book full of errors, not to be put on a level with the light of nature." Quoted in McGahagan, "Cartesianism in the Netherlands," 327.

77. *"Quam superstites quedam reliquiae imaginis divinae."* The Reformed Protestants distinguished between man's original *virtues*, which were lost in the Fall, and his divine *image*, which remained.

life;[78] "Intelligence" (Greek: *nous*, insight or intuition), the human quality that apprehends fundamental principles, sets out the first principles from which Scientific knowledge makes its deductions and contributes most importantly to the knowledge of the ethical goals for the sake of which Practical Wisdom deliberates; "Theoretical Wisdom" (*sophia, sapientia*) is a supreme union of Scientific knowledge and Intelligence, the highest intellectual virtue of the soul.[79]

Despite these manifold modes of knowledge, Heereboord believed that Aristotle had yet failed to provide for the existence in the mind of the natural light, Natural Law, and indeed, conscience. There are, Heereboord said, in truth only three basic intellectual characteristics or modes: science, practical wisdom, and art. "Theoretical wisdom" should be eliminated because it is superfluous, and Aristotle's "Intelligence" is nothing more than the surviving natural light of the intellect, which because it has divine origins cannot be considered a natural characteristic of the soul in the same sense as the others (669). The natural light may be spoken of as a habit of the intellect only by analogy, for unlike a habit it is inborn, not an acquired modification of the soul. It is by means of the natural light that we can more easily assent to the fundamental principles of morality.[80] The natural light of intellect and so-called Natural Law may either be considered the same thing, Heereboord argued, or else be distinguished only in that Natural Law expresses the fundamental practical principles whereas the natural light is the practical judgment that is drawn from the principles (702–703). The natural light, then, is almost identical with conscience as it was widely characterized by both Catholics and Protestants.

Heereboord supported the traditional argument that the precepts of the Mosaic moral code are part of Natural Law, but at the same time he drew a distinction between these two standards. Natural Law existed prior to Moses in time, was not written down, and was given to all men rather than to the

78. Practical wisdom is a major part of ethics, as will be remembered. It differs from Art in having human action, rather than the making of something, as its end, and from Science in that it cannot begin with unchanging certain and necessary principles because of the changing circumstances in life.

79. *Nicomachean Ethics* VI. iii–vii. 1139b–1141b, xi. 1143b.

80. It is perhaps worth noting that Aristotle had not altogether ignored the supposition that the intuition of first principles, i.e., Intelligence, was divine in origin. "Now, if happiness is activity in conformity with virtue, it is to be expected that it should conform with the highest virtue, and that is the virtue of the best part of us. Whether this is intelligence or something else which, it is thought, by its very nature rules and guides us and which gives us our notions of what is noble and divine; *whether it is itself divine or the most divine thing in us*; it is the activity of this part [when operating] in conformity with the excellence or virtue proper to it that will be complete happiness." *Nicomachean Ethics* X. vii. 1177a. My italics.

Jews alone. It is also less clear, and in consequence the law of Moses much
more effectively convicts the sinner (192*ff*). But in either case the function of
conscience is the same. It spontaneously "applies universal rules to singular
actions," that is to say, it brings concrete judgment (689). Heereboord was
careful to stress that conscience, or "right reason," which is constituted of the
practical conclusions deducible from Natural Law, is not the norm of religious
belief. Right reason remains in man after the Fall, for otherwise we would
have to rely on Scripture alone to live in society at all. But religious dogmas
may not be judged by it. It deals only with natural moral and civil life (703).

Practical philosophy, or ethics, in sum, is concerned with the attainment of
happiness on earth to the degree that it is possible with the aid of natural
powers alone (671). But we must then consider the usual question, In what
does this natural happiness consist? One of the great weaknesses of Aristotle's
ethics, Heereboord asserted, is that it did not correctly assign the ultimate
earthly end of man, nor did it truly explain how virtue was the means to that
end (234). The *summum bonum* on earth is not pleasure, or virtue, or even
happiness as Aristotle defined it: the rational and active life in conformity
with excellence and virtue. For the will of man always seeks an infinite object.
The highest happiness for man, in a formal sense, lies in the glorification of
God, according to Heereboord, and practically speaking this consists in "the
worship of God according to the innate principles of Natural Law" (675). It is
a happiness suitable on earth only and ends with death, and without the addition of revealed truth it does not bring salvation. Like Burgersdyck, Heereboord adhered to the common view that the knowledge of God is to a great
extent innate and that much of true piety, too, may be known through natural
means. In both 1679 and 1684 Harvard *quaestiones* affirmed this opinion.[81]
This pious happiness in God is not at all dependent upon externals, such as
good fortune or riches, ingredients that Aristotle mistakenly believed were
necessary complements of happiness.

Heereboord exceeded Burgersdyck in the precision of his explication of
this happiness, which he said cannot be understood in terms of either contemplation or action alone. It is the soul's *combined love and knowledge* of
God, a "certain vital and immanent action that suits (*conveniat*) or befits man
alone and indeed to that extent is rational" (686). The highest good, true
piety, and happiness consist, then, in the operation of both intellect and will
(in the broadest sense) and more in an act of the will than of the intellect.

Heereboord envisioned an elevated mission for moral philosophy, one that
included a great deal of Christian piety. His views foreshadowed the quasi-

---

81. *An notitia Dei sit homini naturalis?* (Whether the knowledge of God is natural to man?)
(Affirmed by Thomas Brattle in 1679, and Samuel Russel in 1684). John Locke's denial that man
has innate knowledge of God was later to be one of the most controversial of his claims in the
Essay Concerning Human Understanding.

religious virtue-devotion of some eighteenth-century moral philosophies. Clear signs were already present in the *Meletemata* that no simple division between Aristotelian civil happiness and Christian beatitude could hold up for long. It became a question of whether a new, Christianized moral philosophy was going to devour Protestant practical theology or practical theology subsume moral philosophy.

In a separate disputation, *"De Bono"* (On the good), Heereboord advanced the view that all goodness is a matter of "fittingness," or *convenientia*. The common manner of speaking illustrates this, he said, as when we say that something is harmonious or right. Burgersdyck had also held the opinion, Heereboord indicated, that goodness consists in the befittingness or harmony of one being to another. Before the Creation, God's goodness consisted in his befittingness or harmony with Himself. And the goodness of the created world lies in its befittingness to God (159–160). Thus we can say that man's happiness on earth and his capacity for goodness are part of a larger metaphysical relationship, the central character of which is harmony or fittingness.[82]

With regard to the place of the affections or passions in the moral life Heereboord did not differ greatly from the positions we have already analyzed. St. Thomas's *prima secundae* continued to be the basic source.[83] Following Thomas, Heereboord pointed out that a triple motion is discoverable in every affection: cognitive apprehension, the appetitive movement, and a bodily change. The bodily change is not the affection itself but follows from it. The affection, properly speaking, falls between the cognitive event that stimulates it and the motion in the body that follows it. The passions are first of all in the soul, not in the body.[84] Our knowledge of our affections is basically mental, not physiological. We know of them as we know of our other sense experiences, through the *sensus communis* or internal sense (721). The affections are therefore not without judgment, but they may not be identified with judgment or intellectual apprehension as the Stoics claimed. When the reason directly participates in an affection, through the exercise of the rational appetite or will, Heereboord spoke of a "mixed affection," which has no

82. "Suarez, *Meta. Disput.*, 10, sec. 3" was the earliest citation Heereboord gave for this idea. Cf. the similar notions discussed in Leroy E. Loemker, *Struggle for Synthesis: The Seventeenth Century Background of Leibniz's Synthesis of Order and Freedom* (Cambridge, Mass., 1972), 177–202, and see Fiering, *Jonathan Edwards's Moral Thought*.

83. It is curious that despite Heereboord's praise of Descartes at the beginning of the *Meletemata* he does not seem to have read *Les Passions de l'âme* (Paris, 1649). The first treatise in use at Harvard that fully exploited Descartes's important work on the passions was probably Henry More's *Enchiridion Ethicum*.

84. For a discussion of the relation of this Thomist theory to the so-called James-Lange theory in modern psychology, which holds that the experience of an affection is dependent on bodily change, see H. M. Gardiner *et al.*, *Feeling and Emotion: A History of Theories* (New York, 1937), 114–117.

parallel in animals. "Moral" and "natural" affections may also be distinguished, the former being the product of education and training (we might call them cultivated emotional responses), and the latter being the same as animal experience. "Natural" affections, according to Heereboord, are studied in natural philosophy or physics better than in ethics.

Reason in relation to the passions and affections is like a sailor on a storm-tossed ship. But the passions are not all bad, as the Stoics held. Their goodness or evil depends upon the degree to which they are in accord with reason. Thus, Heereboord did not adopt the Augustinian view, which judged the passions in relation to the quality of the love or will out of which they spring. But to establish their essential goodness he used the teleological argument we have seen before. "If the affections were evil, God would not have put them in us." And immediately following this he recognized the intimate relationship between sanctifying grace and the affective life: "Nor would the hearts of the pious be excited by the holy spirit" (726). Heereboord's definition of heroic virtue also pointed to a sanctified, more than a natural, ideal. Heroic virtue, he said, is a combination of right reason and right appetites so that inner conflict is eliminated, which makes virtue excellent or perfect. But, he added, this is a fiction and unrealizable in any person. We should talk about ethics not as it is found in the imagination, but in man (236).

Aristotelianism, which had already been under serious attack in the fifteenth century, was by the middle of the seventeenth century causing great impatience in both students and scholars. It would surely be a mistake, however, to identify all Classical ideals with Aristotelianism. The inspiration of certain elements of Classical moral philosophy persisted into the eighteenth century, but without the formal structure that the *Nicomachean Ethics* had supplied. The most serious deficiency in Aristotle's ethics, as Christians saw it, was the absence of a developed distinction between inward and outward morality. Virtue in Classical philosophy was always close to the concept of a technical skill and, like a skill, was developed by outward practice, not by self-examination with an eye to purity or by the intensification of inner rectitude induced by prayer and meditation. When Aristotle discussed the virtues of liberality and magnanimity, for example, which he valued very highly in the scale of conduct, he did not introduce any qualification suggesting a difference between the vain and selfish and the benevolent exercise of these virtues. In other words, Aristotle showed little apparent concern for the purity of motive behind the act. It has even been suggested that in the Scholastic tradition Aristotelian ethics was preferred for the very reason that it posed no challenge to the core of Christian teaching, unlike Stoic philosophy, which addressed itself more to the inner man and in that respect was able to compete with Christianity.

However that may be, there is no denying that the beauties of Classical moral thought in general were received and appreciated at seventeenth-century Harvard. Perhaps the best proof of this is a 1647 commencement thesis: *"Calocagathia est virtus perfecta." "Kalo k' agathia"* expresses the idea of both internal beauty of character and outward grace and manners and represented the Aristotelian ideal, indeed the highest Classical moral ideal. But the man who has this quality or these qualities, described at length in a famous section of book four of the *Nicomachean Ethics*, is in most respects far removed from the idea of the Puritan saint.

3

Will and Intellect

"Video meliora proboque; Deteriora sequor"
*(I see and approve the better course;
I follow the worse).*[1]

Questions concerning the nature of the will probably engendered more debate at seventeenth-century Harvard than any other topic in moral philosophy. At least thirty commencement *theses* and *quaestiones* before 1700 directly or indirectly pertained to this problem, and repeatedly, antithetical positions were taken, which suggests a certain vitality. This degree of activity alone calls for some attention to the details of the controversy. Beyond that interest, a study of will in its relation to the intellect and the appetites brings one promptly into the midst of some complicated problems of moral psychology, and it is possible to show in this context that there were important connections between these seventeenth-century debates and the more familiar eighteenth-century notions of moral psychology, such as were current, for example, during the Great Awakening.

The difficulty in our time of treating the subject of will is not only the typical one common to terms that have multiple and confused meanings—terms such as, for example, "reason" or "nature"—but also that the meanings of "will" that are particularly relevant to understanding the issues in the seventeenth century are now archaic. It is hard to say what is in the popular mind at present, but most of modern psychology seems to do quite nicely without any concept of the will at all. So profoundly has human psychology and psychological theory changed that talking about will is something like talking about bodily humors and the four elements in medical physiology.[2] We have already mentioned in passing one concept of will (which appears in the work of William Ames among others) that is foreign to modern idiom and

---

1. Ovid, *Metamorphoses* VII. 20.
2. There are signs of some change, however, especially among the psychotherapists. See, e.g., Leslie H. Farber, *The Ways of the Will: Essays toward a Psychology and Psychopathology of Will* (New York, 1966), and Rollo May, *Love and Will* (New York, 1969).

preserved only in the idea of the "man of good will," or of good heart and good intentions, where "will" refers to a basic trait of character or disposition. But what can the notion of will as "rational appetite" mean today, what personal or introspective reference do we have to it? Hardly a verbal echo of the idea survives. Similarly, *the* will, in the nominative, as the faculty of choice or decision is remote from modern connotations of "will." Under these circumstances it is not surprising the whole subject has not received the careful attention it deserves if we are to be faithful to seventeenth-century concerns.[3]

The central problem at seventeenth-century Harvard was not the famous one of free will versus determinism as it occurs in either of its classic forms. Insofar as the free will problem was essentially a theological debate, such as that which took place between St. Augustine and Pelagius, or Luther and Erasmus, or Calvinists and Arminians, it was a relatively dormant issue in New England, where the doctrine of predestination by free grace and man's inability to earn salvation were undisputed dogmas. The other classic form of the problem of free will, that which was provoked by the assertion of the determinist hypothesis based not upon God's sovereignty but upon the law of natural causation in all known phenomena, found its modern expression in English thought principally in reaction to the writing of Thomas Hobbes and did not reach New England until almost the end of the century, thus playing no role in the period we are presently examining. In fact, on the broad matter of human freedom there was considerable unanimity before the rise of naturalistic determinism. Everybody, including Calvin, believed that man was free enough to be held responsible before God for his sins and before other men for his crimes. It was a truism passed on from virtually all of the ancient moralists as well as the Schoolmen that praise and blame implied some degree of moral autonomy. Beyond that consensus there was little need to go. Man was held to be self-actuating and spontaneous, a voluntary creature exempt to some degree at least from the bonds of nature that controlled all the rest of the creation. With the angels and God Himself man was ordinarily moved not by "coaction," to use the terminology of the time, but by "counsel." Or, in other

3. In my discussion of will I have been most instructed by Thomas E. Davitt, *The Nature of Law* (St. Louis, Mo., 1951); Levi, *French Moralists*; E. Gilson, *La Liberté chez Descartes et la théologie* (Paris, 1913); Vernon J. Bourke, *Will in Western Thought: An Historico-Critical Survey* (New York, 1964), a useful book, though not entirely reliable; and Archibald Alexander, *Theories of the Will in the History of Philosophy* (New York, 1898), which studies only the few major figures, most of whom were not key influences on American thought in our period. With regard to early American thought, the theory of the will before Jonathan Edwards has hardly been studied at all. In his 100-page introduction to Edwards's *Freedom of the Will*, in *Works of Edwards*, I, Paul Ramsey accepts the widely held assumption that Edwards's interest in the will dated from his reading of Locke. But Locke himself was writing in the context of the great 17th-century debate concerning the will.

words, freedom was characterized simply by the absence of constraint or compulsion in behavior, and it was assumed that this freedom was not diminished by the exercise of rational choice on any given occasion.

What then was at the core of the controversy that for fifty years agitated the tiny group of scholars and tutors passing through the college in Cambridge, Massachusetts, and to some extent similar classes of men at other university centers in the West? Broadly speaking, the challenging question was not whether or not man is free but wherein his freedom lies. In response to this question there was a choice of only two general answers. It was clear that man's freedom was somehow part of his higher faculties, that is, part of his rational soul rather than his animal or his vegetative soul; for if freedom could be traced to his animal soul (also called the sensitive soul), then the animal kingdom, too, would share in this privileged liberty, which was unthinkable and contrary to accepted observation. Animals by definition were dominated solely by material appetites. With the field accordingly narrowed down to the rational soul, within that focus there were two possibilities only, corresponding to the two faculties of the rational soul: freedom as exclusively an act of the will, or freedom as an act of both intellect and will in inseparable unity. Here was the nub of the problem with surprising ramifications in many directions.

Before looking at the content of this debate and some of its corollaries, it may be useful to devote a few words to a description of those elements in the psychological theory of the time to which nearly all parties agreed. It is particularly necessary to make some effort to provide the rationale for this psychology so that it does not remain insuperably alien. Too often in twentieth-century history books, so-called "faculty psychology" is cursorily dismissed as something that everybody "knows" is bad, and this impressive condemnation serves as an end to any further explication. Frequently, too, in this connection, John Locke's well-known critique of "faculties" is cited, as though *all* past psychological reasoning was easily discarded following upon his magic words and thereby a neat line drawn between old-fashioned and modern. But Locke was addressing himself here, as in several other famous arguments in his *Essay Concerning Human Understanding*, to the common abuses in late-Scholastic philosophy rather than to the best scholarly thinking, which in many of its parts was not so far from his own ideas. Indeed, on the matter of faculties, Locke was close enough in 1690 to the traditional psychology taught at Harvard in 1650 to be used as an excellent example of the inherited teaching regarding the general powers of the rational soul: "This, at least, I think evident," Locke wrote, "that we find in ourselves a power to begin or forbear, continue or end several thoughts of our minds, and motions of our bodies, barely by a choice or preference of the mind ordering, or as it were commanding, the doing or not doing such a particular action. This power which the mind has thus to order . . . or to prefer . . . is that which we call the *Will*."

The other power of the mind that Locke recognized was the intellect, or what he usually called the understanding. Of course, in his analysis of the precise acts of the understanding he diverged from tradition, but it is significant that in accordance with centuries of earlier speculation he conceived of understanding and will as the sole rational faculties. His complaint was against the hypostatization of the faculties, such that "this way of speaking of *faculties* has misled many into a confused notion of . . . distinct agents in us," each with "their several provinces and authorities," and able to "command, obey, and perform several actions, as so many distinct beings." But he ended by affirming what was in fact the standard view: "Faculty, ability, and power . . . are but different names of the same things," a matter which was clear enough in an age of Latin scholarship when *facultas* meant just that: ability or power, and no more.[4] Two Harvard commencement theses from 1675 and 1684, respectively, said as much: "The faculties of the rational soul are distinguished from the soul only notionally," and "Intellect and will are the soul as understanding and as willing."[5]

There was after all nothing mysterious about faculties, nor is there anything intrinsically abhorrent in them. In the Cartesian manner Locke founded the faculty of will on internal experience; it is a power, he said, that we find in ourselves. Yet this explanation is hardly enough to account for the immutability for centuries of the notion that the mind has principally the dual powers of intellect and will. The strength of this model probably depended rather little upon recurrent introspection or observation. Its strength lay instead in its congruence with a series of other unquestioned distinctions. It was a commonplace that the intellect responded to truth, whereas the will responded to goodness. Thus logic and ethics could be distinguished along these lines, the former concerned with the well-ordering of the intellect toward truth, and the latter with the well-ordering of the will toward good. The great ideal ends of man, the true and the good, unknown to the beasts, could be realized through man's possession of a rational soul which had these two special powers. The powers of intellect and will also paralleled the rational functions of reasoning and choosing. The will (*voluntas*), which is directed to the good, makes choices (*arbitria*) in relation to its end, in a similar fashion as the intellect reasons to its special end of truth. At the same time God also, by analogy, has

4. Locke, *An Essay Concerning Human Understanding*, ed. Alexander Campbell Fraser, 2 vols. (New York, 1959 [orig. publ. Oxford, 1894]), Bk. II, chap. xxi, 5–21.

5. *Facultates animae rationalis ratione tantum differunt ab anima; Intellectus & voluntas sunt anima intelligens & volens.*

these two powers of intellect and will. From the creature's point of view, through the first His laws become intelligible, and by the second He determines all things. (Some thinkers, however, notably Descartes, refused to allow a distinction between intellect and will in God.) The distinction found frequently in modern writing between thought and action is a continuation to some extent of the idea behind the division into intellect and will. Of course, there are important differences, too, particularly in that the term "action" lacks the teleological overtone that was nearly always present in the idea of will up to the seventeenth century. But as in the distinction between thought and action it was generally held that the will is blind—the phrase itself reappears constantly—or at least purblind; whereas the intellect is passive, in the sense that it is incapable in itself of sponsoring motion.[6] These independent deficiencies or limitations made intellect and will complementary and unitary. Both were needed for the wholesome functioning of man's higher soul.

In St. Thomas Aquinas, who was very well known in early seventeenth-century philosophy and was cited occasionally in student notebooks that have survived from Harvard in this period, the rational faculties of will and intellect are described in a unified way that might not have failed to satisfy Locke.[7] Will and intellect "include one another in their acts," Thomas wrote, "because the intellect understands that the will wills, and the will wills the intellect to understand." Or, in different terms, Thomas said, "Truth and good include one another, for truth is something good, otherwise it would not be desirable; and good is something true, otherwise it would not be intelligible." Thus, when the mind apprehends an object, it has the power of both considering it as true and willing it as good, but never one entirely without the other.[8] In a work on "physiology" by William Ames there is a similar gloss: "Intellect and will differ neither from the rational soul nor from one another essentially, but only differ formally or by a formal notion, namely, with respect to intrinsic operation. Will is intellect as external, for the purpose of

6. There was also an active side to intellect—its ability to abstract intelligible species from material phenomena.

7. Thomas is referred to and quoted in several places, for example, in John Holyoke's commonplace book of 1662–1663, a manuscript in the Houghton Lib., Harvard Univ. Solomon Stoddard owned a couple of works by Thomas when he was a graduate student at Harvard in 1664. See Fiering, "Stoddard's Library at Harvard," *Harvard Lib. Bul.*, XX (1972), 255–269. In 1682 Noahdiah Russell bought from the Harvard Library some duplicate copies of works by Thomas Aquinas, as did Cotton Mather. See the fragment from Russell's diary in the *New England Historical and Genealogical Register*, VII (1853), 57, and Clarence S. Brigham, "Harvard College Library Duplicates, 1682," Col. Soc. Mass., *Trans.*, XVIII (1917), 407–417.

8. Aquinas, *Summa Theologica*, Pt. I, Q. 82, art. 4; Q. 79, art. 11.

possessing and making what it knows. Intellect is will as immanent, for the purpose of understanding."[9]

Other examples could be given of this widely accepted analysis that will and intellect were simply two facets of the one characteristic of the higher soul, namely reason.[10] But there is more to be said about the will, particularly in its guise as rational appetite. In the traditional view, if man had not a faculty of will, he alone in all the creation would lack a natural inclination to an appointed end. Every animal and every plant has inbuilt instincts, appetites, or tendencies that lead them to perform unfailingly their special vital duties and functions on earth. Man, too, has animal appetites to guide him to preserve his body and to reproduce himself. These lower ends, however, do not encompass all of his purposes. On the other hand, his intellect, which is clearly capable of *knowing* ideal values, can not of itself *desire* them. But in the will is found that exclusive appetite that seeks what is true for higher beings alone. Of the creatures on earth only man has a rational appetite added to sensitive appetites, that is, a will, and this trait is roughly analogous in its role to instinct in lower animals. Such reasoning comprised the background of the dictum that we have already observed was repeatedly expressed in Scholastic philosophy: no person can will evil as evil. The will is always directed toward what appears at the moment to be good.

In anticipation we should note that when this meaning of the will as the appetite directed toward the rationally conceived good was finally abandoned, a process that we will trace here in some measure, the term "will" itself lost a good deal of its former usefulness in philosophical anthropology. What was left was still the idea of the will as an elective faculty, man's *proairetic* power in Aristotle's terms, but this power was easily absorbed into the purely intellective functions of comparison and judgment. And for the rest, namely, the need to account for the active or conative side of human nature, the passions or affections of the sensitive appetite were sufficient. Thus, Thomas Hobbes's well-known definition of the will as simply the "last appetite in deliberating" in effect denied the existence of any such thing as a uniquely rational appetite.

It is clear both from the long-enduring status of will as one of man's specific rational faculties and from its comparatively rapid downfall in the seventeenth

9. The notebook of William Partridge, from 1686, a manuscript in the Beinecke Lib. at Yale Univ., contains a section entitled, *"Gulielmi Amesii Theses Physiologica,"* from which this quotation is taken. See n. 13 below.

10. Thus, Bishop Edward Reynolds in his *Treatise of the Passions* stated that understanding and will together may be called by the one name of "Reason." See Reynolds, *Works*, 633. Reynold's treatise was widely dispersed in New England. See, e.g., Evan A. Evans, Jr., "Literary References in New England Diaries, 1700–1730" (Ph.D. diss., Harvard University, 1934), 149, and Ford, *Boston Book Market*, 74.

and eighteenth centuries as a viable concept, that the idea of the will was almost as much a cosmic as a psychological unit. Its history reflects the most profound changes in outlook about man's place in the universe.

Intellectualism

Enough has been said now in prelude to enable us to consider in greater detail the controversy at Harvard over the relation of will to intellect. We can begin with the more established view by quoting from a notebook kept in 1686 by a Harvard student named William Partridge, who was most likely a sophomore at the time of writing. Partridge's notes were extracted, probably indirectly, from the Aristotelian natural philosophy text of Henricus Gutberleth (d. 1635), a teacher at Herborn in Germany.[11] Partridge opened with a definition in Latin, which may be translated as follows: Will is a human disposition [or quality] by which man freely desires the good known by the intellect.[12] Then follows a scholium in English:

> Even as the understanding is occupied in the knowledge of good and bad; so the will is busied in desiring of that [which] is good, but known by the understanding, whence the rational appetite is called, [whereby] it is differenced from the sensitive appetite, [which] proceeds not from the understanding, but from the sense. For the understanding shows to the will, [what] is to be embraced and [what] to be rejected: then the will desireth and governeth [those] inferiour faculties, to wit, the sensitive and locomotive appetite. Moreover the good [which] the will desireth is either good really or apparently, for as the understanding judgeth, so the will desireth: Sometimes it judgeth that good [which] is evil . . . ; so the will [in that case] desireth [what] is part of man's misery. here the rule is: the error of the will follows the error of the judgment. Oftentimes likewise the vehemency of the appetites antici-

11. There was nothing unusual about using textbooks 70 years old, as we have already seen, nor was there anything anomalous in finding a discussion of the will treated under natural philosophy, which undertook to study man insofar as he was part of the natural world. For the 17th century, when the ordering of the disciplines was quite different from what it is at present, opinion on the will must be gathered from diverse sources, including works on theology, on moral philosophy, and on natural philosophy. According to William Ames, the will should be the last subject studied in natural philosophy, or physics, and the first studied in theology.

Partridge headed this section of his notebook: "*Henrici Gutberleth philosophia naturalis Liber primus, qui est de corpore naturali, in genere.*" This probably refers to Gutberleth's *Physicae, hoc est, naturalis philosophiae* (Herborn, 1613, 1623). "Guthberleth's Physick" was ordered by a Boston bookseller in 1683/1684. See Ford, *Boston Book Market*, 127.

12. "*Voluntas est hominis affectio quâ quod homo intellectu cognovit bonum, liberè appetit.*"

pates and obscures the judgment of the understanding, . . . so that a
man runs to evil with violence. . . . To the will is opposed the aversation
of evil known by the understanding, [which] for the sake of teaching
we may call nilling. from volition and nolition ariseth an intellectual
affection [i.e., a disposition] whereby a man is moved and excited to
follow after that [which] is good, and to avoid that [which] is evil,
[as these are] known to be such by the understanding.[13]

This, as I have said, was the common and more established view of the
relation of will to intellect. The understanding shows to the will what is to be
embraced or rejected. As the understanding judges, so the will desires. The
will is itself never culpable in the case of moral error, since it follows the
judgment of the intellect. But because of the misjudgment of the intellect it
may unwittingly choose the apparent rather than the real good. The will as
the rational appetite ought to govern the lower sensitive appetites, though it
may happen that unruly vehement sensitive appetites, or passions, will carry
one forward independently of intellect and will, anticipating and obscuring
rational judgment. It should be noticed, too, that the standard concept of the
technical opposite to willing and volition, namely nilling and nolition, indicates the degree to which many of the psychologists of the time were quite
free of a reification of the will and were thinking of functions and powers
more than of psychic entities.

This example from Partridge is neither complete nor especially precise, but
it does give us a rough picture of what is broadly termed the *intellectualist*
position.[14] It was the most common opinion in the seventeenth century and
the centuries preceding. It had the support of Thomas Aquinas and figures like
Cardinal Cajetan (d. 1534), who did a major commentary on Thomas, and
Robert Bellarmine (d. 1621), the great seventeenth-century Catholic polemi-
cist, all of whom were highly respected by and influential upon Protestant as

13. Partridge graduated in the class of 1689 at Harvard and died four years later. See Sibley,
Harvard Graduates, III, 416–417. Partridge's notebook, partly in Latin and partly in English, is
exceptionally legible and contains excerpts from three logic systems: Charles Morton's, George
Downame's Ramist logic, and the LeGrand-Brattle logic. It is of some interest that this notebook
came into the hands first of Timothy Edwards, who succeeded Partridge at Harvard by a couple of
years, and then of his famous son, Jonathan Edwards, whose autograph is in the book in several
places with the dates 1718, 1719, and 1720, along with a few pages of unreadable notes. It may
also have been owned by Jonathan Edwards, Jr., in 1751.

14. The term "intellectualism" may also be used to denote a theory of the relation of intellect
to the passions and affections, which is a closely related but not identical concept. A great deal of
clarity is added to discussions of 17th- and 18th-century psychology when the casual use of the
term "rationalism" is sharply curtailed and kept for specific purposes in metaphysical and
epistemological theory. As a psychological term "rationalism" has little use beyond that which is
already better served by the term "intellectualism."

well as Catholic scholars.[15] Among the Protestant theologians themselves, a number of influential figures such as Theodore Beza, Girolamo Zanchius, Johann Piscator, and Johann Gerhard were also intellectualists.[16] A particularly important representative of a subtle type of intellectualism in the seventeenth century was the Scots theologian John Cameron (d. 1625), who taught mostly in France.[17] Of the four Aristotelian moral philosophy texts reviewed in the previous chapter, only that of Eustache de Saint-Paul was directly opposed to the intellectualist structure. Both Franco Burgersdyck and Adrian Heereboord stated unconditionally that there can be no willing without a prior judgment of the intellect.[18] In another student notebook from the seventeenth century, this point was made effectively with a quote from the English bishop Robert Sanderson (d. 1663): "All voluntary actions are done with some deliberation, more or less; because it is the nature of the will to Consist with the Understanding in Every act, else it would be Irrational and bruitish."[19] With-

15. On Cajetan and Bellarmine, see Davitt, *Nature of Law, passim*. An eloquent defense of intellectualism, defined more broadly than usual, is Father Pierre Rousselot's *The Intellectualism of Saint Thomas*, trans. James E. O'Mahony (London, 1935). Rousselot makes intellectualism into a metaphysical doctrine, however, which might better be termed "rationalism." He defines intellectualism as "the doctrine which places the supreme value and intensity of life in an act of intellect, that sees in this act the radical and essential good, and regards all things else as good only insofar as they participate in it" (p. 3). There has been considerable controversy about the degree and nature of Thomas's intellectualism. A good example of his position is in *The Summa Contra Gentiles*, trans. English Dominican Fathers (London, 1923–[1929]), Bk. III, chap. xxvi.

16. Nethenus, Visscher, and Reuter, *William Ames*, ed. and trans. Horton, 183, 202, n. 155. This work is a compilation by Horton of three widely dispersed works about Ames. Reuter is dealing in these sections with the intellectualist conception of faith that Ames opposed, not the psychological issue in particular. He also mentions Maccovius, Ames's colleague at Franeker, and Keckermann. The psychological issue is treated directly on p. 258. See also, Robert P. Scharlemann, *Thomas Aquinas and John Gerhard* (New Haven, Conn., 1964), 161. In Brian G. Armstrong, *Calvinism and the Amyraut Heresy: Protestant Scholasticism and Humanism in Seventeenth-Century France* (Madison, Wis., 1969), there is some useful information on the intellectualism of the controversial French theologian at Saumur Academy, Moise Amyraut (d. 1664).

17. Cameron's ideas are presented in a somewhat biased context in Armstrong, *Calvinism and the Amyraut Heresy*, 42–70. Armstrong also provides a bibliography.

18. See Burgersdyck, *Idea Philosophiae Naturalis*, 100, and Heereboord, *Meletemata*, 692, 712.

19. John Hancock, "Commonplace Book," 1687 to 1751?, Houghton Lib., Harvard Univ. The quote is from an edition of Sanderson's sermons. In an anonymous tract spawned by the Puritan revolution, *The Ancient Bounds, or Liberty of Conscience* . . . , the intellectualist thesis on the relation of will to intellect is used to defend liberty of conscience: "Now this liberty of trying and judging [religious doctrines] is in vain if there be not a liberty of profession; and to hinder this were a most tyrannical usurpation over that connection which God hath made between the act of the understanding and the will, whereby *voluntas sequitur dictamen intellectus* [the will follows the dictate of the intellect], and to put asunder what God hath joined together, and indeed to violate the law of God and nature. A man cannot will contrary to the precedent act of judg-

out its counterpart in intellect the will becomes simply a brute desire and is indistinguishable from sensitive appetite.

The commencement *theses* and *quaestiones* from early Harvard summarized the intellectualist theory in the form of a Latin axiom that was constantly repeated: *"Voluntas determinatur ab ultimo Intellectus practici Judicio"* (The will is determined by the last judgment of the practical intellect). These words appear in some form in 1666, 1671, 1678, 1686, and 1692, and we have only a remnant of what may have existed. The great virtue of this theory was that it grounded human conduct in reason, that is, it demanded at once that (1) all moral decision and action be accountable in terms of intelligible ends or reasons, and that (2) reason be, to use the Stoic term, the *hegemonikon* or the ruler of the soul.[20] The latter proposition followed from the former. If reason alone was capable of participating in the divine mind and of discovering moral norms—whether these norms were considered to be the proper mean between the extremes, as in Aristotle, or some other standard of intelligible good—then this unique capability of reason, knowing the universal good, entitled it to rule in the soul. And it was perhaps also such thinking that led to the firm conviction that in fact reason did always rule in some fashion, even in the case of error or wickedness, when it mistakenly chose the lesser or partial good.

Intellectualism was particularly representative of Classical philosophy, and it has been suggested that an opposing point of view did not develop until the patristic era. The only states of mind that Plato and Aristotle recognized "as immediate antecedents of bad acts," wrote the philosopher Henry Sidgwick, "are (1) predominance of irrational impulse overpowering rational judgment or prompting to action without deliberation, and (2) mistaken choice of evil under the appearance of good." Sidgwick also noted that this intellectualism involved the Classical moralists in a rather uncomfortable and unwelcome determinism, for it established that all action was " 'necessitated'—as Plato expressly says—by causes antecedent in time to the bad volition." But, as we have already observed, it was universal opinion that moral responsibility entailed some kind of freedom; so there arose the possibility of a troublesome inconsistency.[21]

---

ment; he wills weakly without an act of judgment preceding. To force a man to a profession or practice which he wills not, nay which he nills, is to offer unto God a sacrifice of violence on the part of the compulsor, and an unreasonable service on the part of the compelled, and therefore necessarily unacceptable." Reprinted in Woodhouse, ed., *Puritanism and Liberty*, 259.

20. On the Stoic term *"hegemonikon,"* see Bourke, *History of Ethics*, 35–37.

21. Henry Sidgwick, *Outlines of the History of Ethics for English Readers*, 6th ed. enlarged (London, 1931 [orig. publ. 1886]), 69, and 114–117, for further elaboration. Aristotle has been most closely studied in this regard by James Jerome Walsh, *Aristotle's Conception of Moral Weakness* (New York, 1963). Walsh warns against "easy generalizations about 'Greek intellectu-

Whatever the case may have been with the ancients (and the exact nature of Aristotle's intellectualism in particular), by the thirteenth century A.D., shortly after the recovery of the bulk of the Aristotelian texts, intellectualist moral teaching was already causing some disturbance within the Church. In the famous condemnation of 219 propositions by the bishop of Paris in 1277, which counted certain of the teachings of Thomas Aquinas among its objects for censure, the doctrine that "the will necessarily pursues what is firmly held by reason, and that it cannot abstain from that which reason dictates," was expressly cited for heterodoxy.[22]

Scholastic and Augustinian Voluntarism

The condemnation of 1277 was one of the stimuli behind the development in the thought of John Duns Scotus and others of an important rival theory of action, which attributed to the will a self-determining power. The best-known example of the reasoning of this school is the famous case of "Buridan's Ass": when placed equidistant from two equally desirable bales of hay between which there was no intellectual foundation for choice, the animal remained forever paralyzed with indecision. In such an instance, the Scotists argued, only an arbitrary will can take the initiative. An ass, lacking the faculty of will, could not solve this problem, they said, but a human will could. Here one finds the origins of a concept of free will that implies not only the freedom of the agent from constraint or impediment in action but also a total freedom from determinism or necessity.[23] The significance for our purposes of this school of thought, which might be designated Scholastic voluntarism, lies in its vigorous rejuvenation in sixteenth- and seventeenth-century Jesuit theology and its entrance into the philosophical melee between Protestants and Catholics over the nature of the will. About Scholastic voluntarism in the seventeenth century and its influence on the philosophy of mind in America we will have more to say shortly.

There was still another alternative to Aristotelian and Thomist intellectualism, one with roots and results that were quite different from Scholastic

---

alism'" but interprets Aristotle as an intellectualist nonetheless, as did Sidgwick. Cf. also Rudolph Bultmann, *Primitive Christianity in Its Contemporary Setting*, trans. R. H. Fuller (London and New York, 1956 [orig. publ. Zurich, 1949]), 181: "Of course, the Greeks and the New Testament are equally aware that man's will can lead him into disaster. But in the Greek view this is due to the failure of reason to control the will. All that is necessary is to train the reason, and then the will should automatically obey it."

22. Ralph Lerner and Muhsin Mahdi, eds., *Medieval Political Philosophy: A Sourcebook* ([New York], 1963), 350.

23. See Bourke, *Will in Western Thought*, 21, 85.

voluntarism. This school of thought did not grow out of opposition to determinism; on the contrary, it was closely associated with it. We have mentioned that it is sometimes asserted that the development of an alternative to intellectualist moral psychology had to wait until the patristic period. The original inspiration for its appearance at that time, it is said, may be found in the striking lament of St. Paul in Romans 7:14–28:

> What I do is not what I want to do, but what I detest. But if what I do is against my will, it means that I agree with the law and hold it to be admirable. . . . the will to do good is there, the deed is not. The good which I want to do, I fail to do; but what I do is the wrong which is against my will; and if what I do is against my will, clearly it is no longer I who am the agent, but sin that has its lodging in me.
>
> I discover this principle, then: that when I want to do the right, only the wrong is within my reach. In my inmost self I delight in the law of God, but perceive that there is in my bodily members a different law, fighting against the law that my reason approves and making me a prisoner under the law that is in my members, the law of sin. Miserable creature that I am, who is there to rescue me out of this body doomed to death?[24]

Certainly by the time of St. Augustine a psychology of the will was present that was of a quite different character from the prevailing ancient pagan view, which is a matter we will come to shortly. But it is curious that in the seventeenth century, when the intellectualist model was challenged, it was usually neither in the name of Paul nor of Augustine. Strangely, it was rather the Latin poet Ovid whose words were constantly recalled. In the *Metamorphoses* (VII. 20) the author has the dramatic heroine Medea proclaim: *Video meliora proboque; Deteriora sequor* (I see and approve the better course; I follow the worse). Ovid was here only imitating Medea's anguished cry in Euripides' great tragedy, but it was Ovid's lines that were quoted in literally hundreds of ethics and physics treatises in order to illustrate a main difficulty with the intellectualist schema.[25] It seems probable that the challenge to intellectualism did have essentially Judaeo-Christian roots and that the use of Ovid or

24. Quoted from the *New English Bible*. See Alexander, *Theories of Will*, 84: "For the first time in the history of thought, Paul presents from a subjective point of view the conflict of a man between two moral alternatives."

25. A curious example is Benjamin Franklin's "Silence Dogood" Letter, no. 14, printed in the *New-England Courant* (Boston), Oct. 8, 1722, where Franklin quotes from *The Spectator*, no. 185, a long section that contains a reference to "that trite Passage which we see quoted in almost every System of Ethicks, . . . *Video meliore proboque/Deteriora sequor*." Leonard W. Labaree and Whitfield J. Bell, Jr., eds., *The Papers of Benjamin Franklin* (New Haven, Conn., 1959–), I, 44.

Euripides was primarily a matter of convention and convenience, a point that perhaps will become evident further on. On the other hand, E. R. Dodds in his important study, *The Greeks and the Irrational*, has brought out that the internal conflict of Euripides' Medea was already a subject of controversy among the ancient Stoics and that Euripides was almost certainly engaged in a conscious effort to refute the Socratic theory that virtuous behavior is identical with right knowledge.[26] The gist of what may be called the Medean paradox (or of St. Paul's similar dilemma) is, of course, that much experience seems to testify to a human capacity for deliberate, conscious choice made contrary to the continuously known higher good; or, stated differently, much experience testifies to the existence of an independent and sometimes perverse will.

The Medean paradox raised some difficulties for the intellectualists, but they were hardly helpless when confronted with this example, as can be seen in the analysis of Medea's case offered by Franco Burgersdyck and Adrian Heereboord. Both of these men based their reply to the voluntarist interpretation of the paradox on the Scholastic distinction between velleity and volition. A velleity is an unfulfilled action of the will to an object seen in and of itself and corresponds to the absolute judgment of the practical intellect. A volition is a completed action of the will toward an object as it is seen in comparison with other objects; thus a volition follows upon the comparative or relative judgment of the practical intellect. But in both of these cases the action of the will is determined by a previous judgment of the practical intellect, for there can be no willing, according to Burgersdyck, without a judgment of the intellect. The battle in the soul expressed typically in the *"Video meliora,"* he said, does not take place between a rebellious will and the judgment of the intellect, as though the will had departed from the judgment of the intellect. Rather, it results from a conflict or "fluctuation in the intellect when the intellect disapproves of the thing absolutely considered but approves of it relatively or with its circumstances." The will is divided, but the foundation of the division is in the intellect. Sometimes the intellect's conflict was described as "woulding" to do the best, but "willing" to do less. Heereboord supported Burgersdyck's analysis with little variation, stressing that the conflict occurs in the reason alone, between the relative and the absolute judgment.[27] Similarly, a student notebook from the middle of the seventeenth century defined velleity as "an imperfect lazy act of the will," and contrasted it with "intention" rather than with volition. "Intention [*like volition*] is a most perfect, vigorous, and strong act of the will. by this a man dos not will this or that

26. (Berkeley and Los Angeles, Calif., 1951), 186–187, 239–240, particularly the footnotes.

27. Burgersdyck, *Idea Philosophiae Moralis*, 65, 141, 310, 313, and *Idea Philosophiae Naturalis*, 99–100. See also, Heereboord, *Meletemata*, 100, 108, 472–489, 692, 712.

good simply w[ith]out respecting anything, [whereby] it may be attained, as he does by velleity; but he wills its end to be attained by these means."[28] Velleity in this definition is related to judgments that are not only absolute, but also impracticable and abstract.

The most enduring and persistent antagonist to intellectualism in Western thought has been the Augustinian teaching concerning the will, the influence of which is seen in St. Anselm and St. Bernard before Scotus. This teaching was more powerfully at work in the Christian anthropology of the seventeenth century than at any other time before or since, affecting Catholic and Protestant circles equally. In this conception the will is not identifiable as a rational appetite at all, except possibly in some perfected state of humanity. Nor is the will easily confinable to a particular operation of the rational soul; instead it comes to be almost synonymous with the inner essence of the whole man, the battleground of God and the devil. The personal drama of salvation is enacted in the will, and on the will's ultimate orientation depends one's entire fate with God. The biblical term "heart" was used almost interchangeably with will in this sense, and the terms "love" and even "soul" itself were also substituted for it. Augustine called a "right will," "good love" and a "wrong will," "bad love" and insisted that man's salvation hangs alone on the quality of his will or love, or in other words, on the fundamental disposition of his heart.[29]

In this Augustinian tradition it is love misdirected, not intellectual misjudgment, that is considered the source of moral evil in man, and in most respects the distinction between will and affections is obliterated. The sin of concupiscence, which to some extent dominates all men, is expressed in a rebellious will, the primary failing of which is its independent rejection of the dictates of right reason and revelation. In his exchange of letters with Erasmus on the will, Luther employed an image taken directly from Augustine (and also used by Calvin) that dramatically characterized the will's paradoxical situation: "The human will is like a beast of burden. If God rides it, it wills and goes whence God wills. . . . If Satan rides it, it wills and goes where Satan wills. Nor may it choose to which rider it will run, nor which it will seek. But the riders themselves contend who shall have and hold it."[30] Obviously, Luther was not claiming that the will is free; but in relation to any other

28. Abraham Pierson, "Notes of Lectures Attended at Harvard College," MS, Beinecke Lib., Yale Univ.

29. Augustine, *City of God*, IV, *Books XII–XV*, trans. Philip Levine, Bk. XIV, sec. vii; Bk. XII, secs. i–iii, vi–ix. For a well-argued view, however, that the Augustine of the Jansenists and the Protestant pietists of the 17th century was not the real Augustine, see Nigel Abercrombie, *The Origins of Jansenism* (Oxford, 1936).

30. Erasmus [and] Luther, *Discourse on Free Will*, trans. and ed. Ernst F. Winter (New York, 1961), 112. Calvin, *Institutes*, II, iv, 1.

of man's psychological powers or faculties it is wholly autonomous. Its dependency is not on the dictates of intellect, but on God. In this conception the will not only rebels against reason's control, but it also does not by its nature necessarily select the apparent good. For there are perverse or demonic wills, too. In fact, without the assistance of divine grace, all wills tend that way.

As was the case with intellectualism, there were Harvard commencement *theses* and *quaestiones* throughout the seventeenth century that upheld the voluntarist position, usually quite simply by the negative assertion: "The will does not invariably follow the last dictate of the practical intellect" (Aug. 9, 1653, 1658, 1676, 1683, and 1691). From this proposition alone, however, it is impossible to tell whether the graduates supported Scholastic or the quite different Augustinian voluntarism. The related thesis presented in 1647, 1677, and 1682, "*Voluntas non potest cogi*" (The will cannot be coerced), is much more clearly aligned with the Jesuit school, and a thesis of 1691, "*Indifferentia est de essentia liberi arbitrii*" (Indifference is the essence of free choice), extraordinarily so. The so-called "liberty of indifference" was the battle cry of the followers of the Jesuit theologian Luis de Molina (1535–1600) in opposition to both the intellectualism of the broadly defined Thomist school and the divine determinism of the voluntarist Protestants. The several commencement propositions, always in the negative, concerning the *scientia media*, the intermediate knowledge by which God knows future contingent events, also reveal the notice taken at Harvard of Molinism. But it was one thing for a Protestant college to take notice of Jesuit theology for the purposes of refutation, and another for that college to defend it. Certainly more typical of Harvard than the 1691 affirmation of the liberty of indifference was the opposite opinion expressed in the negative response of Timothy Edwards to his master's *quaestio* in 1694, "*An indifferentia sit de Essentia liberi Arbitrii?*"

Augustinian or pietistic voluntarism was unmistakably evident at the commencement of 1658 when Gershom Bulkeley, who later became a renowned physician in Connecticut, took as his master's degree *quaestio* a slight variant of the famous proposition we have already mentioned: "*An Voluntas semper sequatur ultimum dictamen intellectus practici?*" (Whether the will invariably follows the last dictate of the practical intellect?) and answered in the negative. We do not have his full statement, but appended to his *quaestio* on the printed master's commencement broadside for that year is a Latin verse that runs as follows in literal translation:

> How many times does it happen that a prince will spurn the dictates of his council, and though he sees the better way, follow the worse? Who would say that the cause of the angel's fall was the dictate of the mind, since [that dictate] was conducive to our salvation? Or who will tell me the cause of Adam's fall? There was in him no error of the intellect.

There is no demon who was not a [demon] before; nor is there any error in the mind without sin. Therefore, it is the imperious will that drives one into vice, and when the mind offers good advice, the will says, "I don't like it; reason is against it." When will puts itself in reason's place, should you not rather call it nill? Therefore, the will does not invariably follow the dictates of the mind, but resembles Medea more than the deity.[31]

The implication of the last line is that only God possesses perfect integrity of intellect and will. Man's sinful nature is primarily a matter of perverse will, not intellectual error.

When the voluntarist theory first became prominent in Scholastic philosophy in the work of Duns Scotus in the fourteenth century, it is possible that part of the impetus for the introduction of this theory was an aversion to determinism of one kind or another. But we must be absolutely clear that the issue between voluntarists and intellectualists that we are considering here was not over whether or not man was morally free. The intellectualists were unanimous in holding that rationality implies freedom, that one becomes free, as has been said, "simply by taking thought" as to what one will do. Whatever the charges made against them, the intellectualists embraced the belief that to act under the influence of free deliberation is to act freely. In other words, intellectualism was in no sense a form of conscious determinism. The debate between the two groups pertained rather to psychological models, and indeed, we should add, ultimately to theological and political models, since ordinarily the conceptions of God and law adhered to by intellectualists and voluntarists corresponded to their psychology.[32] That is, these parties would also disagree on whether the basis of one's moral obligation was will's obedience to higher will or reason's obedience to higher reason. Is it the "right reason" in God's law or in the king's law that we must respond to or is it the authority of their greater wills? However, it is the psychological issue itself with which we are now concerned.

Before looking at a few lengthier voluntarist statements from early Harvard, we must devote at least a few words to some additional contemporary influences in seventeenth-century New England that bore on the issues. First of all, Harvard College, like almost every academic center in the West for a good part of the seventeenth century, was heavily indebted to the work of the

31. The 1658 *quaestiones* are in Morison, *Seventeenth-Century Harvard*, Appendix B. The Latin contains an intentional pun on the last syllable of "Medea" and the first syllable of "deity."

32. Complicated problems of interpretation arise here, however. See, for example, the excellent discussion of Occam and Biel in Heiko A. Oberman, *The Harvest of Medieval Theology: Gabriel Biel and Late Medieval Nominalism* (Cambridge, Mass., 1963), 63, 92–111. See also, Bourke, *Will in Western Thought*, 87.

Spanish Jesuit Francisco Suarez (d. 1619). The impact of Suarez's writing in his own time has only recently been adequately recognized. Paul Dibon has called him the undisputed master of the art of disputation in an era when nearly all philosophical instruction found expression in this form.[33] As it happened, Suarez was a proponent of the liberty of indifference. It is usually assumed that Descartes came to hold a similar view through the influence of Suarez on the schools.[34] Whether or not that is true, there is no mistaking Suarez's weight in New England. Most of the textbooks specifically mention him, and the *Ethica* of Eustache de Saint-Paul argued the radical voluntarist position in accordance with him. If you argued for liberty of indifference in the seventeenth century, you were probably directly or indirectly following Suarez; and if you argued against it, you were probably directly or indirectly arguing against Suarez.[35]

No doubt even more important than Suarez was William Ames, who himself borrowed freely from the Spanish metaphysician on certain points. Ames treated the question of the relation of will and intellect at length in *Conscience with the Power and Cases thereof*. According to Ames, as we have already seen, conscience is a complex human endowment. But its most significant characteristic in relation to the matter at hand is that it is not in any sense a separate faculty. It is rather a reflexive power of the intellect by which *synteresis* (or universal Natural Law) turns in upon the self and judges whether actions are licit or illicit. The dictates of conscience, according to Ames, sometimes precede and accompany our actions and sometimes follow them.

33. Dibon, *Philosophie néerlandaise*, 42. See José Ferrater Mora, "Suarez and Modern Philosophy," *Jour. Hist. Ideas*, XIV (1953), 528–547; William S. Morris, "The Young Jonathan Edwards: A Reconstruction" (Ph.D. diss., University of Chicago, 1955); Gerard Smith, ed., *Jesuit Thinkers of the Renaissance* . . . (Milwaukee, Wis., 1939); Mahieu, *François Suarez*. Suarez's *Disputationes metaphysicae* (1597) was in a number of early American libraries. Cotton Mather, for example, bought a duplicate of the *Disputationes metaphysicae* from the Harvard Library in 1682. See Brigham, "Harvard Library Duplicates," Col. Soc. Mass., *Trans.*, XVIII (1917), 407–417.

34. Bourke, *Will in Western Thought*, 87–88. The Council of Trent also upheld the liberty of indifference. D. P. Walker, *The Decline of Hell: Seventeenth-Century Discussions of Eternal Torment* (Chicago, 1964), 46, is one-sided when he comments: "The philosophical difficulties of this conception of free-will, the *libertas indifferentiae*, are so enormous that only rather naïf thinkers such as [William] King, or occasionally dishonest ones, such as Descartes, or thinkers that were both, such as [Jean] LeClerc, accepted it." Descartes's position is not easy to sort out. In the *Discourse on Method*, trans. Laurence J. Lafleur (Indianapolis, Ind., 1960 [orig. publ. New York, 1950]), Pt. III, 21, he wrote: "Since our will neither seeks nor avoids anything except as it is judged good or bad by our reason, good judgment is sufficient to guarantee good behavior." By the time he wrote his treatise on the passions in 1645 his theory of the will had become more complicated.

35. Suarez's position is thoroughly treated in Thomas Mullaney, *Suarez on Human Freedom* (Baltimore, 1950), and also more briefly in Davitt, *Law of Nature*.

The intellectual character of conscience raised what Ames himself called "a hard question." "How can a man do any thing against the dictate of Conscience which goeth before, or accompanieth his action?" For "it seems to many," Ames wrote, that the will "cannot will or nill any thing, unlesse *reason* have first *judged* it to be willed or nilled; neither can it *choose* but *follow* the *last practicall judgment*, and do that which *reason* doth dictate to be done: and by consequent, the *will* cannot move against the determination of *conscience*." But to this difficulty, Ames stated confidently, there are answers "so cleare that no man can question it." [36]

When Perry Miller in *The New England Mind: The Seventeenth Century* quoted this exact passage from Ames, he apparently inadvertently failed to notice Ames's opening phrase, "it seems to many," and then went on incorrectly to attribute to Ames himself the intellectualism in the passage! Miller compounded the error by remarking that Ames "wrote this doctrine deep into the New England tradition, and founded the whole ethical system upon it." [37] But the contrary is emphatically the case. Ames was one of the leading figures in opposition to the intellectualist theory. More important, Miller's reading has led historians to introduce an illogical severance of eighteenth-century evangelicalism from seventeenth-century Puritan thought. Many historians, following Miller on this one point, have come to believe the preposterous notion that Jonathan Edwards was the first writer to validate emotion in New England psychological theory and religious experience. [38]

---

36. Ames, *Conscience*, I, chap. 7.

37. *New England Mind*, I, 248. On p. 250 Miller also underestimated the importance of the problem of intellect and will in 17th-century New England, maintaining it was "largely academic." Yet strangely, a few pages further on, he correctly noted that "the deliberate errancy of the will, as against the informed reason," was an emphasis "greater among the Puritans than among many other Protestant communions," and he referred to Augustinian and Scotist influences, even quoting William Ames to this effect (pp. 260, 285). Miller's final thought seems to have been that the issue was one between the physicists, that is, natural philosophers, and the theologians, which may have been correct in the particular case of Ames's own indecision but was not generally true. Miller also fell into the crucial error of confusing the question of the independence of the will in relation to intellect with the problem of the freedom of the will in relation to divine decrees (p. 285).

38. For all its brilliance and artistry, Miller's *Jonathan Edwards* (New York, 1949), is extraordinarily careless in some of its assertions. In this case, see p. 159: "Gradually taking shape in this analysis [of Edwards's] was a radically new [!] definition of the religious man, not as right-thinking, but as 'influenced by some affection, either love or hatred, desire, hope, fear.' " This idea was seconded by Ralph Gabriel in "Evangelical Religion and Popular Romanticism in Early Nineteenth-Century America," in Abraham S. Eisenstadt, ed., *American History: Recent Interpretations*, I (New York, 1962), 434: "Jonathan Edwards in the eighteenth century . . . had introduced the idea of the importance of emotion into what had been a coldly logical intellectual structure. Emotion had made its way in the churches despite a somewhat stubborn conservatism of theologians. The significance of religious feeling ultimately found its greatest exponent in Horace Bushnell." Similarly, Loren Baritz, *City on a Hill: A History of Ideas and Myths in*

Ames stated his case in eight propositions, which I have rearranged and condensed. He is not consistent in his answers, for part of his argument was an attempt to preserve the concept of will as rational appetite despite its separateness from intellect, while in other places he implicitly rejected this notion altogether. In arguing the latter view, which is the one that mainly concerns us, Ames made the point that if the will necessarily follows the judgment of the understanding, "then there should (in proper speaking) be no sin of *malice*, distinct from those sins which are committed through ignorance, or passions. . . . But, it is manifest, that this kind of sin is found in Devils, and likewise in some men." An error of judgment need not precede an evil act. In short, there can be a bad will which rejects the lead of reason. Secondly, if the will necessarily follows the understanding, then in regeneration, the creation of the new man by divine grace, "the will it selfe need not be internally renewed" but the mere "inlightening of the Understanding would be sufficient," which is "repugnant to Faith and Godliness."[39] The implication, then, of intellectualist thinking is that a certain degree of education might suffice for salvation, or that a minister could just as well preach to the head as to the heart.

Finally, along these same lines, Ames advanced the significant idea that the will can "turne away the understanding" from the consideration of any object that it is apprehending and judges to be good at the moment, and turn it instead either toward the consideration of another object or to an earlier consideration and judgment of the same object. "By reason of this commanding power, the *Will* is the first cause of unadvisednesse, and blameworthy error in the understanding," for this action of the will by which it draws away the understanding from that which it has judged to be good, the will "doth by its owne inclination," without any prior judgment that it should do so. Ames's analysis, we may remark, is an especially clear instance of both the Scholastic

---

America (New York and London, 1964), 66: "Almost nothing in the history of New England could assist [Edwards] in trying to teach his people the vocabulary of emotion. The legalistic mentality of covenantal theorists had dominated the New England landscape" for too long. J. Rodney Fulcher, "Puritans and the Passions: The Faculty Psychology in American Puritanism," *Journal of the History of the Behavioral Sciences*, IX (1973), 123–139, also assumes that "a significant change in attitude toward the passions would be possible only with the shift to a new psychological theory by Jonathan Edwards," and that "the task of formulating a theory of the affections that was more in accord with religious experience would be left to the sensitive intellect of Jonathan Edwards . . . bold pioneer in the wilderness of religious psychology." The truth is, the antecedents of the psychological theory that supported the evangelical party in the Great Awakening are so numerous and so common that I am led to doubt that the revival can be given a causal explanation (insofar as this is ever possible) in terms of the history of ideas. One might as well cite the air that was breathed. On the passions, see chap. 4, below.

39. Ames, *Conscience*, I, 19.

and the Augustinian theory of the will combining to break through the Thomist Scholastic structure, a process that was going on generally in the seventeenth century.[40] Ames was inspired in the most fundamental way by the Augustinian tradition; at the same time he made use of the brilliant dialectics of the Jesuit Suarez in order to combat the intellectualists. It should be noted, too, that the activity of the will as described here is hardly to be differentiated from that of the passions or affections of the sensitive appetite in its power to sway the reason according to its inclination. Ultimately this theory of the will would merge with several other strands of thought more or less independent of it and give rise to the so-called sentimentalist school in eighteenth-century ethics.

Another series of arguments in Ames has more of the quality of patchwork and results in only a partial voluntarism. Here Ames relied upon the traditional Scholastic distinction between the "specification" and the "exercise" of an act. The specification of an act is roughly identical to the intellectual substance of it, or its description, and the exercise, to the choice of acting or not acting at all, regardless of the substance. In terms of freedom, the liberty of specification in action was a liberty of contrariety, or the liberty to do something different; the liberty of exercise was a liberty of contradiction, or the liberty simply not to do anything at all in a particular case. The seventeenth-century Thomists (leaving aside the question of how true they were to their mentor) adhered to a liberty in the will of exercise, but not of specification. The Suarezians, or the Molinists and the Jesuits in general, held that the will had liberty in both specification and exercise. This doctrine necessarily gave will a certain amount of cognitive as well as active power. Ames disagreed insofar as he held that the intellect must supply the object or the specification of an act, since the will is blind; but he was in accord with the voluntarists in asserting that "in regard of *exercise* or act of willing, [the will] moveth both it selfe, and the understanding with the rest of the faculties."[41] This same principle of liberty was expressed in the common voluntarist belief that the will had the power of suspending action. As Ames put it, "The *Will* can at pleasure *suspend* its act about that which is *apprehended* and *judged* to be good; without any *foregoing act of judgment* that it should do so; for if to *suspend* an act, and to leave off acting, an act of judgment be necessarily required; then to suspend that judgment, another judgment is requisite; and to suspend that, another, and so *in infinitum*."[42] In other words, every time we

40. This is one of the main themes in Anthony Levi's excellent study, *French Moralists*. Ames was describing what later came to be called the doctrine of attention. Descartes and a number of subsequent writers believed that the power to attend the mind to any particular object was an indication of freedom.

41. Ames, *Conscience*, I, 16.

42. *Ibid*.

stop or start to think, which is itself an action, or to act outwardly, a special judgment of the intellect is not necessary, and it would be absurd to assume that it is.

Ames's defense of this limited freedom in "exercise," or freedom to suspend, was a more moderate stand than his other points about the power of the will actually to undermine rational judgment, though he showed no awareness of the entirely different presuppositions upon which he was arguing. Neither did he seem aware that the Augustinian voluntarism that he also espoused vitiated all his other reasoning about the relation of will to intellect. However, even the sole ability to suspend action, we should note, is a considerable power for the will in ethical situations where timing may be of the essence.[43]

Ames's inconsistency in this area illustrates how much the radical suggestions he made in favor of a nonintellectual will were dictated not by philosophical conceptions but by Puritan religious sensibility. This sensibility insisted on a dichotomous struggle between good and evil in the soul, which swept the intellect along rather than being guided by it. The will was in a sense no more than a symbol for the interiority of this struggle, which encompassed the whole man and over which he had little intellectual control.

The detachment of the will from the intellect as argued by Suarez undoubtedly provided support for Ames. But the Protestant emphasis on the radical dependence of the will on God is not found in Suarez, who considered this idea a Lutheran heresy. The Jesuit theologian upheld the independent freedom of will even from divine coaction, arguing that the relation of God's will to human action is solely a matter of concurrence. The human will accedes to God's grace through its own disposition only and without constraint.[44]

It is significant with regard to how Ames was understood by his contemporaries that Adrian Heereboord, Burgersdyck's successor at Leiden, mentioned Ames along with Suarez as a proponent of voluntarism, a school of thought that both Heereboord and Burgersdyck firmly rejected. At his own University of Franeker in Holland, Ames also tangled on this issue with his colleague Johann Maccovius, who believed that "the will always and necessarily follows the judgment of thought." In Adam, according to Maccovius, sin first established itself in his understanding, and will followed. In redemptive regeneration the process is the same: "God's light enlightens the under-

43. It may be of incidental interest to note that Locke in his *Essay Concerning Human Understanding* considered the power to suspend action "the great privilege of finite intellectual beings" and the only freedom that man has that makes any sense (Bk. II, chap. xxi, 53). Locke did not doubt, on the other hand, that will follows the last judgment of our reason, a fact that he called, as had Burgersdyck 50 years earlier, a "perfection of our nature" rather than a fault (Bk. II, chap. xxi, 48–49).

44. See Mahieu, *François Suarez*, 506–507, 236–240, 453–468.

standing of man and through it first allows virtue to stream into the soul." But Ames believed that the will "is an immediate and original creation of God." Karl Reuter has astutely pointed out that Ames's voluntarism was directed against two distinct enemies: first, against "scholastic intellectualizing for the pleasure of it" among the majority of orthodox Reformed theologians; and second, against "moralizing in the Enlightenment vein on the part of the Remonstrants," or Arminians.[45] Augustinian voluntarism resisted the first by making the intellect relatively impotent to effect personal religious reform, and the second by making the *carnal* will impotent to cooperate with merely rationally conceived moral purposes. What was left, designedly, was only God and the devil. It has perhaps not been sufficiently appreciated in American historiography that Ames's program was revolutionary within Reformed Protestantism (and even within Puritanism itself), which in the course of the sixteenth and seventeenth centuries had become deeply Scholasticized and intellectualized.

If we are to see the true situation in the seventeenth century, we must recognize that the controversy within Protestantism had at least three sides (excluding Molinism, which very few, if any, Protestants could possibly accept, however much they may have borrowed useful arguments from Suarez). A preliminary sketch might look as follows. There was first of all a perfectly orthodox Protestant Scholasticism, characteristic of Theodore Beza and the majority of Reformed theologians after him, whose exponents preferred a moderate Thomist-type intellectualist framework in psychology. These men represented a cautious middle group that resisted hasty abandonment of the central learned tradition built on stable and tested Aristotelian foundations. Secondly, there was a "liberal" group with perhaps a remote tendency toward moralism and Pelagianism, for which intellectualism was an essential doctrine that suited their broadly rationalist outlook. They could be called "illuminationists" insofar as they stressed the importance of intellectual enlightenment as a precondition of both faith and good morals, but they stopped short of Pelagianism in that they denied that the natural man could merit salvation by

45. Nethenus, Visscher, and Reuter, *William Ames*, ed. and trans. Horton, 258*ff.* On Ames's reputation as an Augustinian voluntarist in relation to his contemporaries, see also, Ernst Bizer, "Reformed Orthodoxy and Cartesianism," trans. Chalmers MacCormick, *Journal for Theology and the Church*, II: *Translating Theology into the Modern Age* (New York, 1965), 20, 63, and Stoeffler, *Rise of Evangelical Pietism*, 144. For an illustration of the background to an intellectualism like that of Maccovius, see Oberman, *Harvest of Medieval Theology*, 164–165. Oberman finds that the predominant thinking in the Scholastic tradition, even among the nominalists, supported the maxim, "*Cognitio radix et fundamentum omnium virtutum*" (Reason or knowledge, not good will, is the root and foundation of all virtues), and the primary task of the Church was to "provide the Christian people with the proper information about God, which necessarily leads to moral improvement."

his own endeavors. John Cameron was one of the most influential of these men.[46] Finally, there were the Augustinians, or according to the designation of Ernst Bizer, "reformed pietists." This group found the intellectualist theory theologically unacceptable and were therefore opposed to the Protestant Scholastics on technical grounds but still could (and did) join with them to fight the liberalism, moralism, Cameronianism, Amyraldism, or Arminianism of the second group. The great danger to which the Augustinian voluntarists were themselves subject was above all a fideism that divorced the religious life from both reason and natural morality.[47] The Catholic counterpart of this third movement within Reformed Protestantism was Jansenism, and this, too, had its effect in New England through the ardent propagation of Jansen's *Augustinus* by the English dissenter Theophilus Gale. Gale's *Court of the Gentiles* (1669–1677) was in good part devoted to an admiring exposition of Jansen's thought (as well as to the *prisca theologia* mentioned in chapter 1).[48]

Reasoning such as Ames's, which contained some combination of Scholastic and Augustinian voluntarism, was common enough in Puritanism in the second half of the seventeenth century. A similar confused division may be found in Edward Reynolds's *Treatise of the Passions*, for example, a well-known work in psychology from the same period. And John Flavel's *Pneumatologia* (1685) displays another curious blend. Flavel, the author of the famous *Husbandry Spiritualized*, touched on several possibilities in the course of his exposition and seems to have become increasingly radical. The understanding "is the noble leading Faculty of the Soul" and serves to direct and guide us in life. Philosophers rightly call it the *hegemonikon* "because the Will follows its practical Dictates," but it does not rigorously enforce its

---

46. To call this group "Humanist" as opposed to Scholastic, as does Armstrong in his study of the Amyraldist controversy in France, does not seem sufficiently precise, but the suggestion is helpful. Evidence that the French debate aroused interest in America may be found in an address by Increase Mather to Harvard students near the end of the 17th century: "We find also in the word *Amyraldus, Arminius Redivivus* (Arminius restored to life): for the followers of Amyraut, sometimes called New Schoolmen and Methodists, profess little or nothing but what they have learned from the Arminians." (Quoted by Cotton Mather, *Magnalia*, II, 17.) The problem with the term "Humanism" is illustrated by the case of St. Francis de Sales, a pioneer Augustinian psychologist at the opposite pole from Cameron, who is often classified as part of a group called "devout Humanists."

47. See Levi, *French Moralists*, 324, concerning fideism.

48. On Gale, see chap. 6, below. Bourke, *Will in Western Thought*, fails to say a word about Jansenism. Gilson, *Liberté chez Descartes*, contains a good deal of material on the intellectual background of Jansen's ideas and especially emphasizes the anticipation of Jansen's theory of the will by the little-known figure Guillaume Gibieuf (d. 1650). Abercrombie, *Origins of Jansenism*, has valuable insights into 17th-century Augustinianism but overlooks Gibieuf completely and stresses the work of the Flemish Catholic theologian Michael Baius (d. 1589). A good sense of the Augustinian/intellectualist rift is given in the Zaharoff lecture by Antoine Adam, *Sur le problème religieux dans la première moitié du XVIIe siècle* (Oxford, 1959), and in Levi, *French Moralists*.

dictates "for the Will cannot be so imposed upon." The understanding gives the will only "a directive Light . . . pointing, as it were, with its Finger, at what it ought to chuse, and what to refuse." The will, too, is "a very high and noble Power of the Soul," to which the understanding bears the same relation "as a grave Counsellor doth to a great *Prince*." The will cannot be compelled and forced, "Coaction is repugnant to its very Nature."

All of this would seem to be in accordance with a Scholastic voluntarism. But Flavel revealed that the will has other limitations and other sources of guidance. The will can "open or shut the Hand or the Eye at its Pleasure, but not the Heart." For whatever the decrees of our subjective will, God's intercession must also be recognized. Thus, it is as though there are two wills in Flavel's analysis, one that usually follows the judgments of the intellect and another that can obey only the judgments of God. "The Will," Flavel wrote, "commands the Service of the Tongue, and chargeth it to deliver faithfully such or such Words." But "when it comes to do its Office, the Tongue faulters, and contrary to the Command of the Will, drops some Word that discovers and defeats the Design of the Will." A different power has interceded. The will has not the same command over the inner as it has over the outer man. "It can oftimes perswade the Understanding and Thoughts to lay by this or that Subject and apply themselves to the Study of another" (as Ames had also believed), but when a man's evils are set before his eyes through God's work on the soul prior to conversion, "fain would the carnal Will disengage the Thoughts from such sad Objects . . . but all to no purpose." In the throes of conscientious conviction, the will is helpless to distract the mind. And when Satan is tempting the regenerate man with "hellish Suggestions," though the "sanctified Will opposes itself to them," it has no more success than the carnal will. For the sanctified will no more than the carnal can control the "Thoughts of the Heart." But for all this, the will "is a noble Faculty, and hath a vastly extended Empire in the Soul of Man: It is the Door of the Soul, at which the spirit of God knocks for Entrance; when this is won, the Soul is won to Christ; and if this stand out in Rebellion against him, he is barr'd out of the Soul, and can have no saving Union with it."[49]

We are now better prepared to examine closely the voluntarist treatment of the will in several student notebooks from early Harvard. "An explication

---

49. Flavel, *Πνευματολογια. A Treatise of the Soul of Man* . . . (London, 1685), reprinted in Flavel, *Whole Works*, I, 283–284. Flavel's confusion is apparent when he discusses conscience, which he calls the "Chief *Counselor, Guide* and *Director* in all. . . . Bodily Members are but Instruments, and the Will itself as high and noble a Faculty, or Power as it is, moveth not, until the Judgment cometh to a Conclusion, and the Debate ended in the Mind" (p. 346). It was precisely over the relation of conscience to will that Ames found it necessary to break with the intellectualists. Yet Flavel expressly follows Ames on other matters relating to conscience.

of certain rules in Logick," copied by John Stone in 1653, the year of his graduation, is thoroughly Amesian in thinking. Stone began his report on the will with the comment that "the will is the last thing handled in physicke and the first in theologie, whereof it is the subject; and whose scope it is . . . to close with the chiefe good." Then there is an analysis of "cause by councell," which establishes the freedom of rational creatures. The portion relevant to the relation of will and intellect is as follows:

> After a man understands a thing fully, he chuses or refuseth; the understanding finds out things and presents to the will (which setts as queen) to know her majesties pleasure; some question whether the will or the understanding be the superior faculty, but the will is the supreame, for it hath the casting and determining vote, all the rest are for this, the outward senses are for the inward, and the inward for the understanding (according to that rule nihil est in intellectu quod non prius fuit in sensu), and the understanding is for the will, as an antecedent of her actions, and as a pilote to guid and direct her . . . and [as an] attendant to beare the candle and lanthorne before her: and both understanding and will for god; the will is above the powere of any seconde cause, it cannot be compelled by any; men may force the hand to work and the feet to walk, and the tongue to confesse, but they cannot the will to act because the proper act of the will is to elect; it is a contradiction to say it may be compelled to elect. . . . the will hath the power and dominion over its own actions: voluntas prout uti voluntati. A man can will to will and chuse to chuse, and this liberty is as inseparable from the will as light from the sun.[50]

In this analysis the will is the supreme faculty of the soul because it is within the will that the decisive movement takes place that determines man's final relation to God. As Ames had said, "The will is the true subject of theology since it is the true beginning of life and of moral and spiritual action." And further, because the will cannot be compelled, even by force of logic as is the case with the intellect, it is the center of that free choice by which man determines his eternal condition.[51] The will is the apex of the soul; or better, the free act of willing is the climactic movement of the soul, since the dispute

50. Abraham Pierson, "Notes of Lectures Attended at Harvard College," MS.

51. Ames, *Marrow of Theology*, I, iii, 2–6, II, ii, 4–8. See also, Thomas Hooker, "A True Sight of Sin," reprinted in Miller and Johnson, eds., *The Puritans*, 293–294: "The will of man [is] the chiefest" of all God's workmanship. The body is for the soul, "the mind to attend upon the will, the will to attend upon God, and to make choyce of him, and his wil." The Law is "the rule" of God's "Holy and righteous will, by which the will of *Adam* should have been ruled. . . . By sin we justle the law out of its place," and say we will be ruled "by mine own wil and led by mine own deluded reason."

with the intellectualists here was not simply over the power of rival faculties but also over which faculty best represents what is in the end the quintessential element in both faith and virtue. On this level it is too narrow a category to speak of Puritan or even Protestant moral concerns, for what we see in Ames is simply a wing of the Augustinian tradition. As Eugene Rice has shown, the Italian Renaissance figures Petrarch and Salutati expressed a similar conviction that "the will is nobler than the intellect and that love, which is the act of the will, is nobler and more perfect than contemplation or vision, the act of the intellect." And Rice comments, "This emphasis on will and love is a traditional characteristic of those medieval thinkers who kept their Augustinian fervor undampened by Aristotle's intellectualism. For Anselm, Bernard, the twelfth-century Victorines, Bonaventura, and Scotus it was a position which, they felt, guaranteed the possibility of enthusiasm and kept high the temperature of piety."[52]

Perhaps the most extreme voluntarist statement in a student notebook from seventeenth-century Harvard is found in the commonplace book of John Leverett, who was to become Harvard's most distinguished president in the colonial period. The entry dates from about 1680, twenty-five years later than Stone's notes.[53] "Some make Intellectus to be nobilior voluntate," Leverett began, but this may be proved false for the following reasons:

1. Because the rule of the understanding is Logick, but the rule of the will is divinity: Divinity is more excellent being last art of all, and to which all the rest are subordinate. 2. the subject of the will is bonum, and of the understanding verum; so much is the will better than the understanding; yea the prop[er] object of the will is god himself, because he is summum bonum, but he is not the subject of understanding, for our reas[on] cannot comprehend him. 3. The will is the end of every act ab extra or of things unto us; and the beginning of every act ab Intra, or proceeding from our selves. Every thing is received from the outward sense, from then convey'd to the inward, and thence to the understanding, then to the affections, and last of all to the will, which embraceth it or refuseth it, and the act of the will is the end of all the former acts. 4. W[he]n I do any thing intra, the will is the beginning of the act, and shee like a Queen first com[m]ands, I will have this or that done; then Reas[on] thinkes of means to this end, and those being found, the power doth put the thing in practice; and hence is drawn a similitude to express the mistery of the Trinity; that the father should be compared

---

52. Rice, *Renaissance Idea of Wisdom*, 36–43. Or in the 17th century, see Pascal's *Pensées*, trans. W. F. Trotter, Everyman's Library (London and New York, 1932 [orig. publ. Paris, 1670]), sec. 580: "God prefers rather to incline the will than the intellect."
53. Leverett's manuscript commonplace book is in the Mass. Hist. Soc.

to the will, for that he is the beginning of the action; the Son Reas[on], for to him is given the dispensation of things, and here is the wisdom of his father; the HG to the power of executeing [things] for he is the p[er]fecter of every Act, and is called the power of the most high.

To this analysis of the supremacy of the will Leverett added what at first appears to be a twist. "Some think that Voluntas non cogitur [will cannot be forced] but 'tis not always true. men wrong themselves often times, and sin compelleth the will. It is not I, but Sin in me, [sayeth] Paul." But this concluding remark simply verifies what we have already stressed as characteristic of pietistic voluntarism. The will is not uncoerced with respect to the power of God and Satan; it is free only with respect to the other faculties of the soul.

The most intriguing proceeding in Leverett's student notes—which were probably gathered in preparation for a disputation—is his placing of the will absolutely first in what he calls acts *ab intra*, commanding the reason like a queen to think of means to the end it desires. Here is the will in control of both specification and exercise, with the reason reduced to an ancillary function, or we might say, a pragmatic function. It is not a very great leap from this kind of voluntarism to David Hume's famous dictum, and Francis Hutcheson's earlier, that reason is and only ought to be the slave of the passions. Yet such ideas were not uncommon in seventeenth-century Puritanism. Thomas Hooker, earlier in the century, had maintained that "reason and understanding are the underlings as it were of inferior and lower ranck, and can but as servants and attendants offer and propound to the will and affections."[54]

Leverett's surviving papers fortunately also include two formal statements in Latin regarding the will. The first, on the topic "Indifference is not the essence of freedom," is dated October 3, 1680, and thus was written only a couple of months after he received his bachelor's degree, perhaps for an academic exercise.[55] The second, in the form of a *quaestio*, is dated July 20, 1683, and headed: "Whether the will follows the last judgment of the intellect?" Leverett responded to this in the negative.[56] The notes in English from his commonplace book that I have already quoted may have been composed sometime between these two Latin statements, which appear toward the end of the same commonplace book. In the first exercise the central argument is

54. Hooker, *The Application of Redemption* . . . (London, 1657), Bks. IX–X, 279, quoted in Fulcher, "Puritans and the Passions," *Jour. Hist. Behav. Sci.*, IX (1973), 135.

55. The dates of Harvard commencements are reported in Albert Matthews, "Harvard Commencement Days, 1642–1916," Col. Soc. Mass., *Trans.*, XVIII (1917), 309–384.

56. According to the manuscript, President John Rogers moderated at the occasion: "*Moderante D. Praeside J. R. discussa fuit haec Quaestio.*" Rogers was not inaugurated as president until Aug. 14, but he had been in Cambridge since May. See Matthews, "Harvard Commencement Days," Col. Soc. Mass., *Trans.*, XVIII (1917), 371. This *quaestio* was not the one Leverett chose for his M.A. ceremony that same summer.

that liberty and necessity are not entirely incompatible, and therefore one does not have to speak of indifference in order to have liberty. Like Calvin, Leverett held that there is a kind of *"voluntaria necessitas,"* a voluntary necessity, which is consistent with freedom. Through divine concursus "everything, but especially morals, is brought about by . . . necessity and harmony, but a necessary harmony or a harmonious necessity." When divine concursus necessitates the will it does so with "the greatest harmony, complete fitness, and supreme sweetness."

The compatibility of the will with both freedom of a sort and harmony is apparent from the following facts, Leverett maintained. The will adheres to the highest good when grasped as such, and this is most necessary. But still it is free "because it is the most perfect human act" (*quoniam perfectissimus est actus humanus*). Secondly, the saints and glorified angels are necessarily determined to the one good, but they are free in the choice of it. "Suarez most acutely agreed that the obedience of the saints and glorified angels is necessary though free." Thirdly, Christ's obedience was most free, "otherwise it would not be meritorious," but still his obedience was most necessary. Finally, God himself, the freest of agents, is "most necessarily determined in his acts. For all his acts, with respect to their origin and principle, are identical with his essence, and so external and unchangeable." It is undeniable, Leverett continued, that extrinsic compulsion is inconsistent with liberty. But intrinsic, spontaneous liberty "such as arises from the effective influence of the first cause and last end, God, is connatural with both the essence and existence of freedom." And from this it follows that indifference is not in any way connatural with, let alone essential to, freedom.

Leverett devoted the last section of his argument to a rather complicated analysis of indifference, including the distinction not only between specification and exercise, but also between passive and objective indifference, active and subjective indifference, absolute and conditioned indifference, and actual and habitual indifference, all of which it would not be profitable to explore in detail here. Leverett's aim in this document was to refute the Molinist theory of grace rather than to answer the intellectualists. The liberty of suspension might be admitted when it was a question of the rule of intellect versus the rule of will, that is, purely a natural psychological matter. It might be used, as in the case of Ames, to demonstrate the independence of willing from intellectual domination. But no orthodox Reformed Protestant could attribute to the will the liberty of receiving or rejecting God's mercy. It is in this context that we are able to understand Leverett's remark, toward the end of this piece, on the liberty of suspension: "Indifference to acting or not acting is not essential to freedom. For the Will cannot suspend its act of adherence to the final end when grasped as such. . . . The beatific vision allows of no suspension of acts to the extent that they are love of God and happiness in him." This disputation, then, expressing an opinion on the perfect compatibility of necessity and liberty (when properly understood), in terms precisely like those in Calvin's *Institutes*, was directed to the free will debate and in that area was opposed to Scholastic voluntarism.

But in July 1683, in response to another *quaestio*, Leverett delivered an unambiguous voluntarist statement. This document is highly illustrative of the nature of the controversy as it existed in seventeenth-century America and deserves close attention. Leverett opened his discussion with the comment that the dispute among philosopher-theologians (*"Philosophico-Theologos"*), both in the past and recently, on the question of whether the will is determined by the last judgment of the intellect is a "serious" and "not unmerited controversy." He then outlined the historic positions. Both sides in the issue have "legions" of followers as well as "aristocrats in the republic of letters" doing battle. Among them, Leverett noted, "are the defenders of the absolute power and dignity of the will as queen of the microcosm. These deny that will in any way follows the last dictate of the intellect—not even in its specification, let alone in its exercise." The opposition, on the other hand, "fearing . . . that this mistress . . . might assume despotic control for herself, so limit her power . . . that they maintain that the will does not act except at the bidding of the last dictate of the intellect. So much so, that according to them, the will is determined by the last judgment of the practical intellect not only in specification but even in exercise." Accordingly,

> lest the truth suffer in such a sharp clash of many men equally learned, some of the scholastics desirous of making peace, endowed the will with a kind of mixed monarchy. According to them, the will's inferiors in power neither despise nor hate her, but she, like a queen beloved of faithful subjects, holds her scepter among them. Yet because there is safety in an abundance of advice, the intellect is called into council. It is the first of the will's privy advisors; she does not often act without the intellect's advice. But she is not so bound by its last dictate that she cannot suspend her actions and even sometimes originate actions contrary to its last decree.

Leverett's stance amidst these possibilities was as follows. He did not deny the will's dependence upon the intellect for its specification, even in the will's freest actions. For the will cannot will without an object proposed by the intellect. "In this sense philosophers say the will is not carried into the unknown, and the poet says, *Ignoti nulla Cupido* [there can be no desire for something unknown]."[57] But, Leverett added, *dependence* is not the same as

---

57. This famous phrase, also from Ovid, was often cited in the context of the closely related controversy, which cannot be explored here, over whether love or knowledge must precede in

determination by the last dictate of the intellect. For acts of the will have no need of a practical judgment; "simple apprehension of the object [*apprehensio objecti simplex*] is enough." There are, in effect, indeliberate acts of the will, which is clear in the case of infants and the insane. The apprehended good, whatever it may be, possesses all the conditions required to be an object of the will without the mediation of judgment. The rational appetite, no less than the sensitive appetite, is aroused through the simple apprehension of the object. The same kind of choice independent of the last dictate of the intellect can occur, Leverett said, when two goods are presented, either of which can be chosen. "The intellect judges speculatively that the one is a false the other an authentic good, and then judges practically that the authentic good is to be preferred to the false. But the will, in its freedom, can choose the false good, abandoning the authentic, however much the intellect may judge that the authentic is to be preferred practically, and act in accordance with those words of Medea: I see the better and approve; but I follow the worse." Persons who act against their conscience by doing what they know is prohibited, Leverett asserted, are illustrative of the psychological process in which the will actually rejects the practical judgment.

Leverett's conclusion firmly aligned him with the voluntarists. The will in its exercise may move not only itself but also the intellect. Even in specification, the will is limited only by what has in general been "previously apprehended" by the intellect, not by what is last judged. Inevitably, Leverett had to attribute some degree of cognitive power to the will to replace its lost reliance on the intellect. Leverett also cited in his conclusion the common example of the first sin of angels and man, which could not have required an error of intellect to occur, for if it had, creatures would have suffered a penalty of sin before committing the first sin. According to the common belief, before the first sin the practical judgment was fully, clearly, and innately informed of the moral law. Therefore, it was not an intellectual error that came first but a disobedient act of will. Gershom Bulkeley had used the same argument earlier. Finally, Leverett stated, the will, like the intellect, can err, and if the will necessarily follows the judgment of the intellect, then in the regeneration of man there would be no need for the will's inner renewal through grace (*"intrinsice et in sese renovaretur per gratiam"*); the illumina-

---

human response to God or the world. Though there can be no love for what is not known, neither can there be knowledge without a desire (i.e., a love) to know. The question, like so many ancient philosophical issues, has contemporary relevance. David O. Sears, "Political Behavior," in Gardner Lindzey and Elliot Aronson, *The Handbook of Social Psychology*, 2d ed., V (Reading, Mass., 1969), 415–416, writes: "Affect precedes information. Children express strong positive affect toward leaders, and only later acquire supporting rationalizations." Quoted by Peter Loewenberg, "The Psychohistorical Origins of the Nazi Youth Cohort," *American Historical Review*, LXXVI (1971), 1487.

tion of the intellect would be sufficient for everything. "But this is farther from faith and piety than I am from the truth when I maintain that the will does not always follow the last dictate of the intellect."

One further problem regarding the controversy over will and intellect at seventeenth-century Harvard requires clarification. This has to do with the relation of the theological doctrine of regeneration and reprobation to psychological theory. In this period the question could always be asked, to which of the three possible states of man does any given psychological theory of the faculties apply: the innocent man, that is, Adam before the Fall;[58] the fallen man; or the redeemed man? With respect, for example, to the famous lament of St. Paul, quoted earlier, it was a standing dispute for centuries, and presumably still is, whether Paul was describing a condition before or after regeneration. It has been suggested, but I think erroneously, that the intellectualist position applied to the hypothetical condition of man before the Fall, and to a lesser degree to the regenerate soul, whereas voluntarism, that is, the theory of the rebellious will, pertained peculiarly to man in a degenerate state. There is some evidence in support of this assumption in Puritan literature and outside it. Bishop Edward Reynolds, to mention one instance, following John Cameron, listed among the curative psychological effects of regeneration the irradiation of "the mind and judgment with heavenly light" and "an act of *spiritual inclining and effectual determining the will of man* to embrace the *ultimate dictate* of a *mind* thus enlightened." In another well-known psychological study, *The Passions of the Minde in Generall*, first published in 1601, Thomas Wright described how that "bitter Apple which edged all mens teeth" troubled our wills "with tempests and wicked inclinations," even though it is "connatural" for the will to follow the rule of reason and prosecute virtue and honesty. It was thus only by a kind of "vicious miracle," namely the Fall, that the will behaves contrary to nature.[59]

It must be stressed, however, that there was no necessary relationship between the state of regeneration and the psychology of intellectualism, or between the state of corruption and the psychology of voluntarism. Everybody agreed, it is true, that in the fallen state the ideal harmony of the faculties was profoundly disordered, that in Adam's soul before his sin such a harmony had existed, and that the action of divine grace on the soul in sanctification brings about some restoration of this primitive harmony. But within this consensus there continued to be latitude for different conceptions of the exact nature of the harmony or disharmony in the soul. In fact, quite a variety of beliefs

58. See Oberman, *Harvest of Medieval Theology*, 47ff, regarding the state *"ex puris naturalibus,"* which is the condition of man without infused grace, the hypothetical condition between *"in culpa"* and *"in gratia."* The concept was used by Thomas Aquinas, among others.

59. Miller, *New England Mind*, I, 250. Reynolds, *Works*, 583, 635, 769. Wright, *Passions of the Minde*, 2d ed. rev. (London, 1630), 319.

existed. After all, God's being is perfect, yet His nature was interpreted by intellectualists and voluntarists in contrary ways. Concerning the condition of man in the corrupt state, the intellectualists still tended to argue that the basic problem was not the carnal will, though that may enter in, but the darkness of the rational judgment, its failure to supply the will with the right guidance upon which it depends. At the critical moment, when the will is hesitant to follow the direction of conscience, the understanding ought to step in with additional considerations of the ultimate consequences of the will's rebellion, but this it neglects to do. And thus the will is abandoned to its own blindness. Such an analysis comports well with Burgersdyck's intellectualist interpretation of the Medean paradox, mentioned above. The principal failure evident in man's corrupt state, according to this view, is a failure of understanding. In sum, there was no insurmountable incompatibility between intellectualist psychological theory and the usual conception of the degenerate soul. Nor was it difficult to interpret the redeemed or even the perfect state of the rational soul in voluntarist terms. The issue accommodated itself to existing religious categories; it was not constitutive of them.[60]

Indeed, both kinds of will, will as love and will as intellect, are necessary activities of the soul, and an excess of either leads to pathology. People must be "sufferers," in the old sense, as well as actors, "patients" as well as agents, helpless lovers as well as potent willers, and an incapacity in either of these abilities presages personal disaster.[61] The historic philosophical debate over the nature of the will usually took place within the boundaries of psychological health and was for the most part a matter of emphasis, but emphasis is never a negligible matter.

It can be established, then, that coexistent with theological quarrels, and relatively independent of the question of the freedom of the will in its classic forms, there flourished in seventeenth-century New England a deep-running debate concerning psychological models, which in the end may be assessed as a debate based ultimately on temperamental preferences. With regard to the present historiographical controversy over the degree of intellectuality of the New England "mind," it is helpful to realize that the Puritans themselves

60. In his *The Parable of the Ten Virgins Opened and Applied* . . . (London, 1660), Pt. i, 60–61, Thomas Shepard argued that the will retained a "remnant of malignity" even after conversion, and that the *"Video meliora"* applied both before and after conversion, although less so after.

61. See in the appendix, below, my discussion of the theories of the modern psychotherapist Leslie Farber. For a matchless statement of psychological principles similar to Farber's and those held by Augustinians in the 17th century on the meaning of the prayer "Thy will be done," see Eugen Rosenstock-Huessy, "Hitler and Israel, or on Prayer," *Jour. of Religion*, XXIV (1945), reprinted in Rosenstock-Huessy, ed., *Judaism Despite Christianity: The "Letters on Christianity and Judaism" between Eugen Rosenstock-Huessy and Franz Rosenzweig* (University, Ala., 1969), 178–194.

disputed about how "intellectual" they were or wanted to be.[62] Because of this contemporary debate, it is questionable that the present controversy can ever be resolved in favor of one side or the other. It is enough to understand that the seventeenth-century arguments ran smoothly into certain eighteenth-century issues and were part of the universal clashing motifs of "heart" and "head" in Western culture and in American literature in particular. Puritan voluntarists were not romantics, or even "evangelicals" in the later sense. But there are important and demonstrable connections between certain elements in the psychological theory of some Puritans and the psychological theories implicit in eighteenth-century preromanticism, sentimentalism, evangelicalism, and related phenomena.

This general historical relationship has rarely been brought out. One exception is Walter Jackson Bate's lectures of twenty-five years ago, *From Classic to Romantic*. But Bate also failed to make some essential distinctions. Duns Scotus, he writes,

> sought to demonstrate that the will is not dependent on knowledge but, on the contrary, is completely free and directed of itself to good. But with the will thus deprived of a rational guide, the followers of Scotus were not exactly sure how the will was to know the good; and from his uncertainty ultimately stemmed both the social and empirical determinism and the emotional individualism, unified in origin but diverse in direction, which largely tended to replace rationalism in European moral and aesthetic thought. . . . The will, left rudderless in the empirical world, was increasingly discovered to be determined by material circumstances.

The obvious example of this tendency is Hobbes, for whom the will was governed, as Bate says, "by the chain of events and forces of the empirical

---

62. The historiographical controversy is summarized in Michael McGiffert, "American Puritan Studies in the 1960s," *WMQ*, 3d Ser., XXVII (1970), 50–54. Robert Middlekauff has addressed the issue in "Piety and Intellect in Puritanism," *ibid.*, XXII (1965), 457–470, and again in *The Mathers: Three Generations of Puritan Intellectuals, 1596–1728* (New York, 1971). In the latter work Middlekauff gives more recognition to the role of the affections in Puritan religious life, but I do not think he is correct in assuming that "the process of conversion, most Puritan divines agreed, began with the understanding, which then enlightened the will, and finally ended with the transformation of the affections" (pp. 245–246). This may have been Cotton Mather's position, even though, as Middlekauff notes, Richard Mather put an "unusual" emphasis on the affections in every phase of the conversion process, even those phases "commonly deemed intellectual" (pp. 63–67). Also related to the controversy is Glenn Miller's "God's Light and Man's Enlightenment: Evangelical Theology of Colonial Presbyterianism," *Journal of Presbyterian History*, LI (1973), 97–115, which has valuable perceptions but misses the three-way split in the schools of religious psychology in the 18th century and does not recognize the 17th-century roots of the controversy.

world."[63] What Bate left out, however, is the type of voluntarism we have seen in William Ames, in which it is not the empirical world that ultimately dominates the "will" but spiritual forces greater than the objects of this world.

By the same token, historians have not often recognized that Pelagianism and Arminianism were intimately related to the intellectualist theory, although there has always been a completely orthodox intellectualist tradition in Reformed Protestantism, too. Sometimes it is mistakenly assumed that it is voluntarism that is conducive to a Pelagian potency of will, a confusion that is due to a failure to distinguish between the Molinist liberty of will and the Augustinian liberty that subordinates the will to either divine or satanic influence.[64] But if this confusion between *the will as independent of the dictates of intellect* and *the will as "free"* is unscrambled, then it becomes readily evident that intellectualism can lead rather easily to a belief in salvation by effort and endeavor, whereas the pietistic voluntarist can only wait for divine grace in order for redemption to occur. If the will is corrupt, controlled by Satan, and unmanageable in its concupiscence or self-love, then only a redeeming love from outside can turn it around toward God. The function of the ministry of the Church is to reach the heart or the affections, opening the way for a new will to enter. Intellectualism, on the other hand, may encourage human pride in knowing the way and pride in the natural man's sufficiency for virtue and even salvation. This pride was historically supported by the impressive magnitude of the remaining intellectual endowment of man after the Fall, as the pagan philosophical achievement proved. The Natural Law tradition of morality survived all of the assaults of the Reformation, as we have discussed in the first chapter, which meant that intellectualism had available an advanced and well-established notion of human ability. If, then, the intellectualist belief in a perfectly tractable will that is always obedient to the dictates of the understanding is added to these other factors, it is evident the prerequisites are there for a considerable confidence in what effort and striving by themselves can achieve. All that must be watched for in the struggle to live a pious life are, as the ancient pagans also believed, error in the understanding, and unbridled passions.[65]

63. Bate, *From Classic to Romantic: Premises of Taste in Eighteenth-Century England* (Cambridge, Mass., 1946), 49–52. On p. 23 Bate writes that the removal of reason from control over the will "was to plunge European philosophy, by the close of the eighteenth century, into a disunity which was without parallel in its entire history, and from which it has shown no genuine sign of emergence."

64. Miller, *New England Mind*, I, 285, seems to make this error.

65. Flavel, *Whole Works*, I, 284, quotes from one of Thomas Manton's sermons that emphasizes the intellectualism of Pelagius. Pelagius, according to Manton, "acknowledged no other

The Great Awakening

It has not been adequately recognized that the divisions in American thought during the Great Awakening of the 1740s between evangelicals, so-called "old Calvinists," and incipient liberal "Arminians" were partly a carry-over from the debates of the seventeenth century and in some respects continuous with them.[66] There were some indispensable intermediate steps, too, notably developments in moral psychology (especially in the theory of the passions) that took place between the time of the appearance of Descartes's treatise on the passions and the work of the Scottish moralist Francis Hutcheson, which we will consider below. But even without these essential steps it is remarkable how close the correspondence is between the seventeenth-century Augustinian voluntarist position and the ideas of Jonathan Edwards, and between the seventeenth-century intellectualist position and the ideas of, for example, Edwards's opponent, Charles Chauncy.

Edwards completely identified the will with the affections or passions, that is, he treated the will as though it were itself simply a generalized name for the affections of the heart. Ames and a number of others in the seventeenth century and before had maintained the same position. "Ames feels the kinship between feeling and will to be so close at their deepest point that they are at times for him interchangeable terms," Karl Reuter has observed.[67] Edwards stressed that "the informing of the understanding is all vain, any farther than it *affects* the heart." Like St. Augustine and Ames, Edwards emphasized that our loves and hates, which are the basic actions of the will, are beyond intellectual control. "The soul wills one thing rather than another, or chooses one thing rather than another, no otherwise than as it loves one thing more than another."[68] "The Scripture often teaches," Edwards wrote, "that all true religion summarily consists in the love of divine things. And therefore that kind of understanding or knowledge, which is the proper foundation of true religion, must be the knowledge of the loveliness of divine things." It is that knowledge which is the "proper foundation of love" and is inseparable from love. "It is not speculation merely that is concerned in this kind of under-

---

Grace but outward Instruction. . . . His followers owned some kind of internal Grace; but they made that to consist in some illumination of the Understanding, or moral Perswasion by probable arguments, to excite the Will."

66. See the clarifying article by Gerald J. Goodwin, "The Myth of 'Arminian-Calvinism' in Eighteenth-Century New England," *NEQ*, XLI (1968), 213–237. But Edwards may have understood Arminianism to be something like Cameronianism.

67. Nethenus, Visscher, and Reuter, *William Ames*, ed. and trans. Horton, 190. See Edwards, *Religious Affections*, ed. John E. Smith, in *Works of Edwards*, II, 96, 106, and *passim*.

68. Edwards, *Some Thoughts Concerning the Present Revival of Religion in New-England . . .* (Boston, 1742), 8, 9.

standing: nor can there be a clear distinction made between the two faculties of understanding and will, as acting distinctly and separately, in this matter." That Edwards had in mind a unity of intellect and will somewhat different from the old Scholastic unity is apparent.[69] "There is a distinction to be made between a mere notional understanding, wherein the mind only beholds things in the exercise of a speculative faculty; and the sense of the heart, wherein the mind don't only speculate and behold, but relishes and feels. . . . The one is mere speculative knowledge; the other sensible knowledge, in which more than the mere intellect is concerned; the heart is the proper subject of it, or the soul as a being that not only beholds, but has inclination, and is pleased or displeased." Edwards was describing here not a conative function of intellect so much as a cognitive function of the will conceived of in the broadest possible sense, that is, where it verges into the meaning of "heart."[70]

Like Ames, Edwards believed that only by assuming that the operation of grace is primarily in the will could it be reasonably expected that regeneration would issue in the reformation of practical life, as Christian teaching affirmed should happen. In *Charity and Its Fruits*, a series of lectures preached by Edwards in 1738, he taught that "the immediate seat of grace is in the will or disposition," which shows, he said, that "all true grace tends to practice." For the will, Edwards continued, is "the fountain" of practice, just as the head of a spring is the foundation of the stream that flows from it.[71]

69. Chaps. 4 and 6, below, introduce considerably more background for Edwards's theories than has thus far been presented. In addition, see Fiering, *Jonathan Edwards's Moral Thought*.

70. In his *Religious Affections*, ed. Smith, 266*ff*, some of Edwards's remarks would seem to suggest that he was an intellectualist. For example, "Such is the nature of man, that it is impossible his mind should be affected, unless it be by something that he apprehends, or that his mind conceives of." Similarly in his *Freedom of the Will*, ed. Ramsey, there are entire sections on the liberty of indifference and on "the connection of the acts of the will with the dictates of the understanding" where Edwards seems to be unmistakably arguing the 17th-century intellectualist position: "Every act of the will is some way connected with the understanding, and is as the greatest apparent good is. . . . 'Tis very evident in itself, that the acts of the will have some connection with the dictates or view of the understanding" (p. 217). To demonstrate that these remarks are all ad hoc, or involve certain redefinitions of terms, is a project that cannot be undertaken here. It should be noted, however, that Edwards expressly and deliberately bypassed the great 17th-century debate—"nor is it needful that I should enter into a particular disquisition of all points debated in disputes on that question, whether the will always follows the last dictate of the understanding"—and introduced instead "motive" as the key term in his argument, which he defined as "the whole of that which moves, excites or invites the mind to volition, whether that be one thing singly, or many things conjunctly" (p. 141). See n. 69 above.

71. Edwards, *Charity and Its Fruits; or, Christian Love as Manifested in the Heart and Life*, ed. Tryon Edwards (New York, 1851), 327. Cf. Willard's *Compleat Body*, 562: "All true Obedience is rooted in the Heart, which firstly points to the Will in Man, which is in him the supream Faculty, and unless that be devoted to the Service of God, all else that he doth, though it carry never so fair a shew with it, cannot be properly called Obedience." Willard's sermon was preached at the turn of the century, many years before its publication in 1726.

Edwards was, of course, completely familiar with Ames's writings as well as with those of figures like the Scottish theologian Samuel Rutherford (d. 1661), Theophilus Gale, John Owen, and other exponents of Augustinian voluntarism. He was also devoted to the *Theoretico-Practica Theologia* of Petrus van Mastricht (1630–1706), his favorite work in theology. Mastricht, a professor at Utrecht, was himself much influenced by Ames. Reuter has called Mastricht "hardly more than the expositor of Ames." Indeed, Mastricht stated in the preface to the second Latin edition of *Theoretico-Practica Theologia*: "I have followed the system of the renowned Ames as is laid down in his *Medulla* and his *Casus Conscientiae* which seem so helpful and clear to me that I neither desire nor need any other in its stead."[72] In 1770, in the midst of the controversies over the Edwardsian theology in America, a brief section of Mastricht on the topic of regeneration was translated into English and published in New Haven, Connecticut. A good part of this small volume (which also contains a valuable appendix of statements from various authorities before and after Mastricht who shared his views) concerns the relation of will and intellect, particularly the question of whether divine regeneration is a *physical* process in the will or simply a matter of intellectual illumination and *moral* suasion. Mastricht emphasized that it is the whole man that is regenerated— intellect, will, and affections—but the point at issue was whether a super- natural physical change occurs in the will. It is true, Mastricht responded to the Arminians and Cameronians, that the will "doth naturally follow the *last* dictate of the practical understanding," but, he added,

> only when the understanding, in its last dictate, judgeth agreeably to the *inclination* of the will. . . . If we should make the absurd sup- position of the *understanding's* being most clearly enlightened, and yet the *will* not renewed, the will would not follow the practical judg- ment, because in that case the understanding would not dictate agreeably to [the will's] propensity. . . . It is therefore in this spiritual propensity of the will, that the seeds of all those graces, which are necessary to salvation are contained.[73]

Directly connected with this conclusion is the question of whether the action of God in regeneration is moral or physical, and whether "the physical operation," which Mastricht accepted, affects the will "immediately." The Pelagians and the Socinians, according to Mastricht, "allow nothing but a moral *action* or agency of God in regeneration, in which he *teacheth* what is to be done, and by motives persuadeth to the doing of it." They deny any

---

72. Nethenus, Visscher, and Reuter, *William Ames*, ed. and trans. Horton, 145–146, 177.

73. Peter van Mastricht, *A Treatise on Regeneration . . . Extracted from His System of Divinity, Called Theologia Theoretico-Practica* (New Haven, Conn., 1770), 26–27.

"physical operation" of God in the process. Next to them are the "Semi-Pelagians, together with the Jesuits and Arminians," who allow "some *physical* agency of God in regeneration. . . . But, as they restrain the depravity arising from sin to the *inferior* faculties of the soul, or at most, to the understanding, so they allow the physical agency of God, only with respect to these faculties: while, as to the *will* or free will of man, they hold only to a *moral agency*." Mastricht believed that the semi-Pelagian reservation on this point grew out of a fear that a physical action on the will would vitiate freedom. The Cameronians among the Reformed "allow indeed a physical operation upon the *will*; but that only by the *medium* of the understanding, which God, in regeneration so *powerfully enlightens*, and convinces, that the will cannot but follow its last practical dictate." This was also the position of Bishop Reynolds, as we saw above. Finally, the orthodox Reformed group, to which Mastricht himself belonged, considered the physical operation of God immediately upon the will to be the essential principle in regeneration, an operation that directly "begets in the will a new *propensity* toward spiritual good." [74]

The anonymous editor and translator of this volume of Mastricht was in the Edwardsian camp. In a twenty-page appendix he added the words of a dozen other authorities, Charnock, Twisse, Flavel, Witsius, Ames, Rutherford, and so on. From Rutherford's anti-Arminian tract of 1636, *Exercitationes apologeticae pro gratia divina*, the editor extracted the telling comment: "If the last judgment of the understanding necessarily and of itself determined the will, grace would become mere suasion . . . ; to remove the darkness of the mind and instruct it in what it is ignorant of would be sufficient, *which is the grace of Pelagians*." [75] And in a footnote to Mastricht's seventeenth-century text on the relation of will and intellect, quoted above, the editor introduced the eighteenth-century comments of Jonathan Edwards from his *Enquiry into . . . Freedom of Will* (1754) in support of Mastricht: "In some sense, the will always follows the last dictate of the understanding. But then the understanding must be taken in a large sense, as including the whole faculty of perception or apprehension, and not merely what is called reason or judgment. If by the dictate of the understanding is meant what reason declares to

---

74. *Ibid.*, 35–38. The same thought may be found in Thomas Shepard's *The Sound Beleever* . . . , 6th ed. (London, 1659), 87: In moving the human soul, "the Spirit is not only a moral agent persuading, but also a supernatural agent *physically* working . . . by a divine and immediate act" (my italics). William Ames, also, drew a distinction between "the 'moral' way which presupposes the freedom of man to decide for himself and moves through the insight of reason to the acceptance of grace, and the 'physical' way which begins with the divine influencing of the human will and under the divine influx of strength proceeds to the act of conversion." Nethenus, Visscher, and Reuter, *William Ames*, ed. and trans. Horton, 258.

75. Mastricht, *Treatise on Regeneration*, Appendix.

be the best . . . , it is not true, that the will always follows the last dictate of the understanding."[76] Edwards contended that the dictate of reason, the intellectual factor, was just one thing "put into the scale" as part of "the compound influence which moves and induces the will."[77] The image of the scales or the balance is the pre-eminent model for the theory of volition in Edwards's *Freedom of Will*, and the scales are tipped not by *reasons* but by what Edwards called "motives," a catchall term deliberately chosen to allow for the direct physical action of God on the will (including heart and affections) as well as the direct action of many other imponderables and variables, or second causes, by which God directs human destiny. As one of Edwards's earliest critics, James Dana, pointed out in his *Examination of . . . Edwards's "Enquiry,"* the great Calvinist in his *Enquiry* had in fact skirted the whole question of what human motives were, that is, of what caused one action rather than another or what was really behind our willing this rather than that,[78] but Edwards did establish certainly that practical intellect could not be the sole determinant of will and that in consequence regeneration was not solely or even primarily a matter of intellectual persuasion.

At the same time, the intellectualist opponents of the revival, such as Chauncy, also reiterated some ancient arguments. "Is it reasonable to think," Chauncy asked,

> that the *Divine* SPIRIT, in dealing with Men . . . would give their
> *Passions* the *chief* Sway over them? Would not this be to invert their
> Frame? . . . One of the most *essential* Things necessary in *new-forming*
> Men, is the Reduction of their *Passions* to a proper Regimen, i.e. The
> Government of a *sanctified Understanding*. . . . *Reasonable* Beings
> are not to be guided by *Passion* or *Affection*, though the Object of it
> should be GOD. . . . The plain Truth is, an *enlightened Mind*, and not
> *raised Affections*, ought always to be the Guide of those who call
> themselves Men.

And Chauncy made perfectly clear how differently from Edwards he understood the nature of the will. "There is the Religion of the *Understanding* and *Judgment*, and *Will*, as well as of the *Affections*; and if little Account is made of the *former*, while great Stress is laid upon the *latter*, it can't be but people should run into Disorders."[79] The will for Chauncy remained a rational ap-

---

76. Edwards, *Freedom of the Will*, ed. Ramsey, 148.

77. *Ibid.*

78. James Dana, *An Examination of the Late Reverend President Edwards's "Enquiry on Freedom of Will"* . . . (Boston, 1770). See Ramsey's introduction to Edwards, *Freedom of the Will*, 19.

79. Charles Chauncy, *Seasonable Thoughts on the State of Religion in New-England* . . . (Boston, 1743), 324, 326–327, 422.

petite. All of the disputants in the Great Awakening debate were relying on well-established older arguments, some of which we have not exposed here; but of these arguments the voluntarist/intellectualist debate of the seventeenth century was possibly the most central.[80]

It may be of some interest to notice the position of Edwards's grandfather and predecessor in the pulpit at Northampton, Massachusetts, Solomon Stoddard. Although Stoddard himself had a reputation as an effective revivalist in the early years of the eighteenth century, he adhered to the psychological theory predominant among the anti-revivalists of later years, a matter that came into the open twenty-five years later when Edwards published a direct refutation of Stoddardeanism, his *Humble Inquiry into the Rules of the Word of God*.[81] According to Stoddard, "The Nature of Man is such that the Will always follows the last dictates of the Understanding; the Will it self is a blind faculty, and it follows the direction of the Understanding. When once Men have a Spiritual Sight of the glory of God, they can do no other but serve him." By "sight" here Stoddard seems to have meant an intellectual vision. "Light and Life go together. Before Men know God it is impossible that they should love him, for they are strangers to the reason and foundation of love. . . . But when their eyes are opened and they see the glory of God, they would act against their Nature if they did it not."[82] In answer to this old Scholastic problem of which must come first in human response to an object, love or

80. Many 18th-century Yale College commencement theses pertained to the problem of will and intellect. For example:

1718—(*Logicae*) *Voluntas coactioni non subjicitur* (The will is not subject to coercion). Publicly debated.

1733—(*Logicae*) *Omnis actus hominis, intellectione excepta, est volitio* (Every act of a man, intellection excepted, is will).

(*Logicae*) *Actus intelligendi, quo homo judicium fert de actione sua, volitioni antecedit* (The act of understanding by which a man makes judgment concerning his action precedes volition).

(*Logicae*) *Libertas humana supponit determinationem per ultimum dictamen intellectus esse necessariam* (Human freedom implies that determination through the last judgment of the intellect is needed).

1735—(*Metaphysicae*) *Voluntas est mentis esse determinandi potestas* (Will is the power of the mind's self-determination).

(*Metaphysicae*) *Intellectus non aliud quam dirigit voluntatem* (Intellect [does] nothing other than direct will).

1740—(*Ethicae*) *Prava volitio, absque mentis errore, non esse potest* (There cannot be an evil choice apart from a mistake of the mind).

1750—(*Metaphysicae*) *Voluntas per maximum bonum apparens non semper determinatur* (Will is not always determined by the greatest apparent good).

81. Edwards, *An Humble Inquiry into the Rules of the Word of God, Concerning the Qualifications Requisite to a Compleat Standing and Full Communion in the Visible Christian Church* (Boston, 1749).

82. Solomon Stoddard, *Three Sermons Lately Preachid at Boston* (Boston, 1717), 71–72.

knowledge, Stoddard chose knowledge.[83] "The excellency of the object is the foundation of the duty," Stoddard wrote, "and when that reason is seen, [men] are under a necessity to do it. . . . The sight of the glory of God will necessarily draw forth holy Actions."[84] Edwards's answer, based on the difference between "assent" and "consent," summarized the difference between him and Stoddard well: To own the covenant, Edwards said, "is to profess the Consent of our Hearts to it; and that is the Sum and Substance of true Piety. 'Tis not only a professing the Assent of our Understandings, that we understand there is such a Covenant, or that we understand we are obliged to comply with it; but 'tis to profess the Consent of our Wills." Edwards assumed that inner consent does not necessarily follow intellectual assent.[85]

The editors of an excellent collection of documents relating to the Great Awakening make the point rightly that "the central conflict of the Awakening was . . . not theological but one of opposing theories of the human psychology."[86] It is certainly a mistake, however, to consider Edwards's psychological theory a reformulation of Locke and therefore modern, and Chauncy's theory outmoded. This idea is true only in the sense that Augustinian voluntarism fed into the rising tide of romanticism, which was yet to reach its full height. Moreover, the direct influence of Locke's *Essay Concerning Human Understanding* on the American mind in the first half of the eighteenth century has been almost as much exaggerated as the influence of his treatises on government. The issue in the Great Awakening was not old versus new, but rather the perennial opposition of head and heart, both sides of which have found able supporters in every age.

God's Will and Man's Will

The problem of the freedom of the will, as noted at the beginning of this chapter, was not a live issue in seventeenth-century New England. For both intellectualists and voluntarists man was morally and legally responsible for his acts insofar as he was not forced or coerced by external agencies. This conception of freedom is perhaps easier to understand in terms of intellectu-

83. In opposition to this opinion Ames had given the example of prayer, which he said must first arise out of love without preceding knowledge of the object. Cf. p. 132 and n. 57, above.

84. Stoddard, *Three Sermons*, 72, 74. See also, Thomas A. Schafer, "Solomon Stoddard and the Theology of the Revival," in Stuart C. Henry, ed., *A Miscellany of American Christianity: Essays in Honor of H. Shelton Smith* (Durham, N.C., 1963), 348, n. 88, where Schafer observes that Edwards followed Mastricht, not Stoddard, on the matter of intellect versus will.

85. Edwards, *Humble Inquiry*, 28–29.

86. Alan Heimert and Perry Miller, eds., *The Great Awakening: Documents Illustrating the Crisis and Its Consequences* (Indianapolis, Ind., 1967), xxxix.

alist psychology than in terms of Augustinian voluntarism. As long as one's reason is making uncoerced choices it seems appropriate in everyday terms to speak of real freedom, even though the will is dependent on practical judgment. But the modern mind balks at the voluntarist thesis that a person is also free when God is acting physically on the will like a rider in the saddle. Jonathan Edwards confused some of his readers in the eighteenth century (and still confuses some) by insisting, despite his exhaustive defense of predestination, or divine determinism, that men "are not at all hindered by any fatal necessity, from doing, and even willing and choosing as they please, with full freedom; yea, with the highest degree of liberty that ever was thought of, or that ever could possibly enter into the heart of any man to conceive."[87] John Calvin had, of course, concluded the same.

The mist is at least partially lifted when it is recognized that bringing divine influence into the equation does not really alter "freedom" any more than other influences do. We are just as free and unfree when we are governed by reason as when we are governed by affections. Always, however, there are *motives*, as Edwards never failed to mention. God's influence on the human condition cannot be considered coaction, for He bends the inclinations themselves, not our limbs, just as reasons may bend inclinations. By acting directly on "willing" itself, rather than on the effects of willing, God's effects in man's conduct become simply what we will to do, or incline to do, or are pleased to do, in any given case.

Edwards's argument was not new. "Work out your salvation with fear and trembling," Paul wrote to the Philippians, "for it is God that worketh in you *both to will and to do*, of His own good Pleasure" (2:12–13). Edwards's theological ancestors were fond of dwelling on this idea of God's concurrent power in man's willing. "If ye consider the very instant of time wherein God worketh in us, ye shall find," Theodore Beza wrote, "that the ableness to be willing to receive is given unto us, and also that we be willing to receive, both together in one self same moment. . . . God at once and in one self same moment bringeth to pass, both that through grace we may know and through grace we do know indeed, that through grace we will and through grace we do will indeed."[88] Beza was an intellectualist. In William Perkins's *Treatise of God's Free Grace and Man's Free Will* we see the purer doctrine. "God's will hath a sovereign Lordship over the will of man," Perkins wrote, and man's will is absolutely dependent on it. Where man's will "hath any stroke or action, there God's will formerly had his stroke or action." Yet when God

87. Edwards to John Erskine, July 25, 1757, printed in Ramsey, ed., *Freedom of the Will*, 453.

88. From Beza's *A Book of Christian Questions*, quoted by Lynn Baird Tipson, Jr., "The Development of a Puritan Understanding of Conversion" (Ph.D. diss., Yale University, 1972), 117, an excellent thesis that should eventually see publication.

begins to "regenerate us, He makes us then willing, being otherwise by nature unwilling, and thus He regenerates us not against our wills." Because God works on the will directly, there is no arm bending, just as when we are moved spontaneously by love or any other affection we are not coerced, properly speaking. "So soon as God hath begun" to renew the will, Perkins continued, the will "wills to be renewed." In respect of time, God's grace and man's will "are both together, and concur in the very first moment of our regeneration." To will to be regenerate (as opposed to simply "woulding" to be regenerate) is already "testimony of regeneration begun."[89] Edwards's theory of the will, and the principles of Augustinian voluntarism generally, were simply extensions of the *concursus Dei* of regeneration into a broad psychological theory that called attention to the good things that come to man through patience (in the etymological sense) rather than endeavor.[90]

89. Tipson, "Puritan Understanding of Conversion," 227–237.
90. See appendix, below, "A Note on the Problem of Will in the Twentieth Century."

4

The Passions and the Science
of the Inward Man

'Tis a Point about which the
Divines and Philosophers can never agree . . . ;
whether the Passions *be the Institution of Nature,*
or the Corruption thereof.[1]

Despite all the confusion about the nature of the will, in the traditional view
one thing was supposed to be clear: the will was not a common passion or
affection such as sprang from the sensitive appetite. The will was a function
of the intellect, with the special task, among others, of controlling the passions lodged in the sensitive appetite. The will was the instrument of reason in
the governance of the passions.

It was accepted, nonetheless, that breakdowns would occur, as when the
passions swept reason along and thereby indirectly influenced the will to
choose erroneously. But the will itself was by definition considered to be
immune from the direct effects of passions and affections, though here, too,
there was ambiguity, for some psychologists spoke of the will as being torn
between the pull of the passions and the pull of reason. If the passions could
directly alter the will so that it was no longer an exclusive function of reason
or intellect, then the will itself would become like the passions, sometimes
moving in accordance with reason and sometimes not, without any higher
logic consistently guiding it, responding at the moment in accordance with
whatever apprehension it might happen to have of the good or evil in the
particular object before it. In short, it would be nonrational, or at least as
nonrational as the sensitive appetite, a condition that was supposed to be
impossible for the will as will. This summary delineates the view of Thomas
Aquinas and many others concerning the relation of the will to the passions.
The will was by definition a faculty distinct from the passions; it was the

---

1. Ephraim Chambers, *Cyclopedia: or, an Universal Dictionary of Arts and Sciences* (London,
1728), "P" pagination, 759.

practical and active side of the intellect as opposed to the nonintellectual motions of desire or aversion characteristic of the sensitive appetite.

Without getting into irrelevant complexities, it may be said that this schema of the relation of intellect, will, and passion is found at least as far back as Plato's *Phaedrus* and *Republic*, where there also appears a division into three parts: 1) reason, 2) a supportive auxiliary to reason, and 3) unruly emotional elements in need of control or possibly even suppression.[2] And although it is true that Peripatetics and Stoics as late as the seventeenth century vigorously disputed about the proper place of the passions in the moral life, with the Stoics taking the more severely intellectualist approach, neither of these schools in any essential way broke with the general framework just outlined. On the surface the Stoic psychological structure was different, but the practical effects were the same in that passions were excluded in theory from making any positive contribution to virtue.

In the light of this venerable consensus about the natural organization of the soul, the permanent dissolution of this psychological model, when it occurred in the seventeenth and early eighteenth centuries, can be considered nothing less than a momentous revolution in psychological theory. And insofar as psychological concepts can alter human behavior by changing people's ideas about what is natural or normal for man, one might say that this revolution also changed "human nature." In consequence of this revolution, the will, the former auxiliary to reason, was largely obviated as a leading faculty of the soul. At the same time, the lowly and dangerous passions were tempered, transformed, and elevated to become in some cases not only themselves the auxiliaries of reason, but often also the actual and proper leaders of the soul, the very beacons for reason to follow. The ramifications of this change were enormous and have not been fully traced, though studies of romanticism and preromanticism have been concerned with the subject to some extent. Even less have the roots of this revolution, as they are found in the history of moral psychology, been explored. One of our goals in this chapter is to discover these roots and to follow the transformation of the theory of the passions in moral psychology. We have already shown some of the connections between the voluntarist tradition and "sentimentalism," to use the most convenient term for the eighteenth-century view that the affections of the "heart" are at the center of moral life. Another goal in this chapter will be to show the important contribution that Puritan piety made to the development of the sentimentalist school in moral philosophy.[3]

2. See, e.g., the notes to the edition and translation prepared by R. Hackforth, *Plato's Phaedrus* (Cambridge, 1952), 75–76.

3. The most extensive treatment of the subject thus far appears in the last chapter of Hoxie Neale Fairchild, *Religious Trends in English Poetry*, I, *1700–1740, Protestantism and the Cult of Sentiment* (New York, 1939), 535–576, which also contains a useful bibliography. But Fair-

It is perhaps necessary to stress here that our attention to the origins of sentimentalism and to the theory of the passions in general is not arbitrary. Sentimentalist moral philosophers such as Francis Hutcheson, George Turnbull, David Fordyce, and others played a prominent role in the study and teaching of ethics in eighteenth-century America, particularly in New England. In certain decisive respects the sentimentalist movement may be understood as a translation into the secular realm of particular forms of Puritan emotionality, such as "sensibility" and "zeal." The widespread adoption of sentimentalist tenets in moral philosophy provided for many Americans a desirable, if mainly unconscious, continuity with their religious past. A close examination of some aspects of the changing theory of the passions in the seventeenth and eighteenth centuries in the form that it reached American shores is a subject indispensable to a thorough understanding of American culture in the colonial period.

"Man himself is a great deep," St. Augustine wrote, "and you, Lord, number the very hairs of his head. . . . Yet the hairs of man's head are easier to number than are his affections and the impulses of his heart."[4] This observation is a useful forewarning of the difficulties any student of the passions confronts. The modern author of an intensive study of the theory of the passions in France between 1585 and 1649, Anthony Levi, has called attention to the bewildering variety of opinions to be found concerning the passions, their taxonomy, foundations, influence, and so on. The seat of the passions was variously assumed to be in the body, soul, mind, or heart. In the service of the good life it was believed that the passions should be moderated, eradicated, stimulated, or overcome.[5] Their number was reduced to three, four, seven, eleven, twelve, fifteen, or passed off as uncountable. And as we have already partly seen, conceptions of the relation of the passions to the faculties of reason, will, and imagination, and the definitions of those terms themselves, were constantly shifting and allowed for almost any possible combination. Fortunately, we do not have to make a systematic survey of this complex scene, since our concern is only with what appears to have been significant in early America. The necessary starting point, however, is the Stoic theory, not

---

child's interest is literary more than philosophical and is, of course, not focused on America. R. S. Crane's "Suggestions toward a Genealogy of the 'Man of Feeling,'" *Journal of English Literary History*, I (1934), 205–230, was a ground-breaking essay that continues to be valuable. Norman S. Grabo's "Puritan Devotion and American Literary History," in Ray B. Browne and Donald Pizer, eds., *Themes and Directions in American Literature: Essays in Honor of Leon Howard* (Lafayette, Ind., 1969), 6–23, is brief but very suggestive. Erich Kahler's *The Inward Turn of Narrative*, trans. Richard Winston and Clara Winston (Princeton, N.J., 1973) also contains relevant material.

4. Augustine, *Confessions*, Bk. IV, sec. xiv.
5. Levi, *French Moralists*, 4, 200.

because there is evidence that it was effectively represented in seventeenth-century America—in general, the expressed opposition to the Stoic theory of the passions was everywhere disproportionately large in relation to the number of real proponents of it—but because Stoicism represented an extreme against which other theories may be measured and because the Stoic revival of the sixteenth century seems to have been the greatest stimulus historically to the modern reconsideration of the passions.[6]

Stoicism and Its Critics

One solution to misery and unhappiness in the world is somehow to avoid feeling it, even in the midst of trouble. In the simplest terms this was the Stoic solution. It reflected an approach to life that was apparently widely prevalent in the ancient world. In the tenth book of Plato's *Republic* there is a discussion of the effects of drama and poetry on moral character that illustrates this theme and others adopted by the Stoic moralists. "When we listen to some hero in Homer or on the tragic stage moaning over his sorrows in a long tirade, or to a chorus beating their breasts as they chant a lament," Socrates says, "the best of us enjoy giving ourselves up to follow the performance with eager sympathy. The more a poet can move our feelings in this way, the better we think him." Yet this praise and sympathetic response, Socrates continues, is quite inconsistent with another and higher ideal, namely, the pride we should feel, when such sorrow is our own, in "being able to bear it quietly like a man, condemning the behaviour we admired in the theatre as womanish." Can it be right, Socrates asks, "that the spectacle of a man behaving as one would scorn and blush to behave oneself should be admired and enjoyed, instead of filling us with disgust?" Too few men are capable of reflecting "that to enter into another's feelings must have an effect on our own: the emotions of pity our sympathy has strengthened will not be easy to restrain when we are suffering ourselves." Poetic representations of "love and anger and all those desires and feelings of pleasure or pain which accompany our every action . . . water the growth of passions which should be allowed to wither away and sets them up in control, although the goodness and happiness of our lives depends on their being held in subjection." The result is that "pleasure and pain are al-

---

6. It is a paradox, as H. M. Gardiner has pointed out, that the Stoics did more to classify and describe the emotions than did any other ancient sect and that their system of the passions was the basis of much modern knowledge of the passions until the 18th century, even though the Stoics were the most negative about the role of the passions in life. See Gardiner *et al.*, *Feeling and Emotion*, 75–76.

lowed to usurp the sovereignty of law and of the principles always recognized by common consent as the best."[7] The goodness and the happiness of our lives depend upon keeping the passions in subjection. This is a perfect expression of the Stoic message, though the psychological model presented by most Stoic philosophers was different from the Platonic in that they treated the passions as aberrations of intellect and judgment rather than as products of sense experience alone.[8]

In the patristic age St. Augustine made a special point of qualifying this Classical ideal of "*apatheia*" or "*ataraxia*."[9] All of the pagan schools, Augustine claimed, Stoic, Peripatetic, and Platonist alike, essentially agree despite apparent differences that the wise man must defend his intellect against enslavement to the passions. But Christian teaching concerning the passions is entirely different, Augustine insisted. Scripture subordinates the intellect itself to God, to be governed and succored by Him, and "puts the passions into the keeping of the mind, to be so regulated and restrained as to be converted into servants of righteousness." Consequently, Augustine wrote, "in our system we do not so much ask whether a religious mind will become angry, but rather what should make it angry, nor whether it will be sad, but what should make it sad, nor whether it will be afraid, but what should make it afraid." No one finds fault with anger, Augustine said, when it is intended to bring about the reformation of a sinner, or with sadness on behalf of one who is distressed in order to relieve him, or with fear for one in danger, to save

7. *The Republic of Plato*, trans. and ed. Francis MacDonald Cornford (New York, 1967 [orig. publ. London, 1941]), X, 605–606. Sentimentalist moral philosophy in the 18th century, and the related growth of humanitarian sympathy, had to overcome the charge that it "feminized" moral virtue. But there is probably a connection between the emergence of women into the intellectual world at this time—a world that had formerly been the exclusive preserve of men trained in Latin—and the rise of humanitarianism. The severity of Roman justice went out of fashion in Western society along with Latin training in the schools and the brutal corporal punishment that accompanied it. For the various inter-relations here, see Walter J. Ong, S.J., *Rhetoric, Romance, and Technology: Studies in the Interaction of Expression and Culture* (Ithaca, N.Y., 1971), chaps. 1, 5, 11. Ong has not made the connection to sentimental humanitarianism, but it fits. Cf. Adam Smith's comment in *The Theory of Moral Sentiments* (London, 1759), Pt. III, chap. 3: "Our sensibility to the feelings of others, so far from being inconsistent with the manhood of self-command, is the very principle upon which that manhood is founded." On 18th-century humanitarianism and some of its ramifications, see Fiering, "Irresistible Compassion: An Aspect of Eighteenth-Century Sympathy and Humanitarianism," *Jour. Hist. Ideas*, XXXVII (1976), 195–218.

8. Plutarch's essay "On Moral Virtue" in his *Moralia* contains an excellent discussion of Stoic moral theory and was the source of many later commentaries. See *Plutarch's Morals: Ethical Essays*, ed. and trans. Arthur Richard Shilleto (London, 1898), 99–117.

9. For the Christian predecessors to Augustine in this, see Gardiner *et al.*, *Feeling and Emotion*, 89–96.

him from death. "No doubt the Stoic practice is to condemn even pity. . . . But what is pity except a kind of fellow-feeling in our own hearts for the suffering of others that in fact impels us to come to their aid as far as our ability allows?"[10] These and other emotions are right as long as the will is right. If the will, or one's love, is misdirected, they will be wrong. But if it is rightly directed, such emotions are not only not blameworthy but even praiseworthy. The "citizens of the holy City of God feel fear and desire, pain and gladness while they live in God's fashion during the pilgrimage of their present existence, and because their love is right, all these feelings of theirs are right."[11]

The ancient confrontation over Stoic moral psychology, exemplified here between Socrates and Augustine in archetypal isolation, had an exact counterpart in the seventeenth century, when Augustine's ghost was raised and brought into battle against the Neostoics.[12] The furthest advance of the Stoic revival occurred in the last quarter of the sixteenth century, when the *De Constantia* (1584) of Justus Lipsius and the *Philosophie morale des Stoiques* (*ca.* 1585) of Guillaume Du Vair were both published.[13] But by 1650, it seems to be generally agreed by historians, the Stoic negative attitude toward the passions was in retreat, and the Stoic position became mainly a foil for argument in support or defense of the passions. There continued to be holdouts, nevertheless, and some of the general principles of Stoic philosophy, particularly the opinion that a life of virtue is the summum bonum, remained strong throughout the eighteenth century. The same Antoine LeGrand (d. 1699) who helped to popularize Cartesian physics in New England and whose logic text underlay the *Compendium of Logick* prepared by tutor William Brattle at Harvard, actively propounded Stoic psychology as late as 1662 in a study entitled *Man without Passion: or The Wise Stoick*, which appeared first in French, and then in English in 1675.[14] Yet it is indicative of the prevalent

10. Augustine, *City of God*, III, *Books VIII–XI*, trans. Wiesen, Bk. IX, secs. iv, v. Plutarch, writing against Stoic extremism, defended the passions, too—"anger is useful to courage, and hatred of evil to uprightness"—but only insofar as they "wait on reason and run parallel to virtue" (*Plutarch's Morals*, ed. Shilleto, 117). Augustine referred the worth of the passions neither to reason nor to virtue, but to a fundamental disposition or orientation of the soul, the underlying intention.

11. *City of God*, IV, *Books XII–XV*, trans. Levine, Bk. XIV, secs. v–ix.

12. See Levi, *French Moralists*, 18: "Augustine's anti-Pelagianism made him the natural ally of the moralists who combated the renewed affirmations of stoic virtue, and it is to his strictures that they turned when faced with the flood of Senecan literature which threatened to engulf them." On the other hand, Levi shows that both of these terms, "Neostoic" and "Augustinian," encompass diverse positions with regard to many details.

13. See Rudolf Kirk, "Introduction," in his edition of Justus Lipsius, *Two Bookes of Constancie*, trans. Sir John Stradling (New Brunswick, N.J., 1939). For an important distinction between Du Vair and Lipsius, see Levi, *French Moralists*, 330–332.

14. LeGrand, *Le Sage des Stoiques ou l'homme sans passions. Selon les sentimens de Seneque* (The Hague, 1662).

trend that a few years later LeGrand in a major work contritely reversed himself. He confessed that whereas he had formerly pleaded the Stoic cause, not only maintaining Seneca's opinion but even endeavoring to "advance and exalt it" to the best of his ability, under the influence of Descartes he now rejected the notorious "Virulence" with which the Stoics "inveigh against the Passions."[15]

In his Stoic phase LeGrand was influenced by Justus Lipsius, as were numerous others in the early seventeenth century.[16] The *De Constantia* appeared in twenty-four Latin editions before 1606. It has been estimated that in the seventeenth century Lipsius was a far more powerful cultural force than Hugo Grotius and that his books were more widely sold than those of Bacon or Bodin.[17] There can be no doubt that the waves of the Stoic revival washed on New England shores as elsewhere. More than that, the austere moralism of Stoic thought was intrinsically attractive to one side of the Puritan personality. Indeed, the Neostoic movement consciously exploited just that affinity between certain Christian attitudes and this most virtue-minded of the ancient sects. The French historian Antoine Adam has emphasized that the modern Stoic movement was not simply a resuscitation of the ancients but a living system that fascinated many minds. Individual personalities in every age have found Stoic rectitude suitable to their own temperaments. By and large, however, the Augustinian pietistic emotionality with which American and English Puritanism was imbued served as a barrier against the full absorption of the Stoic spirit.[18]

In the *De Constantia*, which is a dialogue between a fictional Stoic wise man named Languïs and the initiate Justus Lipsius, the affections or passions

15. LeGrand, *Body of Philosophy*, trans. Blome, 367–368. The Latin edition came out in London in 1672 as *Institutio philosophiae . . .* and was widely known in academic circles. LeGrand was a Franciscan Recollect friar who lived for many years in Oxfordshire. He retained a Stoic bias even in this work. See n. 19 below.

16. Three editions prepared by Rudolf Kirk are helpful guides to the Stoic revival. In addition to Lipsius's *Two Bookes of Constancie*, mentioned above, see also Kirk's editions of Guillaume Du Vair, *The Moral Philosophie of the Stoicks*, trans. Thomas James (New Brunswick, N.J., 1951), and Hall, *Heaven upon Earth and Characters of Vertues and Vices*. The standard study of the Stoic revival is Leontine Zanta, *La Renaissance du Stoicisme au XVIᵉ siècle* (Paris, 1914). See also, the introduction by Rae Blanchard to his modern edition of Richard Steele's *The Christian Hero* (London, 1932), xvii–xxv. Blanchard cites the number of translations of Stoic works into English throughout the 17th century as evidence of the continuing appeal of this philosophy, and he puts Steele into the context of the opposition to it. See also, Levi, *French Moralists*, 51–55, and *passim*.

17. Peter Gay, *The Enlightenment: An Interpretation. The Rise of Modern Paganism* (New York, 1966), 300.

18. Antoine Adam, *Sur le problème religieux dans la première moitié du XVIIᵉ siècle*. Adam observes that the anti-Stoic reaction was "one of the most important facts of the spiritual renaissance of the 17th-century."

are identified first with "opinion," as contrasted with "reason," and then with the body, as contrasted with the mind. The picture is of a battle for supremacy in the soul between passion-based opinion on one side and "constancy," which is the expression of reason, on the other. A life in accordance with reason frees itself from the disturbances of the passions, which may also be considered false judgments or opinions. Most of the emotions that men feel, Languis claims, are false or hypocritical, and grief and pity for the sufferings of others are most notably so. When Lipsius cries out in response to this, "How should I not bee touched and tormented with the calamities of my countrey for my countrymen's sake, who are tossed in [a] sea of adversities?" Languis answers, "Commiseration or pittying . . . must be despised of him that is wise and constant." Pity is "a verie daungerous contagion, and I judge him not far from a pitiful state, that is subject to pittying of others." On the other hand, Languis does allow for "mercy," defined as "an inclination of the *minde* to succour the necessitie of miserie of another." But there should be no sorrowing, sighing, weeping with those that weep, and so on. "He that is trulie merciful in deed, wil not bemone or pittie the condition of distressed persons, but yet wil do more to helpe and succour them, than the other. He wil beholde mens miseries with the eye of compassion, yet ruled and guided by reason." [19]

It was this recommendation of feelingless and detached virtue that was hardest to swallow for those sharing in the Puritan cult of sensibility. For those adhering to the Augustinian religious voluntarism discussed earlier, Stoic psychology also represented another more pernicious form of intellectualism in ethics. Indeed, writers on all sides found cause to reject this unsympathetic side of Neostoicism. The author of *The Passions of the Minde in Generall* (1601), Thomas Wright, who was not associated with Puritanism, expressed the typical reservations about Stoic morality:

> Passions are not only not wholly to be extinguished (as the Stoics seemed to affirme) but sometimes to be moved, and stirred up for the service of vertue. . . . Mercie and compassion will move us often to pitty, as it did *Job, Quia ab infantia mea mecum creuit miseratio.* Compassion grew with me from my infancy, and it came with me out of my mothers

19. Lipsius, *Two Bookes of Constancie*, trans. Stradling, ed. Kirk, 88–89, 99–100. The emphasis on "minde" is mine. Copies of this work of Lipsius's were particularly prominent in early Virginia libraries. LeGrand's *Body of Philosophy*, which was partly Stoic and partly Cartesian, reduced the life of virtue to three major elements: the exercise of right *reason* in discovering the good; *constancy* in following the laws of reason; and *resignation*, which is an outgrowth of the ability to distinguish between that which it is possible to achieve by one's free will and that which the individual is powerless to effect.

womb. . . . Ire, and indignation will pricke forward the friends of
God, to take his quarrel in hand, and revenge him of his enemies. . . .
Passions well used, may consist with wisedome . . . and if they be
moderated, to be very serviceable to vertue.[20]

Wright refers to Augustine in several places, but it is also evident that
among vernacular writers he is one of the first English Neoplatonists. In his
book he mentions having traveled to Italy, and he probably came into touch
there with the Florentine school. His Neoplatonist belief in special affections
of the "highest and chiefest part of the soule, not unlike unto the passions of
the minde," appears to have led him to a positive view of the passions in general. The passions that the Scriptures ascribe to God, Wright notes, obviously
have no foundation in the sensitive appetite, that is, in the body and its senses.
And men, too, have loves and hates that are not reducible to "sensitive apprehension." These "reside in the will," differing "much in nature and quality
from those that inhabite the inferiour parts of the soule." The passions of the
will are "immaterial, spiritual, independent of any corporal subject" whereas
those of the sensitive appetite are "material, corporall," and dependent upon
some "bodily instruments."[21] The creature's love for God is the greatest of
these higher order passions, a love that Wright casts in the form of an ascent
from material allurement—such as the beauty of bodies founded on "apt proportion" and just "correspondence" of parts and colors—to a love that has no
material body for its object. It is clear that Wright, like the Catholic Eustache,
wished to encourage some degree of enthusiasm and zeal in religious faith
while yet keeping free of the dangerous carnal passions.

In a style remarkably like the third earl of Shaftesbury's a century later,
Wright addressed himself ecstatically to the loveliness of the Creator:

> For thy harmony, thy consort, thy proportion, springeth from the ad-
> mirable union of all thy perfections: all thy creatures produced and
> producible, in thee are united, the lamb and the lyon, fire and water,
> whiteness and blacknesse, pleasure and sadness, without strife or con-

---

20. Wright, *Passions of the Minde*, 17–18. Editions of this work appeared in 1601, 1604,
1621, and 1630. I am citing the 1630 edition. A copy of Wright is recorded in the Yale Library
catalog of 1743. The inventory of the library of the Rev. John Williams of Deerfield, Mass.,
made in 1729, includes a work entitled "Pashions of the Mind," which is almost certainly
Wright's book. (George Sheldon, *A History of Deerfield, Massachusetts* . . . , 2 vols. [Deerfield,
Mass., 1895–1896], I, 465.) "Passions of the Mynd" was also in William Brewster's library in
the 17th century. See Thomas Goddard Wright, *Literary Culture in New England, 1620–1730*
(New Haven, Conn., 1920), 257.

21. Wright, *Passions of the Minde*, 31–32.

tention, without hurt or injury, in a divine harmony and most amiable beauty, dwell, reside and live in thee.

The whole universall world framed in number, weight, and measure, al parts keeping their places, order, limits, proportion and natural harmony; all these in particular in themselves, and combined [into] one, are inaureled with a most gracious vagisnesse, lustre and beauty: all which proceeded from thee, and resideth in thee.[22]

The significance for us of this type of rhetoric is what it reveals of the belief that the pious and virtuous life required an emotional response to God, not just to His law, but to His beauty. The circle of love which runs from God to man and all of creation and then back again to God finds human expression in man's affective life as well as in the works of intellect. The Stoics wanted to eliminate the primary passions of joy, desire, fear, and sorrow from the wise man's experience, under the assumption that a condition of tranquility or constancy would set him in proper relation to transcendent nature. But to Christians of various hues such a condition was not only impossible, it was also undesirable.

Many scholars have pointed out that the Stoic theory of the passions was widely misunderstood by its opponents. The Stoics meant by "apathy" not feelinglessness but simply governance by reason. They rejected turbulent emotions, but not all affections. By a passion they had in mind something that was excessive by definition. There were also the *eupatheiai* (in Cicero's language, *constantiae*), or good affections, which were always consonant with right reason and nature. Moreover, the Stoic rejection of the distinction between psychological responses springing from the senses and psychological responses springing from intellectual judgment, and the consequent location of all of the passions in the intellectual faculty alone, was the product of a desire to see human nature in a more integral fashion than was typically offered by psychologists. Reason and passion were joined, with the proper division to be made between right reason and wrong. In true Stoic theory the passions do not contend with reason. They are themselves forms of rational misjudgment and misunderstanding regarding what is to be sought or shunned.

It is easy to see how Stoic psychology played a part in the intellectualism discussed in the previous chapter. Some Stoics avoided the problems presented by the faculty of will by eliminating it. A will was not needed to mediate between intellect and sensitive appetites, since there were no sensitive appetites per se. Instead, the Stoics attributed to intellect itself an appetitive function. An interpretation of the Medean paradox as a conflict of velleity and

22. *Ibid.*, 198–199.

volition, as we saw in Burgersdyck and Heereboord, was a form of Scholasticism deeply tinged with Stoic thinking. Similar Stoic-type views can be found in other writers who were at the same time opposed to Stoic "feelinglessness" and detachment. But whether or not the opponents of Neostoicism were fair and accurate is not at issue. Anti-Stoicism, however misguided, was a catalyst for renewed interest and thought about the role of the passions in ethics and religion.[23]

Piety and Emotion in Puritanism

The emotionalism of seventeenth-century Protestantism was no doubt continuous with earlier Catholic movements, such as the Brothers of the Common Life that produced Thomas à Kempis's *Imitation of Christ*, or the meditative tradition found in St. Bonaventure and represented in the sixteenth century by figures such as St. Ignatius of Loyola and St. Francis de Sales. "Meditation is an attentive thought iterated, or voluntarily intertained in the mynd, to excite the will to holy affections and resolutions," de Sales wrote, and he counseled his readers "never to restraine, or with-hold their affections once inflamed with any devout motion, but let them have their free course."[24] But one can also point to specific Protestant sources of emotionalism. The Calvinist doctrine of predestination, for example, brought acutely into consciousness the problem of personal assurance of grace. Ian Breward has argued that, whereas the supralapsarian theology of Girolamo Zanchius and Theodore Beza could defend and elaborate on predestination in Scholastic fashion, the poor sinner could not find in such abstract deductive reasoning any certainty concerning his own state. The belief in a covenant of grace could help one to know rationally that one was saved, but a deeper sense of security was required. Hence, one can detect in early Puritanism a reliance on heightened (although properly

---

23. On Stoic and Neostoic psychology, see Gardiner *et al.*, *Feeling and Emotion*, 64–70; Levi, *French Moralists, passim*; Sidgwick, *Outlines of Ethics*, 73. Plutarch's description of Stoic psychology is one of the best: "They think . . . that the emotional and unreasoning part of the soul is not by any natural difference distinct from the reasoning part, but that that same part of the soul, which they call intellect and the leading principle of action, being altogether diverted and changed by the passions, and by the alterations which habit or disposition have brought about, becomes either virtue or vice, without having in itself any unreasoning element, but that it is called unreasoning when, by the strong and overpowering force of appetite, it launches out into excesses contrary to the direction of reason. For passion, according to them, is only vicious and intemperate reason, getting its strength and power from bad and faulty judgment." *Plutarch's Morals*, ed. Shilleto, 99.

24. Louis L. Martz, *The Poetry of Meditation: A Study in English Religious Literature of the Seventeenth Century* (New Haven, Conn., 1954), 14, 46, quoted from de Sales's *Treatise on the Love of God*, translated into English in 1616.

restrained) feeling as one of the grounds of assurance along with other more outward manifestations of grace. William Perkins, among others, came to believe that, in Breward's words, the "working of the converted heart infallibly revealed the operation of God." Internal witnesses enable one to "leap beyond the doubts of reason," Perkins wrote, "to grasp the proffered hand of God reached out toward him." In general terms, Erich Kahler has claimed that "the release of human emotionality, the differentiation and intensification of sentiment" that arises in eighteenth-century England "sprang principally from the moral conflicts and self-examination of the Puritan soul."[25]

Among Continental Protestants, too, particularly German and Dutch pietists, there was a growing theology of the affections, which both influenced and was influenced by developments in seventeenth-century England. Ernst Stoeffler has called attention to such figures as Jean de Taffin (d. 1602) and William A. Saldenus (1627–1694). "For Taffin the main source of ultimate certainty was not a series of reasoned convictions gathered from the Word as it was to some of the Puritans. Nor was it a theologically based trust in a divine act of imputation of the righteousness of Christ to the sinner. It was founded upon the experience of 'holy affections and desires.' 'If we have these motions, these holy affections and desires,' Taffin wrote, 'let us not doubt, but that we have the Holy Ghost dwelling in us and consequently that we also have faith.'" Stoeffler points out that this form of piety was protected from subjectivism by the biblicism that accompanied it.[26]

Writing in the Netherlands several decades later, William Saldenus produced a major study of religious emotions, *The Very Sad State of a Christian, Consisting in the Deadness and Insensibility of His Heart Concerning Spiritual Things* (*De droevichste staet eens Christen . . .* , 1661), which Stoeffler believes was unequaled until the publication of Jonathan Edwards's study of religious affections nearly a hundred years later.[27]

Johann Arndt's famous work, *Vier Bücher vom wahren Christentum* (1606–1609), a foundation stone of German pietism, placed similar emphasis on inward change and on religious emotion, as opposed to formalism and superficiality. "The Knowledge of God does not consist in Words, or in bare speculative and superficial Science; but in a lively, amiable, pleasant, and sweet

25. Breward, ed., *Work of Perkins*, 94; Kahler, *Inward Turn*, trans. Winston and Winston, 131. In *A Graine of Musterd Seede . . .* (London, 1615), Perkins wrote: "If men endeavour to please God in all things, God will not judge their doings by the rigour of his law. . . . [But] this endeavour must be in and by the whole man; the very mind, will and affections doing that which they can in their kinds: and thus the endeavour to obey, which is the fruit of the Spirit, shall be distinguished from civil righteousness which may be in heathen men, and is only in the outward and not in the inward man." Breward, ed., *Work of Perkins*, 402.

26. Stoeffler, *Rise of Pietism*, 123–124.

27. *Ibid.*, 157–160.

Sensation, in a pure and untainted Pleasure, gently insinuating itself, by the Means of Faith, into the Heart, and penetrating the same with an inexpressible divine Sweetness." By "heart" Arndt meant the "whole Man, both as to Body and Soul," including understanding, will, affections, and memory. He united the will with love and stressed the necessity of submission to the will of God. "If thou wouldest have God to operate more eminently in thee, thou must surrender all the Passions, Affections, and Powers of thy Soul, to be possessed, governed, and directed by Him." In the end, not only "outward Works," but "our whole Religion," must be judged "by the *inward* Disposition and Principle that sways the Heart."[28]

We will concentrate here on English and American Puritanism, however, giving particular attention at first to the transformation in attitudes toward feeling that occurred within a religious context. We will then look at some parallel and, indeed, consequent developments in secular moral theory.

Possibly the most significant work on the passions that emerged from English Puritanism was William Fenner's little-known *A Treatise of the Affections; or, the Soules Pulse* . . . , first published in London in 1641 and subsequently in 1642, 1650, and 1657.[29] No other work in English so clearly points to the connection between Protestant, particularly Puritan, emotional sensibility and the sentimentalist school in eighteenth-century ethics. The book is in the form of a sequence of repetitious sermons, but the contents were the product of original thought and addressed the subject with extraordinary completeness.

In Fenner the unity of will and higher passion is already accomplished. The passions or affections are only "the motions of the will, by which it goes forth" to the embracing of its object as good or the avoidance of it as evil.[30] "I know," Fenner wrote, that "*Aristotle* and most of our Divines, too, doe

28. *Of True Christianity. Four Books Now Done into English*, trans. Anthony William Boehm, 2d ed. rev. (London, 1720), I, 79, 333, II, 378–380, I, 411–412. This English translation was first published in 1712. Earlier English translations are not complete.

29. This important book was not noticed by either William Haller or Perry Miller. My attention was first called to it by Norman S. Grabo's article, "Puritan Devotion," in Browne and Pizer, eds., *American Literature*, 6–23. Fenner's *Works*, including the *Treatise of the Affections*, were published in 1651, 1657, and 1658. Increase Mather owned a copy of Fenner's "Workes" in 1664, and Samuel Willard referred to Fenner in his commonplace book. See Tuttle, "Libraries of the Mathers," Am. Antiq. Soc., *Procs.*, N.S., XX (1909–1910), 280, and Evans, "Literary References," 148. In 1718 Elihu Yale sent to the Yale Library a copy of Thomas Wright's *Passions of the Minde*, William Fenner's *A Treatise of the Affections*, and Jean Senault's *The Use of the Passions*. See Donald G. Wing and Margaret L. Johnson, "The Books Given by Elihu Yale in 1718," in *Yale University Library Gazette*, XIII (1938–1939), 46–67. This gift probably is the source of the volume by Wright that is listed in the printed catalog of 1743.

30. *Treatise of the Affections*, "To the Reader." Quotations are all from the London 1642 edition. Subsequent citation of pages will be in parentheses in the text.

place the affections in the sensitive part of the Soule, and not in the will." But this cannot be so, for a man's affections stir most at "a shame or disgrace; which could not bee, if the affections were in the unreasonable sensitive part: the unreasonable sensitive part of a man is not sensible of credit or esteeme." The affections therefore must be in the heart or the will, which is where they are placed in Scripture. "How could the Apostle command us to set our affections on God, and the things that are above, if the affections were in the sensitive and unreasonable part? Can a man make his materiall stomacke to hunger after God?" Furthermore, how could such religious affections be in bodiless angels? (5)

It is true, Fenner acknowledged, that there are something like affections in beasts and in men that do have their foundation in the sensitive appetite. But these are "analogicall affections" only. Grief in torment, fear of a serpent, delight in pleasant food, and so on, are real. "But the Lord doth not call for these sensitive passions to be seated upon him and on heaven. . . . *The affections of the heart*, these are the affections the Lord doth call for" (6).

Fenner introduced a second distinction among the affections when he asserted that "a carnall man" is unable to set his affections upon God or upon grace (9). For the affections are the wings of the soul, and if they are glued to the ground they cannot fly up. Carnal men are "borne downe with their sinnes, their affections are clog'd, security, deadnesse of heart, selfe-love of things here below, [are] like millstones made fast to their heels" (10). There are then in Fenner's analysis three fundamental classes of affections: in order of ascendancy, animal or analogical affections, carnal affections tied to this world, and regenerate affections inclined toward God. The animal affections are universal but unimportant in the scheme of things, and they are not part of the will. The last two are in the hands of God. The affections are "the bent and inclinations of thy heart," and if a person is inclined to "things that are earthy," he is stuck that way, for "nothing can go against its owne bent and inclination, unlesse by the omnipotent power of the spirit of Christ" (12).

Such an organization of man's affective life is already partly familiar to us, for it was implicit in William Ames's writings, not to speak of Augustine, but it may never before have been spelled out in the detail that Fenner brought to it.[31] Fenner's exclusion of reason or rationality as the criterion of religious virtue and piety inevitably had implications for philosophy. The goodness of a man is not, as in Lipsius, for example, a matter of the degree to which he is influenced by rational judgments rather than opinions (that is, passions). The

31. However, it is a measure of the strength and influence of the Augustinian revival of the 17th century that in the very same year in which Fenner's *Treatise of the Affections* first appeared, Cornelius Jansen published his famous *Augustinus*, which presented some psychological theories very similar to Fenner's. See Abercrombie, *Origins of Jansenism*, 148–149, and Levi, *French Moralists*, 310–311.

higher passions or affections enter into goodness as much as into wickedness, and what matters is not their subordination to a rational norm but their basic orientation in relation to God. The will, as an intrinsically rational appetite functioning as the mistress of the passions and therefore at the center of the moral life, is in this model of the soul rendered superfluous and obsolete. Rational guidance is not what is needed. Only the renewed heart, with its godly love, is required. If the term "will" is still used, it no longer means anything like rational appetite but is simply another term for heart or love and is not strictly an intellectual faculty at all. In the Peripatetic and the Thomist systems the passions were morally indifferent because the good or evil of an act depended not upon the impulse of passion but upon the consent of the will to the impulse. For Fenner the will as rational appetite is no longer the hinge of the moral life. Everything of moral concern hinges upon grace or the spirit— that divine grace that infuses the will (or the heart), with the will understood not as rational appetite but as the seat of the passions. The later secularized version of this moral psychology did not, of course, continue to put divine grace at the center of activity. But neither could it revert back to "reason" as the moral norm. Instead, for the sentimentalist something called "nature" became the new criterion.

It is important to notice that Fenner did not employ the same Neoplatonist gradation of the passions (primarily of the passion of love) that Thomas Wright had presented. Fenner did not directly relate animal or analogical affections to the higher states of passion as he might have done through the concept of sublimation, for example. In fact, Fenner's quick dismissal of animal affections, which in his thinking resembled the Stoic's undesirable "perturbations," may have had something to do with Neostoic influence. As Anthony Levi has pointed out, certain principles of Neostoic psychology infected almost all thought about the passions until after Descartes. In addition, latent dualist tendencies from other than Stoic sources, always present in Christianity, contributed to an exaggerated division between animal affections and higher passions. Yet the Christian inheritance was not unambiguously dualist. The distinction in Augustinianism between the carnal and the regenerate soul was not meant to be the same as the distinction between body and soul, for the Augustinians proposed to describe and classify the condition of the whole man, from top to bottom, soul and body, on the basis of his affective orientation, or his spiritual state. The doctrine of conversion did not refer to some departure of the higher from the lower, soul from body, reason from passion, but to a revolution of the whole. This was an integrated and a dynamic human psychology, some of the principles of which were not utilized in secular thought until the twentieth century.

If Fenner refused to unify analogical (animal) passions and the passions of the heart, he did offer, nonetheless, an elaborate series of gradations between the extremes of carnal affections and the affections of the regenerate soul. Between these poles he found, in all, nine degrees of God's acting on the affections. The first five of them can occur in a carnal man; the last four are beyond the carnal man's experience and are wrought only on the regenerate. Fenner's aim in his analysis of the carnal man's five degrees of affection was partly to show just how far an unregenerate person may be overcome with religious emotion and still remain ungodly. He was concerned, in other words, with the problem of counterfeit religion or hypocrisy, the major theme in Puritan psychology for two hundred years. At the pinnacle of the carnal man's experience "the heart may be stolen away" with affection, "grace is . . . beautifull, and the Word of God hath . . . kinde promises and kinde speeches with it. . . . The affections may be wrought on so farre, that the heart may be hot and inflamed with them. . . . A carnall man may have his affections heated and inflamed towards God and towards grace" (19–20). But for all that he will still be wicked in the eyes of God.

It is significant that Fenner recognized the importance of the affections for the moral life as well as for the holy life. The carnal man has still glowing in his heart, for example, the natural "embers of right reason" with which to "regulate his affections to be chaste, and sober, and kinde, and liberal, and just, and morally humble." In this sense, according to Fenner, the "very Heathen themselves guided their affections with Religion" (25). In support of this point he cited Paul's reference to "naturall affection" as a moral quality available to all.[32] But, of course, for Fenner, no natural affections were saving and in the absence of special grace one remained a "carnallist."

The revolutionary anti-Aristotelian moral psychology latent in the Puritan theory of conversion may be illustrated from Fenner's work. Rather than holding up training or habit as the basis of virtue and piety, a concept that makes one's developed character a kind of ineluctable fate dependent upon environment and circumstances, the theory of spiritual conversion stressed the mutability of the affections, a concept of human nature that allows for the occurrence of radical personality change and salvation for anyone at any time. "Be a man never so crosse and crooked, never so cruelly and implacably bent to transgresse, yet as long as there are affections in him to be wrought, his heart may be wonne," Fenner wrote. In other words, without affections, no one would be susceptible to persuasion. The mutability of the affections, Fenner observed in a memorable phrase, can be "a blessed weaknesse" when a man is evil and wicked. For as long as a man has "any naturall affection left, hee is never implacable" (48–49). In direct contradiction to the prevail-

32. The Greek term for "natural affection," *storgé*, and particularly the term for its absence, *astorgos*, were frequently used in the 18th century to describe affections within the family. The idea was expanded to serve as proof of man's natural moral capacity.

ing pagan ethical theory, the very inconstancy and variability of the feelings are treated as a blessing, for this "weaknesse" assures that one is humanly reachable. Emotional sensibility rather than intellectual purity or correctness is the precondition of salvation, as in later sentimentalist moral theory it would be the precondition of virtue.

Fenner also spoke of a degeneration into what he called "unnatural" affection, which may truly make one unredeemable (48–49). Here, too, he anticipated an important element in eighteenth-century secular theory, which made "unnatural affections" an excuse for the persistence of moral evil in a benevolent world. In fact, in the eighteenth century some of the dynamism of Fenner's psychology was already lost, in that human nature became in theory more fixed, and among secular moral philosophers after Shaftesbury, conversion was hardly discussed. The so-called "balance" of the passions was at the center of discussion by mid-century. The emphasis on the affections was retained, but not, to the same degree, the psychology of personal change, of crises of personal integration that form the basis for morally higher levels of human existence.

Fenner argued forcefully against allowing the sinful use of affections, the corruption and perversion of them, to reflect negatively upon the nature of the affections in themselves. That Adam and Eve had affections in their condition of innocence is proof that they are natural in us without sin (63). There may be some natural affections

> that be sinfull in themselves, as envy and malice, and the like; which can never be regulated or guided by any moderation, but are quite to be rooted out: but these affections are not properly naturall, they are no other otherwise naturall then Lice and Vermine are naturall to Carrion, then filthy and noysome weeds are naturall to a cursed ground; these must be utterly rooted up and stubb'd out of our hearts, because to speak properly they are unnatural affections and sinfull in themselves, but our naturall affections are not sinfull in themselves. Nay more . . . , the affections are not onely not sinfull, but it is an infinite blessing of God, that God hath given us affections. . . . If we had not affections at all, we should be like stocks, and like senselesse stones (66).[33]

33. A play upon the words "stoic" and "stock" was fairly common by the 17th century. See, e.g., Shakespeare's The Taming of the Shrew, I, i, 17–41: Lucentio announces his intention to study "Virtue, and that part of philosophy / Will I apply, that treats of happiness / By virtue specially to be achieved." Tranio replies: "I am in all affected as yourself; / Glad that you thus continue your resolve / To suck the sweets of sweet philosophy. / Only, good master, while we do admire / This virtue and this moral discipline, / Let's be no stoics nor no stocks, I pray; / Or so devote to Aristotle's ethics, / As Ovid to be an outcast quite abjured: / . . . No profit grows, where is no pleasure ta'en: / In brief, sir, study what you most affect."

And Fenner also employed a commonplace image found dozens of times later, which sees the passions "as the wind to the sailes of a ship," without which a man would be immobilized (66–67).[34]

Fenner's treatise, in sum, was a storehouse of images and ideas that would achieve much greater currency in the eighteenth century. One wonders how many ministers, both Anglican and Puritan, must have borrowed from it. He called the affections the "sympathies" and "antipathies" of the soul, thus bringing together the physical principle of "sympathy," as an occult quality of some forms of matter (such as magnets), with psychological notions. This comparison was a step toward seeing in human nature laws of order that were like the laws in the physical world, a step essential to the confidence of the great moral philosophy enterprise of the eighteenth century.[35] The moral possibilities of "sympathy" were to be fully exploited in the eighteenth century. Fenner also had a preliminary concept of reason-in-the-heart that approached Pascal's contemporaneous idea (84). He thoroughly depreciated "understanding" as a factor in the religious life and warned ministers against preaching to it, and he held, as would Jonathan Edwards in the next century, that the affections are "the maine matter of grace . . . the material of grace" (51). "Grace runnes along in the affections," Fenner said, "as water in the pipe" (53–54). In sentimentalist moral psychology it was virtue that was believed to

34. This simile may have first been used by Plutarch. Alexander Pope's lines in the *Essay on Man* are undoubtedly the most famous modern instance: "On life's vast ocean diversely we sail, / Reason the card, but Passion is the gale" (II, ll. 107–108). See also, *Spectator* no. 224, Nov. 16, 1711 (in Donald Bond, ed., *The Spectator*, II [Oxford, 1965], 373, plus Bond's notes on the subject), sometimes attributed to Pope. Earlier, in Fontenelle's "Hérostrate et Démetrius": "It is the passions that do and undo everything. If reason were dominant on earth, nothing would happen. . . . Passions in men are winds which are necessary to put everything in motion, although they often cause storms." Quoted by Lester G. Crocker, *An Age of Crisis: Man and World in Eighteenth Century French Thought* (Baltimore, 1959), 220. On p. 231 Crocker expresses the opinion that this was the single most frequently employed metaphor to describe the passions. See below, pp. 176–177, 185.

35. Sympathies and antipathies were commonly discussed in physics texts in the 17th century. It should be noted that both the terms "passion" and "affection" had wider meanings, through their Latin origins, that were gradually being lost in 17th-century English. An affection could be the property, quality, or attribute of anything, and human affections, in the sense of emotions, were modifications of the soul or properties of it at certain moments. Modern translators from the Latin sometimes confuse the general concept of an affection with the specific concept of human emotion. For example, Morison, *Seventeenth-Century Harvard*, 262, mistranslates a thesis from the commencement of 1647, *Cardinales quas vocant virtutes, virtutis affectiones sunt, non species*. A passion, too, still had the general meaning of passive reception as opposed to active agency. The word passion aptly described the passivity of a soul as it undergoes an emotion. But as was often pointed out in the 17th century and before, all sense impressions, seeing, hearing, etc., were also passions in this general meaning, as were all external effects insofar as a thing or person passively received the effect. This very unity of terms contributed to the making of a "science" of psychology that paralleled a science of matter.

run along in the affections as water in the pipe. All in all, Fenner's book was a remarkable performance for 1640.

The Study of the Passions in New England

Because a theory of the passions was not an integral part of Aristotelian ethics, and because the passions only gradually became the focus of discussion in moral philosophy in the course of the seventeenth century, the surviving manuscripts from Harvard do not include a large literature on the subject. Most student notebooks from the period have relatively little discussion of the passions. The first commencement thesis to state anything significant about them does not appear until 1689, probably under the influence of Henry More: "The passions of the soul are in themselves naturally good."[36] Generally, a crippling division persisted, wherein the nature of the passions, their number, origin, types, and so on was studied in the context of physics and physiology while their moral status and the problem of governing them were studied in the context of ethics. Descartes took the lead in attempting to treat the subject more comprehensively, but the texts at Harvard did not catch up with him immediately. We will examine only a few examples of the discussion in seventeenth-century Massachusetts of the role of the passions in the moral and religious life.

Among Fenner's American readers can be numbered Jonathan Mitchell, minister at the Cambridge church and the subject of a chapter in Cotton Mather's *Magnalia*.[37] A sermon Mitchell preached before Harvard students in 1664 on Galatians 5:24 seems to follow Fenner closely, though as was typical in sermons of the time there is no explicit acknowledgment of sources.[38] We should labor to rectify and sanctify our affections, Mitchell told his audience. Our affections should be "taken off from sinfull objects, moderated toward earthly [objects], and set principally [toward] heavenly [objects]." The affections "are excellent and glorious things being kept right, but pernicious if abused." We have some ken of God by the understanding but "we possess him by the will and affections." Grace itself "hangs much" on the affections. "So many affections sanctified so many graces." When Mitchell described the affections as "the handles of the soul, on which God takes hold when he would work on us for good," he was virtually quoting Fenner. And

36. *Passiones animae sunt sua natura bonae.*

37. Mather, *Magnalia*, II, 54–96.

38. Solomon Stoddard took brief notes on this sermon in his notebook of sermon abstracts of 1664, a manuscript at Union Theological Seminary in New York City. For some description of this notebook, see Fiering, "Stoddard's Library at Harvard," *Harvard Lib. Bul.*, XX (1972), 255–269.

so also in the statement, "The affections are the hands and feet of the soul whereby it comes to God and takes hold on him." Mitchell also touched on the relationship between an ethics of intention and the affections. Good affections, he stated, "are many times accepted of God for good actions" because actions proceed from the affections "as the stream from the fountain." In conclusion, "affections oil the wheels of a christian."

Only one surviving student notebook contains an extensive array of thoughts about the passions and affections. Indeed, this notebook, kept by John Holyoke in 1662–1663, includes comments and analyses more sophisticated than one would ordinarily expect to encounter in college teaching in mid-seventeenth-century New England.[39]

Holyoke was especially interested in hope and fear as the mainsprings of action, a sort of hedonic approach to motivation resembling somewhat the Hobbesian emphasis on desire and aversion. He took seriously and literally the religious commandment to fear the Lord, and he made fear the basis of conscience. "Upon Knowledge and due considerat[ion] of the prevalence of this passio[n] of feare towards the Guiding [of] Man . . . it seemed good in the eye of divine wisdom to ranke his service, and al our returnes of duty and obedience, as under that Motio[n]." It is curious that Holyoke, or his unidentified authority on this matter, did not speak of God first implanting the emotion of fear in man in order to bring about His divine ends, but rather of God observing the prevalence of fear in human motivation and thereafter making use of it. Holyoke believed that God not only expresses his commendation of those who have been "dutyfull and obedient unto him" in terms of their having "feared" Him, but also that for the increase of such duty and obedience He is "wont to promise a new increase and implantat[ion] of feare into the hartes of those partyes and people fro[m] whom he expects it, as being the only steady grace that is effectual herein[.] Hope and feare are the two maynspring passio[n]s of the soule." Fear is the only steady grace; that is, it is the most reliable and fundamental passion that God can employ for His purposes.

Holyoke further explained the meaning of fear in a discussion of conscience:

> In Reference to the essential support and relat[ion] which feare Carrieth towards the establishment of subject[ion] and Obedience, we may call Obedience . . . [the] deportment of the inferiour, according to the Com[m]and of the Superiour, through the sense of duty and feare: For as sense of duty or Conscience must keep up obedience, soe sense of fear must keep up Conscience[;] by which definition we may know how to distinguish between that obedience and subject[ion] the other Crea-

39. John Holyoke was the uncle of Edward Holyoke, president of Harvard between 1737 and 1769. The manuscript is in the Houghton Lib., Harvard Univ.

tures give, who obey out of feare onely, and not out of sense of duty, as wanting understanding to apprehend it.

Holyoke's meaning here seems to have been that the original passion behind all obedience is fear; but in man, as distinguished from "other Creatures," the fear is transmuted into conscience or a sense of duty, perhaps because man alone can anticipate the future. Holyoke did not explain the exact psychological process, but his next comment adds a little clarity. From what has already been said, he continued, we may also perceive that since it is the sense of duty that "must bring on a submission of wil, therefore hope can be very seldome and Love never made the proper Cause of obedience." Hope of benefit or hope of advantage from a command is the "proper end and motive" by which a superior or commander is led. "It must therefore follow, that hope of benefit cannot be also directly assigned as an end to him that obeyes." The inferior who obeys does not see the end and does not necessarily know the benefit to him, if any, of obedience. In consequence, he must obey out of duty and fear alone, not interest or hope of advantage. "The two great Motives to obedience," according to Holyoke's notes, "are a sense of benefit and Interest, and sense of Conscience and duty." For want of "true Knowledge and experience" of these two basic motives, "Kingdoms . . . come to be troubled with mutynys and insurrect[ions]."

Holyoke's hope and fear are comparable in effect to reward and punishment, or rather, hope and fear may be described as emotional responses in the present to the future possibilities of reward and punishment: one has hope of reward in the future and fear of punishment in the future. The "Com[m]anding passio[n]s of hope and feare" are the forces by which, through "meanes of rewards and punishment," all the other passions are kept in line. A sense of honor and a sense of shame are sublimated versions of the same distinction as it exists in any present moment of moral decision. Conscience refers properly to that which is to come hereafter, whereas shame and punishment "regards the sentence and judgm[en]t of them as have present powers." Conscience refers to "the com[m]ands and power of those . . . that judge for the future," and one sort of good conscience, Holyoke noted, may simply be want of memory, namely, the want of memory of what divine expectations are.

For the strengthening of good conduct in adulthood, Holyoke continued, childhood training in obedience is most important. "Swathings of precepts and discipline help greatly to a streightness of mind, whereby we have the irregularitys and rebellions of nature rectifyed by parental Laws and Rules. According as we are habituated to duty and submission in our Oeconomical [i.e., domestic] relat[ions], so proportionably we act in our political relat[ions]." In short, training at home makes obedient citizens.

Holyoke had a rudimentary concept of psychological association, which probably came to him from a Cartesian source, and this theory formed the basis of his idea of emotional habituation, or conditioning. Affections arise, he wrote, not from present objects alone but from their relation to our "Collect[ions] and memory" of their former effect upon us, "which is not grounded on one but many observat[ions], except that one [may] be equidistant [equivalent?] to many in strength." Those collections that arise from "real figurate and perceptible (bodys) objects" are properly called "science" and are "thereupon gathered into notio[n]s, and thence into affect[ions]." But many affections have not so solid a basis in real experience with objects. "Discourse and argum[en]ts upon subjects not figurable [i.e., not visually conceivable], produce nothing but mazes and intoxicat[ions], as . . . in some metaphisical notions and specula[tions]." Moreover, the frequent repetition of anything to us "under the classis of hope or feare, prevailes towardes the beliefe of what is thereupon offered and presented, in as hygh [a] manner, as if it had beene presented impressed by a fygurate object of its owne." In other words, certain concepts that have no visible referents—heaven and hell might be good examples—when frequently presented in association with the emotions of hope and fear, may strike one as forcefully, or more forcefully, than a loved or feared concrete object, let us say, for example, a snake. In fact, Holyoke argued, because a merely imagined object cannot be contradicted by any "sensible," that is, sensory, example of its converse, such notions will affect us even more enduringly and convincingly than something that we can see.

Holyoke evidently acquired from somewhere the greatest respect for the power of the passions to shape thoughts.[40] In another section of the notebook he entered into a comparison of logic and rhetoric. Much of this type of comparison was quite conventional and has recently been well described by Wilbur Samuel Howell.[41] Holyoke's conclusions in favor of rhetoric, however, were not so conventional. The blows of logic may strongly affect the hearer, Holyoke noted, yet the repeated strokes of rhetoric on the passions and affections may "rayse an impression or swelling" equal to them. Thus, he said, repeated light strokes upon the forehead with an egg or the like will eventually create as great a swelling as a much greater blow with a stronger object that raises a great contusion. "A syllogisme can give but one blow," the effect of which will decline in time. Wise men may, on the basis of observation, contradict it, and fools for want of observation not apprehend it. "Whereas relying and grounding upon the strength of affect[ions] already made, a discreet pressure can never fayl of receipt and increase." The skilled rhetorician can through the affections play upon the prejudices, or the built up emotional associations, of his audience.

40. That Holyoke used the vernacular for most of his discussion is also remarkable and suggests that he was reading English rather than Latin sources in this area.
41. Howell, *Logic and Rhetoric in England, 1500–1700* (Princeton, N.J., 1956).

Logicke must cleare its way to.the wit by the understanding, and must appeal to the Indicative mood before it can make use of the Imperative; whereas those thinges that enter as Retoricall impressions, by that insinuat[ion] and mixture with those affect[ions] and passions that already rule and Com[m]and us, cannot fayle of a Constant power to governe and guide us alsoe: and thereupon they, depending not soe wholly on sense but being usually above its controule, are not in like danger of a defeat by a negative fro[m] [the]nce. For Logicke must ascertain us by the rule of all or none, whereas the other [i.e., rhetoric] needs but Looke like truth, and, by joyning with that which hath beene soe fully assented unto already, standes always [*illegible word*] proved, where it is not totally contradicted.

At this point the theory of persuasion and the comparison of the functions of logic and rhetoric clearly connect with Puritan religious concern about effective preaching. From a different starting point Holyoke arrived at a position identical to that held by Fenner, Ames, and numerous other Puritan ministers who stressed the necessity of getting to the heart of the listener: "Nice . . . speculat[ions] cannot with all fine subtiltys of accurate delivery, be reasonably presumed halfe so efficacious for Convict[ion]" as "more familiar insinuat[ions] . . . made suitable to the affect[ions] of the present auditory."[42]

The importance of moving the affections through the use of rhetoric had been emphasized by Francis Bacon a generation earlier.[43] Bacon drew upon an aspect of the Platonic tradition (also occasionally stressed by Cicero) that the Stoics had ignored. "Virtue," Plato wrote, "if she could be seen would move great love and affection."[44] But since the beauty of virtue cannot be shown corporeally, Bacon said, the next best thing "is to show her to the imagination in lively representation: for to show her to reason only in subtilty of argument, was a thing ever derided in . . . many of the stoics; who thought to thrust virtue upon men by sharp disputations and conclusions, which have no sympathy with the will of man." If the affections were truly pliant and obedient to reason, Bacon continued, there would be no need for the use of "persuasions and insinuations to the will, more than of naked propositions and proofs." But, unfortunately, " '*Video meliore, proboque; Deteriora sequor.*' " Therefore, eloquence must bring about a confederation between the reason and the imagination against the whims of the affections, lest the affections

42. For the Puritan position, see, e.g., Haller, *Rise of Puritanism*, 26, 30, 45, 93.

43. Bacon was a relatively popular author in 17th-century New England.

44. The statement is in the *Phaedrus*, trans. [and ed.] Hackforth, 250. Plato's influence was exerted both on those who thought in terms of sublimating the passions and on those who wanted only to suppress them.

rule without guidance. Bacon believed that the affections, like the reason, inherently moved toward the apparent good: "The difference is, that the affection beholdeth merely the present; reason beholdeth the future and sum of time. And therefore the present filling the imagination more, reason is commonly vanquished; but after that force of eloquence and persuasion hath made things future and remote appear as present," then reason can prevail.[45]

On the recurring issue mentioned earlier of whether or not the appetite for knowledge must precede its acquisition, Holyoke sided with those who favored appetite.[46] "I must have sense of want before I can have Instigat[ion] to attaine the meanes of Content. . . . The more sense of want the more enquiry and the more enquiry the more wisdome. . . . Wisdome is generally found of such as seeke her. Soe in Every particular, men are more or less knowing and wise, as their desire to the thinge hath made their diligence and attent[ion] to Exceede." The Stoic wise man or sage was one who had eliminated affections or passions from his judgment. For Holyoke, one could not even begin to be wise without the impetus of the passions. "The wisest men," Holyoke wrote, "(altho it be a part of wisdome to conceale them) have the most and [the] most eager affect[ions] [and] passions, which may be easyly proved by their breaking out [under?] pressure or sudden occasions, [where]in discret[ion] cant or is not warned of concealing of them."

On this matter of the relation between desire and knowledge, Holyoke introduced some qualifications, too, with the express citation of the Ovidian tag *ignoti nulla cupido* (ignorance knows no desire), and with the comment that "observations and knowledge of thinges doe grow into affect[ions] and appetites." "He that is Content and cant give a reason of his content is a foole and the more content the more folly." The discovery of anything in the world is made first "in the braines bec[ause] in there as in the first sentient the figures of things are first impressed and a discriminat[ion] made by comparison, before any of the more inward partes can be Consentient and stand affected therewith." But if it should be asked

> fro[m] whence the . . . ajudicat[ion] and determinat[ion] towardes action doth proceed, which is in us the guide of all our essays, it must be answered, fro[m] the hart and affect[ions]; for fro[m] those the braine is instigated to rayse figures and to continue and pursue them as they shal be judged to be of Concern. . . . For the braine may be sayd to regard and apprehend objectes, as they are in [themselves] separate and absolute, but the hart as they are modall and respective to ourselves; it is a different knowledge to know a man as a man, and as he is a friend an enemy or the like.

45. Bacon, *Advancement of Learning*, ed. Kitchin, 147.
46. On this issue, see also pp. 132, 143–144, above.

In sum, the brain is "the seat of the understanding and discourse, and the hart of the will: we may place natural philosophy in the one and Morall in the other, bec[ause] this [moral philosophy] points to Good, that [natural philosophy] to truth." It was not uncommon in Holyoke's day to locate moral philosophy with the will and logic with the intellect. But to center moral philosophy, not just piety, in the *heart*, and make it a matter of affections, was unusual in 1663. On the other hand, Holyoke noted that with respect to the "contemplative Part" of moral philosophy "the braine is the seat of morall knowledge . . . bec[ause] when any[one] is to deliver anyth[ing] on that subject the methode by which he proceeds is first conceived in his owne braine."

The heart, Holyoke wrote, is the source of all knowledge that points to action. For the desire to know is either for honor's sake or for other benefits, but in any case for some "selfe end," and these ends begin with "some affec-[tion] of the hart." All action springs from the affections of the heart, self-love being one of the most prominent such affections. God's wisdom in so creating man as a creature of affections as well as of reason was easily defended by Holyoke. "The assignement of wisdome and knowledge to the hart may very well be good. When God Cal[ls] for and claimes mens harts to be exercised in his worship and service and when Solomon prayes for an understanding hart to Know Good and Evil[,] noe doubt both of them very well know when[ce] our actions and Endeavours tooke their source and original; that is fro[m] the affect[ions]." For God's chief aim for men is that they practice "moral observances" toward one another and carry themselves "in a right and steady Course of subject[ion] towards God," not that they engage in "Phylosophical speculation." Had Solomon had sufficient fear of offending God, a fear that would have acted as a "Counterpoise" in his personal judgment, calling him to a "deliberate examinat[ion] before execut[ion]," he would then have been as happy and celebrated for the wise guidance of himself and for giving "a right sentence betweene his passions and affections" as he was for the famous sentence he gave the harlots.

The concept of counterpoised affections referred to in the case of Solomon brings up a final point to be stressed concerning Holyoke's notes on the passions. Holyoke believed that all actions proceed from the passions, as we have already observed. That this is not more evident, he maintained, is because of the counterpoise of the passions in the soul, which leads to intellectual deliberation before the release of one side or the other. In line with this theory of action, Holyoke distinguished between affections and passions. Affections are more "inward," passions more "outward." Thus, one's affections are revealed by one's passions, just as passions become known by "actions." The "affections" of the soul, then, are like fundamental dispositions or inclinations. Actions that appear to take place without passion differ from passionate actions "but in measure, for al proceed fro[m] affect[ions]." Those seemingly without passion "proceed fro[m] affect[ions] counterpoised by compariso[n] of one another, which we cal discourse and Reason," while passionate actions spring from "our violent affect[ions] alone." Finally, if our diffused observations of particulars in the world did not collect themselves into affections, "it would not be possible to have any promptness towardes p[ur]suit and desire." This statement is very much like Descartes's belief that the passions, by serving as vehicles of spontaneous action in many critical situations, endow rational and deliberative man with an enhanced capacity to survive in the natural order. We should note, too, that the concept of counterpoise foreshadowed the prevalent eighteenth-century idea of a balance of the passions as a moral ideal.

There is nothing in John Holyoke's post-collegiate career that reveals intellectual distinction. He died unmarried in 1712 after having served in most of the important local political offices in Springfield, Massachusetts. His library was valued at £10 upon his death, and he seems never to have published a word.[47] Yet his student notebook is distinguished. It would be of exceptional interest to know what he was reading in the early 1660s that helped to shape his thought.

In 1660 in London, under the auspices of Jonathan Mitchell in America, who did the editing, and a leading group of English Puritan divines, Thomas Shepard's *The Parable of the Ten Virgins* was posthumously published.[48] Shepard's ultimate goal in preaching this series of brilliant sermons in Massachusetts in the late 1630s, like Fenner's, was to establish the criteria for distinguishing between true Christians and mere hypocrites (the wise from the foolish virgins). Necessarily he devoted much space to the nature of holy affections and related matters. Whereas today hypocrisy connotes deliberate deception of others for private ends, in the seventeenth-century meaning the hypocrite might be as unknown to himself as he was to others. Like a counterfeit coin without consciousness of its admixture of base metal, hypocrisy was more an accidental quality of the soul than an intentional deception. In Shepard's work we once again encounter the major Puritan concern with finding the means of testing or proving the authenticity of souls. The *Parable*

47. Sibley, *Harvard Graduates*, II, 102–103, devotes less than a page to Holyoke. The value of his library is mentioned by Evans, "Literary References," 67. Thomas Weld's library, which contained 170 volumes in 1702, was priced at £12. Robinson and Robinson, "Three Massachusetts Libraries," Col. Soc. Mass., *Trans.*, XXVIII (1935), 156–175.

48. The subtitle reads: "Being the substance of divers sermons . . . now published from the authors own notes . . . by Jonathan Mitchell and Thomas Shepard, Jr." (London, 1660). Thomas Shepard, Jr., was the author's son. These sermons were originally delivered between June 1636 and May 1640 in Massachusetts Bay.

of the Virgins will serve as a final example of American Puritan treatment of the passions.

Shepard drew a principal distinction between external "affectionate expressions" and the "inward bent" or "byas" of the whole soul. (His terminology clashes with Holyoke's.) Expressions of feeling can be misleading about the "bent" of the soul—also properly called heart or will—which is by definition an enduring state, as opposed to the variableness of feeling. Of course, the affections often do accurately reveal the true inward disposition, but not always. It is also often difficult to know whether saving grace is in the soul "when acts are not seen or felt. . . . 'Tis in this case, as 'tis in sin. Though the act of sin ceaseth, yet there is a bent of heart still toward it; and a carnal heart will return to his old Byas and bent again." Similarly, though the "act of Grace" may momentarily cease, "yet there is an inner man, a gracious bent and frame put upon the will, that though for a time it ceaseth acting, yet it will return to its old bent again, to its own nature, which is called the seed of God."[49]

New England theology emphasized that saints are distinguished by their having a "new inward principle," which is lasting, in contrast to "immediate actings of the spirit," which occur on occasion only. Shepard regarded the denial of the doctrine that saints have graces "peculiar unto them" a "delusion digged and hatcht out of the steam of the lowest sink in Hell." "It transcends my capacity," he wrote, "from whatever I have read, or have heard, or have felt, or can imagine, how the power of sin can be taken away, but where the spirit infuseth the contrary grace" (Pt. i, 177). Behind this defense, clearly, was the Augustinian notion of the two contrary and exclusive wills or inclinations, which determine one's fate with God. "Before the Lord justifies the soul, every man living seeks himself as his last end and good. . . . After it, the Lord sanctifies the soul with such a measure of his Grace as makes the Lord his utmost end. . . . As there is abundance of self-love, that men are eaten up with it; so there must be much love, which must be abundantly shed in the heart, so as to eat up that" (Pt. i, 215–216). Rather than assigning the task of keeping concupiscence under control to the rational faculty, it is necessary to set passion against passion. No principle is more characteristic of the Judaeo-Christian heritage in moral philosophy as compared to the Classical. It is a rule in nature, Shepard said, that "a man's affections like streams must run some way." And it is a rule in theology, "stop the affections from running to the Creature, and in a sincere heart [they] will run unto Christ" (Pt. i, 56).

Yet the problem remained of being able to distinguish clearly and confidently between transient feelings and lasting inclinations. Shepard could write, " 'Tis nothing else but love the Lord looks for, or cares for. Love [from

49. Pt. i, 144. Subsequent page references will appear in the text in parentheses.

God] looks for nothing but love, *Prov.* 8.17. and this is the end of all Election, to be holy before him in love. . . . He desires only love, only the heart. . . . After all, is this all? Yes, no Portion he cares for, and when he hath this he hath all" (Pt. i , 25). But the same word "love" could be used to describe a range of emotions, some more, some less enduring. Shepard did not doubt that the basis of the religious life lay in the heart; nonetheless, the task before him was so to define the gracious heart that it would be as stabilized in theory as he believed it was in actuality. "Many that have had mighty strong affections at first conversion, afterwards become dry, and wither, . . . and die away. . . . You shall have some ignorant creatures awakened by some thundering ministry, weep and mourn for sin, and after vanish into smoak. . . . Many are affected with Christ, and with joy of the Gospel . . . , but they wanting depth . . . of conviction, die away again. . . . There may be greatest hypocrisie under greatest affections" (Pt. i, 149–150).

The solution was to retain as part of the concept of "the heart"—that is, the "new inward frame," the "new principle of the will"—an intellectual component, yet not a component so defined that it could be confused with intellectualist theories. Shepard warned his hearers not to "worship every Image in your own Heads. . . . There are many men of great knowledge, . . . and yet their hearts are unsound." And he dismissed offhand as false sources of ultimate religious truth such things as knowledge from "the light of nature," knowledge from "education," from "the law, whereby men may know their sin and evils," and from "the letter of the Gospel." "Many may know much, and speak well, and so in *seeing see not.*" But beyond all these false lights there is "a Light of Glory, whereby the Elect see things in another manner; to tell you how they cannot[;] its the beginning of light in Heaven, and the same Spirit that fills Christ, filling their minds" (Pt. i, 151).[50]

The difference between the "hypocrisie of the heart" and evangelical truth lies in "saving illumination in the understanding," but "understanding" must be interpreted in a very restricted sense. Shepard denied that it was necessarily true that all "fulnesse and clearnesse of light in the mind" brought about corresponding changes in the will. Even in the redeemed soul there remains, he said, a "remnant of malignity not yet removed" (Pt. i, 146, 61).[51] But the "Divine Light of Glory," in contrast to natural intellectual illumination of any

---

50. "There is a spirit of light, illumination, or revelation, let into the mind, which is peculiar to the beloved of Christ. . . . [To babes] doth the Lord reveal some things that the wisest in the world never knew. I do believe that the greatest scholar that ever lived, never had one such thought or apprehension of the Lord and the things of the Lord as the saints have" (Pt. i, 200).

51. Pt. i, 61: "Before conversion the main wound of men is their Will, *Video meliora proboq; deteriora sequor*: Hence John 8.44 *His lusts ye will do.*" But men are rightly punished for their wrongdoing because there is "a double impotency" in the will, "*ex infirmitate*" and "*ex malignate.*" In the latter case, men will not; in the former, they cannot.

kind, "is ever powerful through Christ to change the heart. . . . As Iron is drawn to the loadstone by a secret hidden vertue, so there is a secret vertue of Divine Light that drawes the most Iron heart" (Pt. i, 147).

Although the conversion of the mind or the understanding is the decisive criterion of regeneration, the process is altogether supernatural and affects the heart simultaneously and irresistibly. The basic difference between receiving the teaching of men and receiving the teaching of God is that in the latter case the light, the Gospel truth, "comes in power, it comes in demonstration; whereby the heart is mightily overpowered, that it cannot but fall down before God, whose voice and truth it hears." The teaching of mere men, which Shepard called "*bare* light," cannot change the will. "But the Lord doth it by the power of his Truth and Light: And as 'tis with water coming through some mines, there is a healing vertue in it, so Light coming from everlasting love, it heals men of their eviles" (Pt. i, 147). The ostensibly intellectual illumination that is at the core of true conversion for Shepard paradoxically begins with love and ends with love. In short, it brings about total change in the personality. This theory assured that wild affections, enthusiasm, private voices, impulses, and the like, would not rule the direction of religion. Yet at the same time Shepard, like Fenner, left much room for emotionality.[52] The function of intellect is not to suppress or control the affections from a lofty height of rationality. Carnal intellect in fact has no prerogatives over the sanctified heart. The divine light, which is ineffable, alters understanding and heart together, for the "one great reason or Original of both lies in the mind." Shepard could revert as needed to the old Platonic metaphor—"The eye or mind of a man sits like the Coachman and guides the headstrong Affections," and if the eye is blind, "there will be falls and deviations into crooked waies." But he also maintained that the relation between heart and mind is reciprocal, for "the heart makes the eyes blind, and mind makes the heart fat" (Pt. i, 146). Shepard's idea of divine illumination conformed to neither of the two traditional functions of reason in Classical ethical theory—reason as the executive or *hegemonikon* in the soul and reason as the source of moral norms (the first may be called the intellectual function, the second the rational). Because of its inseparable connection to the "heart," it represented a departure from anything in Classical pagan theories.

Shepard's theory can perhaps be restated in modern terms as follows. True conversion as compared to hypocrisy is integrated change; it includes affec-

52. For example, he wrote, " 'Tis strange to see some people carried with mighty affection against sin and Hell, and after Christ. And what is Hell you fear? A dreadful place. What is Christ? They scarce know as much as Devils do; . . . Oh trust them not! . . . It's rare to see Christians full both of light and affection. . . . I never liked violent affections and pangs, but only such as were dropt in by light; because [the former] come from an external Principle, and last not, but [the latter] do" (Pt. i, 150).

tions as well as mind. There is new understanding—which is known from direct experience only (Shepard used the traditional comparison to the taste of honey)—a new inclination of the heart or will, and appropriate feelings or affections. The hypocrite, the man who is as yet unresolved in his relationship to God, may have passing affections that resemble those felt by the converted, but he is still disposed at least half the time to put self ahead of God, and his mind has not yet been changed. "Hypocrites have awakening grace, and are much troubled; they have enlightening grace, and know more than many Christians; they have affecting grace, and are wonderfully taken with the glad tidings of the Gospel; but satisfying grace, or that grace which brings them to full rest, and satisfying sweetness in God . . . this they never come to" (Pt. ii, 81).

Some Relations between Religious and Secular Theory

The workings of the "spirit" in the religious sense and the workings of passion or emotion are similar in this important respect: human beings experience them both passively. Both the Holy Spirit and natural emotions roll over one like waves, take possession of the soul during their time of influence, and are so personal that they are self-authenticating. When Thomas Shepard was discoursing on the question of how much direct effort can be expected of the Christian in seeking salvation, he made use, not surprisingly, of the "wind" metaphor commonly applied to describe the effect of the passions. When waiting for saving grace, Shepard said, the soul must *try* to act even though there is inner deadness. Yet at the same time one may not trust one's own powers. The right approach, he said, is "ever hold up sailes, but look for a wind."[53] No person can fully control their emotional states any more than they can their spiritual states. Thomas Fuller, a seventeenth-century Anglican divine, used the same metaphor of the ship at sea. Adversely commenting on William Perkins's thought, Fuller claimed that Perkins's doctrine "referring all to an absolute decree, hamstrings all industry, and cuts off the sinews of man's endeavours toward salvation. . . . Ascribing all to the wind of God's spirit (which bloweth where it listeth), [Perkins] leaves nothing to the oars of man's diligence, either to help or hinder to the attaining of happiness."[54] The commonplaces for describing emotions and spiritual influences were so alike, in short, as to be almost interchangeable.

Reformation theology raised anew the crucial question of the degree to which men can take an active part in their own conversion, and inevitably,

53. Shepard, *Parable of the Ten Virgins*, Pt. i, 32.
54. Fuller, *The Holy State (The Profane State)* (Cambridge, 1642), 90.

this theology introduced more general questions concerning the active and passive sides of human experience, questions with certain parallels to problems of natural psychology and the passions. The etymology of the word "spirit" is related to the words "breath," "wind," and "air."[55] In the eighteenth century, when educated men talked less of the wind of God's spirit than they had in earlier times, the wind of the passions or the affections was the substitute, because it, too, moved the soul independently of human intentions or purposes. Since both spirit and passions transport the soul, it was hardly a great leap to begin to see in the passions and affections significant revelations of God's will. The tie was cemented by the richness of meaning surrounding the word "love," which was both a commonly recognized gift of the spirit and a common affection.[56]

Some of the relations between the religious concept of spirit and the sentimentalist view of the passions are illustrated in the well-known transformation in meaning of the word "enthusiasm." Prior to the seventeenth century, enthusiasm, which in Greek meant literally "god-possessed," did not have a strongly pejorative connotation and was sometimes a term of praise. To be possessed by the spirit of God was a claim to distinction. In the wake of the subjectivism unleashed by the Reformation, however, and later during the Interregnum, enthusiasts were more likely to be social or religious radicals who claimed a personal inspiration, and the tendency in the seventeenth century was to disparage such claims as the result of madness, or, at the least, of a crazed mind and wild emotions. The passionate intensity of enthusiasm was to be feared, as a deluded maniac was to be feared.

John Locke's condemnation of enthusiasm, added to the fourth edition of his *Essay Concerning Human Understanding*, is only the most famous of many other attacks, but already when Locke was writing, enthusiasm in the good sense was in the process of being restored, although in altered form. Writers like Henry More, whose *Enthusiasmus Triumphatus* was published in 1662, and particularly the third earl of Shaftesbury some forty years later, wanted to preserve the emotional energy of enthusiasm for the cause of religion and virtue without the taint of antinomian madness. They set about deliberately to redefine the word in secular terms, which meant, in effect, to make

---

55. Cf., for example, James Fitch's description of the Trinity. "God . . . knows himself and is known of himself and . . . he is breathed after by himself. . . . The God-head with a relative and individual property is a divine person, and is either persons breathing or breathed, *spirante* or persons breathing, as Father and Son, *Spirit*, or breathed as the Holy Ghost." Fitch, *First Principles*, 10–12. See also, Heppe, *Reformed Dogmatics*, ed. Bizer, trans. Thomson.

56. Cf. Arndt, *True Christianity*, trans. Boehm, I, 429: "For till thou art brought to this pass, O Christian, that thy Mind be merely passive, and that thou purely sufferest the Operation and Will of God, 'tis evident that God is hindered by thee." Secular moralists in the 18th century later spoke of unnatural emotions hindering the flow of good or benevolent affections.

enthusiasm a kind of directed emotional excitement capable of supporting good causes. Shaftesbury went so far as to define virtue itself as "a noble enthusiasm justly directed and regulated." Enthusiasm, Shaftesbury said, is "what inspires us with something more than ordinary, and raises us above ourselves," clearly desirable qualities in the pursuit of virtue. The dangers of enthusiasm were all to be found only in the superstitions, religious and other, often associated with it, but not in the passions themselves.[57] This naturalized enthusiasm, no longer a divine manifestation of the Holy Spirit in any orthodox sense, was more or less what Emerson meant in the nineteenth century when he argued that "every great and commanding moment in the annals of the world is the triumph of some enthusiasm." Natural affections, properly enlivened and focused, became the substitute for the infusions of spirit of an earlier time.

None of the writers on the passions that we have thus far commented on succeeded in introducing clear and consistent distinctions between momentary feeling-states, which could also be called bodily sensations; settled dispositions or tendencies of the personality; instincts rooted in biological needs; appetites or conations rooted in rational conceptions, such as social goals; and tastes or sentiments that in some way combine delicate judgments with affections. The great strides in the modern interpretation of the passions did not begin until Descartes's treatise on the subject was published at mid-century, followed by the basic work of Nicolas Malebranche, and then by the essays of the third earl of Shaftesbury, his disciple Francis Hutcheson, and the other Scottish moralists. The Cambridge Platonist Henry More was also a crucial figure in this development, as we will see in chapter 6.

The passions have for several reasons always been extremely difficult to subordinate to theory: 1) diverse coordinates can validly be used to describe them, 2) it is uncertain that a single structural model can be applied to them at all times and in all societies, and 3) the sorting out of such extraordinarily subjective and elusive phenomena is inherently difficult. With regard to the

---

57. Shaftesbury, *Characteristics*, ed. Robertson, II, 176, 174. Henry More's *Enthusiasmus Triumphatus* . . . (London, 1662) is available in a modern reprint distributed by the Augustan Reprint Society, *Publication* no. 118 (Los Angeles, Calif., 1966). More distinguished between "enthusiasm in the *better* sense" and false fanaticism, and probably influenced Shaftesbury. E. C. Walker, "The History of 'Enthusiasm' As a Factor in the Religious and Social Problems of the Eighteenth Century" (Summary of Thesis), Institute of Historical Research, *Bulletin*, IX (1931), 123–126, gives a short bibliography of 17th- and 18th-century works on enthusiasm. Enthusiasm was mostly in disfavor throughout the 18th century, despite Shaftesbury's efforts. There are many good studies of the subject of enthusiasm. Two brief works are Oliver Elton, "Reason and Enthusiasm in the Eighteenth Century," *Essays and Studies by Members of the English Association*, X (1924), 122–136; and Joe Lee Davis, "Mystical versus Enthusiastic Sensibility," *Jour. Hist. Ideas*, IV (1943), 301–319.

first problem, for example, Fenner classified the affections according to their degree of carnality or holiness. Others ranged them on the basis of their dependence on bodily change, that is, from passions that cannot be imagined to exist at all without concomitant effects on blood pressure, respiration, and so on, to affections that appear to be entirely mental and quiet. It was also possible to classify the passions according to whether their objects are good or evil, present or distant, attained with difficulty or easily reached. And there has always been much effort to distinguish so-called primary or irreducible passions from secondary passions that can be reduced or broken down into more elemental parts.

The all but universal view in the early seventeenth century, as in the preceding centuries, was that a passion, emotion, or affection—the terms did not have uniform meanings—was some modification, in the soul, of an appetite or aversion. The typical taxonomy made love the primary passion (or perhaps, love and hate) and derived the other emotions from this beginning. Fulfilled love to an object is joy, an emotion that is experienced only in relation to a present good. Love to an attainable object that is not held in the present evokes desire. If an obstacle is introduced that raises some doubt about the attainability of the object, hope might follow; though if the obstacle is very great, despair may be the result. In Thomas Aquinas's influential scheme, those passions that are the result of confrontation with difficulties—such as hope, despair, courage, and so on—were known as the "irascible" passions, perhaps because anger was the typical one. Those that related directly to the object without an intervening difficulty were known as the "concupiscible" passions. It can be seen without introducing further detail that the passions were understood within a framework of motion toward or away from an object, or as variations in the soul and body in consequence of elementary conations. The modern psychologist H. M. Gardiner has noted that in general the Scholastics included under affections and passions "very diverse psychological phenomena—pleasure and pain, sudden and transient emotions, more or less permanent tendencies, dispositions, habits both of feeling and behavior, virtues and vices," and in particular they tended to identify the affections and passions with "modifications of conative tendencies."[58]

In comparison to the moral psychology that developed in the eighteenth century, this failure to distinguish adequately a feeling or sensation from a conation or desire was very primitive. The seventeenth-century theory of the passions did allow for virtuous moral impulses that had an affectional basis, as we have seen. But without an independent notion of non-conative feeling, such as the eighteenth-century concept of "sentiment," there could be no psychology of moral *judgment* (as distinguished from the psychology of moral

58. Gardiner *et al.*, *Feeling and Emotion*, 103, 188, 197.

action) that was nonintellectual, or affectional. A major step in this direction in secular philosophy was taken by the third earl of Shaftesbury, who brilliantly made use of an analogy with aesthetic appreciation to argue that there can also be a form of moral appreciation and judgment that is affectional and sensory in its nature rather than intellectual, and yet is not identifiable with, or simply reducible to, desire. Thus, after Shaftesbury it was possible to work out a complete system of nonintellectualist ethics. In this system, the source of moral knowledge and judgment is not in the reason, however conceived; and the moral faculty in the soul, which is the basis of both the discrimination and the pursuit of the good, is not in the intellect. Feeling, affections, and passions, variously defined, are sufficient, or nearly sufficient, to describe and prescribe all of moral behavior.

Three general notions from seventeenth-century religious literature that seem particularly to have fed eighteenth-century moral psychology, in addition to the concept of enthusiasm we have already mentioned, are sensibility, zeal, and heart. The terminology is not in itself as important as the substance of the ideas. All three suggest a unity of primary sensations with discrimination and judgment and imply that an agent with these traits has reserves of affective energy ready to be directed toward a moral goal. Religious sensibility was easily converted into moral sense and moral sentiment; zeal into disinterested benevolence and related impulses toward feelingful moral reform and the pursuit of virtue; and heart was all-encompassing for the expression of knowledge, affection, and conduct.

It is significant that Fenner put zeal at the summit of affective life. God created man "upright and good" and gave him affections "so to twist and hamper his heart upon good, that it might be harder to loosen it." God gave men love to embrace the good, hope to expect it if it is wanting, grief if it is lost, hatred to deal with obstacles to its attainment, and so on. But in addition to these conventional passions, God gave man zeal, which is "*a high strain of all the affections*, whereby the heart puts forth all its affections with might upon that which it absolutely affects." Zeal was "the extremity of the affections" for Fenner. "What the soule is zealous unto, that is the predominant temper of the soule." In zeal a man is "transported out of himself," so that "the passion hath command of him, and not he of his passion."[59] Dozens of passages in Shaftesbury, urging moral enthusiasm, closely compare to these statements of Fenner's.

Although "heart" was sometimes used almost interchangeably with "will," it was a term laden with meanings closely connected to feeling. It was above all in the religious notion of heart that the foundation was established for the introduction of another "rational" faculty beyond intellect and will. A modern

59. Fenner, *Treatise of the Affections*, 129, 141, 151, 167.

historian of the will, Vernon Bourke, speaks of the special way of looking at divine and human willing that results in "heart-language." The source of heart-language is principally the Old Testament, but there was a school of Greek medicine that used similar terminology.[60] The Greek emphasis seems to have been more on the unity of heart and "ruling will," whereas the Bible in both Hebrew and Greek parts attributes to heart an extraordinarily wide range of meaning, including a cognitive quality (for the law of God is written in the hearts of men), without in any way reducing its emotional side. As we noted earlier, Augustine frequently availed himself of the idea of the heart as a moral and religious concept, and it is later found in Calvin as well as many other writers before and after him.[61]

By the seventeenth century the condition of a man's heart could refer to his thinking, his intention, his will, his faith, his affections, his desires, his faculty of choice, or his inclinations. But it is the heart as the paradoxical faculty of *intelligent feeling*, or *rational emotion*, that particularly interests us because, along with zeal and sensibility, it forms the background for some key ideas in eighteenth-century moral philosophy. The heart had the potential to be an all-purpose moral faculty: the seat of the deepest innate moral knowledge, which was yet feeling more than idea; and at the same time, the spring of action like the will and passions.[62] Here, too, as in the case of zeal, a concept that had fundamentally Judaeo-Christian origins rather than pagan would play a major role in eighteenth-century moral thought, despite the alleged Classicism of the age of enlightenment. Of course, heart and zeal were closely related ideas. The heart was the source and guide of zeal in the same way as the moral faculty or the moral sense would later be the source and guide of benevolence.

Introspection and the Science of the Inward Man

The renewed interest in the nature of the passions, which appears in a variety of forms in the seventeenth century, and the defense of the passions as moral instruments are both phenomena in the history of early modern Europe and Britain that may be subsumed under the grander topic of the rise of introspective techniques and the extraordinary expansion of the psychology of man's inward life. One of the surest marks of modernity is increased consciousness of subjective events and their influence, culminating in writings

60. See Bourke, *Will in Western Thought*, 13–14, for the term "heart-language" and the Greek medical school.

61. See, for example, Calvin, *Institutes*, III, ii, 7–34, and vi, 4.

62. For the heart-language of Pascal and the Jansenists, see Levi, *French Moralists*, 323–328.

like those of Dostoevski, Freud, and Joyce. Although the Greek tragedians, notably Euripides, and some other Classical authors began to explore the inner world of consciousness, and although St. Augustine is beyond question one of the great masters of introspective observation, it was not until the sixteenth century that the subject burgeoned into a cultural tendency of first-rate importance, giving rise to wholly new forms of literature and philosophy. One of the distinctive marks of the new moral philosophy, as we have already noted, was its psychological awareness.

The expansion of man's inner world cannot be ascribed alone to the appearance of new psychological realities or singly to the sudden discovery in consciousness of internal realities that have always been present. The two seem rather to have worked together, as Erich Kahler has suggested. Man's new awareness of his internal processes has in turn widened his internal world and given rise reciprocally to consciousness of that world, which in turn becomes a fuller world, and so on with spiraling reflexive growth.[63] Underlying this process of growth, and perhaps the most fundamental explanation of the seemingly new ability of human beings in the West to study their interior makeup, was the rise of literacy and the new availability of printed matter. Puritan consciousness of inner self was probably closely related to the remarkably high literacy rate within the sect. The spread of reading and writing skills, Walter J. Ong has explained, made it possible for people to objectify themselves to themselves, which is a prerequisite of the exploration of interior life.[64]

However the process occurs, in the modern world it has usually been stimulated by the special conditions that arise in one of three circumstances: courtship and affaires d'amour, diplomacy, and religion. All have in common the imposed necessity of sharply distinguishing between outward conduct or behavior on the one side and inner feelings that must be concealed, such as desires, intentions, or fears, on the other. On the one side there are external constraints, such as the etiquette prescribed by one's social position, or the fear of the enemy, or the duties enjoined by God's word; on the other there are passions of love, or schemes and subterfuges to ensure survival in the negotiations between princes, or sinful inclinations.

63. Kahler, *Inward Turn*, trans. Winston and Winston, 5–6, 67: "Consciousness changes its world and changes itself." "Realms of the external world which were previously obscure, with which man communicated naively and unconsciously, with which he was entangled in the confused depths of his being, are gradually subjected to observation and analysis. . . . Not only the external realms but also man's internal realms are thus objectified."

64. Of Ong's numerous brilliant writings related to this subject, the most recent is "Reading, Technology, and the Nature of Man: An Interpretation," *Yearbook of English Studies*, X (1980), 132–149.

Concentrating primarily on changes in fictional narrative, where the reciprocal influence of consciousness upon reality and reality upon consciousness is especially apparent, Kahler has noted "the necessity for self-discipline in the course of protracted intrigues" in a crowded royal court or prince's domain, where "subtle positional battles mark life" and encourage, "in fact compel introspection." Under such circumstances, "one's fellow men as well as one's own inner life become objects of conscious observation." [65]

In the case of diplomatic intrigue, Machiavelli immediately comes to mind. An original student of the techniques of deception, pretense, feigning, and other devices that separate inner purpose from outward performance, Machiavelli opened to full consciousness aspects of human nature that were hardly examined before his time. Once such a process of investigation was started it could not be contained. Machiavelli may be seen as a predecessor of Hobbes, who was equally secular-minded and experienced in the practices of statecraft, and one of the masters of psychological observation in the seventeenth century. Hobbes expressly undertook to search the "characters of man's heart," which are "legible," he said, "only to him that searcheth hearts" rather than books. His method was partly introspective, for to search hearts "without comparing them with our own . . . is to decipher without a key." The words "of an Aristotle, a Cicero, or a Thomas" may be believed by faith, but knowledge comes from direct experience. [66]

In the affairs of love as they are depicted in fiction there are similar developments, as Kahler has shown. A novel like Madame de La Fayette's *La Princesse de Cleves* (1678) portrays characters of enormous internal complexity, which the author dwells on, exploring every nuance of feeling and reflection. The external circumstances of marriage, propriety, honor, and duty are set off against an intense emotional life with inclinations often powerfully in conflict with the outside demands. The richness of the internal life that La Fayette brought out had the effect not only of revealing facets of consciousness already in existence in her social set but also of increasing human sensitivity in

---

65. Kahler, *Inward Turn*, trans. Winston and Winston, 26.

66. Thomas Hobbes, *Leviathan . . .* , reprinted in Edwin A. Burtt, ed., *The English Philosophers from Bacon to Mill* (New York, 1939), 130, 143, 158. See also, Hobbes's *Human Nature . . . A Discovery of the Faculties, Acts, and Passions, of the Soul of Man . . .* , in William Molesworth, ed., *The English Works of Thomas Hobbes of Malmesbury*, IV (London, 1840), 73: "Those men who have written concerning the faculties, passions, and manners of men, that is to say, of *moral philosophy*, . . . whereof there be infinite volumes, have been so *far from removing doubt* and controversy in the questions they have handled, *that* they have much *multiplied the same*: nor doth any man at this day so much as pretend to *know* more than hath been delivered two thousand years ago by Aristotle. . . . The reason whereof is no other, than that in their writings and discourses they take for principles those opinions which are already vulgarly received, whether true or false; being for the most part false."

general to delicacies of feeling, thus making possible a more sophisticated moral psychology. Manifestations of this tradition in France are seen earlier in the maxims of La Rochefoucauld, and in both France and Britain in the eighteenth century there was a large outpouring of fiction committed to exploration of the self at a deep level. Rousseau's autobiography represents a landmark in this social passion for self-knowledge.

Finally, an equally remarkable growth of religious self-consciousness occurred between 1500 and 1700. This is the area of psychological analysis that had the greatest effect upon changes in the conception and writing of moral philosophy. Three movements in the general area of religion were underway in the period, each conceptually distinct but impossible to keep entirely separate in actuality: the Humanist, the Roman Catholic, and the Protestant. Our interest is primarily in the Puritan foundations of the new moral philosophy and particularly of the sentimentalist ethics found in Shaftesbury and Hutcheson, but the broader context must be considered lest it be assumed that the Puritan quest occurred in miraculous isolation.

The foundations of the Humanist investigation of internal processes were partly religious and partly philosophical. It was a pursuit inspired both by St. Augustine's *Confessions* and by Socrates' famous dictum that a person must know himself before he can begin to seek truth, especially moral truth. The crucial figure in this movement, which is conventionally said to have begun with Petrarch, was the Spanish expatriate Juan Luis Vives, a friend of both Erasmus and Thomas More. Vives's *De Anima*, published in 1538 (when Montaigne, that other great student of the self in the sixteenth century, was but a child of five), was essentially a treatise on the passions, written in the belief that only through such a study of man's internal nature would moral reform be possible. "The soul is the spring of all our blessings, as well as the source of all our evils. We must, therefore, know our soul as deeply as possible; then by purifying the fountainhead we can secure a constant flow of clean and pure operations."[67]

Vives believed that the psychological study of the emotions was "the foundation of all ethics, private and public." He considered himself (apparently with some justice) to be the first person to undertake the study of "the internal mechanism of man's operations" with the sole purpose of deriving from such an investigation a sound basis for moral improvement. Aristotle, Vives noted, was strikingly deficient in his treatment of the passions insofar as they pertained to ethics.[68]

Antipathy to Aristotle and to Scholastic education is one of the identifying

---

67. Vives, quoted by Carlos G. Noreña, *Juan Luis Vives* (The Hague, 1970).
68. *Ibid.*, 270, 290.

traits of Humanism, and Vives was a leader in this anti-Scholastic drive.[69] Like Erasmus, Vives looked upon Christian revelation as a source of moral guidance rather than as the basis of a dogmatic theology subject to essentially intellectual treatment.[70] Scholasticism and Aristotelianism in ethics (basically the same thing) were derogated both for excessive intellectuality (as was Stoicism) and for superficiality, that is, for failing to support the investigation and cultivation of inward virtue.

Not surprisingly, the two archrebels against the Scholastic tradition, Bacon and Descartes, also had something to say about the deficiencies of the Classical authorities in the area of moral psychology. Moral philosophy, according to Bacon, should "set down sound and true distributions and descriptions of the several characters and tempers of men's nature and dispositions; especially having regard to those differences which are most radical in being the fountains and causes of the rest, or most frequent in concurrence or commixture." Bacon, who may have been influenced by Vives, considered the study of the affections to be essential to this inquiry. The mind ordinarily is temperate and stayed, but the "affections, as winds . . . put it into tumult and perturbation," which makes it vital that their nature and effects be understood. Bacon found it "strange," as we have noted, that Aristotle "should have written divers volumes of ethics, and never handled the affections, which is the principal subject thereof." [71]

Bacon recognized that in the *Rhetoric* Aristotle did touch on the subject of the affections, but not adequately. "For it is not his disputations about pleasure and pain that can satisfy this inquiry, no more than he that should generally handle the nature of light can be said to handle the nature of colours; for pleasure and pain are to the particular affections as light is to particular colours." The best sources of knowledge of the passions, Bacon pointed out, are literature and history, where one may find "painted with great life, how affections are kindled and incited; and how pacified and restrained; and how again contained from act and further degree; how they disclose themselves; how they work; how they vary; how they gather and fortify; how they are inwrapped one within another; and how they do fight and encounter one with another." The last study—how the affections may battle one another—was especially important in Bacon's mind, since "as in the government of states, it is sometimes necessary to bridle one faction with another, so it is in the government within." [72]

69. One of the most influential critics of Aristotle in the 17th century, Pierre Gassendi, was initially awakened to the defects of the Peripatetic philosophy by reading Vives.

70. Noreña, *Vives*, 171.

71. Bacon, *Advancement of Learning*, ed. Kitchin, 171.

72. *Ibid.*, 172.

Descartes wrote a major treatise on the passions that had a profound effect on the study of the subject, and his dualist metaphysics, which isolated a world of exclusively mental phenomena, provided a great impetus toward the study of the inner self.[73] Like Vives and Bacon, Descartes pointed out that "there is nothing in which the defective nature of the sciences which we have received from the ancients appears more clearly than in what they have written on the passions." And, as with everything else, Descartes advocated trying to start afresh. "That which the ancients have taught regarding them is both so slight, and for the most part so far from credible, that I am unable to entertain any hope of approximating to the truth excepting by shunning the paths which they have followed."[74] By the "ancients," Descartes meant, as did Bacon, some vague combination of the Classical writers plus the thick Scholastic accretions upon them, but this was one area of the humanities in which there seems to have been broad agreement that the moderns could and did exceed pagan achievements.

In France, aside from Descartes, figures such as Montaigne, Pascal, and Pierre Charron were also turning away from practices in Scholasticism, or academic philosophy, that seemed to issue only in objective learning rather than in self-improvement along moral lines. In two different English translations— Samson Lennard's of 1612, which by 1670 was in a sixth edition, and George Stanhope's of 1697—Charron's *Of Wisdom* had a wide distribution in America (like Lipsius, Charron was particularly well represented in colonial Virginia libraries). On the very opening page Charron declared the moving principle behind the later endeavor of the new moral philosophy: "No folly can be compared to that which draws off mens attention, and employs their diligence and pains in the search of other objects, and fixes them every where, any where, rather than upon themselves: For when all is done, the true learning is at home, and the proper science and subject for man's contemplation, is *man* himself." Self-knowledge meant for Charron the systematic and intimate study of human nature:

> A true, long, constant study of man's self; a serious and diligent examination, such as shall observe and nicely weigh, not only his words and actions, but even his most secret thoughts, and that . . . critically. . . .
> No motion of his mind must escape his notice; no, not his very dreams: He must view himself near, must be eternally prying, handling, pressing,

---

73. Descartes's work on the passions is discussed in more detail in chap. 6, below.

74. Descartes, *The Passions of the Soul* (Amsterdam, 1649), in Elizabeth S. Haldane and G.R.T. Ross, trans. and eds., *The Philosophical Works of Descartes*, rev. ed., I (Cambridge, 1931), 331. The work was written in the winter of 1645–1646, and was the last book to which Descartes turned his hand.

probing, nay, pinching himself to the quick: For there are many Vices
in us, that lurk close, and lie deep; and we know nothing of them because
we do not take the pains to search far enough, and ferret them out.[75]

The Humanist philosophical program for attaining moral wisdom through the
intimate knowledge of the self may be looked upon as an enterprise of gen-
tlemen and scholars with no roots in popular religion. That it was a quasi-
religious movement in itself, especially in the case of figures like Vives and
Charron, cannot be doubted, but it lacked the zealousness and life-or-death
urgency of more devoutly orthodox Catholic and Protestant scrutiny of the
soul, and it was not as directly focused on personal concern for salvation.

The specifically Roman Catholic contribution to systematic self-examination
in the sixteenth and seventeenth centuries has probably been underestimated
in favor of the better-known Puritan exercises of this sort, as Louis Martz has
pointed out. "Intense concentration on the 'motions' of the self is not a peculiar tendency of Puritanism," Martz observes. "The fact is that both Catholic
and Puritan, while accusing the other bitterly of neglecting the inner life, were
pursuing the art of self-knowledge by methods equally intense and effective—
methods that had, on both hands, developed a subtlety of self-awareness that
went far beyond the popular achievements of the Middle Ages."[76] Both faiths
encouraged the growth of affective piety and sanctioned the arousal of emotions in the service of godliness, but did so by disparate techniques.[77] The
techniques of Franciscan and Jesuit meditation were specifically designed to
bring the affections into harmony with intellectually known goods, as we
have noticed earlier in quoting from St. Francis de Sales, and for that purpose
great emphasis was placed on concrete and sensuous imagining of Christ's
Nativity and Passion. At the same time, worshipers were expected to purify
their souls by combating tendencies toward sin and the concupiscent strivings

75. Pierre Charron, *Of Wisdom* . . . , trans. George Stanhope, 3d ed. (London, 1729), I, 1,
14. The book was first published in French in 1601. It is extraordinary that more than 200 years
later in 1815 Thomas Jefferson could tell George Ticknor (so Ticknor recorded in his journal) that
Charron's *De la Sagesse* was the best treatise on moral philosophy ever written. See Adrienne
Koch, *Power, Morals, and the Founding Fathers: Essays in the Interpretation of the American
Enlightenment* (Ithaca, N.Y., 1961), 32–33.

76. Martz, *Poetry of Meditation*, 121.

77. Cf. the Jesuit Robert Southwell's *Marie Magdalens Funeral Teares* (London, 1591): "For
as passion, and especially this of love, is in these daies the chiefe commaunder of moste mens
actions, . . . so there is nothing nowe more needful to bee intreated, then how to direct these
humors unto their due courses, and to draw this floud of affections into the righte channel.
Passions I allow, and loves, and loves I approve, onely I would wishe that men would alter their
object and better their intent. . . . There is no passion but hath a serviceable use eyther in the
pursuite of good, or avoydance of evill, and they are all benefites of God and helpes of nature, so
long as they are kept under vertues correction." Quoted by Martz, *Poetry of Meditation*, 185.

of lower appetites. Of Lorenzo Scupoli's *Spiritual Combat*, one of the most popular devotional works in seventeenth-century England, Martz writes that "the subtlety of effort expanded in this battle leaves no corner of the mind unexamined: the whole treatise is one astonishing tribute to the psychological penetration of the sixteenth-century masters of self-analysis." [78]

Puritan self-scrutiny was also dedicated to inner purification, but since Calvinist theology did not permit reliance on any autonomous technique as a meritorious work of grace, most of the energies of the Puritan went into self-examination for the purpose of discovering signs of one's eternal status. The raising of the affections in Puritan devotional exercises was the outcome not of presenting to the mind pictures that were deliberately contrived to arouse strong feelings, but of the anxious and perhaps self-fulfilling hope that one would find already lodged in the heart the strong and steady feelings indicative of grace. A warm heart and zeal were themselves important tests of faith. Richard Baxter's *The Saints Everlasting Rest* (1650), which Martz shows was a landmark volume in encouraging among Puritans some of the Catholic techniques of meditation, criticized the Puritan doctrine of passivity insofar as it "caused some to expect only Enthusiastick Consolations" regarding their state. Active meditative techniques could bring more stable comfort,[79] as the subtitle of Baxter's book indicated: "a Directory for the getting and keeping of the Heart in Heaven: By the diligent practice of that Excellent unknown Duty of Heavenly Meditation."

Another school of Catholic introspection, distinct from the meditative tradition, namely Jansenism, has so many parallels to Puritan religious and moral psychology and had so many direct and indirect connections to English and American thought in the seventeenth century that it is hardly necessary to comment on it independently of English Puritanism. Both religious movements, Puritanism and Jansenism, were obsessed with the need to ferret out

78. Martz, *Poetry of Meditation*, 128. Scupoli's work was first published in Italian in 1589 and translated into English in 1598 and again in 1652.

79. *Ibid.*, 155, 157, quoting Baxter. Although one cannot quarrel in general with Martz's argument that there were "striking similarities" between Catholic and Protestant methods of self-scrutiny and self-reform (p. 123), he does not appreciate all of the differences. Most of the Catholic manuals he cites are intellectualist in approach—"When an object presents itself," Scupoli wrote, "let the understanding weigh its merits with mature deliberation before the will is permitted to embrace it"—and incremental in method. The conquest of sin and the attainment of holiness is accomplished in small steps. Although the Puritan believed that growth in sanctification was slow and necessarily had to continue throughout one's life, he emphasized rather the instantaneity of the total renovation that occurred through the action of the Holy Spirit at the moment of conversion. A redeemed heart was a substitute for rational control and the necessary foundation of moral and spiritual growth. Some of the Catholic treatises also show evidence of Stoic influences. On the incremental approach, see Fiering, "Franklin and Virtue," *Am. Qtly.*, XXX (1978), 199–223.

hidden sins, and in both France and Britain the intense scrutiny of the natural man that these sects encouraged left a valuable legacy of objective knowledge, a legacy that could be detached from the original concern with the differences, both subtle and obvious, between holiness and depravity.[80]

In the case of the Puritan, although it was believed that the creature might gain some assurance of his good standing with God, no devout person could ever allow in himself that degree of security that might end in complacency. The true Puritan was often in a state of oscillation brought about by his endless self-scrutiny. As Michael McGiffert has commented in the best short essay on the "Puritan paradox," the opportunities to misjudge the marks of grace "were virtually infinite," which therefore meant greater and greater self-examination. On the one hand, the Puritan considered anxiety about one's condition to be salutary, for it guarded the believer against presumption, pride, and complacency. On the other hand, one of the great boasts of Reformation theologians was that they had abolished once and for all the futile and anxiety-producing human effort to please God characteristic of the Romanists, and by casting all in terms of dependence on divine will, were able to give the creature the peace of assurance that could be found in no other way. Assurance, then, was both the Protestants' glory—against the alleged vanity and futility of Roman struggling and endeavoring—and at the same time, their great temptation, since a mere creature was never to let himself fall confidently into believing that he knew what a hidden God had in store for him. "It became the great problem of Puritan piety to maintain anxiety while simultaneously converting it into assurance. . . . Those who were not assiduously anxious . . . were almost certainly bound for Hell. It followed that the sound believer could measure his assurance by his anxiety: the less assured he felt, the more assurance he actually had." No passage in all Puritan literature more vividly illustrates this paradox, McGiffert writes, than Thomas Shepard's "almost offhand note" in his journal that "the greatest part of a Christian's grace lies in mourning for the want of it."[81]

Through it all, as we have noted, the constant inward searching contributed to the accumulation of an enormous amount of subtle, if rather random, psychological lore, particularly about the workings of the affective life, that is, the ins and outs of love and hate, desire and aversion, pride and ambition, lusts and longings. There is "no prisoner so slippery, no chapman so cunning

---

80. The social basis of Jansenist ethics, its opposition to the vainglory of aristocratic concepts of honor and morality, is brilliantly brought out by Paul Bénichou's classic work, *Man and Ethics: Studies in French Classicism*, trans. Elizabeth Hughes (Garden City, N.Y., 1971), originally published as *Morales du grand siècle* (Paris, 1948).

81. Michael McGiffert, ed., *God's Plot: The Paradoxes of Puritan Piety, Being the Autobiography and Journal of Thomas Shepard* (Amherst, Mass., 1972), 17–25.

and able to deceive us, as a man's heart is," John Cotton wrote, but the quest for self-knowledge was too fateful to be ignored.[82]

The problem of self-deception—with all the psychological devices for which we now have a terminology, such as rationalization, projection, displacement, reaction formation, and so on—was the particular subject of one of the earliest Puritan masterpieces of moral psychology, Daniel Dyke's *The Mystery of Selfe-Deceiving*, first published in London in 1615 (posthumously by the author's brother) and in an enlarged edition in 1628, followed by new editions in 1630, 1633, 1634, and 1640. Dyke's work, published a generation before Hobbes's *Leviathan*, is worth examining more closely as a major example of the specifically Puritan contributions to a new moral science of the inward man. Few other productions by seventeenth-century religious figures were more acute or penetrating. A copy of *The Mystery of Selfe-Deceiving* was in John Harvard's library, which was given to the college, and it is highly probable that the work was well known in New England. In addition, there was both a German and a French translation. A. O. Lovejoy and others have suggested that the latter may have influenced La Rochefoucauld and other French cynics and satirists who in turn later influenced English thought.[83] One of the ironies of the period is that cynics and libertines borrowed Calvinist insight into the worst qualities of human nature without also borrowing the inherent optimism of the theory of conversion.[84]

Dyke was mainly concerned about the same problem scores of other Puritan writers before and after him suffered with, including Jonathan Edwards: How can the sincere Christian, or the sound Christian, be distinguished from the

---

82. John Cotton, *The Way of Life* . . . (London, 1641). The ironies implicit in Puritan attitudes toward the self and self-examination are discussed with great perceptiveness in Sacvan Bercovitch, *The Puritan Origins of the American Self* (New Haven, Conn., 1975), 8–34.

83. According to Arthur O. Lovejoy, *Reflections on Human Nature* (Baltimore, 1961), 31, Dyke's book was "translated into French in 1634 by a Huguenot refugee in England, Jean Verneuil, under the title *La Sonde de la Conscience*, and the French version was apparently known and admired in Jansenist circles." Jacques Esprit's *De la Fausseté des vertus humaine* (Paris, 1678), published in English in 1706 in a translation by William Beauvoir as *Discourses on the Deceitfulness of Human Virtues*, was "probably inspired" by Dyke's *The Mystery of Selfe-Deceiving. Or a Discourse and Discovery of the Deceitfulnesse of Man's Heart* (London, 1615), according to Lovejoy. Ernest Stoeffler, *Rise of Pietism*, 75, has commented about Dyke's work: "Protestantism has produced no other treatise in which the psychology of sin was more exhaustively treated."

84. Bernard Mandeville's French sources, as described by F. B. Kaye, may themselves have derived understanding of the subterfuges of human nature from Calvinist and Jansenist writers. Unlike Puritan students of the heart, however, who needed constantly to gauge their purity in order to measure their standing in the economy of salvation, the French libertines scrutinized themselves and others solely to gain power through psychological manipulation. See, e.g., Loyd Ramond Free, "Crébillon fils, Laclos, and the Code of the Libertine," *Eighteenth-Century Life*, I (1974), 37. See also, Benichou, *Man and Ethics*.

hypocrite, what Dyke called the "temporary" as contrasted with the "true" believer? The temporary believer may resemble the true believer to such an extent that "even the most judicious and discerning Christians, cannot perfectly distinguish between them."[85] And the problem of self-deception is such that the sinner can as easily delude himself as he can fool others. Like Edwards (and dozens of other Puritan writers earlier), Dyke proposed test after test for distinguishing true from false, sound from counterfeit. As always, one of the signs of grace was "a practicall, a feeling and experimentall" (that is, an experiential) knowledge, not just intellectual comprehension of religious truth. The knowledge of faith is a "heating knowledge" that "stamps goodness in the heart," whereas the knowledge of the temporary believer "is onely a flame that gives light by blazing, but no sound and durable heat by burning." A good heart "loveth, favoureth, and affecteth things spirituall" and hates sin. It is by these internal standards, Dyke said, that we must "narrowly examine our selves."[86] It is notable that amidst much exploration of the "foldes of our hearts" for the evidences of Satan, the plumbing of that "deepe dungeon" where the devil "sporteth himselfe" like a leviathan in the ocean depths, Dyke could also counsel a search of the heart for positive signs of grace. If a sin lies covered by the merely "outward flourishing show" of graces, it will poison and rot all, and therefore must be cut out. But if the signs of grace lie buried, they will help to conquer the heart for God, and grace will work its way to the surface, repairing what is corrupted.

Dyke's trust in sincere intention as the most meaningful measure of goodness was perhaps greater even than Puritans typically allowed. "God regards not so much the matter, as the forme of our obedience, not so much the thing that wee doe, as the affection wherewith wee doe it." "Sincerity is the highest perfection attainable in this life."[87] This emphasis, although not without

85. Dyke, *Mystery of Selfe-Deceiving*, 67.

86. *Ibid.*, 69, 119–120. The copy of Dyke that I used contained an error in pagination, in which 10 page numbers (117–126) were repeated, although the text itself was in proper order. This citation refers to the second group of pages numbered 117–126.

87. *Ibid.*, 368, 362. The Anglican bishop Robert Sanderson was a notable opponent in the 17th century of the doctrine that a good intention is sufficient for a good action. In a sermon delivered in 1634 Sanderson particularly emphasized this "remarkable difference, among many others, between Good and Evil," that to make a thing good "there must be a concurrence of all requisite conditions," but for something to be evil, "a single defect in any one condition will suffice." *"Bonum ex causa integra, malum ex partiali."* Sanderson continued: "If we propose not to ourselves a right end, or if we pitch not upon proper and convenient means for the attaining of that end, or if we pursue not these means in a due manner, or if we observe not exactly every material circumstance in the whole pursuit, if we fail but in any one point, the action though it should in every other respect be such as it ought to be, by that one defect becometh wholly sinful." Quoted by Kevin T. Kelly, *A Thomistic Appraisal of the Concept of Conscience and Its Place in Moral Theology in the Writings of Bishop Robert Sanderson and Other Early English*

precedent—Peter Abelard centuries earlier had tried to work out an ethics of intention—was strongly opposed to the tenor of Classical ethics. It laid the groundwork for eighteenth-century sentimentalism, whether of the pessimistic type, like Mandeville's, that weighed all action in terms of its degree of self-regard, or of the optimistic type, like Hutcheson's, that placed maximum value on benevolence, or good will, ahead of either rational or utilitarian criteria. Dyke would certainly not have denied that obedience to the commands of God was essential for piety or virtue, no matter how sincere one's intentions—in fact, by sincerity he specifically meant a respect for God's glory and the interest of the church in all conduct. So Dyke retained formal, external criteria for goodness or holiness. But his concern with the inward condition of the agent, and particularly with the condition of one's will and affections, which is what "heart" signified for him, was easily expropriated by more secular moralists who captured this precise Christian spirit without the dogmatic framework. An emphasis such as Dyke's on sincerity of intention was an antidote to the cynical libertine standard represented in Dyke's mind by that "mischievous Machiavilian precept," that "vertue it selfe should not be sought after, but onely the appearance; because the credit is a helpe, the use a cumber."[88] In a system in which only internal emotional states mattered, placing value on the mere appearance of virtue without regard for a deep foundation of piety and goodness was not only contemptible but also dangerous, leaving one open to eternal damnation.[89]

Since inward condition was the paramount concern in religion, Dyke offered his readers every help for detecting the possible camouflages of the devil in their hearts. Reform had to take place in the heart first of all; no attack merely on the outward manifestations of sin would do. "It is impossible, the outward man, or actions thereof should be reformed, as long as the heart remains unpurged." That "must first be reformed, which was first deformed." Eve's heart was poisoned before her eye was.[90]

Protestant Moralists (London, 1967), 57. This book was also published in the same place and year with a different title, *Conscience: Dictator or Guide? A Study in Seventeenth-Century English Protestant Moral Theology.*

88. Dyke, *Mystery of Selfe-Deceiving*, 28.

89. Lovejoy, *Reflections on Human Nature*, brilliantly traces in political thought the decline of the emphasis on inner states. When civic obedience was accepted as sufficient for an orderly state, as in the Classical tradition, politics and morals parted ways, except for utilitarian morals.

90. Dyke, *Mystery of Selfe-Deceiving*, 308. Dyke wrote: "I doe not so well like their advise, that wish men in repentance to beginne with outward abstinence from sinne, as the easier, and so by degrees to come to the inward mortification of it." Cf. this point of view with the contemporary advice of the Jesuit Robert Southwell, quoted by Martz, *Poetry of Meditation*, 123: "I must not think to get al vertues at once, or cut off all imperfections togither, but having a generall resolution to get vertue, and leave all vice, begin with some one, endeavouring to breake my selfe of some one faulte, which I am most inclined unto, and procuring to get the contrary vertue."

Dyke's cataloging of man's deceits toward both himself and others is a testimony not only to his own perceptiveness but also to St. Augustine's, whom he cited and quoted repeatedly. Dyke also exploited the Bible as a record of human deviousness. A few examples of Dyke's analyses will suffice. The most secret deceits, he believed, are those which are "mantled and masked with the disguised pretences of special love and kindnesse" toward others, and the first part of his book is devoted to deceitfulness of this kind. Dyke recorded such particular types of deceitfulness toward others as dissimulation practiced before one commits wickedness; concealment of intentions and feelings; concealment after a crime; and so on. He fully recognized the importance of praise from other men as a motive to virtue, observing that a hypocrite is capable of going as far as any Christian in self-sacrifice, even undergoing martyrdom, so long as the esteem of others is forthcoming. It is for this reason that St. Paul could write, "Though I give my body to be burned, and have not charity, I am nothing."

> Marke the best of the Temporaries in their sufferings, and you shall see, that for all the thornes of persecution, wherewith the adversaries pricke them, they still continue pricking their own soules with the thornes of covetousness, pride, and vaine-glory. . . . The coole winde not of Gods, but of mens praises, is that which refresheth them in the skorching of this sunne. . . . Let us not then please ourselves overmuch, if we have suffered something for the truth, because even in suffering, the heart is deceitful.[91]

Dyke divided self-deceptions into those that exist in the mind and affections jointly and those that exist in the affections alone. When the mind is part of the self-deceit there are errors, for example, of judgment, whereby men convince themselves intellectually that they are not as bad as they actually are. In the event, "great sinnes are made little sinnes and little sinnes no sinnes. And here especially doth the cunning deceitfulnesse of the heart excell. It doth so straine and stretch its wits, even as it were on tenter-hookes for to finde out excuses. . . . The heart of man is so subtle, that if it can find out any other thing or person, that in the least sort may seeme to be but the least piece of an occasion, that shall be sufficient to free it selfe of all manner of blame."[92] Men blame other men, they blame the times, they blame conditions, and so on. They invent elaborate distinctions to protect themselves from self-accusation. Justifications are invented for gouging or otherwise injuring others. For Dyke,

---

Southwell was reflecting the injunctions of St. Ignatius's *Spiritual Exercises*. See also, n. 79 above.

91. Dyke, *Mystery of Selfe-Deceiving*, 87.

92. *Ibid.*, 130, 133.

the very meaning of Original Sin is that every human creature contains in himself or herself all the seeds of all possible sins.[93]

The deceitfulness of the affections taken alone, without the assistance of intellectual judgments and promises, is especially dangerous, Dyke maintained. The affections are capable of changing so swiftly that "the face of the heavens is not so divers, nor the sea or weather so inconstant, nor the Camelion so changeable as they." When once an affection is moved toward a personal gain, then presently that gain takes on the aspect of "godlinesse." If a thing be "gainfull, then though never so vile, it shall be coloured over as good and lawfull. Our affections when they would have a thing, sharpen our wits and set them on worke to devise arguments to serve their turne."[94] What better description of rationalization.

Puritan anxiety about the state of one's soul, and the consequent interest in the facts of human psychology such as is apparent in works like Daniel Dyke's *Mystery of Selfe-Deceiving*, may have ineluctably pushed religious-minded men toward anthropocentrism, in the same indeliberate way that the rise of modern science, or the new natural philosophy, involved the representatives of the churches in debates, issues, and studies that were beyond the capacities of religion to deal with in its own terms.[95] By the middle of the eighteenth century, in any case, nearly all of the meaty psychological insight and schematizations of the churches, Protestant and Catholic, had been picked clean by the secular moral philosophers, leaving the clergy simply dry bones. The fertile period of Christianity in terms of moral psychology was over, at least inasmuch as that psychology could be transferred into secular thought without destruction. This was the situation that Jonathan Edwards, with only partial success, attempted to rectify.

In the theory of the passions Edwards confronted two problems. After a century or more of the conflation of the workings of the spirit with the workings of emotion, the question was now urgently presented, Are there such things as specifically religious affections? Or was it enough to say that in the area of the emotions God works entirely by second causes and natural means, whether the circumstances are religious or not? Secondly, Edwards had to

93. "All evill, the whole body of sinne, that is, the seedes and spawnes even of the vilest corruptions are in the heart of man. Naturally the best of us have an inclineableness even to the most odious, and loathsome sinnes. As in that *chaos* at first creation there were the seedes of all the creatures, fire, aire, water, heaven, earth, so in mans heart of all sins. Upon which let but the spirit of Sathan move, as once the Spirit of God upon the *chaos*, and with the warmth of his temptations heat it, and no lesse ougly monsters will proceede out of our hearts, then did once goodly creatures out of that *chaos*" (*ibid.*, 305).

94. *Ibid.*, 280, 283.

95. I am indebted to Tipson, "Puritan Understanding of Conversion," for the suggestion that Puritan psychologizing compelled a drift toward anthropocentrism.

combat the everpresent tendency in human institutions, not least religious denominations, toward deadness, formalism, and legalism, and the justification for this state in dry intellectualist theories that would deny any significant place for emotional excitation in religion. The second campaign was much easier to conduct than the first. There will always be a party of sentiment in religion that will guard against the loss of emotional vitality. The first problem, however, that of proving the existence of a unique kind of emotion in religion substantively distinguishable from the whole array of natural emotions that men and women may feel in the course of edifying activities not conventionally considered religious, was a near-impossible task. Edwards could not win back for institutional religion what religion had already given to the world for the use of all.[96]

Yet in one way the religious theorists and the secular philosophers of human nature were engaged in a cooperative enterprise in the eighteenth century. It was a period when natural theology flourished as never before or since, and one of the axioms of the age was that knowledge of man was a direct preliminary to knowledge of God, who was the maker of man, the "author of our being" in the fashionable phrase. It was a period, indeed, when psychological theory, or philosophical anthropology, deeply influenced theology. Almost all the schools of thought shared in this effort to explore the central fact of creation—human nature—for the study of man could reveal the nature and purposes of the deity. By 1739 this new faith had become an academic commonplace. A Yale College thesis in that year stated, *"Philosophiae studium homine dignissimum, est humanae naturae scientia"* (The philosophical study most worthy of man is the science of human nature).

After the discrediting, in various quarters, of the model of the psyche that had put will as "rational appetite" at the axis of conduct, the resultant vacuum in psychological theory was filled by several divergent ideas. Four in particular can be adverted to here. (1) The religious-minded in the Reformed tradition clung to the rather imprecise notion of the "heart" and, for the regenerate, the new "inward nature" that underlay motivation and assured not only morality but also piety. This group used the word "will" in a different sense than was characteristic of its use in the Scholastic vocabulary. (2) British sentimentalist moral philosophy, which was first articulated in secular terms by Shaftesbury, derived in large part from the pietist tradition, I believe, with the Cambridge Platonists as essential intermediaries and contributors. The sentimentalists also did away with the idea of rational appetite, of course. Such notions as the moral sense, benevolent affections, moral taste, sensi-

96. Edwards's encounter with the secular moralists is the subject of Fiering, *Jonathan Edwards's Moral Thought*.

bility, and sentiment replaced reason and intellect as the source of moral norms and as executors in right conduct.

(3) The school of thought most closely allied to the old psychological theory of rational will was the intellectualist. The main figure in this school in the early eighteenth century was Samuel Clarke, the Boyle lecturer. But Clarke did not dwell much on the will as a moral faculty (although he was intensely interested in the problem of the freedom of the will), since the will as rational appetite was out of fashion. Instead he simply attributed motivational efficacy to reason itself.[97] Clarke and his followers, in other words, did not agree that moral choices were always the product of affections of some sort. Not so clearly in Clarke, but among later intellectualists such as John Balguy very definitely, the analysis of moral terms like "duty," "obligation," and "ought," which do seem to be distinct from affections and yet which effectively serve as motives for conduct, gave credence to this theory.

(4) Finally, a fourth response to the need for a new theory of the psychology of moral conduct was the revival of ancient hedonism, presented now with greater ingenuity and subtlety than hitherto. These modern hedonists attempted to show how the inescapable passion of self-love was translated into virtue via the human need for approval and praise. This theory more than any of the others was rooted in sophisticated conceptions of social psychology and the dynamics of social interaction. Like the sentimentalists, these men (who might be called constructive cynics) held that it was psychologically impossible for reason as such to move the will or the affections and thus motivate to action.[98] It was nevertheless important that men act and behave reasonably. The Creator, therefore, implanted in mankind an unsuppressible need for praise and approval and a dread of rejection and contempt. A leading formulation of this theory was Jacques Abbadie's *L'Art de se connoitre soy-meme* (1692).[99] Abbadie argued that God gave man for a judge of his actions not only his reason or conscience (which has the unfortunate defect of allowing itself to be easily corrupted by self-love and pleasure seeking in general), but also the critical reason of other men, "which is not so easily seduced," since "they are not so partial to us as we are to ourselves." God placed this *"penchant"* for approval in man for the good of society.

97. In 1728, in his *Essay on the Nature and Conduct of the Passions and Affections . . .* , 31n, Francis Hutcheson observed that some writers in his time seem to have forgotten about the will as the appetitive function of reason, "by ascribing to the understanding not only ideas, notions, knowledge; but [also] actions, inclinations, desires, prosecution, and their contraries." For Clarke, see below, chap. 7, nn. 4 and 5.

98. Lovejoy, *Reflections on Human Nature*, 162–163.

99. (Rotterdam, 1692). Abbadie's book was published in English at Oxford in 1695 as *The Art of Knowing One-self . . .* , with a second edition in 1698.

For it is this desire of being esteemed that makes us courteous and considerate, obliging and decent, makes us wish for decorum and gentle manners in social relations. Who, moreover, does not know that it is to this natural desire of glory [or fame] that we owe the fine arts, the most sublime sciences, the wisest governments, the most just institutions, and in general all that is most admirable in society.[100]

In all four systems the traditional compartmentalization between Christian ethics and pagan ethics, based on the alleged special inwardness of the former, was either weakened or broken down completely. Having appropriated a developed moral psychology of the passions, secular philosophy was itself prepared to engage and reform the whole man, with or without the aid of religion. Antoine LeGrand's secular ethics, published late in the seventeenth century, was explicit on this point, reversing all of the older rationales for the teaching of moral philosophy. Ethics, LeGrand wrote, "is a right way or course of thinking, in order to the obtaining of Human Felicity." It is not "conversant about any External Matters, nor considers Bodily Actions; but is intirely employed and concern'd about the inward Operations of the Will." External conduct was to be considered only so far as it is the effect of "internal Actions and the product of the Will." The virtue of liberality, for example, does not consist principally in "the relieving of our Friend, but in the care and desire we have to assist him, which is the peculiar property of a generous and vertuous Mind." Outward actions are but the "instruments . . . whereby the Will executes her decrees, and performs what she hath resolved upon."[101] LeGrand's concept of will was secular and intellectualist, which would set it miles apart from, let us say, William Ames's conviction that "the prime and proper subject of divinity is the will" and that virtue is a "habit whereby the will is inclined to doe well." Yet both men were aiming at the same end, the control and reformation of the inner person. In this struggle the party of religion and piety was obviously doomed to failure; the heart of man was not to remain absorbed in the problem of attaining salvation through piety so much as it was to become absorbed, in the eighteenth century, in the attainment of natural virtue, the religious revivals notwithstanding. Nonetheless, when it is understood that the very preoccupation with inner cure and reformation and with sentiment and emotion was itself a Judaeo-Christian legacy to modern philosophy, we may believe that the practical theologians did not fail altogether.

In the eighteenth century, theologians attempted to maintain the superiority

---

100. Abbadie, quoted by Lovejoy, *Reflections on Human Nature*, 163. In his *Thoughts on Education*, John Locke also stressed the moral efficacy of shame and praise.

101. LeGrand, *Body of Philosophy*, 348.

of religious virtue over sentimentalist secular virtue, but as we noted in the case of Jonathan Edwards, this was not an easy task. The theologians tended to look for something psychologically unique in the moral performance of the pious, which was, at best, an elusive goal. At the very beginning of the eighteenth century William Whiston, who was a significant figure in the history of mathematics as well as religion in Britain, still argued in the old way that the "virtues and good Actions of the Heathen Moralists," though brave, prudent, and valuable in themselves, were still "never done from a real Principle of Holiness, or a Divine Life: were not, generally speaking, intended for Instances of Love, Gratitude, Submission, and Obedience to the God of Heaven; had no regard to the Authority and Love of the Blessed Redeemer of Mankind; and were generally without inward Influence of the Holy Spirit of God." The heathen moralists, according to Whiston, had only mundane ends, mainly riches and worldly reputation, in view.[102] Some twenty years later, in 1728, Peter Browne, the bishop of Cork, a vigorous opponent of Shaftesbury, emphasized the psychological superiority of Christian virtues more than the theological differences:

> All that were merely moral virtues before, are by . . . [Christian] Revelations heightened and exalted into Evangelical Graces, as the merit of all instances of virtue and goodness is thereby transferred from the outward actions and deportment only, to the inward disposition of mind and conscience, formed and regulated by an evangelical faith. For neither Jew nor Heathen had any true and proper notion of internal holiness, which consists in an habitual state and temper, and inclination of the whole heart and mind to all virtue and goodness.[103]

Browne's emphasis on "true and proper" notions and the "whole" heart and mind may be interpreted as an effort merely to go one better than the preaching of Shaftesbury and Hutcheson.

Hutcheson's Theory of the Passions

The first systematic and consolidated presentation of the findings of the preceding century's investigation of the passions was Francis Hutcheson's *Essay on the Nature and Conduct of the Passions and Affections*, published in 1728. Although Hutcheson was an eighteenth-century figure, it will be clarifying to conclude this chapter with a short description of his theory of the passions,

---

102. Whiston, *Sermons and Essays upon Several Subjects* . . . (London, 1709), 106.

103. Quoted from Browne's *The Procedure, Extent, and Limits of Human Understanding* (1728), in *Present State of the Republick of Letters*, I (London, 1728), 129.

since it will serve to synthesize much of the foregoing material as well as to indicate generally the direction of thought about the passions and affections between 1650 and 1725. Moreover, Hutcheson was probably the most influential and respected moral philosopher in eighteenth-century America, both through his own writing and that of his followers, such as David Fordyce.[104] The high place given to Hutcheson as a moral philosopher may partly be explained in terms of certain inherent parallels between his thought and seventeenth-century religious doctrine. Thus, by briefly looking at Hutcheson's work on the passions, we are also looking at a profound extension of some aspects of seventeenth-century Puritanism.

There were two great innovations in Hutcheson's theory of the passions, both of which became immensely important in the course of the eighteenth century and beyond. It would be difficult to say to what degree these innovations were entirely original—there are always anticipations—but it is in Hutcheson's work that these principles were first stated definitively.

Hutcheson's first innovation was the introduction of a clear distinction between desire and aversion, and all other sensations. As we have seen, the traditional conception of the passions or affections, inherited from the ancient schools and restated by Thomas Aquinas, had treated all passions as modifications of desire, without differentiating those that were in no way related to desire. Passions, affections—or, to use the modern word, emotions—were responses to apprehended good or evil, or to present or anticipated pleasure or pain. In the widely held Stoic classification, associated with Zeno of Citium, good (or pleasurable) objects incite love, evil (or painful) objects incite hatred. Beginning with this basic principle of motivation, four primary passions were educed according to whether the objects are immediate and present or only anticipated. A distant good arouses desire; a present good evokes joy; a distant evil arouses fear; and a present evil evokes sorrow. In one form or another, this classification of the passions dominated all psychological theory until Hutcheson.

Hutcheson pointed out—and he noted with surprise that even his mentor in some of these matters, Nicolas Malebranche, had not made this observation—that joy and sorrow are more like sensations or perceptions than they are like affections because they do not incline the mind to action, or volition of mo-

104. The pertinence of Hutcheson's thought to America and his extensive influence here are discussed in Caroline Robbins, " 'When it is that Colonies May Turn Independent': An Analysis of the Environment and Politics of Francis Hutcheson (1694–1746)," *WMQ*, 3d Ser., XI (1954), 214–251, and Robbins, *Eighteenth-Century Commonwealthman*; Fiering, "Moral Philosophy in America, 1700–1750, and Its British Context" (Ph.D. diss., Columbia University, 1969), and Fiering, *Jonathan Edwards's Moral Thought*; David Fate Norton, "Francis Hutcheson in America," *Studies on Voltaire and the Eighteenth Century*, CLIV (1976), 1547–1568; and Garry Wills, *Inventing America: Jefferson's Declaration of Independence* (New York, 1978).

tion. Hutcheson accepted the ancient definition of the passions and affections, that they are always related to motion toward or away from an object, but then insisted that there is, in fact, a whole range of feeling-states that cannot be accommodated to that definition. The distinction between "affections," which are conative, and "sensations," which are not, was seldom made, Hutcheson noted, because in the emotive life the two almost always occur together. Yet, he said, they are logically distinct, just as "the will is [distinct] from the understanding or senses. . . . The simple idea of desire is different from that of pain . . . or from any sensation whatsoever: Nor is there any other argument for their identity than this, that they occur at once." But so also do color and figure, or incision and pain, Hutcheson observed.[105]

The significance of this distinction will be clearer after we consider Hutcheson's second major innovation in the theory of the passions, namely his extraordinary extension or enlargement of the meaning of sensation or perception. For too long, he said, has it been accepted that all sensations or perceptions must be mediated by and reduced to the external senses. Locke, of course, was particularly guilty of this among the moderns. Hutcheson, on the contrary, took hold of the traditional concept of "internal sense," which the Aristotelians had regularly acknowledged but not developed, and stressed that we have perceptions of enormous variety, reaching far beyond the external senses. Beginning with the perceptions commonly attributed to the internal sense, such as duration and number, and extending to perceptions of aesthetic order, such as proportion and balance, Hutcheson called attention to moral perceptions of virtue and vice, perceptions of honor and shame (such as the constructive cynics like Abbadie had stressed), sensations of sympathy, pain and pleasure, and many more. Some sensations include an image or representation plus feelings of pleasure or pain. In other cases the sole perception is merely pleasure or pain without an image, like the pleasures of smell or the pains of hunger.

This great number and variety of irreducible sensations or perceptions is part of man's God-given endowment, Hutcheson argued. They cannot be explained beyond this, though we can attempt to interpret them teleologically, that is, to understand their purpose in the design of human society. It is also a simple fact that sensations are generally either agreeable or disagreeable, pleasant or painful. Hutcheson then delineated a broad classificatory scheme of human senses, which included five major categories. He has often been wrongly criticized for introducing a multiplicity of "*senses*," but it is apparent

---

105. *Essay on the Passions*, 3d ed. (London, 1742), with an introduction by Paul McReynolds (Gainesville, Fla., 1969), 24. Subsequent citations to pages in this book will appear in parentheses in the text.

that he began his studies with the realization that human beings have a multiplicity of "*sensations*," or kinds of perception. Only after this discovery did
he proceed to assign hypothetical "senses" that corresponded to the "sensations." The idea of "senses" does not have to be taken literally, or understood
in terms strictly analogous to the five external senses. It need merely be recognized that there are categories of knowledge not reducible to the data derived
from the familiar external senses of touch, taste, smell, sight, and hearing.

Hutcheson's five types of "sense," then, are as follows:

1. The familiar external senses.

2. The aesthetic sense, which he called, following Joseph Addison, the
"pleasures of the imagination," and which includes "pleasant perceptions
arising from regular, harmonious, uniform objects; as also from grandeur and
novelty."

3. The public sense, namely, "our determination to be pleased with the
happiness of others, and to be uneasy at their misery," which includes the
involuntary feeling of compassion and other forms of sympathy.[106]

4. The moral sense, "by which we perceive virtue or vice, in ourselves or
others." This is distinct from the public sense in that there are some "who are
strongly affected with the fortunes of others" but who reflect little upon virtue
or vice.

5. The sense of honor or shame, "which makes the approbation, or gratitude of others, for any good actions we have done, the necessary occasion
of pleasure," and their condemnation of us the occasion of shame and pain
(4–5).

Just as the functioning of the external senses is determined by "nature," so
these other senses are part of the "frame of our nature." Neither the sensations themselves nor the pleasures and pains associated with them are matters
of volition or are controlled by intellect. These are happenings in the soul that
are largely independent of what we might wish for ourselves had we much
choice in the matter.

The pleasures and pains associated with each of these five types of sensation in turn arouse desires or aversions. For all men are so constituted that they
naturally seek pleasurable and avoid painful sensations. The "pleasures of the
imagination, or of the internal sense of beauty, and decency, and harmony, . . .
regularity, proportion, and order in external forms will as necessarily strike
the mind, as any perceptions of the external senses," although we may have
no "uneasiness of appetite previous to the reception of those grateful [i.e.,
pleasing] ideas" and are not necessarily miserable in their absence. It is note-

106. On the development of the theory of sympathy and compassion in the 17th and 18th
centuries, see Fiering, "Irresistible Compassion," *Jour. Hist. Ideas*, XXXVII (1976), 195–218.

worthy about the aesthetic sense, according to Hutcheson, that when un-corrupted by false associations, the "sense and desire of beauty" can exist entirely abstracted from desire for possession or property (103).

The pleasures and pains of the public sense also arise in us "necessarily," that is, of necessity. "Men cannot live without the society of others, and their good offices; they must observe both the happiness and misery, the pleasures and pains of their fellows: Desire and aversion must arise in the observer" (104). Moral ideas, too, necessarily arise in our minds, for we cannot avoid observing the affections of those we converse with and observing also our own affections. Although we have no "proper appetite toward virtue, so as to be uneasy . . . antecedently to the appearance of the lovely form," as soon as the image of virtue appears to any person, "as it certainly must very early in life, it never fails to raise desire, as vice does raise aversion" (106). And, finally, there are peculiar pains and pleasures associated with the sense of honor and shame.

As there are five classes of pleasure related to the five classes of sensation, so there are also five classes of desire. "Desires arise in our mind, from the frame of our nature, upon apprehension of good or evil in objects, actions, or events, to obtain for ourselves or others the agreeable sensation, when the object or event is good [i.e., is conceived to be good]; or to prevent the uneasy sensation, when it is evil" (7). From the external senses we have desires of "sensual pleasure," connected mainly with pleasures of taste and touch, and an aversion to the opposite pains. We have desires for the pleasures of the imagination, and an aversion to ugliness; desires for the pleasures arising from public happiness, and an aversion to the misery of others; desires for virtue, and an aversion to vice; and desires for honor, and an aversion to shame. These desires may also be called "affections," so that it would be equally correct to speak of five broad classes of affections. These, too, are involun-tary, in that affections also cannot be raised in us directly by our volition or by our desire to have a particular affection (17). Each of these five classes of affections may also be subdivided into those directed to one's own personal benefit and those directed to the public good or the good of others. Thus one could speak of public or private affections in relation to each of these: honor for others or for ourselves, sensual pleasure for others or for ourselves, and so on.

According to Hutcheson's arrangement, joy and sorrow, as we have noted, are properly sensations rather than affections, although earlier commentators had always considered them affections. Indeed, strictly speaking, desire and aversion themselves are the only pure affections. Everything else is some combination of a sensation with either of these two (60). But desire and aversion never exist alone, since we always feel desire or aversion toward some particular thing, that is, in combination with a sensation or perception.

On the other hand, and this is the important point, there are sensations that are logically separable from desire. It was Hutcheson's conception of these sophisticated sensations—such as those of the moral sense—that revolutionized moral philosophy and aesthetic criticism and placed religious psychology on new foundations, by creating the psychological categories or domains for modes of knowledge independent of ratiocination and intellectual judgments. These modes of knowledge are not reducible to wild passions, and yet can provide the basis for intelligent judgment and action. It had formerly (since Aristotle at least) been psychological dogma that rational action, or one might even say, all acceptable human conduct, had to proceed from intellectual deliberation of some sort that in turn informed the will, which then motivated the action. When this process was short-circuited, and the sensitive appetite, or the passions, moved the will, human behavior was assumed to be operating on an essentially subhuman level with results that were likely to be destructive. Hutcheson introduced his own short circuit from sensations to action. He used as the mediating faculty neither intellect nor will but these rather complex sensations that contain within themselves standards of taste, discrimination, and judgment and that can serve constructively as substitutes for will and intellect in guiding action. Perhaps the best word to describe these sorts of sensations is "sentiments," though Hutcheson rarely used this term. In any case, Hutcheson's refined and complex sensations united certain cognitive qualities with immediate and direct sense experience, and also with affections or desires that prompted action. This model of behavior cut completely across the traditional Scholastic organization of the psyche into intellect, will, and passion.

As we have indicated, Hutcheson did not write without precursors from whom he borrowed here and there. In philosophy the main influences upon him (excluding Classical sources, which he mined thoroughly, particularly Cicero), were Henry More, Malebranche, and the third earl of Shaftesbury. Equally important, however, were the unsystematic psychological theories generated by religious experience in the seventeenth century. Protestant and Catholic theologians working in the Augustinian tradition compelled the formulation of an alternative model that was virtually complete by the time Hutcheson began to write.[107] But no one before him had synthesized and systematized the results. Consider, for example, these parallels to Hutcheson's theory that may be found in religious literature. Hutcheson's complex and discriminating sensations of shame, honor, virtue, vice, compassion, and beauty were secularized versions of the intuitive and essentially nonintellectual taste and relish, illumination and heart, holy affections and gracious dispositions of

---

107. Hutcheson had himself been trained as a Presbyterian minister and was the scion of two generations of ministers.

the saints. The difference was, of course, that Hutcheson did not regard supernatural intercession as the precondition of these. In both Hutcheson's and the religious theorists' systems, the responses engendered by moral sensations or new inward dispositions were determined or involuntary, that is, they were not produced by conscious will or controllable by will. In both cases intellectual illumination or "light" was somehow an integral component of heart or feeling, so that blind emotion was excluded. And in both cases, though the parts were distinct, these sensations, holy or otherwise, aroused desire or inclination toward the particular good objects apprehended, as well as aversion to the evil. "All men feel something in their own hearts recommending virtue," Hutcheson wrote (xiv). And our approbation or dislike of certain affections, tempers, sentiments, or actions on the basis of moral perceptions cannot be controlled any more than we make "the taste of wormwood sweet; or that of honey bitter" (3).

Hutcheson argued, too, in opposition to Hobbes, that all desires are not reducible to self-interest; many desires are implanted in us independently of calculated personal interests. In the same way, it is clear, the saint is inclined toward God. It is not a prior sense of insufficiency or pain that creates desire, Hutcheson maintained, but the pre-existing and necessitated desire that creates the sense of insufficiency or uneasiness. He took Locke to task in particular for defining desire as an "uneasy sensation in the absence of good." Just as the saint wishes for heaven because he loves God, and does not love God because he wishes for heaven, and just as he does good out of a holy desire to do good irrespective of anticipated rewards, so in Hutcheson's view were disinterested benevolence and other social virtues independent of both preceding uneasiness and subsequent pleasurable self-congratulation or other reward. "The uneasy sensation, accompanying and connected with the desire itself, cannot be a motive to that desire which it presupposes" (16). The desire is raised prior to the uneasy sensation. And the "peculiar pleasant sensation of joy, attending the gratification of any desire," which may exist *in addition to* the "sensation received from the object itself, which we directly intended," is never the goal of the desire (16–17). It is the thing itself we want, not the concomitant pleasure of getting it. Men who love or desire God for what he can give them simply do not love God, but some lesser thing. The commonness of such misguided love does not prove that it is impossible to love God for Himself.[108] "We have not in our power," Hutcheson wrote, "the modelling of our senses or desires, to form them for a private interest: they are fixed

108. In opposition to Locke Hutcheson pointed out that we can "desire to remove uneasiness," which indicates that desire is independent of preceding uneasiness. He also observed that there are moments of neutrality, so to speak, in our feelings, when we can desire some alteration in conditions without there being prior uneasiness (p. 44). "There is a middle state of our minds, when we are not in the pursuit of any important good, nor know of any great indigence of those

for us by the Author of our nature, subservient to the interest of the system"
(118).

In sum, the structure of Hutcheson's theory of the passions intersects everywhere with the earlier formulations of his Puritan ancestors. It seems likely
that he was indebted to this legacy for his ability to approach the problem of
the passions in a manner distinct from the Scholastic tradition.

One other comparison between Hutcheson and some of the theories of
seventeenth-century religious psychology may be made. For both pietists in
religion and for sentimentalist moralists like Hutcheson, motivation had to
be basically affectional, not intellectual. There still remained, however, the
danger of unbridled, irrational passions. It was necessary in both religion and
morals to differentiate proper zeal and emotionality from dangerous passions.
Hutcheson joined to the scheme already outlined two additional forms of
emotionality: one kind even more refined than the ordinary affections and
desires; the other less refined and directly connected to bodily responses. The
former he referred to as "calm and extensive desires," the latter as "passions," though he did not always use the term "passion" in this restricted
sense. The "calm desires of good" are influenced directly by reason and
reflection, and extend beyond the immediate desires that arise in response to
the sensations evoked by particular goods or evils. Indeed, in Hutcheson's
description these calm and extensive desires resemble the old notion of rational appetite or will that moves at the command of reason and guides the
passions to the rational good as defined by the intellect. Will in this sense is
"a constant natural disposition of the soul to desire what the understanding
represents as good." But these calm and constant desires have an even closer
resemblance to Thomas Shepard's "inward bent and inclination" of the soul,
and to many other Puritan descriptions of the holy love that infuses the regenerate and remains with them for life. Calm, universal benevolence, in
Hutcheson's system, is the very height of virtue and is a great support for the
ordinary virtuous affections of a slightly lower order. This calm, universal
benevolence has a counterpart, perhaps, in the finest kind of saintly holiness.

At the other extreme, the "passions" are violent impulses of the moment,
defined by Hutcheson as "a confused sensation . . . occasioned by some
violent bodily motions, which keeps the mind much employed upon the
present affair, to the exclusion of everything else, and prolongs or strengthens

---

we love. In this state, when any smaller positive good to ourselves or our friend is apprehended to
be in our power, we may resolutely desire and pursue it, without any considerable sensation of
pain or uneasiness. Some tempers seem to have as strong desires as any, by the constancy and
vigor of their pursuits, either of publick or private good; and yet give small evidence of any
uneasy sensation. This is observable in some sedate men, who seem no way inferior in strength of
desire to others." This debate between Hutcheson and Locke has a parallel in the 20th century in
the antithetical views of the humanistic and the behaviorist psychologists.

the affections sometimes to such a degree, as to prevent all deliberate reasoning about our conduct" (28). Following Descartes and Malebranche, Hutcheson indicated that the duration and intensity of passions are tightly meshed with bodily motions, such as respiration, circulation, and so on, that make them all the more difficult to control. All affections, in fact, occur with bodily concomitants, except for pure desire and aversion and joy and sorrow, which theoretically, at least, could be felt by bodiless angels, since these affections or sensations are purely mental or spiritual and "seem to arise necessarily from a rational apprehension of good or evil" (63). But it is a law of nature (57), so far as humans are concerned, that certain motions in the body accompany all affections and passions, which is where physical temperament comes into play as an influence on moral character. In the end, it is only the violence or the intensity of the passions that distinguishes them from the more sedate affections. Physiologically and psychologically there is no qualitative difference. The corruption of morals (or of religion, for that matter) is caused not by the influence of passions per se but by imbalances that result from allowing certain kinds of desires, such as those related to the pleasures of external sense, to overweigh the desires related to the public sense, the moral sense, or whatever. Fundamentally Hutcheson, like Augustine, found no fault with the affections or passions in themselves, which after all were given by God for definite purposes. Rather, he criticized the mismanagement or indulgence of some passions at the expense of others morally more desirable or worthy.[109]

109. In addition to calm and extensive desires, regular affections, and turbulent passions, Hutcheson also recognized the existence of instincts and propensities that exist without reflection on good or evil (p. 63). This includes both animal instincts and traits of character, like a propensity to anger, that persist without any good in view.

5

A Harvard Teacher
of Moral Philosophy:
Charles Morton

Change not in things divine,
keep what is old[.]
[But] *in philosophicalls you*
may be bold.[1]

If emigré professors can be considered Americans, Charles Morton (1627–1698) was America's first professional philosopher. Though a member of the clergy, his interests were predominantly pedagogical and naturalistic rather than homiletic and religious, and he achieved distinction primarily as the head of a well-known dissenting academy (Newington Green, near London), not as a minister. Among his pupils had been such notables as Samuel Wesley (a commendable poet and father of the founders of Methodism) and Daniel Defoe, both of whom unreservedly lauded him in later writings. When Morton came to America in 1686 at nearly sixty years of age, it was with the prospect of stepping into the presidency of Harvard, but the political situation following the loss of the Massachusetts Bay charter prevented his assuming the office. Apparently the college would have risked its survival by appointing so conspicuous a dissenter. Instead, Morton became the minister of the church in Charlestown. He also immediately began to tutor in his home, and for a short while it looked as though he would establish an academy that would rival Harvard in attracting students. But by the mutual agreement of all concerned parties, Morton included, it was realized that this development would not be in the best interests of higher education in New England, and Morton took no more students. Beginning in 1692 he served as a fellow of the college and in 1697, shortly before his death, was named vice-president, a newly created office. According to the college records, at a meeting of the Harvard Corpora-

1. See n. 6 below.

tion in 1693 Morton raised the question, "How may the Colledge be made greater and better?"[2]

Coming directly from the metropolis, Morton must have brought to the educational scene at Cambridge, Massachusetts, a degree of urbanity and progressivism that was quite unsettling, although not necessarily unwelcome. He had deliberately used the vernacular in all of his lectures at Newington Green, and according to J. W. Ashley Smith he was probably the first educator anywhere to teach English as a subject for study. He undertook to prepare in the vernacular short compendiums of all the parts of learning, which would make knowledge available, he said, to all persons of "either sex, who have not the Command of Learned Languages, nor have had the opportunity to attain them." "What a pity it is," Morton wrote in the introduction to the vernacular logic that introduced the series, "that Reasonable Souls should languish for want of matter to work upon." This conviction about the use of English, his association with Samuel Wesley, and his friendship with the bookseller John Dunton, who visited New England on Morton's suggestion, all point to the likelihood that Morton had more than a little to do with the origins of the Athenian Society in London, a peculiar but highly innovative educational group that Dunton began in about 1690, shortly after his return from America.[3]

Most of the American interest in Morton thus far has been in connection with his widely distributed manuscript physics text, used at Harvard from the 1680s until about 1728, of which more than a dozen student copies have sur-

2. Morton is treated authoritatively in the *Dictionary of American Biography* by Wilbur J. Bender, and also in considerable detail in a biographical sketch by Samuel Eliot Morison, which prefaces vol. XXXIII of the Col. Soc. Mass., *Colls.* (1940). This volume contains Morton's *Compendium Physicae* . . . edited from manuscripts by Theodore Hornberger. Morison also treats Morton in *Seventeenth-Century Harvard*, 236–237. None of this early biographical work had the benefit of J. W. Ashley Smith's excellent study of the dissenting academies, *Birth of Modern Education*. Also valuable is McLachlan, *English Education under the Test Acts*. A useful bibliography of Morton's writings, with references to some of the older sources pertaining to his life and career, is in George C. Boase and William P. Courtney, *Bibliotheca Cornubiensis*, I (London, 1874), 371–372. Two recent short studies are F. L. Harris, "Charles Morton—Minister, Academy Master and Emigrant (1627–1698)," and F. A. Turk, "Charles Morton; His Place in the Historical Development of British Science in the Seventeenth Century," Royal Institution of Cornwall, *Journal*, IV (1963), 326–363.

3. On Morton's use of English, see Smith, *Birth of Modern Education*, 58–59, 70, 238. On Dunton and the Athenian Society in relation to Morton, see Fiering, "The Trans-Atlantic Republic of Letters: A Note on the Circulation of Learned Periodicals to Early Eighteenth-Century America," *WMQ*, 3d Ser., XXXIII (1976), 642–660. Dunton wrote of Morton with characteristic hyperbole: "His Memory is as vast as his Knowledge, which is so great, that in the Firmament of Learning, the Name of Morton will shine like a Bright Star of the first Magnitude to all Posterity: and as tho' he were the Epitomy both of Aristotle and Descartes, he is the very soul of Philosophy."

vived.[4] But other extant examples of Morton's teaching are also noteworthy, namely those in logic and moral philosophy. In moral philosophy three important items have come down to us: two manuscripts in the Harvard Archives (one on "Ethicks" and one on "Pneumaticks," or pneumatology); and a published book, *The Spirit of Man* (Boston, 1693). The last two works are properly studies preliminary to ethics, pneumatology treating the study of spirit or mind independent of the body, and *The Spirit of Man* treating the subject of character or temperament (including the body) as it influences moral behavior.[5]

Morton himself was quite interested in "method," or the proper ordering and framing of the disciplines, and wrote on the subject. It would be an injustice to him to approach his work unmethodically. Yet, he did not have the intellectual capacity or perhaps the inclination to systematize his own writing to the degree that all inconsistency would be removed. So the reader should expect some paralogisms and lacunae in this account of Morton's thought.

Morton's strength was his ability to reduce philosophical material to simple and clear formulations, and he perfected a technique, at which he was remarkably persistent, of versifying basic knowledge in couplets. One student notebook from the late 1680s contains a piece entitled "The Memorial Verses of the Logick System," undoubtedly originally from Morton, which reduces an eclectic system of logic to 350 lines of rhyming couplets.[6] The section on method concludes as follows:

> By sense, observance, and experience
> Adding induction, Arts arose from hence.
> Change not in things divine, keep what is old[.]
> In philosophicalls you may be bold.
>
> .   .   .   .
>
> If in good method [a]ught you would express,
> Take what is needfull nothing more or less.

4. Morton, *Compendium Physicae* . . . , ed. Hornberger (Col. Soc. Mass., *Colls.*, XXXIII [Boston, 1940]), hereafter cited as Morton, *Compendium Physicae*.

5. Miller, *New England Mind*, I, 121–122, calls Morton the "one figure of importance in the intellectual history of 17th-century New England who adhered to the Peripatetics. . . . His treatise on physics reflects many new developments, but his logic was a reactionary Aristotelian manual." Miller's term "reactionary" structures the teaching of logic in terms of a dialectic of progressive and retrogressive that has no real application to the study of logic in early America or perhaps anywhere. Morton was, in fact, an eclectic in logic as was almost everyone at Harvard and Yale in the first quarter of the 18th century.

6. These 10 pages of verses on logic are in William Partridge's notebook, MS, Beinecke Lib., Yale Univ. It had long been common to use Latin verses as mnemonic aids. Morton may have been one of the earliest to try this system in English.

Let every part in method well agree
Not one to other contradicting be.

.   .   .   .

That always must precede which is most fitt
To make you understand what follows it.
When paragraphs are apt, distinct, and clear,
Connections of the parts will best appear.

.   .   .   .

Upon the prickly bush of Logick grows
Of other Sciences the fragrant rose.

All of Morton's surviving manuscripts of academic lectures, including the *Compendium Physicae*, are sprinkled with couplets like these, which he called "epitomes." At the end of the lecture, for study purposes, the student could put them all together to make a continuous rhyming epic that summarized the fundamentals of Morton's arguments.

"Change not in things divine, keep what is old. But in philosophicalls you may be bold." We do not know exactly what Morton meant by "philosophicalls," nor even how he conceived of the relationship between philosophy and theology, which entered a critical phase in the seventeenth century with the publication of the controversial works of Descartes and Hobbes. The Cambridge Platonists, whose writings were all well known to Morton, consciously strove to renew those philosophical traditions and ideas that they felt would "draw an Exoterick Fence, or exteriour Fortification about Theologie," as Henry More put it.[7] Their presumption was that true philosophy could never be injurious to the interests of true Christianity, a belief vague enough to leave ample room for individual interpretation. Morton may have had something like this program in mind when he encouraged boldness in "philosophicalls." Although he was not himself an outstandingly bold or original thinker, he was conversant enough with the works of the leading philosophers of his time to give Harvard students a more up-to-date education than would ordinarily have been the case without him. It was possibly Morton who introduced Henry More's ethics and metaphysics at Harvard, a change that effectively brought the Scholastic era to a close in Massachusetts. A close look at Morton's work can provide valuable understanding of the state of moral philosophy in New England in the last decade of the seventeenth century. We will look first at Morton's pneumatology.

7. Quoted by William C. DePauley, *The Candle of the Lord: Studies in the Cambridge Platonists* (London, 1937), 119–120.

"Pneumaticks"

The history of pneumatology as a distinct discipline has not been written. When it is, its story will illustrate neatly how a discipline may rise into prominence, perform a service to the state of knowledge for nearly a century, and then ultimately be reabsorbed into some broader or more stable area of study.[8] The discipline had already been defined in the early seventeenth century in the work of Bartholomaeus Keckermann and was also delineated in Alsted's famous *Encyclopaedia* of 1630. Although numerous works with the title "Pneumatology" or "Pneumatics" followed in the course of the seventeenth century, every writer seems to have had a different idea of what the subject was supposed to be. The Puritan pneumatologies, like John Owen's *Πνευματολογια, or, A Discourse Concerning the Holy Spirit* (London, 1674) and John Flavel's *Pneumatologia: A Treatise of the Soul of Man* (1683), were devoted primarily to theology and the doctrine of grace and did not purport to be philosophical treatises, although they often contained much information relevant to a philosophical treatment. Other scholars denied that pneumatology was a valid discipline in its own right. Alexander Richardson, for example, commented in the notes on "physics" appended to the 1657 edition of *The Logicians School-Master* that Keckermann "would have a special art of Spirits, scilicet πνευματίκε, and let him, but yet 'twill be a branch of natural philosophy." Richardson meant that pneumatology, if one wanted to give it any credence at all, belonged under physics (or natural philosophy), not metaphysics.[9] William Ames, of course, agreed, since he was particularly concerned about the danger of naturalistic studies encroaching on the domain of revealed truth. In Ames's schema physics was by definition concerned only with natural beings, which meant that by subsuming pneumatology under it, the subject would be confined simply to the study of the human soul as it could be understood without the aid of revelation. It is doubtful that Ames would have accepted the subdivision of *Physica* presented in Thomas Govan's *Ars Sciendi sive Logica* (1682), which posited two major branches, *Somatologia*, the science of material bodies, and *Pneumatologia*, the science of spiritual beings, and then further divided *Pneumatologia* into *Theologia*, the doctrine of God; *Angelographia* (including *Demonologia*), the doctrine of angels (and devils); and finally *Psychologia*, the doctrine of human souls. In this conception of pneumatology, revealed truth and naturally derived truth seem wholly intermixed.

8. In this respect the history of doomed disciplines is somewhat analogous to the history of third parties in American politics.

9. Richardson, *The Logicians School-Master: or, A Comment upon Ramus' Logicke . . .* (London, 1657), p. 89 of the appended notes.

Equally objectionable to Ames was the different arrangement proposed by Keckermann and Alsted, which treated pneumatology as a basic science of nature equivalent and parallel to physics rather than subordinate to it. In this schema metaphysics comes first as the study of being qua being; then follow pneumatology and physics, the one treating being as incorporeal, the other as corporeal. Working along these lines, Jean LeClerc at the beginning of the eighteenth century comprehensively covered the principal parts of knowledge by writing a logic, an ontology, a pneumatology, and a physics. A little earlier Henry More's *Enchiridion Metaphysicum* of 1679 had in effect eliminated metaphysics or ontology altogether by treating it as identical to pneumatology. More argued that everything else was either logic—the categories and predicaments of being—or plain physics, the study of the behavior and nature of material things.

The standing of pneumatology during Morton's lifetime was sufficiently at issue, in any case, for Heereboord to include in the "Index Quaestionum" of his *Meletemata* the *quaestio*, *"An pneumatica sit distincta specie scientia a Metaphysica?"* (Is pneumatology a science different in kind from metaphysics?)[10] Master's *quaestiones* more or less identical to this query were answered in the affirmative at Harvard in 1688, 1709, and 1715, indicating at least that the subject was taken seriously.

The relationship of the science of pneumatology to the rise of the new moral philosophy is both important and complex. The study of the soul or psyche in Aristotelian philosophy was by no means concentrated under moral philosophy. To pull together an integrated science of man from Aristotle's thought as a whole it would be necessary to bring together elements from his *De Anima*, from his rhetoric, and from several smaller works in addition to the material in his ethics treatises. In the seventeenth century the study of man remained similarly fragmented. The development of pneumatology was, perhaps, symptomatic of the increased attention to human psychology we have already noted, or at least of a desire in the seventeenth century to study the nonphysical side of the creation in isolation from its association with material bodies. The common inclusion of the study of angels and God along with human spirits in pneumatology testifies to this special concern with what might be called, somewhat anachronistically, mental phenomena. Aristotle's interest in psychology, on the contrary, had always been physiologically oriented.

Throughout the seventeenth century speculation under the aegis of pneumatology went on separately from work in ethics, as though the two were not intimately related. Ethics continued to be thought of primarily as a normative discipline subordinate to divinity, but the weakening of theological authority

10. Heereboord, *Meletemata*, 1014.

was already causing philosophers to search for ethical foundations independent of revelation. These foundations, it came to be believed, were primarily lodged in human nature itself, and when that assumption was made, pneumatology, as the science of man's psyche, suddenly became quite central to the enterprise of moral philosophy. This whole process of change can be traced in considerable detail in the thought of Samuel Johnson of Stratford, Connecticut, early in the eighteenth century. "I thus define *Moral Philosophy* in a larger sense than is usual," Johnson wrote in 1731, after fifteen years of reflection on the subject, "comprehending under it, the Doctrine of Spirits, or Moral Agents, which, I think, truly belongs to it; because the Knowledge of our Duty is so necessarily connected with the Knowledge of the Nature of Spirits, or Intelligent Free Agents, and entirely depends on it, that it cannot be understood or explained without it."[11] Johnson in effect decided that pneumatology, the "Doctrine of Spirits," was a branch of moral philosophy. Johnson's conclusion represented the American version of the process that had already gone on in England in the work of Richard Cumberland, Henry More, the third earl of Shaftesbury, and others. In the pneumatology of Charles Morton we see this same process at an early stage.

Morton defended the existence of a separate discipline of pneumatology on the grounds that every species of being has a distinct science by which it is studied. "It is to be wondered at," he said, that "Spirit, the most noble species of the most noble creature," should still lack the dignity of a particular science and be thrust into a corner of metaphysics, especially when "Body, much below it, and divers accidents much below that again have bin so ample treated of."[12] His explanation for this neglect was that the heathen philosophers who first molded the sciences knew little of the subject, and the Schoolmen, out of "superstitious respect" for those heroes, followed suit. Morton no doubt was sincere in his desire to give every species its due, but underlying his concern for pneumatology was the goal of establishing a reasonably independent science of man based upon man's most salient characteristic, his mind. Pneumatology included more than psychology, however. It was also the science of angelic minds and the divine mind. A crucial question that faced Morton and every proponent of pneumatology, until the time that it was

---

11. Johnson, "An Introduction to the Study of Philosophy, Exhibiting a General View of All the Arts and Sciences," *Present State of the Republick of Letters*, IV (London, 1731), 389. See Fiering, "Samuel Johnson," *WMQ*, 3d Ser., XXVIII (1971), 199–236, for a full account of the evolution of Johnson's thought on the place of moral philosophy in the curriculum. On pneumatology in the 18th century, see McLachlan, *English Education under the Test Acts*, especially p. 276.

12. Morton, "Pneumaticks," MS, 1, Harvard Univ. Archives, Cambridge, Mass. Hereafter references to pages in this manuscript will appear in parentheses in the text.

converted simply into human psychology, was whether it was to be the empirical (including the introspective) study of man or the inherited postulates concerning God and angels that would define the subject. The eventual absorption of pneumatology into moral philosophy in the early eighteenth century signaled the victory of human studies over divine in the determination of the nature of spirit.

Morton distinguished pneumatology (or pneumatics) from metaphysics on the basis of the former's exclusive concern with nonmaterial being. Metaphysics, which takes being per se as its object, must necessarily treat the nature of matter as well as of spirit. Pneumatology differs also from theology in that its sources are wholly natural; theology takes as its principles of knowledge "Revelation and faith by the light of grace, manifested in the Scriptures" (3). Pneumatology may draw some things from the light of grace, for Scripture is used in reasoning for purposes of "illustration and confirmation," especially with regard to angels, but there was no confusion in Morton's mind about these distinct sources of understanding.

> Pneumatic is a science quite distinct,
>   From Metaphisick and Theologie,
> God, Angels, Souls, are plainly handled in't,
>   But in a way that has diversity.

Spirit may be defined in several ways: "immaterial substance" or the Cartesian "thinking substance" were both acceptable to Morton. He first discussed spirit in general, and then specifically as theology, angelography, and "psycologie." Rationalist Cartesian influences are evident immediately when Morton established that the first proof of "spirits being is from the soul of man, as neerest to us and therefore best perceived by us." Intellect is a primary power of spirit and "most nearly conjoyned thereunto, if not the same[;] therefore spirit is more knowable than body, which is but the object of sense, a more inferioure faculty of the soul." The soul's thinking "shows its activity, whereby we first perceive it" (5).

The most frequently mentioned authority in Morton's pneumatics is not Descartes, however, but Adrian Heereboord, whose *Meletemata* contained a "Pneumatica" that Morton was indebted to. Heereboord was a popular author at Newington Green as well as at Harvard, if we may judge from the Latin verse Samuel Wesley wrote to describe his course of studies under Morton in the late 1670s:

> Stahlius, et Suarez, Gassendus cum Zabarella,
>   Et Keckermannus, tuque Hereborde Pater!
> Hisce Opus immortale tuum, Venerande Cracanthorp!
>   Scheiblerique ingens, Smiglecijque Labor.

Carolus et Morton; Mortonius inclytus, et Tu,
Carole! etc.[13]

But Heereboord, in addition to being an authority, was often a foil for Morton, too: an author Morton's students would familiarly know from whom he could meaningfully diverge in his teaching.

One difference between Morton and Heereboord concerned the question of whether spirit is a univocal or equivocal species, in other words, whether the term "spirit" has one meaning or several throughout all its applications. Heereboord held it was univocal; Morton, that it was equivocal. Among Morton's replies to Heereboord was the argument that "Spirit ascribed to creatures [and not to God], though it be Immaterial, yet it has this in common with matter, that it has *Passibility* (an attribute that is very near to the essence of matter), but God has not passive power, being pure act" (6). Possibility meant the capability of being passively affected as an object rather than as an agent. God is never an object, and His spirit, unlike man's, is never passible. Matter, as distinguished from spirit and form, is pre-eminently passible; but in man, spirit, too, is affected, as by the passions, and therefore passible. Because it allowed for the discussion of the differences between spirit in man and spirit in God, Morton's assertion of the equivocality of spirit was a step in the direction of removing pneumatology from under the aegis of metaphysics and theology and placing it under moral philosophy. With regard to all *created* spirits, however, that is, angels and human souls, Morton agreed with Heereboord that spirit is univocal.[14]

God as a spirit differs from man's spirit in other respects than passibility, of course, particularly in degree of perfection: God's infinity, immensity, eter-

13. Morison, "Charles Morton," Col. Soc. Mass., *Colls.*, XXXIII (1940), xvii, quoted from Wesley's *A Defence of a Letter Concerning the Education of Dissenters in Their Private Academies* . . . (London, 1704). Heereboord was one of the most widely used authors in the dissenting academies. Most of the other authors mentioned—Stahlius, Suarez, Gassendi, Zabarella, Keckermann, Cracanthorpe, Scheibler, and Smiglecki—were well known at Harvard, too.

14. The modern temptation to ridicule the study of angels should be somewhat checked by Dom David Knowles's comment in *The Evolution of Medieval Thought* (Baltimore, 1962), 242: "Strange and unreal as may seem to us the care devoted by medieval theologians to a consideration of the angelic beings, the matter is of crucial importance to those who are convinced of the reality of another kind of spiritual being, the human soul, for in the 'angels' the being of an incorporeal spirit can be isolated and discussed without the complications caused by a material body." Even in modern reductionist behavioral science, angels may be thought of as a kind of psychological "model." In *Le Thomisme* (Paris, 1922), 56, Étienne Gilson has commented that St. Thomas's study of angels cannot properly be looked at as a strictly theological study. The workings of inferior creatures like man could be fully understood, it was believed, only in comparison to, or in contrast with, that of angels. See Léon Brunschvicg, *Le Progrès de la conscience dans la philosophie occidentale* (Paris, 1927), I, 115. See also, Increase Mather, *Angelographia; or a Discourse Concerning the Nature and Power of the Holy Angels* . . . (Boston, 1696).

nity, and so on. But Morton was enough of a rationalist, as was everyone who ventured to write on pneumatology, to hold strictly to the belief that the assumed analogy between God and man was real, and that it was not only possible to make deductions pertaining to both based upon knowledge of one or the other spirit, God's or man's, but necessary and right to do so. Those writers who denied the validity of this analogy were either self-blinded fideists or skeptics, Morton believed. The constant necessity to square knowledge of the human spirit (psychology) with angelology and theology was the greatest handicap to the development of pneumatology. The subject was a peculiar mixture of empiricism and dogma. One of the heuristic benefits of deist thinking in the eighteenth century was that it emancipated the study of man from its earlier close ties to theology. The new question in moral philosophy was: What can be observed about the world of man and human nature independently of inherited assumptions about God and the theological image of man?

In his treatment of the will, Morton, like Heereboord, was an intellectualist. Will is always conjoined to intellect, otherwise even the most perfect intellect would be "but an Idle Speculator." The existence and nature of the will may also be demonstrated by "simile." All natural beings tend by their natural form to some natural good. Brutes have their "sensuall forme" and by sensitive appetite tend toward what is right for them. Rational spirits, by their "Intellectuall forme (if it may be called)" have a rational appetite, or will, which seeks good and shuns evil.

Morton took what appears to be a rather naive view of the ontological standing of will and intellect. He disagreed with Heereboord on the question of whether these faculties and underlying spiritual substance ought each to be considered real beings in themselves. In accordance with the Occamist principle that "entities are not to be multiplyed without necessity," Heereboord had rejected a distinction between agent, power (or faculty), and act and ascribed simplicity to the soul. Morton, on the contrary, believed that it is necessary "for the clear and distinct apprehension of the souls operations to allow that they come from Powers, which are distinct from their own acts: And therefore, to say, the soul *thinking* is Intellect, the soul *willing* is Will, seems . . . very unphilosophicall." Heereboord's position, according to Morton, "makes the creature to understand and will by essence (while the very substans is immediately applyed to the acts) a thing which by themselves was reserved to God onely" (17).[15]

Morton was content with the definition of liberty characteristic of intellec-

15. Henry More, like Heereboord, also maintained that the soul is a single, complex unit, and it is always the whole soul that thinks or wills, not a faculty somehow "separate and distinct from the Essence they belong to." See *The Immortality of the Soul . . .* (London, 1659), Bk. II, chap. iii, sec. 8.

tualism, that it is simply a matter of "rational spontaneity," or unconstrained action taken after intellectual consideration. Liberty of indifference he emphatically rejected for both God and man. God "must in al things doe best and what he has done in al things is best,—therefore it is necessary he should doe what he has done."[16] In God and angels, there exists simultaneously both the greatest freedom and the greatest necessity. This proves that freedom consists in the absence of "coaction," or coercion, rather than in the absence of necessity; necessity is consistent with freedom when it is an intellectual or a rational necessity spontaneously arrived at. "That old notion of the popish schoolmen, of suspending the Act of the Will, after the Dictate of Reason, I think tis a useless figment. They may as well fancy that the Intellect may suspend its act of Assent or Dissent when truth or falsehood is made manifest unto it" (17–18, 60, 102). Thus Morton took a strict intellectualist position and denied that the will has either liberty of specification or liberty of exercise.

Morton discussed the relationship between the divine will and the human will under the pneumatics of theology, the first of the three special parts of the general science of spirits. The Molinist concept of the *scientia media* (or middle science) was predictably unacceptable to Morton, but in its stead he outlined a comparably dense Scholastic framework of divine knowledge.[17] God's "reall knowledge" is divided into "possibles" and "futures" and into "necessary" and "contingent." Contingent future knowledge is either "absolute" or "conditional." In Morton's epitome: "Absolutes and Conditionates are Known, / And yet we middle science need not own" (52–55). God's will may also be divided into secret and revealed and into antecedent and consequent. The antecedent will, which is sometimes called "velleity," or suspended will, is a concept that has been much abused by the Pelagians, according to Morton. Belief in antecedent will gives credence to the *scientia media*. But such a velleity is "unworthy of God," for it suggests He is "impotent to accomplish what he would" and makes Him "depend on mans Will," as if it were man's will that causes God to act (59).

The providence of God over man and all of His creation consists of three operations: conservation, concurse, and government. Morton's analysis of these three is very similar to other Puritan statements, such as one by Urian Oakes in 1682.[18] Conservation "is a transient act of God whereby the creature is preserved in existence and caused to persevere therein." As Morton noted, Thomas Aquinas calls conservation simply *"continued creation,"* and both

16. It seems unlikely that Morton knew anything of Leibniz's work, but in this brief statement he summarized the "principle of sufficient reason" that underlay Leibniz's *Theodicée*.

17. A number of Harvard *theses* and *quaestiones* rejected the *scientia media*. This concept is discussed more fully in chap. 3, above.

18. See Oakes, *The Soveraign Efficacy of Divine Providence . . .* (Boston, 1682), part of which is published in Miller and Johnson, eds., *The Puritans*, 350–367.

creation and conservation are "one indivisible act, only distinguished by our thoughts. . . . Creation and Conserving are the same / But by our thoughts obtain a diverse Name. / The world may be annihilated hence / If God withdraw sustaining Influence" (70).[19] Jonathan Edwards throughout his life placed considerable emphasis on the doctrine of conservation, but the great antiquity of this teaching is sometimes forgotten. The modern impetus behind interest in the subject derived from Descartes.

The doctrine of concurse has particular bearing on questions of ethics. "Concurse or Cooperation, is an external transient act of God, whereby he does cooperate with all second causes in their actions and producing their effects." The most important distinction within this definition is between physical and moral concurse. Physical "truly gives effectuall influx." Moral "perswades to, or from an act, . . . puts or removes objects, and opportunities"(72). This difference is the same as that which divided Augustinian voluntarists and intellectualists on the matter of conversion. Was conversion a moral process, proceeding through the understanding and then the will, or a physical process directly affecting the will? Neither position put God very far out of the texture of human events, and Morton did not address himself to the issue at any length. Interestingly, at this early date the clock analogy was sufficiently prominent for Morton to reject it explicitly: God "deals not with his creatures, as men doe by machines (such as clocks) put them a going and then let them goe by their own frame, or as brutes doe by their young when grown. . . . In those things their is no such dependence of the effect on the external cause, as is necessary in the creature on God, the first cause" (73). The concurse of God, in other words, is everpresent in human affairs.

An interesting comparison to Morton's thinking on the relation between divine will and human will may be drawn with the lectures of the English dissenter Henry Grove, who taught ethics and pneumatology at Taunton Academy from 1698 to 1738. Grove was fifty years Morton's junior chronologically, and in the evolution of ideas he represents perfectly the next stage of academic philosophy in the dissenting academies after the disappearance of Morton's generation. When Grove was himself a student at Taunton under Morton's contemporary Matthew Warren, he studied Burgersdyck and Eustache, but in addition he read Cumberland, Locke, and LeClerc. Grove's lectures differ strikingly from Morton's in a number of conclusions. Regarding the doctrine of continuous creation, Grove asked: If by this is meant

> a kind of contrived and successive creation, a positive volition that it [the world] remain in being, in the absence whereof it would presently fall

19. Morton's defense of the doctrine of continuous creation is also iterated in his *Compendium Physicae*, 190. Many Protestant Scholastics adhered to this doctrine. See Heppe, *Reformed Dogmatics*, ed. Bizer, trans. Thomson, 256–262.

back into nothing, it is hard to conceive in what the necessity of this should be founded. If there be such a necessity, it must proceed from a supposed tendency of all created beings to become nothing; which inclination in something to become nothing, is to me, I confess, equally difficult to apprehend, as an inclination in nothing to become something.

Grove also rejected the idea that God concurred or cooperated in all human actions, and particularly the belief that God sometimes determines the will to action "by a positive, immediate, and irresistible influx," as distinguished from "that which is moral, and influences the will by an address or application to the understanding." Whoever was the author of this "ill-favored opinion," Grove wrote, "he has had too many followers, as well among the Protestants as among the Romanists." He listed among his objections to the doctrine that it is "perfectly opposite to the nature of man as a rational agent," that God did not need to use this kind of influence to raise particular desires in man, and that physical predetermination "will not consist with human liberty." The worst consequence of this doctrine was that it made God the author of sin. God's rule, according to Grove, consists only in "creating and maintaining a being, and its powers of action, and ordaining the objects and circumstances, which are the *occasional* causes of action."[20]

Morton's pneumatics was in general more concerned with theology than with either angelology or psychology. We will pass by the angelology except to note that in his arguments Morton cited, among others, Thomas Aquinas, Scotus, Cajetan, Suarez, and Heereboord. He referred with approval both to Glanvil's famous attack on Sadduccean skepticism toward spirits and to some of Henry More's theories in defense of spiritual entities, which is simply one more confirmation of the support that learned men gave to the belief in witches in seventeenth-century New England and elsewhere. As has long been noted, some of the roots of the infamous witchcraft trials at Salem, Massachusetts, in 1692 may be traced to the philosophical opposition to Hobbesian materialism maintained strongly by the Cambridge Platonists. The revived interest in demons at the end of the seventeenth century was the result not of archaic superstition but of the seriousness of the materialist challenge. As Henry More once wrote, "That Saying is not more true in Politicks, *no Bishop, no King*; than this is in Metaphysick, *no Spirit, no God.*" The issue, as a recent

---

20. Grove, *Moral Philosophy*, ed. Amory, 221, 224–228. Published posthumously, this book was comprised of Grove's lectures during his years as a teacher. From internal evidence it is clear that most of the book was written in about 1710, with occasional signs of updating to the 1720s. Despite its datedness, Grove's work was widely read in American academic circles upon its publication in 1749. Jonathan Edwards read it in the 1750s. It was also in use at Princeton in 1752, according to Francis L. Broderick, "Pulpit, Physics, and Politics: The Curriculum of the College of New Jersey, 1746–1794," *WMQ*, 3d Ser., VI (1949), 42–68. A copy was ordered by the Library Co. of Philadelphia in 1752. See Labaree and Bell, eds., *Franklin Papers*, IV, 351.

historian interprets it, was simply this: "If one believed in spirits, then he must also believe in evil spirits; and if one denies evil spirits, then he will be led to deny all spirits, and ultimately to deny the Godhead itself."[21]

Most of what appears in the psychology section of Morton's manuscript on pneumatology was quite commonplace at the time. He dismissed the Aristotelian doctrine that there are three souls in man—a rational, a sensitive, and a vegetative. "Reason, Sens, and Vegetation are all but powers of the same Spirit, which is the Form of Man." "What need three Souls when one with its various faculties will doe?" (95–96) As a good example of proof of the soul's immortality by the use of natural reason alone, Morton, interestingly, cited Ficino (97). The soul's operations are divided into "proper" and "common." "Proper" activities of the soul, such as intellection, do not depend upon its conjunction with the body. "Common" activities, such as sight, do require the body. The point that Morton wanted to emphasize is that in some cases the understanding does not depend upon the "imagination," that is, upon the images conveyed by external sense-data. "Suppose the soul has the species of materiall things otherwise than by phansy [phantasm, image] namely by infusion, can it not understand them?" (98) At the conclusion of his "pneumaticks" Morton included a review of the powers, habits, and acts of human souls in a separated state, that is, as separated from the body, a subject about which there was much disagreement. The moral habits remain in the separate soul, but some merely subsist without being used, such as the virtues of fortitude, temperance, and liberality, which "require some materialls to complete them" (100). Special circumstances must exist in which such moral

---

21. Samuel I. Mintz, *The Hunting of Leviathan: Seventeenth-Century Reactions to the Materialism and Moral Philosophy of Thomas Hobbes* (Cambridge, 1962), 41. In an appendix to his "Ethicks" Morton referred to Hobbes by name in a different context. Morton's role in the Salem witch trials is briefly discussed in Morison, "Charles Morton," Col. Soc. Mass., *Colls.*, XXXIII (1940), xxv–xxviii. See also, Rosalie Colie, *Light and Enlightenment: A Study of the Cambridge Platonists and the Dutch Arminians* (Cambridge, 1957), 106, concerning demonology. Hobbes's banishing of superstitious beliefs in witches and evil spirits was celebrated by some authors. See the poem by John Sheffield, earl of Mulgrave and duke of Buckingham (1648–1721), *On Mr Hobbes, and His Writings*: "While in dark ignorance we lay, afraid / Of fancies, ghosts, and every empty shade, / Great Hobbes appear'd, and by plain reason's light, / Put such fantastic forms to shameful flight." Quoted by Fairchild, *Religious Trends in English Poetry*, I, 3. A Harvard thesis in 1689, perhaps under Morton's influence, stated: *"Dantur Veneficia"* (There is such a thing as sorcery). Clarence Gohdes, "Aspects of Idealism in Early New England," *Philosophical Review*, XXXIX (1930), 546, quotes Ralph Cudworth's *The True Intellectual System of the Universe* . . . , 2d ed., 2 vols. (London, 1743 [orig. publ. 1678]), as follows: "As for wizards and magicians, persons who associate and confederate themselves in a peculiar manner with these evil spirits for the gratification of their own revenge, lust, ambition, and other passions; besides the Scriptures, there hath so full an attestation been given to them by persons unconcerned in all ages, that those our so confident exploders of them in this present age can hardly escape the suspicion of having some hankring towards atheism."

habits are required. In his physics, which was cross-referenced to his ethics and pneumatology, Morton dealt with some of the operations of intellect more fully, including the internal senses (which he called *"interior"* senses) of "common sense," "phantasy" or imagination, and memory.[22]

Morton's most interesting psychological concept was not presented in the section on the soul. He introduced it in his discussion of how man is able to know God. Human beings, he said, have both subjective-innate knowledge of God and objective-acquired knowledge. (The philosophical belief that the existence of God is directly knowable to man without the aid of external sensation was widely held prior to the publication of Locke's *Essay Concerning Human Understanding*, and Locke's opposition to this belief was one of the main grounds on which the *Essay* was criticized.) The presence of this subjective "impressed" idea of God in the soul, which is perceived as soon as the soul perceives itself, was, for Morton, man's most essential characteristic. That "a sentiment of Deity is first in [man] even before any acts of Reasoning," is good cause to describe him as an "Animal *Religious*, or an Animal after the Image of God," rather than as an "animal rational" (27–28). One of the benefits of such a definition is that it distinguishes man more decisively from brute creatures, who, Morton argued, are also rational to some degree.[23] In an appendix to the "Pneumaticks," "The Soules of Brutes," which dealt with the great question raised by Descartes of whether animals are merely machines, it becomes clear that Morton was pressed to his new definition of man after rejecting the Cartesian position. "Tis to me a very inconceivable thing that [animals] have noe more perception and passions than a machine. Certeynly if Brutes act only as machines then machines act as Brutes; and then the moustrap is as angry as the mous, which nibles at the Chees when it knocks him on the pate" (118). Morton held outrightly that "the

22. See Morton, *Compendium Physicae*, 180–184. Morton's definition of "phantasy" was conventional: "Phantasy, or fancy is the [second] interior Sens, the Seat [hereof] they place in the middle part of the brain. tis defin'd a Sensative power, whereby the Animall Soul can Apprehend, Compare and Estimate Phantasms, which are Images ([hence] tis Cal'd Imagination,) or representations of things that have been some way or other perceived by [outward] Senses; Without Sens can be no Imagination. . . . But what has appeared and been perceived by the Senses, has made an Impression upon the Animall Spirits in the brain which Signature is retain'd for Contemplation long after Sensation is Ended." There is further discussion following this. On the operation of the intellect and the nature of the will, see also, pp. 198–205 in Morton.

23. In the *Spectator* no. 201, Oct. 20, 1711, Addison wrote: "It has been observed by some writers, that Man is more distinguished from the Animal World by Devotion than by Reason, as several Brute Creatures discover in their Actions something like a faint glimmering of Reason, though they betray in no single Circumstance of their Behaviour any thing that bears the least affinity to Devotion." Bond, ed., *Spectator*, II, 287–288. In a footnote Bond adds: "Cf. Edward, Lord Herbert of Cherbury, *De Veritate*, chap. vi: 'But the most significant point is that no form of religion exists among beasts. It is through these differences that we are distinctively human' (trans. Meyrick H. Carre [Bristol, 1937], 174)." Vives earlier had had a similar notion.

soules of Brutes are True *Spirits*, or thinking substances, because we find in them such operations as cannot be ascribed to meer matter." Therefore, the *"difference* between these Spirits and that of man is rather Religion and sense of Deity than either reason or speech; for . . . some Rudiments of these are in brutes, and the difference in *Degree* is more manifest than the difference in *Kind"* (122).

The ascription of higher powers to brutes—Morton believed the dog has "a kind of conscience"—also has certain humanitarian and practical value. It encourages "mercy and justice" toward them, Morton claimed, and truly moral arguments may be drawn from their behavior: "Goe to the ant thou sluggard." And "as the moralls of heathens doe shame and incite Xtians, who have more and better light to guide them, to walk more regularly than they doe, so the brutes moralls (if we may so call them) may incite men who have clearer intellectuals and greater obligation lying upon them" (126).[24]

The Spirit of Man

In 1693 Morton published in Boston the major fruit of his psychological and moral speculation, *The Spirit of Man*. The subject of this volume was clearly of deeper concern to him than pneumatology, the study of separated souls. *The Spirit of Man* was a full-length metaethical investigation into the subject

---

24. Morton's 25-page appendix on "The Soules of Brutes" referred to Hobbes, Gassendi, Boyle, More, Antoine LeGrand, and Thomas Willis (*De Anima brutorum*, 1672), as well as to Descartes. In the *Compendium Physicae* Morton also treated extensively both the matter of whether brutes have souls and the definition of man (see pp. 145, 149–151, 187–190, 196–198, and 205). Morton seems to have been preoccupied with these problems—not without reason, given the uncertainty of the age. "Most Phylosophers have been very Shy of allowing Spirits to brutes lest thereby they Should render them immortal, or Incorruptible because of their indivisibility. [Des]Cartes tells us [that objective] motion is no more than pulling the tricker [trigger] of these machines. . . . Thus when I Whistle my Dog, all his Spirits are put in motion, by the Small touch of the Timpanum or Drum of the Ear, from the Air Vibrated by the Whistle. And So by the motion of the finger, a taught Eliphant has his whole [vast] body put into motion, the tricker being in his Eye beholding the fingers little motion. All this they Say is possible because of the Immense knowledge of the Oppificer of the machynes, and therefore mens Impotens to make an Engine like this hinders not its probability" (p. 188). Continuing, Morton made some shrewd observations about the difficulties inherent in this approach. One of his goals, it seems, was to preserve intact a graded chain of being with only a small gap between animals and man. Regarding the definition of man, in the *Compendium Physicae*, 196, Morton wrote: "For [animals] Seam to have a sence of fault, and guilt if they have offended, and Some [Kind] of [Self] Satisfaction, and pleasure when they have obeyed their immediate Lord (man) and done as they have been bid: But no Sentiment of a deity or worship could ever be observed in them, and therefore Some learned men are inclined to think religion, and not reason is the Essentiall difference of a man from a brute. Shaddows of reason in a brute we Spie / But no religious Sens of Deity."

of temperament or character, necessarily deeply affected by the body. But in only slight respects was Morton's approach a return to the old Galenic theory that temperament shaped moral character. He was attempting to draw up something new for his time, something much broader, that would contribute to the human self-knowledge that is essential for moral virtue.[25] *The Spirit of Man* is one of the earliest instances of "original" philosophy attempted in America.

Morton's first task was to delimit the meaning of "spirit," or *pneuma*, so that it could be a useful term in moral analysis. He intended, he stated, always to use the term in relation to the human body, unlike its use in pneumatology. The "spirit" of man refers to the "whole man . . . both Soul and Body," and is "a more *General* and comprehensive word" than is sometimes assumed (4–5). Morton took pains to show how spirit in this sense may be distinguished from soul, mind, will, and so on. He agreed that it is also possible to speak of spirit outside of man, such as the Holy Spirit; but in man, spirit denotes "some *Qualifications*, or *Inclinations* of the mind as *United* to the Body, and *Conformed* much thereunto." It is synonymous with the "*Genius*, *Temper*, or *Disposition*" of a man, that which is as "peculiar to himself in this respect" as his features, stature, carriage, and "whereby he is Distinguished from any other" (15). The modern counterpart of Morton's "spirit" might be "personality," "character," or "temperament."

The spirit, or the genius, of an individual is an "Aggregate . . . of divers things." Four elements enter into its formation: the soul's faculties, the body's temperament, acquired habits, and outward circumstances. The faculties of the soul, "as Understanding, Will, Sensitive Appetite or Passions," are all "ingredients as the *Substrate Matter* of this *Spirit* in Man." But Morton assumed that souls are all equal in this respect, or that these faculties are constants in the development of individual spirits. In consequence, the vast differences among men must be due to variations in the other ingredients (19). Of these, temperament is undoubtedly the most important in Morton's estimation. Thus, the famous Galenic tag, "*Manners of the Mind follow Temperament of the Body* is true if rightly understood." By manners, however, we must understand "not the *Vertues*, or *Vices* themselves; But the *Genius and Inclination*, which leads and Disposes to them." This definition reveals that Morton was hoping to get behind ethics to a kind of pre-ethics based on the determinants of personality. Temperament is only one ingredient, though; so Morton's investigation is not in the end a physiology of morals. And he explicitly recalled the old critique of the Galenic theory, that if morals were

---

25. *Spirit of Man*, 89. Hereafter page references to this volume will appear in parentheses in the text. Morton's *Spirit of Man* has a preface signed by Increase Mather, James Allen, Samuel Willard, John Baily, and Cotton Mather. Some background to one element in Morton's approach is in chap. 9 of Levi, *French Moralists*, "Medicine and Morals."

alone a matter of temperament "skilful *Physicians* (who may perhaps have the worst Manners) might be accounted the best Moralists, and they could easily mend all the world, who cannot mend themselves." Moreover, it is the soul, not the body, that is the "active" part in man. The sense in which the soul is influenced by the body is always passive. In "exerting its own proper power," the soul is simply "helped or hindered by the *Bodys* good or ill Temperament" (20–21).[26]

The third ingredient in individual spirit, after the soul's faculties and the body's temperament, is acquired habits, which "do much Alter the *Genius* or *Spirit*, from what it would be, if men were left to their Pure Naturals." The sources of acquired habits are several: instructions and rules that we learn in our youth, including the academic subjects in higher education, which train the mind in various ways; example and converse with people, which can make a greater impression than rules alone; and finally, the customs and habits of the place one lives. Country people are plain hearted and may have a rough rusticity. The city breeds "Civility, Sagacity, and Cunning. One who lives where News is frequently Talked, Gets somewhat of a Publick Spirit: Amongst good natured People, a Candid Spirit" (23–24).

Fourth and last, "Outward Circumstances do also Exceedingly vary *mens spirits*, and that in a shorter space of time, then *Habits*." Prosperity may make a man bold and brisk; poverty contracts and emasculates the spirit. And if such circumstances continue for a long time, they may "fix" our genius.

All of these factors "do some way concurr to Constitute and Represent the Man." But the internal force of temperament is the chief one. The others are "Accidental Inherents, and Adjacents," which modify the basic constitution but can never submerge it altogether. In modern terminology, it is biological inheritance (perhaps nerves and metabolism) that counts most, and Morton hammered the point home with one of his couplets: "Drive Nature out with Pitche forks; twill Return, / And act its part, as sure as fire will Burn" (26). It is somewhat ironic that Morton delivered these thoughts on the pre-eminent importance of inheritance in the very decade that John Locke's *Essay Concerning Human Understanding* and his *Thoughts on Education* were advancing cogent arguments in support of nurture and environment. It should be noted, however, that Locke's and Morton's concern with the problem of nature versus nurture was principally in connection with *moral* development, that is, with the problem of the attainment of virtue. The similar twentieth-century debate over inheritance versus environment is much more preoccupied with the conditions of *intellectual* development (in many respects a more

26. Cf. the Harvard *quaestio* in 1704, responded to affirmatively by Israel Loring: *An mores animi sequuntur temperamentum corporis?* (Whether moral character is dependent upon [i.e., follows] the temperament of the body?)

superficial and much narrower question). Thus, Morton and Locke both mini-mized inherited differences in mental faculties, since even if there is some variance in intelligence from person to person at birth, it is hardly likely to be great enough to influence moral character.[27]

Morton's idea of "temperament" is roughly included in what Henry Grove in his ethics called "inclination." Inclination, according to Grove, may be defined as "a kind of bias upon nature, by the force of which it is carried towards certain actions, previously to the exercise of thought and reasoning about the nature and consequences of them, whether they are good or evil, beneficial or hurtful." Grove distinguished between natural and acquired in-clinations and observed that the former are seen clearly in children. "It is not improbable," he added, that this "variety of inclinations has its foundation in different temperaments and complections of body; according to that maxim of Galen, *Mores animae sequuntur temperamentum corporis*." But Grove did not explore the relation between temperament and virtue in any detail, be-cause, he argued, the moral value of any "purely natural" inclination toward good is nil. The true test of the strength of one's virtue lies in overcoming obstacles. Beyond that, man's moral life should be ruled by the dictates of reason, not by mere natural inclinations.[28]

After introductory material most of Morton's short treatise on *The Spirit of Man* is concerned with an analysis of temperaments, which he defined in terms of hot, cold, and medium. He rejected the coordinate humors of hot, dry, cold, and moist for the study of spirits, since they are properly applied to medicine and physiology only. In "Humane and Moral Actions" hot, cold, and "mean" alone have "the greatest Influence." Another broad principle of analysis in Morton cut across the metaphors of temperature and was equally determinist, namely the religious condition of the individual. Any given tem-perament may be either sanctified or unsanctified, and these conditions will respectively determine the goodness or the badness of a temperament neutral "in itself." Temperament "in itself" is a state that Morton never clarified. Is this pure state something merely hypothetical? Is there an area of nature somewhere between sanctification and corruption such as the Adamic state before the Fall? Morton did not directly answer these questions, but the whole unwitting tendency of his *Spirit of Man* was toward the establishment of a secular psychology of temperament considered in terms of constant human types.

---

27. For some of the issues and opinions at the time, see J. A. Passmore, "The Malleability of Man in Eighteenth-Century Thought," in Earl R. Wasserman, ed., *Aspects of the Eighteenth Century* (Baltimore, 1965), 21–46, and Fiering, "Franklin and Virtue," *Am. Qtly.*, XXX (1978), 199–223.

28. Grove, *Moral Philosophy*, ed. Amory, 137.

Hot spirits act warmly; cold spirits act cooly; and some people are in the middle. Cheerfulness is a trait of some hot spirits, along with activity, courage, and zeal. But the cheerful spirit when unsanctified is grossly abused in levity, froth, vanity, and foolish jesting. If sanctified, the cheer becomes "Spiritual Joy" (29). Another type of temperament among the hot spirits is what Morton called "Activity," or the active spirit. In its natural state, or in itself, activity has these qualities: willingness to be employed, strong inclinations, great inquisitiveness after things that are out of view. But when this condition is unsanctified it makes a man like "a brisk Monkey"; it leads to idle busybodies, meddlers, restlessness, and so on. It makes "*Seekers* in Religion; never satisfied with settled Truths, but *Scepticks*, Rambling and Uncomposed sectarys, tossed about with every wind of Doctrine." On the other hand, when the active spirit is sanctified "then none so *Serviceable* to God, or Man" (32). Morton analyzed zeal in a similar fashion. The spirit of zeal itself is "a *Natural Passion*, and therefore (in it self) neither *Good* nor *Bad*" (41). It is what happens to zeal under divine or satanic influence that determines its value. Perhaps these samples provide a sufficient taste of Morton's methods.

Morton's appreciation of the natural diversity of temperaments led him to appreciate also the necessary diversity in religious qualities. For the best outcome, nature and grace must cooperate. "*Zeal* for God, which is every mans *Duty*," may not "Comport so well with every mans *Spirit*." Also, "many good Christians, by Reason of a *Natural* Infirmity, are not always able to manage a *Zealous Spirit*" (47–50). Thus, Morton believed that meekness of spirit is the best *unsanctified* temperament to have, for though "it does *no good*, so it does *Least Harm* and *Mischief*" (71).

More desirable than any hot or cold temperaments is the mean between them, the "well-balanced spirit." In discussing this personality type Morton again revealed his intellectualism. In this individual "the *Will* is Benign, and the *Passions* Regular. The *Will*, and all the *powers under* its Commands are Disposed to Subjection unto Right Reason." Such a person governs himself and is most fit to govern others. Titus Vespasian was Morton's surprising example of such a man and leader "so far as *Nature* can go." But this same middle spirit is the most dangerous when it is unsanctified, even though it is "so very good *in it self*" (75). "Its *Wisdom* and *Prudence*, if *Unsanctified*, is (at best) but *Worldly Wisdom*, and Imployed wholly to serve Worldly Interests," which often end in "Devilish Policy." It is the well-balanced unsanctified temperament that is behind "the Smoothbootes that look Demure, who can think and contrive, and are not in over-great Haste; The Wolves in Sheepscloathing; (in a word) The close and undiscerned Hypocrites. . . . These under their *seeming Vertues*, have advantage to act their secret Vices." Such men are also very hard to convert to Christ (76–78). When the well-balanced temperament is sanctified, however, it is the best possible combination, for "this *Governable* Spirit is under a *Twofold* Government; That of [his] *own*, and that of God too" (80).

The significance of this little book of less than one hundred pages lies not so much in the interesting nature of its contents as in its approach to the problem of morals. Despite its many references to Scripture and the use of the dichotomy between regenerate and unregenerate natures, the author's aims do not seem to have been exclusively religious. Nor, incidentally, does *The Spirit of Man* fit into an Aristotelian mold, except perhaps for the influence upon it of the genre of Theophrastian "charactery."[29] Rather, the emphasis in the work is naturalistic and constitutes an early investigation into the psychology of inherited temperament as a factor in moral behavior. It is perhaps related to the Cartesian drive to reduce morals to medicine, the belief, in Descartes's words, that "the mind is so dependent upon the humors and the condition of the organs of the body that if it is possible to find some way to make men [in general] wiser and more clever than they have been so far, . . . it is in medicine that it should be sought."[30] Such an approach necessarily bypasses religious determinants as much as possible, notwithstanding Morton's division into sanctified and unsanctified temperaments. Above all, Morton's idea of the spirit in man positively eliminated by implication the role of reason as a motive in moral conduct, a consequence that it is doubtful he ever faced squarely.[31] Thus, despite his general conservatism of thought, Morton, too, writing in a Puritan milieu, was searching for naturalistic means of expression that would capture in secular moral philosophy something of the psychological insight into the nonrational forces of the soul that had characteristically been recognized in the religious tradition. If we leave aside his taxonomy of hot, cold, and medium, Morton's *Spirit of Man* reduces to a rather sketchy theory of the affections, which are understood as calm and constant dispositions. In this one respect, his book fits into the line of development from Shepard and Fenner to Henry More, Shaftesbury, and Hutcheson. But most of Morton's work cannot rightly be included in this development.

29. For discussion of this genre in English literature, see Kirk's introduction to Joseph Hall's *Heaven upon Earth and Characters of Vertues and Vices*; Gwendolen Murphy, *A Bibliography of English Character-Books, 1608–1700* (London, 1925); and Murphy, ed., *A Cabinet of Characters* (London, 1925).

30. Descartes, *Discourse on Method*, trans. Lafleur, 46.

31. On p. 28 Morton wrote that no man can act contrary to his "peculiar *Genius*" except by "a special hand of the Good or Evil Spirit upon him; some special Instigation, and Assistance, upon a particular Occasion."

"Ethicks"

Morton's skill at drawing up short compendia of learning is apparent in his manuscript system of "Ethicks."[32] This academic piece is a seventeenth-century semi-Aristotelian system, very much like Heereboord's, reduced to forty succinct pages. No other work of ethics in English can provide us with so exact a picture of the treatment of the subject typical at Harvard throughout the later seventeenth century. A review of Morton's ethics will provide us with a last glimpse of the "old" moral philosophy.

Morton devoted the largest amount of space by far to the nature of man, and within that area he directed the most attention to the problem of the will. The organization of the work follows the Peripatetic tradition: ethics is first defined in terms of its "end"; second, man is studied as the "subject" of ethical conduct; third, the "means" of attaining the end is investigated, such means being necessarily dependent on the nature of man. We will review Morton's ethics in the order in which he presented it to his students. He defined ethics in general as "a Prudence, Directing a man absolutely taken, by morall virtues to Ethicall felicity."[33] Felicity is the end; man "absolutely taken," that is, man as man, is the subject; virtue is the means. In sum, man's end of true happiness is attainable only through the practice of virtue.

Morton defined felicity, or "happyness," as "an *operation* of the *Rationall Soul*, according to the most perfect virtue, in the most Perfect life." Each part of the definition requires individual explication. Felicity is an *operation* because "*Action* is the perfection of everything." Powers are perfected by habits, and habits by acts. Without the actions, habits cannot even be discovered or praised. Habits are sought because they give rise to actions, but actions are sought for themselves. Above all, action most assimilates us to God, "who is purely and all together Act." Here is the famous Aristotelian emphasis on happiness as an activity, which we have noted on several previous occasions. It is an idea that Henry More took issue with, as we will see. And Morton himself did not quite hit the right Classical note when he elaborated on the concept: "Tis not [there]fore in Idleness, Cessation, Sensual Ease or pleasure, but the Complacence, Contentment, and Satisfaction, which we take in virtuous actions, the excusings of our thoughts, the comforts of a natural conscience; for w[he]n one has done wel he has contentment and satisfaction in

---

32. This appears in the same manuscript notebook as his "Pneumaticks," with separate pagination. Page references will appear in parentheses in the text.

33. Cf. Grove, *Moral Philosophy*, ed. Amory, 52, who also structured his ethics along Aristotelian lines: "Ethicks or Morality is a science directing human actions for the attainment of happiness." Grove's discussion of happiness is much more complex than Morton's.

him self. . . . This is a felicity." This description of the joys of a clean conscience is not what Aristotle had meant by happiness as an activity. It derived rather from Stoic and Christian sources.

"Rational soul" is, quite simply, understanding and will, or the mind. The "whole man" is not the subject of ethical felicity because circumstances may restrict the man in some parts while he still acts virtuously "in Inward Inclinations." For example, there may be a lack of opportunity for the exercise of some virtues: a poor man cannot practice liberality, nor can a sick man be valiant.

"Felicity is an operation of the rational soul according to the most perfect virtue, in the most perfect life." Perfect virtue is here meant to be only an ideal to be "pressed after." The "nearer to perfect virtue, the nearer to felicity [that] is perfect." Finally, a perfect *life* refers to the importance of external conditions in happiness, a point that the Peripatetics stressed and the Stoics minimized. The fullest happiness cannot exist without good bodily health, good habits, some degree of good fortune in money matters, in friendships, and so on, all of which Aristotle had discussed in the *Nicomachean Ethics*.

The subject of ethics is man insofar as he is "capable of Ethical direction." He has three faculties that are susceptible to ethical precepts: intellect, will, and sensitive appetite. In physics these are studied simply as faculties; in ethics, "as governable."

> Three Powers in Man, by Ethicks are Set Right,
> Intellect, Will, Sensitive Appetite (4).

We have already spent enough time on the human faculties to enable us to run through Morton's conventional views fairly quickly. His analysis is strictly intellectualist. Of the two kinds of intellect in the rational soul, speculative and practical, it is the function of the latter to consider things "as good or evil, to be proposed to the wil, either to be inclined to, or turned from." The speculative intellect is concerned with the truth of speculative propositions, matters of being and essence, rather than with practical propositions of good and evil. "Practicall judgment" is comprised of four steps or acts: apprehension, judgment, deliberation, and empire.

Apprehension of the object is necessary before it can be presented to the will, for the will is a blind power and knows nothing by itself. "Its Eye is the Intellect." *Judgment* of the object apprehended is of either its "goodness" or its "possibility." The goodness may be judged either in itself, in absolute terms, or in terms of the convenience of the object for us. Practical judgment then acts on the will and "willing, or *volition*" follows, or "as some say rather velleity, *wishing* or *woulding*," or willing without deliberation concerning the means. "Possibility" refers to one's judgment of the attainableness of the object by means, and from this follows "Intention, Purpose, or a Compleat and full willing."

Deliberation, or "Consultation about means," is the consideration of which of several possible means "is most conducible to the end." Only after deliberation can there be "consent" in the will. It was on the basis of such a psychological analysis that in the Thomist tradition consent was considered a necessary precondition of sin and virtue. Without the consent of the will arising from rational deliberation, no action was fully human: it was at least partly mindless and an action for which a man could not be held fully responsible.

The fourth and last step in practical judgment is *Empire*, which Morton defined as the "intimating to the will [that] it prepare it Self to the work, [and] stir up the Inferiour faculties [such as] motion, speech, etc. to the execution." The act of the will after this process is called its "use." If the will attains its object, the use results in "fruition."

After discussing the practical intellect, Morton turned to the will itself. Its acts *with regard to the object or end only*, he said, are three: volition, intention, and fruition. Volition occurs without respect to means. It is simply the choice of the end as good. Intention considers the attainability of the object. It is obviously impossible to intend something that is in no way attainable. Fruition is "a delight or satisfaction in the End when obtained." There are also three acts of will pertaining to the *means* chosen: consent, which is the approval by the will of the means propounded by the judgment; election, which is the approval of one means (commended by the judgment) rather than another; and use, or exercise, which is the implementation of the act and the stirring up of the inferior faculties to performance. Volition, intention, consent, election, use, and fruition are in practice intermeshed. Taken as a whole, Morton's theory of action may be summarized as follows: "Understanding as the Director. Will as the first mover. Inferiour facultyes as executors."[34]

In his physics Morton went so far with the notion of man as the "religious animal" as to add to the primary faculties of the mind (i.e., understanding and will) a third power, "Conscience." The absence of this idea from his ethics is hard to explain, except as a deficiency in the extant manuscript. "I know," Morton wrote, that conscience "is accounted an act of the practicall Judgment, concerning a man's Self and his actions," ordinarily defined as "the Judgment of a Man Subjected to the Judgment of God," in which the word "subjected" "carryes a yielding and Subjective act of the will." Perhaps, Morton ad-

---

34. Grove, *ibid.*, 158, runs through the same six acts of the will and notes that this division into six rather than the usual two was introduced by Pufendorf. It seems probable that Morton also borrowed from Pufendorf. See, *De Officio hominis et civis juxta legem naturalem libri duo*, trans. Frank Gardner Moore (New York, 1927 [orig. publ. Cambridge, 1682]), chap. 1.

vanced, it would be more accurate to think of conscience as "a Complex" of both will and intellect, which may be defined as "an Aptitude for, and Inclination to religion" and as a "higher facultye" comprehending both will and intellect. It may then be seen as "the Differentiall power in man, whereby he Acknowledges God," putting "intellect, will, and all other facultyes Subservient thereto." For, Morton emphasized, it is "piety (rather than Science [i.e., speculative knowledge] or prudence) [that] does Commend a man as transcending other Creatures."[35] Heereboord, it will be remembered, had also defined piety as a combination of will and intellect.

Morton's proposal of a new leading faculty and his definition of man the "religious animal" may be interpreted as signifying two important trends in Puritan or dissenter psychological theory in this period. First, the very adoption of the idea that conscience is a faculty comprehending both will and intellect is indicative of the fluidity of psychological theory at this time (following the collapse of Aristotelian authority) and of the realization that something of a philosophical vacuum existed. Secondly, Morton's stress on conscience and piety as the qualities by which man transcends the animals illustrates the growing concentration on problems of moral psychology in particular and also parallels the trend among the Reformed pietists, such as Ames earlier, toward unifying all of man's powers under a central principle of conduct such as "living to God."

The third human faculty that Morton discussed was the sensitive appetite and its passions. Under the will's command there are two sorts of inferior powers, those that respond without reluctance, such as the members of the body, which are "governed magisterially, by absolute command," and those that do the will's bidding reluctantly, the passions, which are all seated in the sensitive appetite and which must be governed "politically, by persuasion" (5–7). The passions are common to men and lower animals, but only analogously. In beasts the sensitive appetite is directed entirely by "phantasy," or by sense impressions, for beasts have no rational appetite or will that is directed by intellect and that can in turn govern the passions.

The passions, according to Morton, which are the "acts" of the sensitive appetite, can be treated in four different disciplines. Physics studies "[their] *Nature* and *Order* among the faculties of the soul." Medicine considers them as "arising from the Exorbitancy of humors, and considers of their cure: as Mad and Melancholy persons, etc." Rhetoric "indeavours to Excite and stir

35. One thinks here of Jonathan Edwards's note on conscience: "Besides the two sorts of assent of the mind, called will and judgment, there is a third arising from a sense of the general beauty and harmony of things, which is conscience." Edwards, "The Mind," no. 39, in Harvey G. Townsend, ed., *The Philosophy of Jonathan Edwards from His Private Notebooks* (Eugene, Ore., 1955), 41. Edwards's changing ideas about conscience are discussed in Fiering, *Jonathan Edwards's Moral Thought*.

them up to a vigorous activity, which is good if the judgment be first rightly informed and the wil well Inclined." Finally, ethics is concerned with "their moderation to keep them in a propper mean and due subjection to the Higher faculties."

Ethicks the Passions dus Suborm to Reason
Bounding them to [their] measure, place and season (12).

A passion is "an intense (or vehement) act of the sensitive appetite, by which it inclines to, or shuns, a good or evill, perceived by the sense, proposed by the Phantasie, and [that] with some non-natural change in the body." There is nothing unconventional in this definition. Morton did take care to stress that a passion is not an "opinion," as the Stoics believed, "for that's in the mind, these in the appetite." Moreover, "against the Stoicks, Passions are not Evil in [their] own Nature but only as they are irregular. In their Nature they are good and may (yea must) be in a good man; They are given to the animall by nature for its preservation and in man may be [the] helper and furtherer of virtue, as Love of good, Hatred of Evill. Yea affection that is Regular makes Virtue Eminent." Such defenses of the passions were becoming more and more common at the end of the seventeenth century, following the publication of Descartes's work on the subject.[36] Morton advised his students that "vivid affections, and warmth of spirit, are much more suitable to godly youth than a cold and grave formality."[37]

Morton drew a distinction between passions "partially" in the sensitive appetite and passions "totally" in it. Those affections unique to man and not in brutes, such as envy, gratitude, shame, indignation, revenge, emulation, and commiseration, are "intimately conjoyned with some rationall act of the mind" and are therefore of a "mixt Nature," partly in the mind and partly in

36. Cf., for example, Charles Hickman, *Fourteen Sermons* (London, 1700): "Nay, tho' it were a possible thing for a Man to force his nature, and divest himself wholly of his passions, yet 'tis a question whether the thing were desirable or no. They are the proper season of our souls, which would be very insipid and flat without them: The proper motive to encourage and stir us up to good works, without which (as our constitution now stands) our reason would be too weak to support our vertue, and man at best would be but a heavy, sluggish, unactive creature. But to this a stoick may object, that our passions incline us to evil works, as well as to good: That they lead us into dangers, and betray us unto sin, and therefore 'tis fit they should be rooted out." But, says Hickman, a man without passion, though "he does not hate his brother . . . he does not love him neither. He does not oppress his neighbour, perhaps; but withal, he neither pities, nor relieves him." Quoted in Lois Whitney, *Primitivism and the Idea of Progress in English Popular Literature of the Eighteenth Century* (Baltimore, 1934), 22.

37. "Mr. Morton's Advise to Young Scholars Ingadgeing in the Work of the Ministry under the Present Discouraging Circumstances," MS, Harvard Univ. Archives. In support of this advice Morton recommended Richard Baxter's *Gildas Salvianus . . . The Reformed Pastor . . .* (London, 1656) and William Fenner's *Christ's Alarm to Drowsie Saints . . .* (London, 1646).

the sensitive appetite. (Heereboord earlier had also spoken of "mixed" affections.) On the other hand, passions common to man and beast, such as love, hatred, and fear, "belong wholly to the sensitive appetite, and are seated organically in the heart." The traditional distinction between Morton's so-called partial passions and his so-called total passions was based on the individual passion's degree of complexity, rather than on its admixture of mental elements. Love, hate, joy, desire, fear, and grief were often considered primitive or fundamental emotions; envy, gratitude, shame, and so on were compounds made up of primitive emotions plus special circumstances having to do with their peculiar objects. What is perhaps most notable about Morton's treatment of the passions is that he made no reference to Descartes's treatise on the subject. For Descartes, all human passions strictly speaking have a mental and a physical component. Morton's passions that are totally in the sensitive appetite, or those passions common to men and animals, might better be designated simply bodily appetites or instincts, such as hunger, lust, and so on, rather than passions.

Morton himself returned to the more usual distinctions immediately following his excursus on partial and total passions. He listed the four Stoic primary passions of desire, joy, fear, and grief and asserted that all other passions are mixtures of these. He also presented the Thomist classification into eleven passions. In this context he noted the common confusion respecting the terms "irascible" and "concupiscible": whether they both properly refer to good and evil objects, or whether an irascible passion is a response only to evil (hate, fear, etc.) and a concupiscible passion only to good (love, desire, etc.). The original Thomist position had been the former, that an irascible passion involves the overcoming of a difficulty (hope, despair, etc.), whereas a concupiscible passion is a response without any intervening obstacle or difficulty (love, hatred, desire, etc.).[38]

Morton's rather cursory treatment of the passions suggests that he had comparatively little interest in them, perhaps because his essay on *The Spirit of Man* was a kind of substitute. As compared to Henry More's handling of the subject, which we will discuss in the next chapter, Morton's was very elementary.

In the context of his discussion of human nature, Morton also took up the

---

38. In the *Compendium Physicae*, 185–186, there is another short discussion of the passions, somewhat more technically constructed but not significantly different from Morton's treatment in his "Ethicks" manuscript. There is this note, however, concerning the terms "affection" and "passion": "Affections, and passions are common names to all[,] yet Vulgar Use appropriates affections to Love, and the other concupiscibles, and passions to the Irassibles Especially in Anger and Griefe[.] but though we Speak with the Vulgar we must think with the Wise. The like also may be Said of the Equivocall name of passions ascribed to those which are indeed actions of the will, or appetite, and those vehement in their kind."

subject of the liberty of will. Morton's strength in analyzing this problem lay in the pedagogical simplicity of his presentation, not in his acuity. On the vexed subject of the will Harvard undergraduates were probably quite appreciative of Morton's qualities. Most of the traditional distinctions and terms we have already seen were discussed in Morton's presentation.

Liberty is of two kinds, freedom from coaction and freedom from necessity. Both animals and men may be free of coaction, that is, may be governed by "inward Inclination" alone. But animals can never be free of natural necessity in their behavior, since they lack rational counsel. "A hungry Horse seeing Oates within his reach, cannot forbare to eat, tho' he should not, when it belongs not to his Master, is not his allowance, or he has been newly drenched. But a hungry man can forbeare, if it be anothers meal to which he is not invited, he is in physick, or that sort of food does not usually agree with his stomach" (8). This liberty from necessity is divided by the Schoolmen, Morton noted, into a liberty of contrariety and a liberty of contradiction, or a liberty of specification and a liberty of exercise. Here, in Morton's view, is where the "Schooles" and "Reformed Philosophy" part company. The usual teaching of the Scholastics "in the darker times of Popery" was in defense of the liberty of contradiction, that is, the liberty of exercise or suspension. The will is not free with regard to specification, they maintained, "for it cannot will evil, or nill good, as such." But when it apprehends evil, for example, though it cannot will it as such, yet it is possible that it may not nill it; the will may "suspend its nilling Act"; and though the will cannot nill a recognized good end, yet it may suspend its act of willing it. But in Reformed philosophy, according to Morton, liberty is not in "Indifference to opposites (willing or not willing; nilling or not nilling) *But in Rational Spontaneity*."[39]

"Rational spontaneity" refers to the will's "unenforced" following of the dictates of the practical understanding, or the doing of a thing spontaneously "for a Reason." "The word 'for a Reason' differing this spontaneitys from a Brutes, which act not deliberately at all, but according to present appetite, excited by present sensible objects." In Reformed Protestantism, then, according to Morton, both the liberty of contradiction and the liberty of contrariety are denied, for the Reformed hold that it is impossible the will should not incline to a good proposed by the understanding. "The will always must follow the last dictate of the Practicall Judgment." If the will acts without a reason it "ceases to be a rational power . . . ; and then also the Act of Willing is not a Humane action, tho it may be the Action of a man; for humane actions are done with the Deliberation of the Judgment" (9).

39. For a fuller discussion of the difference between the liberty of specification and the liberty of exercise, see above, pp. 123–124, 130–131.

We have seen earlier that the liberty of suspension was in fact espoused by many Reformed Protestants, despite Morton's disclaimers. On the other hand, the liberty of indifference was not. Morton's generalization holds with regard to the Molinist liberty of indifference; but many Protestant scholars, with Thomas Aquinas, allowed for the liberty of exercise, which is the same as the liberty of suspension and the liberty of contradiction. Morton's analysis failed to keep the types of liberty distinct. We must bear in mind, however, that we have no more than a corrupted student version of Morton's ethics.

In summary, the necessities to which the human will is subject are two: God's decree of all things that shall certainly come to pass; and the last dictates of the practical judgment. These necessities, Morton suggested, may be called the will's "Immutability," a term that comprehends the will's liberty-despite-necessity. Man's acts are free insofar as they are rationally spontaneous and because "man is an Arbiter of his own Acts." He is "conscious" of what he does and "chuses to do it." This consistency of liberty and necessity is also demonstrated by the nature of God, angels, and blessed souls, "who are most free and yet act most necessarily."

> Man from necessity of force is free
> And yet his acts Immutable may be.
>
> . . . .
>
> God and His Angells have the freest will,
> And yet [their] acts are necessary still.

Morton's final word to his students on the problem of the will was an exhortation: "Study this point of liberty, in Rational Spontaneity, Consisting with necessity of events, and you will easily over come Arminianisme and Popery" (10–11).

The third and last of the major parts of Morton's ethics concerns the means by which ethical ends are realized. The primary means is virtue. In ethics, Morton wrote, it is principally moral virtue, not intellectual virtue, that is studied, and prudence is the intellectual basis of this virtue. "Prudence . . . is the string that goes through the bracelet of other virtues, because Prudence determines the virtuous mean, in every moral virtue." The defects or opposites of prudence we are already familiar with from the seventeenth-century Latin ethics texts: "craftyness" or cleverness, which is using good means to achieve an evil end, or evil means to achieve a good end; ignorance; neglect of the opportunity to perform a good work; and vehement passions, which lead to actions taken without due deliberation (16–17). Moral virtue is seated in the will, not in the sensitive appetite, even though it is true that the habit of virtue depends upon the moderation of the rebellious passions.

Virtue in Will is seated, [there]by
It makes unruly Passions to comply.

As was typical of Christian Aristotelianism, however, Morton did not accept the doctrine of the ethical mean in pure form. The essence of virtue lies in the will's "agreement with, or conformity to the dictates of right Reason," not simply in the choice of the mean. And right reason for Morton meant "the will of God revealed in his Morall law [and] the Light of Nature." Therefore, the rule of virtue for Morton is transcendent, a necessary corrective to Aristotle's position. It is first of all "Gods Law and Will," and secondly, "the Dictate of Right Reason, which is a transcript (tho now obscure) of the moral law in the mind of man." "Mediocrity," or the mean, is not the essence of virtue but only one of its properties and is a relation respecting the "Latitude" of affections, vicious extremes, and the object or matter of action.

In a discussion of the causes of virtue, Morton was able to bring in his theory of "spirit." God is the first "extrinsick" cause. He influences human actions by His general concurse afforded to all creatures, which sustains them in their being and action; by special influences toward virtue; and "by giveing a Happy temperament and good natural disposition, [where]by a man is fitted for all virtue, in general, or eminently, for some particular virtues in special." This last Morton designated "the Spirit or Genius of a man." In addition, God providentially disposes men's birth and education, so that some will live at times and places where virtue flourishes. Lastly, God protects men from "Evil spirits who obstruct virtuous actions, by darkening the understanding, blinding the mind; perverting the will; stirring com[m]otions in the passions," and this God does "by wonderfull insinuations into the humours and spirits of the body" (20). After God, education is another extrinsic cause of virtue. Through natural and ordinary means it "hath great influence on the lives and actions of men."

Intrinsic causes of virtue are in the soul and the body. With regard to the former, the attainment of virtue depends upon the government of the will by right reason, such that the actions of the will in accordance with right reason are "frequent, constant, spontaneous." The emphasis here, as in Aristotle, is on the formation of habit. Morton cataloged and described all of the eleven Aristotelian virtues—liberality, magnificence, modesty, magnanimity, comity, and so on—and also the four cardinal virtues. He added one or two others, but most of this discussion is of little interest and was entirely commonplace.

Morton also considered moral weakness, or what he called "semi-virtue" and "semi-vice." Here he presented the problem of the incontinent man, who "against his mind [is] drawn to Unlawful Pleasures, his right reason (or natural Conscience) in the meanwhile disallowing." This man, according to

Morton, acts with partial knowledge in that he recognizes in general that the pleasures are unlawful, but he does not apply his general knowledge to the present particulars. "Therefore he condemneth the pleasure *in its self*, and yet approves it in the *present circumstances*, as was said of *Medea* in another case—

> Medea when she did her conscience force,
> Cry'd, I see better things and follow worse" (34).

Morton's solution to the Medean paradox was like Aristotle's and that of intellectualists such as Burgersdyck and Heereboord. Two kinds of rational judgment were posited, one of which may be temporarily inoperative.

One of the great supports of virtue, according to the Aristotelian tradition, is friendship. It may thus be considered one of the ancillary means by which ethical ends are realized. The subject of friendship takes up two famous chapters of the *Nicomachean Ethics*. By the general term "friendship" Aristotle meant what in modern times might be called a theory of human relationships. This was also Morton's meaning. According to Morton, friendship is properly called the "secondary means of felicity." It is a complement to virtue itself, which is the primary means of finding happiness, because through friendship "virtue is better exercised [and] felicity most comfortably enjoyed." But Morton gave relatively little space to this subject. What he did say was directed to an explication of Aristotle's point that friendship, which is ideally a union of two or a very small number of persons in virtue, can never exist in relationships with many. "Tis hard to *know* [many] so *exactly* as we should a freind. . . . Tis hard to *love* many so intirely as we should a freind. Tis hard to *live* and intimately converse with many as we should a freind," and so on. These inescapable restraints on social virtues, which Aristotle had analyzed so brilliantly, tended to be forgotten in eighteenth-century benevolist theories of virtue, when men were supposed to be friends of all mankind. Aristotle's ethics was criticized for, among other things, lacking an adequate treatment of social virtues like benevolence, and as we have noted, giving insufficient attention to the passions. In the next chapter we will see in the ethics of Henry More a prototype of the new non-Aristotelian moral philosophy, which easily superseded Morton's conservative approach.

In the end, it is impossible to find a simple classification for Morton as a thinker and writer, except perhaps to categorize him vaguely as an eclectic teacher. In any case, the key to placing him in the New England context is to be found not so much in an assessment of how much he was an Aristotelian and how much a Cartesian, but in observing the breadth of his "philosophical" interests independent of theological concerns. That Morton can legitimately be called a philosopher (a term that immediately signifies a large measure of secular intellectual interests) is more important than the conservatism of his Aristotelian ethics. For at the end of the seventeenth century, "philosophy" connoted a degree of openness to ideas and speculation, and a spirit of innovation, that for New England was unprecedented.

6

The Break with Scholasticism: More and Gale

Be more of a Christian, than to
look on the Enchiridion *of [Henry More] as,*
Next the Bible, the best book
in the world.[1]

It had been the hope of William Ames that his new "practical theology" would make moral philosophy in the traditional form a superfluous discipline. In a partial and indirect way this hope was realized, at least in America, though Ames could hardly have accepted the results. The traditional arid commentary on Aristotle, along with the variety of rationales that were used to keep pagan moral thought alive but at the same time unmistakably distinct from Christian piety, was largely abandoned at Harvard before the end of the seventeenth century. Ames would have been pleased with that change. But the new synthesis that followed must be described as a subtly Christianized or Protestantized moral philosophy rather than as a practical theology in the Amesian mode. This step was ironically far more subversive to the older religious order than the former candid education in Aristotle and Cicero had been, when these and other pagan moralists were kept in compartments segregated from Christian truth.

The adoption of Henry More's ethics text in the last decade of the seventeenth century signified the final abandonment at Harvard of the Scholastic commentary on Aristotle as the pre-eminent model for introducing the study of moral philosophy. We will briefly review the manifold intellectual forces from abroad that compelled this change, taking into account what seems to have been most decisive in New England reasoning and experience. There was, first of all, a long-standing dissatisfaction with the conventional schism between moral philosophy in the pagan mode and moral theology based on Christian revelation and tradition. The ethics of the Cambridge Platonists,

1. Cotton Mather, *Manuductio*, 27.

by drawing on the Neoplatonic tradition—which in any case was already pervasive in certain areas of Puritan theology—seemed to point the way to exactly the kind of new integration of philosophy and religion that was needed to overcome the schism. Since the fifteenth century the metaphysics of Platonic idealism had been proclaimed by some writers as being far more compatible with Christian teachings than Aristotelianism. But Henry More offered more than a better metaphysics. Like the work of the other Cambridge Platonists, his writing was suffused with pietistic warmth, even an evangelical strain. Although More was not doctrinaire or militant about any specific denominational teaching, his ethics was suffused with religiosity. The young John Norris, who was a great admirer of More and in later life was Malebranche's most important English disciple, wished that his education had been at some of the Cambridge colleges where Platonism flourished, rather than at Oxford, for he missed teaching and books that were "sapid, pathetic, and Divinely relishing, such as warm, kindle, and enlarge the interior and awaken the divine sense of the soul."[2] The need for texts with warmth and divine relish, which More could supply, was also strong in New England.

Yet warmth alone was not enough. If it had been, a practical theology would have sufficed. The second force inducing change, then, was the challenge of the new philosophical methodologies of the seventeenth century, or more generally, the new logics (using the term logic in the more comprehensive seventeenth-century sense).[3] Ramus and Bacon were harbingers of the seventeenth-century revolution in philosophic methods, which culminated in the writings of Descartes above all. It was a revolution supported also by the work of Galileo and Gassendi and by the tremendous stimulus to fresh thought given by Hobbes. More's writing in one way or another was shaped by all of these predecessors. This revolution in method, in style, and in substance was well underway, it should be noted, before John Locke had published a word.[4]

2. Quoted by Muirhead, *Platonic Tradition in Anglo-Saxon Philosophy*, 74.

3. The discipline of logic in the 17th century included study of the means of gathering knowledge (for example, scientific method) as well as study of the laws of reasoning and of the organization and presentation of knowledge once gained. Both Malebranche's *Treatise Concerning the Search after Truth* and Locke's *Essay Concerning Human Understanding* were classified as logic texts. The term "epistemology" was not coined until the middle of the 19th century.

4. No greater mistake can be made in gaining a precise understanding of the New England mind in the period from, say, 1675 to 1725 than to believe that the publication of the *Essay Concerning Human Understanding* in 1690 was a great turning point. Locke confirmed some already existing trends in philosophic method, but beyond that he was viewed in more or less the same light that Hobbes was, namely, as a dangerous obstacle to be gotten around. This assertion may be validated by the simple exercise of trying to name one American writer before about 1750 who thoroughly reflected Locke's views in the *Essay*. It is seldom understood that Jonathan Edwards was a critic of Locke, both directly and by implication. To write about Locke in America, one must take each of his works separately, since each had a somewhat different reception. Locke's *Thoughts on Education*, for example, was undoubtedly read with less initial

The changes that occurred in American thought were not as radical as some that occurred elsewhere, because the essential drive in the colonies throughout the seventeenth and eighteenth centuries was not toward extreme naturalism, skepticism, nominalism, or anticlericalism, let alone toward materialism or atheism. The long-term impetus in America was toward philosophical structures that would reinforce and protect the essential elements of the inherited religious tradition. This tradition appeared to be gravely threatened by thinkers like Hobbes and Spinoza. Americans in the eighteenth century favored naturalistic explanations and studies only insofar as they strengthened orthodox trust in divine goodness, intelligence, and design. Generally, colonial New England intellectuals favored rationalist idealism in metaphysics, not empiricism or nominalism. Moreover, they were in sympathy with the opinion of the Cambridge Platonist John Smith, who believed that "God is not better defined to us by our understandings than by our wills and affections," and that "He is not only the eternal reason, but He is also that unstained Beauty and supreme good to which our wills are perpetually aspiring."[5] The main consequence in New England of the challenges from materialism and radical naturalism was a marked broadening or expansion of the foundations of thought. The New Englanders neither fell back on dogmatic reliance on Scripture nor diluted their essential theism, but they added the evidence of God-in-nature, including human nature, to their former trust in revealed truth. The program of studying the book of nature as well as the book of divine writings was not a new one—it had been heralded by Bacon—but it came fully into its own only after Descartes and Hobbes.

Cartesianism stood for many things, obviously; at Harvard, as elsewhere, it meant rejecting mere textual erudition as the prime means of uncovering truth, and it encouraged the procedure of beginning with self-evident clear and distinct axioms. In metaphysics it meant abandoning the study of inherent qualities in nature and substituting mechanical and mathematical explanations, but immediately added to this conception was a definition of matter that installed divine spirit as an essential force in all natural activity; in ethics, finally, it meant building a new semi-secular study of man, and in a sense re-doing the work of the pagan moralists, using better foundations, foundations that drew instinctively from a millennium and a half of Christian thought and practical experience. "I compared the ethical writings of the ancient pagans to very superb and magnificent palaces built only on mud and sand," Descartes wrote. "They laud the virtues and make them appear more desirable

---

antagonism than the *Essay*. The one published work thus far that makes any attempt to examine accurately the reception of Locke's "logic" in America is Elizabeth Flower and Murray G. Murphey, *A History of Philosophy in America*, I (New York, 1977), 365–373.

5. Muirhead, *Platonic Tradition in Anglo-Saxon Philosophy*, 29, quoting from Smith's *Discourse of the Existence and Nature of God*.

than anything else in the world; but they give no adequate criterion of virtue, and often what they call by such a name is nothing but apathy, parricide, pride, or despair."[6]

I have mentioned the pietistic desire to establish morals on an integrated basis and have noted some of the philosophical developments that compelled a move away from mere theological reassertion. These developments led Henry More, for example, to believe that Hobbes must be refuted in his own terms, those of nature and reason, and that Descartes's metaphysics, suitably modified, provided the means for doing so. A third factor that helps to explain both the Puritan affinity for Henry More's ethics and also the broad dissatisfaction with the Aristotelian commentary that existed by the end of the seventeenth century was the great progress in the psychological theory of motivation and morals that had been made in the preceding two hundred years. Henry More's *Enchiridion Ethicum* offered a secularized theory of the sources of virtue that closely paralleled the Puritan belief that the holy life is won and sustained not only by an illuminated intellect but by a unique combination of will or affections and divine grace.

Philosophical Liberalism at Harvard

The dangers to orthodox religion notwithstanding, the thirst for modern learning struck Harvard College no less than other intellectual centers in the West in the latter half of the seventeenth century. Immensely seminal writers like Grotius and Bacon were important from the beginning in stimulating changes in outlook. Far more decisive was the impact of Descartes, both from the direct reading of his work and from the propagation in New England of some of his key ideas by Cartesians like Heereboord, Antoine LeGrand, More, and others. This influence was undoubtedly already felt a decade or two before Nathaniel Mather wrote from Dublin in 1686 that he had perceived from the commencement theses of that year and the year before that "the Cartesian philosophy begins to obteyn in New England."[7] Nothing was more of a solvent to the old thinking and nothing more infectious than the Cartesian emphasis on starting afresh by abandoning the received authorities from the past and basing everything on "clear and distinct ideas" and a plain style. This

6. Descartes, *Discourse on Method*, trans. Lafleur, 5.

7. Quoted in Wright, *Literary Culture in New England*, 103. Marjorie Nicolson, "The Early Stage of Cartesianism in England," *Studies in Philology*, XXVI (1929), 356–374. By mid-century Descartes was already famous as a thinker. On some of the less-known conduits of ideas to New England in this period, see Fiering, "Transatlantic Republic of Letters," *WMQ*, 3d Ser., XXXIII (1976), 642–660.

was the decisive addition to the anti-Scholasticism already present to a greater or less degree in Ramus, Bacon, and Gassendi. We must infer, then, more than the ordinary Ramist animadversions from the Harvard thesis of 1693, "*Secta Peripateticorum non est omnibus aliis praeferenda*" (The school of the Peripatetics is not to be preferred to all others). The only alternative at Harvard to going forward with the new anti-Scholastic trend would have been the renunciation of the hope of distinction as a college of the liberal arts and sciences and a consequent quick descent to the status of a Protestant parochial seminary. Thus, the famous *crise de la conscience* between 1680 and 1715 on the European continent about which Paul Hazard wrote had its modest counterpart in New England, triggered by different but not unrelated factors. In every area of study it was necessary to make some adjustment to new thinking, although this adjustment cannot appropriately be called a convulsive revolution in thought.[8]

The process of irremediable fragmentation in intellectual authority inevitably increased the dependence of American thinkers on those outside voices that seemed to have some answers to current philosophical problems. To whatever extent the American colonies were becoming more self-sustaining and characteristically "American" in the course of the seventeenth century, there was greater need than ever in the realm of ideas for the guidance of recent British and Continental writers who had responded positively to some of the changes in thought and yet preserved a degree of continuity with the early generations of Reformed Protestantism. The intellectual baggage that had been carried over in the first migration was rapidly becoming obsolete. The small body of New England intellectuals was in the position of the old alumnus who finds his previously acquired concepts inadequate in a changed philosophical milieu and is eager to return to alma mater for summer courses or get what news he can in order to refresh his thinking.

The specific situation at Harvard in the last twenty years of the seventeenth century was appreciably affected by two internal events: the appointments of the "liberal" tutors John Leverett in 1685 and William Brattle in 1686, and the arrival in Massachusetts in 1686 of Charles Morton, who began to lecture at the college in 1692. Either of these occurrences may have been behind the introduction of Henry More's ethics text, *Enchiridion Ethicum* (1667), at

8. Paul Hazard, *The European Mind: 1680–1715*, trans. J. Lewis May (Cleveland, Ohio, 1963), originally published as *La Crise de la conscience européenne (1680–1715)* (Paris, 1935). Elisabeth Labrousse, *Pierre Bayle*, II, *Heterodoxie et rigorisme* (The Hague, 1964), 43, warns against "l'image fallacieuse de la 'révolution cartésienne.'" That Descartes opened a new era cannot be doubted, but eclecticism was the prevailing attitude at the end of the 17th century, and most contemporaries, Labrousse writes, perhaps out of intellectual inertia, tended to think of Cartesianism as falling within a traditional framework of thought.

about this time, although Morton's thinking was not distinctively Neoplatonic and his own compendium of ethics did not show More's influence.[9]

In his tribute to Leverett and Brattle, Samuel Eliot Morison has probably underestimated the diffuse forces compelling the modernization of learning at Harvard at the end of the seventeenth century, but his comment is worth noting: "It is largely owing to Brattle as tutor and to Leverett both as tutor and President that Harvard was saved from becoming a sectarian institution, at a time when the tendency of most pious New Englanders was to tighten up and insist on hundred-per-cent puritanism in the face of infiltrating ideas that heralded the Century of Enlightenment."[10] Leverett was a tutor for twelve years and beginning in 1708 was president of the college for sixteen years. His and Brattle's effectiveness was partly a consequence of the extended absences of the official president, Increase Mather, between 1685 and 1701. It is not altogether certain, however, that the curriculum would have been substantially different from what it was under the leadership of the tutors if Mather had been actively leading the college. The so-called "tolerant and enlarged Catholic Spirit," typified by the enormously popular sermons of Archbishop John Tillotson in England, was in the air, and the Mathers breathed it, too. If old England had always had such archbishops as Tillotson, Increase Mather is reputed to have said, "New England had never been."[11] But according to Perry Miller, Leverett and Brattle "entertained notions still more 'enlarged' " than the college president would have supported.[12] One of the debates between the tutors and Mather apparently involved how much of the fashionable Anglican or Anglicizing literature the students should be exposed to.

In Increase Mather's favor, possibly, is the example cited by Cotton Mather of an oration to the students delivered by the president sometime before 1697:

> It pleaseth me greatly that you, who have been initiated in the Liberal Arts, seem to savour a liberal mode of philosophizing, rather than the

9. There were other Latin editions of More's ethics in 1668, 1669, 1679, 1695, and 1711. See the bibliography in Flora I. MacKinnon, ed., *Philosophical Writings of Henry More* (New York, 1925), 234–245.

10. Morison, *Three Centuries of Harvard*, 46.

11. When Increase Mather was in England he was assisted by Tillotson. See Clifford K. Shipton, "The New England Clergy of the 'Glacial Age,' " Col. Soc. Mass., *Trans.*, XXXII (1937), 24–54. Few works are found in as many American libraries as editions of Tillotson's sermons. Possibly no other Anglican writer was more widely read in America, North and South, with the exception of the author of *The Whole Duty of Man*. To mention one example, Joseph Green (1675–1715), later minister at Salem Village, wrote a letter to his brother, a seaman, in 1696, requesting help in getting some books. Among the books Green wanted was "Dr. Tillotsons sermons." Samuel E. Morison, ed., "The Commonplace Book of Joseph Green (1675–1715)," Col. Soc. Mass., *Trans.*, XXXIV (1943), 223.

12. Miller, *New England Mind*, II, 237–238. See Miller's various discussions of the "liberal"-"conservative" split on pp. 249, 447–450, 465.

Peripatetic. I doubt not that the *Exercitationes* of Gassendi are familiar
to you; in which he sheweth with many proofs that there are many deficiencies in Aristotle, many excesses, and many errors. . . . How much
in [Aristotle's] writings are redolent of their author's paganism! He
would have the world uncreated; he denieth a possible resurrection of
the dead, he declareth the soul mortal. To Aristotle some prefer Pyrrho,
father of the Sceptics; others, Zeno, father of the Stoics; many prefer
Plato, father of the Academics. You who are wont to philosophize in a
liberal spirit, are pledged to the words of no particular master, yet I
would have you hold fast to that one truly golden saying of Aristotle:
Find a friend in Plato, a friend in Socrates (and I say a friend in
Aristotle), *but above all find a friend in* TRUTH.[13]

But such rhetoric is hard to interpret. The famous motto paraphrased from
Aristotle at the end of Mather's address has been called "a party slogan of the
Ramists" and should perhaps not be taken too seriously.[14] If all that Increase
Mather meant to convey in his oration was Ramist anti-Aristotelianism, his
message is not very startling and might even be interpreted as regressive. But
before he quoted from his father Cotton Mather took the trouble to emphasize
that though the Ramean discipline was preferred to the Aristotelian, the students did not confine themselves to that school either, to the extent that it
would lead to depriving themselves "of that *libera philosophia*, which the
good spirits of the age have embraced, ever since the great Lord Bacon show'd
'em the way to 'the advancement of learning:' but they seem to be rather of
the *sect*, begun by Potamon, called ἐκλεκτίκοί, who adhering to no former
sect, chose out of them all what they lik'd best in any of them."[15] Neverthe-

13. See Cotton Mather, *Magnalia*, II, 21, for the Latin version. I have quoted the translation in
Miller and Johnson, eds., *The Puritans*, 721. Gassendi, influenced by Vives and by Ramus to
some extent, had attacked Aristotle in his *Exercitationes paradoxicae adversus Aristoteleos*
(Grenoble, 1624). Mel Gorman, "Gassendi in America," *Isis*, LV (1964), 409–417, is concerned
almost exclusively with the influence of Gassendi's astronomy.

14. Miller, *New England Mind*, I, 152. There is a similar statement in Grotius's *Prolegomena
to the Law of War and Peace* (Paris, 1625): "Among the philosophers Aristotle deservedly holds
the foremost place, whether you take into account his order of treatment, or the subtlety of his
distinctions, or the weight of his reasons. Would that this pre-eminence had not, for some centuries back, been turned into a tyranny, so that truth, to whom Aristotle devoted faithful service,
was by no instrumentality more repressed than by Aristotle's name! For my part . . . I avail
myself of the liberty of the early Christians, who had sworn allegiance to the sect of no one of the
philosophers, not because they were in agreement with those who said that nothing can be
known—than which nothing is more foolish—but because they thought that there was no philosophic sect whose vision had compassed all truth, and none which had not perceived some aspect
of truth." See the translation by Francis W. Kelsey (New York, 1957), 27.

15. Mather, *Magnalia*, II, 21. On Cotton Mather's growing ecumenicalism in the opening
years of the 18th century, see Middlekauff, *The Mathers*, 226–229. According to Middlekauff,

less, one could wish that Increase Mather had been as explicit in his listing of friends as the Acts of the University of Leiden in the later seventeenth century: "*Amici nobis sunt Socrates, Plato, Aristotles, Conimbricensis, Suarezius, Ramus, Cartesius, sed magis amica veritas*" (Our friends are Socrates, Plato, Aristotle, the school of Coimbra, Suarez, Ramus, Descartes, but our greatest friend is truth).[16]

If the Mathers may not be termed wholly "liberal" in the 1690s, Leverett himself cannot casually be called "liberal." He was certainly perfectly orthodox in religion despite his reputation for latitudinarianism and Anglophilia. The best recent work on the man finds it necessary to use the term "paradox" to describe the inconsistencies in his thought and character. Leverett's thinking reveals "the very deeply rooted ambiguities of orthodox Puritan theology writ large." And his confusions "demonstrate how certain assumptions of seventeenth century Puritan orthodoxy grew up to devour the elaborate religious synthesis based on them." Whatever his liberalism, in other words, it was not something entirely alien or imported.[17]

Leaving aside the exact meaning of "liberalism" in New England at the end of the seventeenth century—and philosophical and religious "liberalism" should probably be sharply distinguished, for men orthodox in religion turned to philosophies that promised to be helpful to their cause, regardless of that philosophy's tenor—More and some of the other Cambridge Platonists had unusually attractive reputations for piety. "The holiest person upon the face of the earth," was the description of More given by a contemporary.[18] Similarly, it was said of Benjamin Whichcote that he continually practiced "universal charity and goodness," and John Smith was described as "incomparable as well for the loveliness of his Disposition and Temper, the inward ornament and beauty of a meek and humble Spirit, as for the extraordinary amiableness of his outward person."[19] In addition, despite such divergences from Cal-

---

Mather held that "if we prefer a man not of the 'Best Morals' who supports our notions of Church polity to one of eminent piety but of different ecclesiastical persuasion," we are guilty of sectarian spirit.

16. Quoted in Mora, "Suarez and Modern Philosophy," *Jour. Hist. Ideas*, XIV (1953), 540. College texts from the university at Coimbra (Conimbricensis) in Portugal were widely used in the early 17th century.

17. Arthur Kaledin, "The Mind of John Leverett" (Ph.D. diss., Harvard University, 1965), 138. There is also useful material on Leverett and Brattle in Clayton H. Chapman, "The Life and Influence of Reverend Benjamin Colman, D.D. (1673–1747)" (Ph.D. diss., Boston University School of Theology, 1948).

18. Quoted in John Tulloch, *Rational Theology and Christian Philosophy in England in the Seventeenth Century*, II (Edinburgh, 1872), 350.

19. The description of Whichcote is from a funeral sermon by Tillotson in 1683, and that of Smith from the introduction by John Worthington to Smith's *Select Discourses* (London, 1660). Both are quoted in C. A. Patrides, ed., *The Cambridge Platonists* (Cambridge, Mass., 1970), 16.

vinism as the qualified rejection of predestination among most of the Cambridge group (Nathaniel Culverwell, Jeremiah White, and perhaps, Peter Sterry were exceptions), a dislike of sectarianism in religion, a broad toleration of a variety of goodwilled religious beliefs, and an emphasis on God's love that was almost Universalist, these Neoplatonists had a close historical and philosophical kinship to New England Puritanism. It is essential to remember these ties if we are to understand how Henry More fit so comfortably into the state of learning and religion at Harvard in the last decades of the seventeenth century.

The rather extreme antagonism between the Cambridge Platonists and Puritanism that Ernst Cassirer sets up in his *Platonic Renaissance in England* would seem to make the adoption of Henry More's text tantamount to a total reversal in thought. According to Cassirer, "Puritan" moral law was based on God's arbitrary will and power as expressed in divine decrees. Both the validity of the law and one's obligation to obey it were derived from God's eternal sovereignty and man's subordinate relation to Him, not from any recognition of the intrinsic rightness of the decrees. Starting with this sort of definition of Puritan ethics, as radically theocentric and voluntarist rather than, as we might say, "logocentric" and rationalist, it was easy for Cassirer to show innumerable passages in the work of More and the other Cambridge philosophers that emphatically disagreed. Thus, from Ralph Cudworth's *The True Intellectual System of the Universe* (written in the early 1670s though not published until 1678), Cassirer quotes the author's vigorous rejection of that false doctrine "which deprives the ideas of good and evil of all sense and value in their own right by deducing them from the absolute will of God, bound by no inner law." For Cudworth, ideas of good and evil were "intelligible entities. . . . No power, not even omnipotence, can destroy these eternal and immutable natures, and make good bad or bad good."[20]

More's *Enchiridion Ethicum* contains a number of similar passages: right reason "knows what in every Case is good and bad," and what right reason sees as good or bad is such in its own nature. The "rectified Mind takes in . . . the Essence of the thing it self, painted in the Understanding: and so a Triangle, in its own Nature, is nothing else but what Right Reason conceives to be such. . . . Hence it plainly follows, that there are some unchangeable Ideas or Impressions of Good and Evil, even as of Figures in the Mathematicks." "All Men do agree, that the supreme Law is *Right Reason*: and this Reason, being also a Divine Thing, is therefore immutable, always constant and like unto it self."[21]

20. Ernst Cassirer, *The Platonic Renaissance in England*, trans. James R. Pettegrove (London, 1953 [orig. publ. Leipzig, 1932]), 79–80.
21. Henry More, *An Account of Virtue: or, Dr. Henry More's Abridgment of Morals, Put into*

Cassirer is obviously right about the element of Platonic rationalism in the Cambridge philosophers. Yet we can speak of no philosophical turnabout attendant upon Harvard's adoption of More's work (aside from the rejection of Scholasticism and Aristotle) because Cassirer oversimplifies seventeenth-century Puritanism. The antithesis he reports between the "ethical conscience of the Cambridge school" and the "fanatical worship of the mere principle of power" among the Calvinists has relatively little application to New England.[22]

Within the context of the teaching of moral philosophy (if less so, perhaps, in theology) a well-established doctrine of innate Natural Law was part of the fabric of thought in New England, with historical roots in both Thomist-Scholastic and Stoic sources.[23] Even William Ames gave it some recognition, as we have seen. In accordance with scriptural authority it was universally accepted that all men possessed at least sufficient natural moral knowledge to be convicted of sin, although many doubted that this knowledge could be useful to lead to virtue. But since this natural knowledge was the possession even of pagans outside the Judaeo-Christian revelation, its basis had to lie to some degree in unchangeable reason.[24] The Puritans attempted to get around the inherent difficulty of reconciling God's freedom and power with His absolute goodness by believing that God *chose* to limit Himself to rational rather than arbitrary judgments. Thus Thomas Shepard (d. 1649) wrote impenetrably: "For it is the sovereign will of God . . . to make every moral law good, and therefore to command it, rather than to make it good by a mere commanding of it."[25] If the New England Puritans worshiped power, it was a a power subtly tempered by reason.

English (New York, 1930 [orig. publ. London, 1690]), 81, 114. This work was originally published in Latin in 1667. See n. 9 above.

22. Cassirer, *Platonic Renaissance*, 81.

23. Miller, *New England Mind*, I, 185–186: "The Puritans did not really believe that the law of nature was extinct or useless, whatever harsh things they said in their more pious moods. There was something left of innate knowledge, . . . reason could still make out a few all-important letters in the faded text. . . . One of the most pronounced and widespread characteristics of Puritan thought in the seventeenth century is the constantly increasing emphasis put upon the remains of God's image in fallen men." See also, Lee W. Gibbs, "The Puritan Natural Law Theory of William Ames," *Harvard Theol. Rev.*, LXIV (1971), 37–57.

24. Perry Miller has pioneered in showing the extent and depth of Puritan rationalism, though he also comments on its "elusive" quality.

25. Quoted by Miller, *New England Mind*, I, 198. Miller's entire chap. 7, "The Uses of Reason," gives many examples. However, see also, pp. 486–487: "By logic or rhetoric or the federal theology [the Puritans] managed to support the principles of reason and intellect in spite of their absolutist doctrines, but we should not so misread their minds as to decide that they had no genuine allegiance to the absolute ideas, or that these were not sincerely felt. They achieved marvels by their artful device of securing God's assent to His own delimitation." In the medieval

Discussions of the moral law in relation to God's will were always marked by ambiguity. Henry More could assert that no virtue and no moral philosophy exist that are "beyond the Compass and Meaning of *Right Reason*; nor exceed the Professions and Memorials of the most Excellent of the *Heathens*," an opinion that few New Englanders could have agreed with. But More qualified the startling rationalist moralism of this passage in the very next paragraph by reference to the *prisca theologia*, which immediately made everything all right. "That Religion may not be defrauded of her due Honour," More declared his belief that nothing is found in the writings of the heathen philosophers that was not owing "either to the very Doctrine, or to the Ancient *Cabala* or Tradition of the most Primitive Church of God; Or else to the *Eternal* Son, that *Logos*, or WORD *of God*; Who has, in all Ages past, endow'd every Man with some Sense of *Honesty*."[26] Similarly, in 1706 one Harvard *quaestio* implied that Natural Law is in itself unchangeable, a proposition that opened the way to a rationalist foundation for morality. But in the same year the response to another *quaestio* asserted that the virtues of the *Ethnicae* (i.e., the pagans) were not true virtues, a proposition that proclaimed the limitations of mere reason.

One of the things that Plato "left unexplained about his theory of ideas," Harry Wolfson has observed, "is the question of how these ideas are related to God." Is the moral law in some sense external to God, whether produced by Him or coeternal with Him? Or is this law internal and properly speaking simply the "thought" of God?[27] In their complex responses to these questions in the seventeenth century, questions that inevitably also touched on the doctrine of the Trinity because of the problem of the Father's relation to the Logos, Henry More and a large number of the New England clergy were probably not as far apart as may appear on the surface. Heinrich Heppe has pointed out that "Reformed dogmaticians as a whole" were occupied with the question of "whether goodness is good because God wills it, or whether God wills the good because it is good." The opinion of a Polanus that "God is a law to

nominalist tradition there was a similar compromise based on the distinction between "the ordained or ordinary power of God (*potentia dei ordinata*) by which He chooses to regulate his activity in the world in accordance with the revealed and natural laws that He has established, and the absolute power (*potentia dei absoluta*), by which He can do anything that does not involve a formal contradiction." See Oberman, *Harvest of Medieval Theology*, 30–56. Many other examples could be given of this effort at balancing law and power in the attributes of God. Miller assumed the Puritans were more unique than they were in fact.

26. More, *Account of Virtue*, 266–267. Of course, since God is Himself unchanging, His law will be unchanging, which does not itself settle the question of the relation between will and intellect in the divine mind.

27. Harry A. Wolfson, "Extradeical and Intradeical Interpretations of Platonic Ideas," *Jour. Hist. Ideas*, XXII (1961), 3–32.

Himself," and that "whatever He wishes done, it is right by the very fact that He wills it," was hardly the dominant opinion in the seventeenth century.[28]

The Platonism implicit in many Ramist ideas was another medium that created an affinity between New England Puritans and the Cambridge Platonists. This affinity is especially apparent in natural theology, as expressed principally in the Harvard emphasis on technologia, on the one side, and some of the common metaphysical ideas of the Cambridge philosophers, on the other. Alexander Richardson, who was at Cambridge University early in the 1600s, prefaced his *Logicians School-Master* with a statement on the "ideas" of God visible in the world. The same "Idea," he said, that was

> in the making of the thing . . . is in the governing of it. . . . Hence it follows, that every rule of Art is eternall . . . every rule of Art is most true . . . as it answers to that Idea that is in [God]. . . . Now it is in God as in the fountaine, and it is in the creature, too, but there it is by a refraction: for this wisdom coming to the creature, according as the creature is . . . will be divided into parts: and as in a looking-glasse that is broken, looke how many peeces it is broken into, so many images shall you see.[29]

A nearly identical Platonic theory is in John Smith's discourse on "The Excellency and Nobleness of True Religion":

> God made the Universe and all the Creatures contained therein as so many Glasses wherein he might reflect his own Glory: He hath copied forth himself in the Creation; and in this Outward World we may read the lovely characters of the Divine Goodness, Power and Wisdom. In some Creatures there are darker representations of God, there are Prints and Footsteps of God; but in others there are clearer and fuller representations of the Divinity, the Face and Image of God. . . . That Divine *Wisdome* that contrived and beautified this glorious Structure, can best

28. Heppe, *Reformed Dogmatics*, ed. Bizer, trans. Thomson, 93–94. After both Descartes and Hobbes reduced the standard of goodness to will alone—Descartes maintained (for technical reasons in his metaphysics) that even such eternal truths as those of mathematics, like two plus two equals four, were contingent on God's will—Calvinists were more ready to dissociate themselves from stark theological voluntarism so as not to be implicated in such radical views. Descartes did maintain, however, like some Calvinists, that the eternal truths are fixed and immutable because the divine will is itself immutable. See Gilson, *Liberté chez Descartes*, Pt. I, chaps. 1, 2. Cf. Samuel Willard, *Compleat Body of Divinity*, writing in *ca.* 1700: "Whatsoever God wills us to do, is our Duty, and nothing else but what he so wills; and the supream Reason why it is our Duty, is because he wills it." Willard defined the moral law as "a Divine Unchangible Rule given to Man, and accommodated to his Nature, as he was created by God, obliging him to serve to God's glory as his last End" (pp. 561, 565).

29. Richardson, *Logicians School-Master*. On Neoplatonism in England, see also, Costello, *Curriculum at Cambridge*, 18–19, 30.

explain her own Art and carry up the Soul back again in these reflected Beams to him who is the Fountain of them.[30]

Many related notions may be found in More's work. The point to be emphasized is that there was a continuous tradition of rationalist theology in New England, a tradition that certainly did not exclude piety and devotionalism, although it did eschew fideism or any suggestion that God is altogether unintelligible. To be more specific, two kinds of rationalism vied for authority in the early seventeenth century, the Aristotelian Scholastic and the Platonist, the latter of which is evident in Richardson. With the universal repudiation of Scholasticism after mid-century, Platonism expanded to fill the vacuum in metaphysics left by the disintegration of the Aristotelian synthesis. Platonism had the virtue, moreover, of being historically compatible with affectional religion, even with mysticism, which made it quite congruous with existing tendencies in New England religion.

There were also some concrete connections between the Puritans who came to America and the Cambridge philosophers. Emmanuel College at Cambridge was for both groups an academic nucleus, though later Christ's College became the home of Platonism, principally because More was there. Benjamin Whichcote, John Smith, Nathaniel Culverwell, and Ralph Cudworth had all been associated with Emmanuel in the 1630s. Some of the views of John Preston, a well-known Puritan minister and master of Emmanuel from 1622 until his death in 1628, resemble those of the Platonists. During the period of Puritan political domination in England many of the men associated with the Platonist group received positions of preferment.[31] Henry More and some of the other Platonists had been raised as strict Calvinists, and though they ultimately turned away from the doctrine of predestined reprobation in particular, much of their work shows traces of their Puritan background. More's moral psychology, as we will see, was in the Augustinian voluntarist tradition and emphasized divine control of the "will" by the power of grace as the key to virtue.

Whatever the case may be concerning the inner affinities between New England Puritanism and Cambridge Platonism, the success of More's ethics in New England is undeniable. The *Enchiridion Ethicum* seems to have been used continuously at Harvard until about 1730.[32] Even Cotton Mather,

30. Smith, *Select Discourses*, quoted in Patrides, ed., *Cambridge Platonists*, 184.

31. Marjorie Nicolson, "Christ's College and the Latitude-Men," *Modern Philology*, XXVII (1929–1930), 35–53. See also, Vivian de Sola Pinto, *Peter Sterry: Platonist and Puritan, 1613–1672* (New York, 1968 [orig. publ. Cambridge, 1934]), and Colie, *Light and Enlightenment*, 22–23. See also, chap. 1, n. 77, above.

32. The Harvard Univ. Archives owns a manuscript abstract or condensation of More's ethics prepared by John Leverett in the early 1690s. This copy, no doubt one of several made by various students from Leverett's original, was owned first by Thomas Symmes, class of 1698. Also on

strongly opposed to an ethics course independent of theology, relented slightly in the case of More. Writing in his *Manuductio ad Ministerium* (1726), Mather conceded that it may not be amiss for the young candidate for the ministry simply to know what pagan ethics is, and he allowed a "short Reading upon a Golius, or a More." "But be more of a Christian," he warned, in a comment that reveals much about the esteem in which More was held, "than to look on the *Enchiridion* of the Author last mentioned, as *Next the Bible, the best book in the world.*"[33]

In contrast to Harvard, Yale did not turn to using More for the teaching of ethics until the early 1720s. "When my Father was in Coll.," Ezra Stiles tells us, "they recited Mori Enchiridion Ethicum." Stiles's father, Isaac, was at Yale between 1719 and 1722.[34] That the book was not used for recitations before 1719 may be gathered from the appearance of the title in the personal catalog of reading kept by Samuel Johnson of Stratford, Connecticut. Johnson's catalog lists the books he read "since I left Yale College, *i.e.*, after I was Tutor of the College." According to this list, he completed reading his own copy of More in July 1720. If More's ethics had been included in the Yale curriculum when Johnson was either a student or a tutor there (between 1710 and 1719), he would probably not have read the book in 1720, though we cannot be sure it was not a second reading.[35] There is no question that the book was available, of course. In about 1713 Sir John Davie, who had graduated from Harvard in 1681 and later succeeded to a baronetcy in England, sent

---

the manuscript is the signature of "James Cushing, 1726." Many students must have relied heavily on their personal copy of this 50-page abstract and never glanced at More's full text. The title on the abstract is: "Doc:[ris] H. Mori Enchiridion Ethicum ad theses contractiores redactum. In usum Pupillorum. p[er] D. J.[ohn] L.[everett]." Similar manuscript précis exist of More's *Enchiridion Metaphysicum* (London, 1671).

33. Mather, *Manuductio*, 38. The manuscript diary of Henry Flynt, tutor at Harvard for more than 50 years prior to his death in 1760, shows that More's ethics was lent out to students as late as 1730. This diary runs from 1724 to 1747 and is in Houghton Lib. at Harvard Univ. Ebenezer Pemberton owned a copy of More's ethics in 1717, as the catalog of his books, published in that year, indicates, and in 1700 Samuel Sewall ordered a group of academic books, probably for the college, which included More's *Immortality of the Soul*, his metaphysics, and his ethics (*Letter-Book of Samuel Sewall* [Mass. Hist. Soc., *Colls.*, 6th Ser., I (Boston, 1886)], 237). In Virginia, William Byrd II owned an English translation of More's *Enchiridion Ethicum* (John Spencer Bassett, ed., *The Writings of "Colonel William Byrd of Westover in Virginia, Esqr."* [New York, 1901], 442). The Bray Collection in the Maryland Hall of Records in Annapolis, deposited in the 17th century, has all of More's works. Such references to the dispersion in America of More's works, his ethics in particular, could be easily extended. The Cambridge Platonists, especially More and Cudworth, had a special appeal to some American intellectuals in the 19th century. For the interest of Emerson and others, see F. O. Matthiessen, *American Renaissance: Art and Expression in the Age of Emerson and Whitman* (New York, 1941), 104–105.

34. *Diary of Ezra Stiles*, ed. Dexter, II, 349.

35. Johnson's catalog is in Schneider and Schneider, eds., *Samuel Johnson*, I, 497–526.

to the Yale Library, along with nearly two hundred other volumes, a copy of More's ethics bound together with the *Ethices Compendium* of Daniel Whitby. The well-known Dummer gift to Yale also included More's ethics as well as copies of all of his other works.[36]

In addition to the American colleges, several of the dissenting academies in England, such as Sheriffhales, Rathmell, and Bethnal Green, adopted More's ethics in the second half of the seventeenth century, and it was used or recommended at Cambridge University by 1730 if not much earlier.[37]

Henry More's ethics struck a harmonious chord in New England. Yet it must be understood that some of the characteristics of the Cambridge Platonists were the outgrowth of specific responses to problems in old England that had no analogs in America. The Cambridge group's well-known latitudinarianism in matters of religious doctrine was directly opposed to internecine sectarian rivalry and was a reaction against the religious dissidence in seventeenth-century Britain. Their philosophical idealism, their conviction that true philosophy and Christianity are in necessary agreement, and their belief that genuine altruism is possible were systematic responses to the threat presented by Thomas Hobbes's philosophical materialism, implicit atheism, and psychological egoism. It is important to note, too, that in general a man of More's intelligence and learning was moved by intellectual goals that in both depth and breadth went far beyond the ambitions and abilities of anyone in America at the time.

There is no evidence that the works of Hobbes were studied in seventeenth- or eighteenth-century America, but the drift of his thought was well understood because Hobbes was so frequently and widely written against.[38] "Hardly

36. There is a manuscript list of Davie's gift in the Beinecke Lib., Yale Univ. The Beinecke at present owns Daniel Whitby, *Ethices compendium* . . . (Oxford, 1684) and bound with it, paginated separately, More's *Enchiridion Ethicum* (London, 1667). For an annotated list of the Dummer gift, which was sent from England in 1713 but not available for use for several years after that, see Louise May Bryant and Mary Patterson, eds., "The List of Books Sent by Jeremiah Dummer," in *Papers in Honor of Andrew Keogh, Librarian of Yale University*, ed. Staff of [Yale University] Library (New Haven, Conn., 1938).

37. McLachlan, *English Education under the Test Acts*, 302; Smith, *Birth of Modern Education*, Appendix A; Christopher Wordsworth, *Scholae Academicae: Some Account of the Studies at the English Universities in the Eighteenth Century* (Cambridge, 1877), 129–132. According to J. W. Ashley Smith, John Smith, Whichcote, Cudworth, and More "exercised a profound influence on the academies" (p. 32). A copy of Nathaniel Culverwell's *An Elegant and Learned Discourse of the Light of Nature* (London, 1652) was in New England before 1702. See Robinson and Robinson, "Three Massachusetts Libraries," Col. Soc. Mass., *Trans.*, XXVIII (1935), 168.

38. Copies of Hobbes's *Leviathan* were extremely hard to come by in any case, the book having been partly suppressed by the Stationers' Company and under the threat of a parliamentary ban. See Mintz, *Hunting of Leviathan*, 61. In a pamphlet on money written by Cotton Mather in 1691 there is a reference to "Hobs his state of nature" (Miller, *New England Mind*, II, 162); and, of course, Charles Morton referred to Hobbes. George Lawson's *Examination of Hobbs*

has there been seen again such a ferment of popular feeling and learned opinion round the thought of one man till . . . Darwinism touched the same human interest in a manner not wholly dissimilar," James Martineau wrote of the author of the *Leviathan*.[39] Without a glance at Hobbes it is impossible to understand the particular emphases in More's ethics and the character of most subsequent moral philosophy in the eighteenth century. As with Darwin, without necessarily intending it Hobbes changed the course of religious thinking, for in replying to Hobbes in his own naturalistic terms the clergy and other pious minds sometimes found themselves defending novel positions in moral philosophy that inevitably penetrated into theology and Christian anthropology. The responses to Hobbes were often reaffirmations of traditional notions familiar to all the learned. But on occasion he jarred original and unexpected results out of his opponents.[40]

Hobbes

Hobbes antagonized his age by his methods and his conclusions, but both were extremely fruitful. He began in the Cartesian manner by denying the worth of most prior speculation in the field of ethics, proclaiming that careful observation of men, particularly one's own self, is the proper foundation for moral philosophy. The "characters of man's heart . . . are legible only to him that searcheth hearts." Yet "to do it without comparing them with our own . . . is to decipher without a key." This approach immediately forced the questions of ethics onto empirical ground such as had not been quite the

---

his Leviathan (London, 1657) was in the Harvard College Library before 1723 (see Morison, *Seventeenth-Century Harvard*, 260n.). According to John Bowle, *Hobbes and His Critics: A Study in Seventeenth Century Constitutionalism* (New York, 1952), 100, Richard Baxter called Lawson "the ablest man of almost any I know in England." Richard Lee of Westmoreland County, Virginia, owned two works by Hobbes when he died in 1715 at age 68: something called "Elements," which could be any of three possible Hobbes titles, and *Philosophical Rudiments Concerning Government and Society* (London, 1651). Lee's library has been analyzed and the titles identified in Louis B. Wright, "Richard Lee II, a Belated Elizabethan in Virginia," *Huntington Library Quarterly*, II (1938–1939), 1–35. The Amsterdam 1670 Latin edition of the *Leviathan* in the Bray Collection, Md. Hall of Recs., may have been the earliest copy of that work to arrive in America, in about 1697.

39. Martineau, *Types of Ethical Theory* (Oxford, 1885), quoted by Frederick J. Powicke, *The Cambridge Platonists: A Study* (Cambridge, Mass., 1926), 120.

40. If Hobbes's philosophical work had provoked only Cudworth's *True Intellectual System* and Richard Cumberland's *A Treatise of the Laws of Nature* (1672), those two cornucopias of ideas from which everybody borrowed for decades, his work would have been well justified. For references to some of the specifically benevolist opinions growing out of anti-Hobbesianism, see Mintz, *Hunting of Leviathan*, 142–146.

case since the time of St. Augustine. To answer Hobbes, psychological evidence equivalent to his was required.

Hobbes was a major contributor to the extraordinarily rich blossoming of psychological investigation that occurred within the context of moral philosophy in the late seventeenth and early eighteenth centuries. The force of Hobbes's ideas complemented and joined with the Cartesian interest in introspection, with the quite independent Puritan obsession with scrupulous plumbing of the depths of the heart, and with the cynical, libertine-type exposé of amour propre as found in La Rochefoucauld, to produce this unusual intellectual harvest.[41]

What Hobbes claimed to have discovered in human nature through his introspective and empirico-deductive method was rather disconcerting: predominantly selfish instincts redeemed only by an ignoble capacity to calculate one's way toward a practical accommodation with others. The summation and the height of moral knowledge, "intelligible even to the meanest capacity," is the golden rule in negative form: "Do not that to another, which thou wouldst not have done to thyself." It is self-preservation alone that obliges us to social decency and civil obedience, and self-preservation is the sole justification for such standards of conduct. There is an ironic parallel between Hobbes's image of man and the Christian concept of Original Sin, which also proclaims human self-love and depravity. But the Christian's wickedness is measured in relation to an objective moral standard applicable to all men at all times and available to them through right reason and Scripture, the divine law. Sin in the Christian tradition is defined by an absolute. For Hobbes, on the contrary, the only objective standards were the clear dictates of rational self-interest and the positive laws of one's State.[42] "The desires, and other passions of man, are in themselves no sin. No more are the actions that proceed from those passions, till they know a law that forbids them: which till laws be made they cannot know." Where there is no political sovereign, there is no law; "where no law, no injustice. . . . Justice and injustice are none of the faculties neither of the body nor the mind."[43] Human beings carry with them no private lading

41. Thomas Hobbes, *Leviathan* . . . , ed. Michael Oakeshott (Oxford, 1946), 6, 22, 41–42. See chap. 4, above.

42. Some 20th-century commentators have found an absolute morality in Hobbes, but his 17th-century critics certainly found none. See, typically, John Tutchin (1661?–1707), *Satyr against Vice*, who lashed out against Hobbes as "the Malmesbury Devil," who "sin's Columbus" meant to be in viewing "the Orb of large Iniquity." Hobbes, he said, is "the goodliest Brand that ever burnt in Hell." Quoted by Fairchild, *Religious Trends in English Poetry*, I, 65.

43. *Leviathan*, ed. Oakeshott, 103, 83. "Men, vehemently in love with their own new opinions, though never so absurd, and obstinately bent to maintain them, gave those their opinions also that reverenced name of conscience, as if they would have it seem unlawful, to change or speak against them; and so pretend to know they are true, when they know at most, that they think so" (p. 41).

of moral law, no conscience in Ames's sense, no right reason in harmony with divine law such as Cicero described.

Yet it was still necessary after these claims for Hobbes to deal with the existence of moral judgments themselves. Men do in fact constantly praise and blame in moral terms and strive to separate right from wrong, and seem to do so without reference to (and sometimes against) the conventions of their society. Could not this behavior be interpreted as the effect of a moral disposition and perhaps even of innate moral standards? Hobbes's reply is the classic subjectivist-relativist argument:

> Moral philosophy is nothing else but the science of what is *good*, and *evil*, in the conversation, and society of mankind. *Good*, and *evil*, are names that signify our appetites, and aversions; which in different tempers, customs, and doctrines of men, are different: and divers men, differ not only in their judgment, on the senses of what is pleasant, and unpleasant to the taste, smell, hearing, touch, and sight; but also of what is conformable, or disagreeable to reason, in the actions of common life. Nay, the same man, in divers times, differs from himself; and one time praiseth, that is, calleth good, what another time he dispraiseth, and calleth evil. . . . And therefore so long as man is in the condition of mere nature [i.e., without a State to define morality] . . . private appetite is the measure of good, and evil.[44]

Among the implications of this passage is the view that moral judgments have little if any rational or transcendent content; they are merely emotive statements or linguistic conventions that record transient pleasure or displeasure with a person or an event.

If we add to the above opinions, outrageous for the time, Hobbes's corporealism or materialism, his mechanical determinism and behaviorism, his Erastianism in politics, and his alleged atheism, it is easy to understand why Bishop Warburton in 1741 described the philosopher of Malmesbury as "the terror of the last age" upon whose "steel cap" "every young Churchman militant would needs try his arms."[45]

Hobbes challenged conventional ethical views in a number of areas. More's response was primarily a defense of human nature and a reaffirmation of the rational and absolute foundations of moral good and evil. In addition, he inevitably attempted to integrate many elements of Christian theology into his ethics.

44. *Ibid.*, 104.

45. Warburton, *Divine Legation of Moses* . . . (London, 1738–1741), quoted by William R. Scott, *Francis Hutcheson: His Life, Teaching, and Position in the History of Philosophy* (Cambridge, 1900), 153.

More particularly attacked Hobbes's egoistic or cynical theory of human nature.[46] The Cambridge philosopher found sources of "natural" human goodness in the intellect, in the will, in the passions, and in an apparently new human endowment, the "Boniform faculty." How all of these are related to one another is one of the major problems in understanding More's ethics. It is highly significant that More, like Descartes and Hobbes, claimed to have "dived" for the rules of morality "into the intimate Recesses of his own Soul and Experience." What he discovered in this way, he hoped, "will not pass for less, than had he barely transcrib'd from Books, and from the Authorities that went before him."[47]

More's belief that man has an absolute standard of virtue derived from intellect or reason was familiar to the Harvard student of the 1690s, since on this point the Cambridge philosopher mainly reiterated traditional arguments going back to the ancients: Reason is man's special endowment, which places him above all other creatures, and is his best attribute; it is proper for man to live in accordance with his highest nature, that is, reason; reason provides him with knowledge of virtue; therefore it is proper and natural for rational men to be virtuous. With Marcus Aurelius, More maintained that God's divine will is found in human reason, and thus men are under a "common rule" with God and are His "fellow-citizens."[48] But this conventional reliance on the law of nature and right reason as a source of morality in human conduct played a

---

46. The terms "cynical" and "cynic" are used here and throughout in the modern sense and without any reference to the ancient philosophical school. There is a good discussion of the 17th-century "cynics," those psychologists who saw little that was altruistic or edifying in human nature, in the introduction by F. B. Kaye to Bernard Mandeville, *The Fable of the Bees: or, Private Vices, Publick Benefits*, I (Oxford, 1924), lxxvii–cxiii. Kaye uses the term "anti-rationalists." See also the admirable study by Lovejoy, *Reflections on Human Nature*, 1–34. It seems to me preferable to retain the traditional term "egoism" despite Bernard Gert's criticism in "Hobbes and Psychological Egoism," *Jour. Hist. Ideas*, XXVIII (1967), 503–520. Gert argues that a true egoism—defined as the view that "men *never* act in order to benefit others, or because they believe a course of action to be morally right"—is almost never explicitly defended. Gert would prefer the term "pessimism" for the view that "most actions of most men are motivated by self-interest."

47. More, *Account of Virtue*, Epistle to the Reader.

48. *Ibid.*, 5, 14–19, 96. Subsequent references to page numbers in More's *Account of Virtue* will appear in parentheses in the text. In addition to the works by Cassirer, Powicke, Colie, Tulloch, Nicolson, MacKinnon, and Patrides already cited in this chapter, see also, on More: Gerald R. Cragg, ed., *The Cambridge Platonists* (New York, 1968); Eugene M. Austin, *The Ethics of the Cambridge Platonists* (Philadelphia, 1935), a published dissertation 86 pages long; Grace Neal Dolson, "The Ethical System of Henry More," *Philosophical Rev.*, VI (1897), 593–607, which is quite good; Basil Willey's classic work, *The Seventeenth Century Background: Studies in the Thought of the Age in Relation to Poetry and Religion* (New York, 1950 [orig. publ. London, 1934]); and Aharon Lichtenstein, *Henry More: The Rational Theology of a Cambridge Platonist* (Cambridge, Mass., 1962).

comparatively small role in the whole of More's ethical thought, as we will see.

Hobbes had also appreciated the powers of reason, but it was a different kind of reason. In More's argument and in the Stoic Natural Law tradition, "reason" meant intuitive or noetic reason, the mind's inchoate or manifest possession of the great principles of divine law, as in the endowment of *synteresis*. For Hobbes, on the contrary, "reason" only and explicitly meant instrumental reason, the ability of the mind to calculate toward an end without also being the possessor of ends.[49] As is well known, Locke broadly followed Hobbes in this type of naturalistic nominalism (though Locke deliberately exempted moral knowledge, which he believed could be made as rationally demonstrable as mathematics), and the consequence has been that for a large segment of modern thought "reason" refers not to substantive knowledge that God has given mankind, a direct line to the eternal verities, and the foundation of the moral consensus, but to a restless, probing, critical reason, a skeptical faculty that denies all authority except its own and easily becomes the victim of itself.[50] Reason, which had formerly been the defensive bulwark of old authority, thus came to be the challenger to it. Henry More, however, did retain a firm belief in noetic reason, and in general the direction of moral philosophy in early America was always away from the type of critical rationalism exemplified by Hobbes and Locke.[51]

49. See Hobbes, *Leviathan*, ed. Oakeshott, chap. 5: Reason is "nothing but *reckoning*."

50. Locke was not beyond referring to "the candle of the Lord . . . set up . . . in men's minds, which it is impossible for the breath or power of man to wholly extinguish," showing the influence of the Cambridge Platonists in favor of intuitive reason, but there may have been a subtle difference. The scriptural phrase "candle of the Lord," popularized by Benjamin Whichcote, the father of the Cambridge school, had "only a technical meaning" for Locke, according to Ernest Tuveson, "referring to that light which illuminates the ideas so that the understanding can distinguish them, rather than to a spiritual and moral radiance which gives certainty in the dilemmas of life." Ernest Tuveson, *The Imagination as a Means of Grace: Locke and the Aesthetics of Romanticism* (Berkeley and Los Angeles, Calif., 1960), 47.

51. Perry Miller in *New England Mind*, I, 190–191, distinguishes two senses of "reason": "From scholasticism, from Thomistic philosophy, and ultimately from Aristotle, came the conception of reason as a principle of action, a power or faculty by which truth was discovered in the sensibles, an aptitude for discovering it; from reformed theology, from Augustine, and ultimately from Plato, came the conception of reason as itself the source of truth, the container and giver of ideas through inward intuition or recollection. Much of the Puritan's thinking must be explained as an effort to relieve the tension between the two meanings." Neither of these notions is the same as 18th-century critical reason, which was a form of skepticism. In *New England Mind*, II, 417–436, in a chapter on "Reason," Miller at one point seems to be arguing that the prevailing development in the 17th century was from an original concept of reason as "an ability to handle logic," a "function, not something with content," to a later concept in which reason has "a large capacity" to formulate "its own premises and [argue] from them rather than from externally given data" (pp. 427–429). In other words, there is a progression from the predominant notion of discursive or syllogistic reason to noetic reason. Such a notion of progression seems to me

Critique of Aristotle

We have seen that Increase Mather in a public address defending "liberal" philosophy had warned against the impieties of Aristotle, his denial of personal immortality, his pagan belief in the world's eternity, and so on. But Hobbes was also a denigrator of Aristotle, and one of the concerns of the Cambridge Platonists was to point out, as Ralph Cudworth emphasized, that no matter what, Aristotle was "infinitely to be preferred" over Hobbes. Hobbes exceedingly disparaged Aristotle, Cudworth went on to say,

> yet we shall do him [Aristotle] this right here to declare, that his Ethicks were truely such, and answered their title; but that new model of ethicks [Hobbes's], which hath been obtruded upon the world with so much fatuosity and is indeed nothing but the old Democritick doctrine revived, is no ethicks at all, but a mere cheat, the undermining and subversion of all morality, by substituting something like it in the room of it, that is a mere counterfeit and changeling; the design whereof could not be any other than to debauch the world.[52]

It is significant that More's *Enchiridion Ethicum*, despite the label "Platonist" attached to it, called upon Aristotle for direct support of arguments on 65 out of 268 pages and Plato and Platonists on only 15 pages.[53] In other words, More launched no sustained attack on Aristotle, and among the continuities he offered with the past study of moral philosophy was a moderate Aristotelianism in some matters.

Yet on the whole, the essential thrust of More's thought was toward a modification of the Aristotelians' single-minded intellectualization of ethics. More conceded that "Rectitude of Conjecture" and "Right Reason" are truly essen-

---

to be quite unsustainable, since both of these concepts of reason, along with several variants, existed throughout the 17th century. Yet it is true that Scholastic logic, which pervaded the curriculum, lost influence in favor of new logics of inquiry, while at the same time various modes of noetic intuitionism became increasingly influential. The great problem in ethics after Hobbes and Locke was how to counteract their nominalism and empiricism and securely reintroduce intuitive moral knowledge.

52. Cudworth, *True Intellectual System*, I, 53. "Democritick" refers, of course, to the ancient atomist, Democritus.

53. The figure for Aristotle includes some early followers, particularly Andronicus. More cited Cicero on 54 pages and various "Pythagoreans," a nebulous school existing from the first century B.C. to the second century A.D., on 36 pages. The Pythagoreans might be combined with the Neoplatonic school, which they influenced. I do not mean to suggest by these figures that the underlying influences in any philosophical work can be determined by counting affirmative quotations. My purpose here is merely to introduce some cautions against facile judgments regarding Aristotelianism and Platonism. See also, Powicke's comment that the Cambridge Platonists "drew far more from the Bible" than from Platonic or Neoplatonic sources. *Cambridge Platonists*, 21.

tial elements in "prudence." And since Aristotle makes moral virtue "nothing else but, *A fit Habit of pointing or aiming at that just Medium which, in acting and in suffering, is to be wish'd for*," which "habit" is the same as prudence, it is clear that moral virtue requires the intellectual habits of judicious conjecture and right reason as well as others (98–103). Nevertheless, certain familiar problems arise in this formulation. According to Aristotle, More observed, "*Right Reason is that which is conformable to Prudence.* But then he himself elsewhere defines *Prudence, To be a true Habit, exerting it self in what happens to a Man good or bad, according to Reason.* But surely this sounds very odd, and is no better than a trifling Circle, to define Right Reason by Prudence, and Prudence again by Right Reason" (152–153). The way out of this dilemma for More was not a repudiation of Aristotle but rather a reinterpretation of the Philosopher's moral thought. More put the *Eudemian Ethics*, the most Platonic and the most religious of Aristotle's ethical works,[54] in the forefront of his treatment, and by a highly selective method of quoting, metamorphosed Aristotle into a Christian Neoplatonist. A closer look at some of these modifications will bring us nearer to the center of More's ethics and reveal also the process by which certain Puritan ideas invaded and reshaped moral philosophy.

First of all, More asserted, virtue cannot properly be considered a habit at all. It is rather an "*intellectual Power of the Soul*" that "*easily pursues what is absolutely and simply the best.*" It is not essential to virtue that it be a habit. If a man had the right intellectual power "born in him, he would doubtless be virtuous, tho it came not to him in the way of repeated Actions, such as constitute a Habit. . . . It is not the external Causes, but the internal, which make the essence of a thing" (11–12). What is this after all, we may ask, but the Scholastic notion of an infused habit, which enters the soul through grace, though More did not use those terms. Virtue, More wrote, is "a quick and vigorous heat," which "*irresistibly*" moves the mind to do good and honorable things. Through this power the mind is elevated and inclined "*to love*" virtue (12).[55] The inward possession of the power of virtue leads one to love all virtue. The power is termed intellectual, More tells us, not only because it is in the intellectual part of the soul but also because "it is always excited by some Principle which is *intellectual* or rational." But More wanted to emphasize equally the idea of "pursuit." If the soul "had not that force to pursue, it would not be Virtue, but only a Disposition towards it" (12–13). According to More, Aristotle himself seemed to point to such a specific faculty of virtue (as something distinct from the more general intellectual faculties) insofar as

54. Lichtenstein, *Henry More*, 64, draws this judgment about the *Eudemian Ethics* from Werner Jaeger.

55. Italics mine. Note the determinist element contained in the word "irresistibly."

he recognized that when men discover what is best in any subject they do so "not as they are *knowing*, but as they are *Good*." Aristotle would have done better, More held, if he had more correctly styled this faculty "*The very Eye of the Soul*," rather than "to call it that sort of Natural *Industry*, which seems too much bordering upon *Craft*" (14). In short, More rejected the prevalent Greek analogy between skills and virtues, or between techniques and essential goodness, which the metaphor of "habit" served to reinforce. Virtue for More was in no way reducible to a series of acts, however much transformed into habits.[56] Rather, it is an irresistible inclination in the soul. Its character is not that it is successful at manipulating externals but that it possesses the essential inward quality. It might even be called a kind of zeal.

But how does one break the problem of circularity in Aristotle? Not only is there the problem of defining right reason in terms beyond its individual representation in the prudent man, but also the question, which Aristotle himself hardly confronted, of how this criterion is to be elevated above the moral standards of the mundane social or political reference group within which one lives. "We must have recourse," More said, "to some middle Principle to serve as *Mercury* did of old, and be an Interpreter between God and Man" (14). For this purpose, right reason, "*which is in Man . . . a sort of Copy or Transcript of that Reason or Law eternal which is registered in the Mind Divine*," is the obvious choice. More introduced, then, a transcendent standard and defined virtue as the constant pursuit of that which seems best to right reason (15). Such a standard is not entirely unlike what Aristotle envisioned, More believed, but the Philosopher failed altogether to remember "that the Divine Life was not a matter of Sapience only, but was principally to consist in Love, Benignity, and in Beneficence or Well-doing. For these are the Fruits of that Celestial Particle of the Soul, which we term the *Boniform*; and by which, above any other Accessions, we are made most like unto Almighty God" (18–19). As one reads on in More, it quickly becomes apparent that his idea of "right reason" does not at all resemble reason or intellect in any ordinary sense. Like Thomas Shepard's "divine Light," it is a principle of love and beneficence in the soul; it is a celestial particle; and above all it is resolvable into "an *inward Sense*, or an *inward Faculty of Divination*," and not into "certain and distinct Principles, by which a Man might judge of that which in every thing were the best" (17). The validity of More's effort to demonstrate that this idea of virtue was also implicitly Aristotle's need not concern us, though the effort itself is significant. It is More's concept of the inward moral sense that is more important, for in the end it subordinates even right reason.

56. Some of the ambiguities in the 17th-century notion of moral habits are discussed in Fiering, "Franklin and Virtue," *Am. Qtly.*, XXX (1978), 199–223.

Not only did More thoroughly renovate the ancient concepts of habit and right reason; he also revised the Aristotelian concept of happiness. He introduced no obstacle to the prevailing conviction, which continued unbroken throughout most of the eighteenth century, that happiness is inseparable from virtue; but he changed the traditional nature of the relationship. *"Happiness is that pleasure which the mind takes in from a Sense of Virtue, and a Conscience of Well-doing; and of conforming in all things to the Rules of both."* Unlike Aristotle, More defined happiness as "a *Pleasure* of the Mind rather than an *Operation* of it." It is a fruition, according to More, rather than an activity (4). Charles Morton had argued similarly. More tried to show that Aristotle implicitly supported him in this opinion in that the Philosopher defined pleasure as a restitution of a creature from an imperfect or preternatural state to its own proper nature. Now, said More, "a true Feeling and Possession of Virtue, is also the conversion or bringing a man about, from what is contrary to his Nature, to that which is conformable to it" (5). Depravity is not natural to man. "Virtue is natural to human Nature, and born as a twin therewith . . . ; it was Sin only that brought Death into the World" (6). Therefore, the restitution to a state of virtue is man's most intrinsic and peculiar pleasure, and happiness is that pleasure. Thus, the greatest happiness is not activity in accordance with virtue, as Aristotle held, but the pleasure one feels when one is virtuous or has virtue.

This pleasure in fruition, which the modern scholar Ronald Crane in a classic article called the concept of the "self-approving joy," was to have an important career among the sentimentalist moralists of the eighteenth century. Its effect was to ground the happiness of virtue in a distinct sensation and hence to expand further More's notion of an inward moral sense.[57] The pleasure of possessing virtue was designed to be not simply a subjective experience, but a standard and criterion of the strait path. Thus, it closely resembled William Perkins's good conscience. It is notable, too, that More expressly spoke of *conversion* to a virtuous state, a "bringing a man about" to his proper condition from unnatural depravity.

57. Crane, "Suggestions toward a Genealogy of 'The Man of Feeling,' " *Jour. English Lit. Hist.*, I (1934), 205–230. In this article Crane showed the many 17th-century roots of Shaftesburian thought. Anticipations of Shaftesbury's ideas were particularly common among the liberal Anglican divines opposed to the severity of both the Calvinist and the Hobbesian view of human nature. Crane isolated four concepts that together, he said, characterized the sentimentalist ethics of Shaftesbury and later Hutcheson: (1) virtue defined as universal benevolence; (2) benevolence as a form of feeling; (3) benevolent feelings as natural to man; and (4) the self-approving joy.

The Boniform Faculty

Morality then, for More, cannot be founded on intellect, as Aristotle seems to have intended, for virtue is not an intellectual habit; "right reason," despite the name, is partly love and inward sense; and happiness is not intellectual activity in accordance with virtue but pleasure taken in a special moral sensation. All of this novelty required new terminology, which More provided with his concept of the "Boniform Faculty" of the soul. This faculty has correctly been seen as an anticipation of the idea of a "moral sense," which arose more definitely some years later in the work of the third earl of Shaftesbury and Francis Hutcheson.[58] It has not been so common, however, to notice the resemblance of the boniform faculty to certain Puritan notions of the psychology of the regenerate. As opposed to the naturalistic "moral sense" concept of the eighteenth century, More's boniform faculty retained quite openly its link to the divine and thus was an important transitional concept in the progress toward naturalistic ethical systems. The boniform faculty was also universalist or democratic in import, as was the moral sense, and represents a stage in the movement away from sectarian exclusiveness in moral theology. Finally, the boniform faculty was one more variant in the tradition of Augustinian voluntarism, for it was above all a type of affective/cognitive will or a sense of the heart.

The desires of the soul, More noted, do not fly to their object as it is intelligible or known, but as it is good or "congruous." "Supreme Happiness," which comes from closing with the good object and taking pleasure in it, is not in the intellect, the faculty that "knows." The proper seat of this happiness must be called the "*Boniform Faculty of the Soul*: namely, a Faculty of that divine Composition, and supernatural Texture, as enables us to distinguish

58. See, for example, W. R. Sorley, *A History of English Philosophy* (Cambridge, 1920), and especially various studies by Ernest Tuveson. In *Imagination as a Means of Grace*, 51, Tuveson writes: "The moral sense is for [Thomas] Burnet a naturalized version of what . . . Henry More called a 'boniform faculty.'" Tuveson has shown Burnet to be an intermediate figure in the development of the theory of the moral sense. In an article on "The Importance of Shaftesbury," *Jour. English Lit. Hist.*, XX (1953), 267–299, Tuveson discusses the moral sense as the descendant of More's idea. He also sees a resemblance between the boniform faculty and the "*mens*" or "*intellectus angelicus*" of Ficino, a suggestion which needs follow-up. See also, Tuveson, "The Origins of the 'Moral Sense,'" *Huntington Lib. Qtly.*, XI (1947–1948), 241–259. In More's *Divine Dialogues*, the obvious model for Shaftesbury's *Moralists*, Hylobares, one of the characters in the dialogue, refers to a "quicker sense . . . whereby we discern *Moral* good and evil," and Sophron, another character, speaks of "a *sense* in a Man, if it were awakened, to which these *moral incongruities* are as harsh and displeasing as any incongruous object . . . is to the outward senses." Philotheus, also, speaks of "a living sense of the comeliness and pulchritude of grace and virtue" that is the property of the virtuous. See More, *Divine Dialogues . . .* , 2d ed. (London, 1713 [orig. publ. 1667]), 146, 147, 170.

not only what is simply and absolutely the best, but to relish it" (6). (Charles Morton's idea of conscience as a third intellectual faculty was not dissimilar.) The verb More used most frequently in connection with this new faculty is "relish," a term later used by Shaftesbury and Jonathan Edwards and one that Puritan theologians earlier in the century, such as Thomas Hooker, had frequently played upon. The idea of relish connoted effectively the irreducible element of a singular and ineffable taste in the sensibility of the graciously regenerated and had antecedents in Christian literature going back for centuries.[59] The boniform faculty "much resembles that part of the Will which moves towards that which we judge to be absolutely the best, when, as it were with an unquenchable thirst and affection it is hurried on towards so pleasing an Object; and being in possession of it, is swallowed up in satisfaction that cannot be exprest" (6–7). To act in accordance with this faculty, More wrote, is to conform to *"the best and divinest thing that is in us."* This divinity in the soul cannot be in the intellect, as Aristotle would have it, for happiness in contemplation alone "can be no *moral* Happiness." Worst of all, it would be a happiness "confined to a few speculative Men and Philosophers, and . . . shut out the Bulk of Mankind, who could never be partakers thereof" (7). The democracy of souls posited by More, it should be noted, was opposed not so much to the exclusiveness of the doctrine of election as to intellectualism in ethics. The "Study and Improvement of [the boniform faculty] is common to all men. For it is not above the Talent of the meanest, to love God, and his Neigbour very heartily. And, if this be done with Prudence and Purity of Life, it is the Completion of this Happiness, and the very natural Fruit of this *exalted Faculty*" (8). The egalitarianism of the moral sense, based upon its independence from attributes of superior intellect, would more than once be similarly emphasized by Hutcheson.

The boniform faculty, we can see, was a device for integrating will, affection, intellect, and sensation into a hypothetical unified moral force in the soul. The sensory element in this unity is extremely prominent. This novel faculty, More wrote, provides mankind with a "Sense of Virtue," not simply "bare Definitions" (8–9). But since virtue is "in it self an inward life, not an outward shape," it cannot be discovered by the ordinary eye, or, we might say, the natural eye. One must first be "transformed into this life of Virtue, then indeed you behold the Beauties, and taste the Pleasures thereof." As Plotinus said, *"If you ever were the thing it self, you may then be said to have seen it"* (9).

The principle that inward purification or reformation is necessary preparation for establishing new levels of vision and understanding in the soul, levels

59. See Terrence Erdt, *Jonathan Edwards: Art and the Sense of the Heart* (Amherst, Mass., 1980).

that are unattainable by a carnal nature, was common to all the Cambridge Platonists. According to Cassirer, the doctrine that the soul "contemplates the divine, not by virtue of a revelation which comes to it from without, but by creating the divine within itself and thereby making itself like the divine," was at "the core" of English Neoplatonism.[60] This notion has obvious similarities to the religious doctrine of regeneration and to the Pauline description of the gifts of grace and is hardly unique to Protestantism. As More put it, by the subjection of our passions and the purification of our bodies and souls, "there springs up to us, as it were, a new *Sensibility* in the Mind or Spirit," through which we receive special powers of moral discernment (101). The source of this new sensibility and relish is God. "For who, as a mere Creature, can sincerely and constantly prosecute that which is best? This must be the Gift of God, and the Effect of a Divine Sense or Spirit" (105). The boniform faculty must be "replenish'd with that Divine Sense and Relish, which affords the highest Pleasure, the chiefest Beauty, and the utmost Perfection to the Soul." It is, after all, "by this supreme Faculty that we pant after God, that we adhere unto him, and that (as far as our Nature does admit) we are even like unto him" (106).[61] In More's ethics the religious sense, or devotion,

60. Cassirer, *Platonic Renaissance*, 27–28. See Thomas à Kempis, writing early in the 15th century, *The Imitation of Christ*, trans. Richard Whitford, ed. Harold C. Gardiner, S.J. (Garden City, N.Y., 1955), 37: "A good life makes a man wise toward God and instructs him in many things a sinful man will never feel or know." A similar theme that makes true knowledge partly a moral attainment is found in Ficino. See Paul Oskar Kristeller, *The Philosophy of Marsilio Ficino*, trans. Virginia Conant (New York, 1943), 301–303. In both Kempis and Ficino, as in More, the end or goal of this moral purification is not mystical contemplation but practice, or the right moral guidance of the soul. Thus, philosophy begins and ends in the moral life.

61. Norman Pettit, *The Heart Prepared: Grace and Conversion in Puritan Spiritual Life* (New Haven, Conn., 1966), is in error, I believe, in drawing a dichotomy between what he calls the Platonic mystical concept of preparation for grace—that man "through an effort of the will, may move from one level of spiritual activity to another until at last he becomes one with God"—and the Puritan conviction, seen in William Perkins, for example, that man "cannot ascend by his own will to a state of union with [God]" (p. 15). The extremes may exist, but for practical purposes the gap between the English Neoplatonists of the 17th century and the Puritans in this matter was negligible. Shading and nuance are more significant here than stark distinctions, especially since it was so widely believed that after the initial converting divine influence, God's will and man's will worked concurrently. Cf., for example, Thomas Hooker, *Application of Redemption*, 410: "That Dispensation of God which gives ability and a Principle to the will for to work[,] that act and dispensation must be before the ability of the will and act of it, and so cannot be caused by it. . . . But this Preparation and pulling away from sin, is to make way for a spiritual ability to be given to the will for to work, and therefore it is before the will and work, and either of them as any cause. . . . This is to be Observed against a wretched Shift and cursed Cavil of the Jesuits; [who] . . . pretended to give way to the Grace of God; and yet in truth take away what they give: . . . they yield freely and fully, That *it is God who gives both the will and the deed*. And Grace is required of necessity unto both, and neither can be without it; nor will nor deed. But in truth this is nothing but a colour of words, when the sense which they follow sounds quite contrary. For ask but their meaning, and when they have opened themselves, al comes to

merges totally with the moral sense, and the irresistible inclination to the good in the redeemed will, or the boniform faculty, is identical to the inclination toward God. Indeed, More's deepest declared purpose in the *Enchiridion Ethicum* was to demonstrate that "*Virtue, Grace,* and *the Divine Life,*" though they may seem distinct, "if *rightly* ponder'd . . . are all but one and the same Thing" (Epistle to the Reader). In the middle of the next century Jonathan Edwards would maintain the same position.

We mentioned above that More ultimately subordinated even right reason to the higher standard of inward sense, which is finally the sense of the boniform faculty. There cannot be found in the whole compass of nature a greater good, More wrote, than "*Intellectual Love.*" Nothing can more "fill, elevate, and irradiate the Soul . . . , nothing is more exalted or Divine, nothing more ravishing, and complacent, nothing more sharp in distinguishing what in every Case is decorous and right, or more quick in executing whatsoever is laudable and just." Intellectual love ought to be the rule and standard of all else, and "nothing should pass, or be accounted, for Right Reason, which from this Divine Source and Fountain did not take its Birth." And what is this intellectual love, More asked, "but an inward Life and Sense, that moves in the *Boniform Faculty of the Soul*? 'Tis by this the Soul relisheth what is simply the best" (156). Therefore, "this most simple and Divine Sense and Feeling in the *Boniform Faculty of the Soul*, is that Rule or Boundary, whereby Reason is examin'd and approves her self." Anything offered by reason that is "contrary to the Sense and Feeling 'tis spurious and dishonest"; if congruous to this divine sense, it is orthodox, fit, and just. No other "*external* Idea of Good" need be invented, no remoter object, so long as the inward life and sense is pointed "singly at that Idea, which is fram'd not from exterior things, but from the Relish and intrinsick Feeling of the *Boniform Faculty* within." All the shapes and modes of virtue derive from this one idea and all may be resolved into it again (157). This interior "idea" is, of course, nothing other than the love of God.

It is unmistakably clear that the core of More's ethics is the Augustinian

---

thus much; That the Lord hath a Concourse and a co-working in the Will and Deed, sends forth an influence into the act of the Will, and of the work done: and leads forth and guides both unto their end. And this is no more than he doth with the act of any Creature; the first cause concurring with the second. . . . As it is with Two men that draw a Boat or a Ship together, each man hath a principle and power of his own whereby he draws, both these meet, and concur, and co-work together in the drawing. . . . [But] this gives no more to the work of God's Grace in Conversion, than it doth to the Act of Providence upon, and with the act of any Creature reasonable. Whereas this must be observed carefully, and for ever maintained as the everlasting Truth of God, That the Lord gives a power spiritual to the work, which it had not before he Concurs with the act of that power when it is put forth, he gives him a being in the state of Grace, before he leads out the act of that being. He first lets in an influence of a powerful impression upon the Faculty of the Will, before he Concurs with the Act or Deed." See also, pp. 145–146, 217–219, above.

conception of redeemed will, which is the same as love, and which takes precedence over any conception of intellect or reason. The boniform faculty is predominantly affective rather than intellectual.[62] Can it be doubted that what was radical in More for many New England Puritans was not Platonic rationalism but a conception of the revivified will that bordered on antinomianism and enthusiasm? More's kinship to the devotees of the Holy Spirit within Puritanism is evident. In More's system the restraints set by Scripture as well as by reason and law seemed to be threatened with inundation by spirit.

More himself was sensitive to this problem. He engaged in long debates with and about Quakers in order to distinguish finely his own philosophy from the teaching of the Friends.[63] One of his most influential works was a learned attack on religious enthusiasm, which he called the "misconceit of being *inspired*," wherein he warned also against fancies not tried by the "known Faculties of the Soul."[64] But even in this work he was careful to differentiate from religious pathology that "*true* and *warrantable Enthusiasm* of devout and holy Souls, who are so strangely transported in that vehement *Love* they bear towards God. . . . To such Enthusiasm as this, which is but the triumph of the Soul of man inebriated, as it were, with the delicious sense of the divine life, that blessed Root and Originall of all holy wisedom and vertue, I must declare my self as much a friend, as I am to the vulgar fanatical Enthusiasm a professed enemy."[65]

In the *Enchiridion Ethicum* More anticipated the criticism from the orthodox right that would classify him with the enthusiasts and tried to counteract it without also relinquishing his preference for a true and warrantable enthusiasm as the key to genuine religion and virtue. There will be those, More said, who will claim that he erects all the "splendid Fabrick of the Virtues . . . on a weak and tottering Foundation," namely on "Passion, such as they may suppose this our *Love* to be" (158). In addition, his prudent man, it will be said, is necessarily given up to "Inspirations and to Enthusiasm" in the bad

---

62. Cassirer, *Platonic Renaissance*, 124, makes this point very effectively. James Martineau's classification of the ethics of the Cambridge Platonists as belonging to the "dianoetic type" is incorrect, Cassirer observes. "The ethics of the Cambridge School, in spite of all its intellectual and discursive aspects, can never be diverted in the direction of mere intellectualism. For it conceives the fundamental power of the intellect itself as the pure power of love." And on p. 30 Cassirer writes that the "Cambridge conception of religious reason cannot be derived from the power of thinking alone. . . . They combat logical as well as theological dogmatics, and dogmatics of the understanding as well as those of faith. For in both they see an obstacle to that pristine grasp of the divine which can spring only from the fundamental disposition of the will."

63. See, for example, Marjorie Nicolson, "George Keith and the Cambridge Platonists," *Philosophical Rev.*, XXXIX (1930), 36–55, and DePauley, *Candle of the Lord*, 126–127.

64. More, *Enthusiasmus Triumphatus* (Augustan Reprint Soc., *Pubs.*, no. 118 [Los Angeles, Calif., 1966]), 2.

65. *Ibid.*, 45. On enthusiasm, see above, pp. 177–178.

sense, because it must ensue that one who believes his mind is "reform'd and purg'd" will ever afterwards imagine that everything that occurs to him is right reason itself "merely because he thinks so" (155). To such predictable charges More had several answers. He could, as occasion demanded, emphasize the rational aspect of the boniform faculty, which, he said, "hath nothing in it that savours of Fanaticism" (17). "The Measure of *Right Reason* is to imitate the Divine Wisdom, and the Divine Goodness, with all our Might" (19). In this statement More referred to an external rational standard beyond inward sense. And he offered many similar formulations, some of which we have already quoted. Significantly, however, another approach that More took to this problem was the outright defense of the passions as contributors to the moral life. The *Enchiridion Ethicum*, in fact, was a landmark in the psychological revolution of the seventeenth and eighteenth centuries that laid the basis for sentimentalist ethics and the romantic view of the passions.

The Passions

Sometimes More treated the passions in the conventional fashion, as the challengers to intellect that for the sake of virtue must be controlled—"Virtue *is an intellectual Power of the Soul, by which it over-rules the animal Impressions or bodily Passions; so as in every Action it easily pursues what is absolutely and simply the best*" (11)—but he equally often gave them surprisingly unreserved approbation. He explicitly rejected the alleged Stoic wish to root up all passions in order to free the soul from discord. The passions are "of their own Nature . . . good." The trick is to "temper them aright" (34). "Passionate affecting is the most intimate and immediate Fruit of Life." Without the passions we are capable of but superficial and imaginary approval; with them we are enabled "to wed" the good and "to intermix it with our Sense and Life." The nature of true virtue is "to love the best things, and hate the worst," so that "the whole man" is carried up to God and heaven in "the firy Chariot of his Affections" (40). Thus, the passions are "not only good, but singularly needful to the perfecting of human life." And in them "the true Characters and Images of Virtue, are made the more resplendent." The "principal part of Virtue" is in the "due Commixture" of passion and reason (83).

Statements parallel to these of More might be found in the work of William Fenner and others in the Neoplatonist and Augustinian tradition. But More went beyond his Puritan predecessors in his incorporation of certain principles from Descartes's *Traité des passions de l'âme* (1649). More admired this work exceedingly; it is the one modern book that he admitted to having relied upon in his ethics, and he must be credited with being one of the first to bring Descartes's work on the passions into the mainstream of British and American thought.[66] His dependence was selective, however, in that he drew from Descartes only what seemed useful for his own ends. The role that the French genius assigned to the conarion or pineal gland, as the specific locale at which body and mind interconnect with each other, More dismissed as "a witty conceit . . . insufficiently grounded" (38), and perhaps because of Puritan influences, More generally went much further than Descartes in emphasizing the importance of holy affections for the moral life. What More derived from Descartes, or at least found cogently affirmed in his treatise (in addition to many particulars in the analysis and classification of the passions), were several basic ideas: the great importance to ethics of an adequate theory of the passions; the value of the passions as revelations of "nature's" (or God's) intentions regarding man's conduct; their necessary self-authentication; and the significance of the self-approving joy.

The theory of the passions was the one area in moral philosophy in which the moderns could feel confident of their originality and superiority, as we have already noted. Like Bacon before him, Descartes called attention to the deficiencies of the ancients on this subject: "That which the ancients have taught regarding [the passions] is both so slight, and for the most part so far from credible, that I am unable to entertain any hope of approximating to the truth excepting by shunning the paths which they have followed."[67] In the face of this deficiency, and despite the considerable confusion in terminology and theory in the various Renaissance studies that preceded his own, Descartes succeeded in introducing greater precision and clarity than had been the case before.[68]

Descartes spoke of the functional and the survival value of the passions and affections and tried to indicate the purposes of each of them. Implicit in

66. Descartes's treatise on the passions also had a profound effect on Nicolas Malebranche, perhaps the greatest student of the passions in 17th-century France. Malebranche, in turn, had a major influence on British and American theories of the passions, both directly and through John Norris of Bemerton. Hutcheson, for example, expressly credited Malebranche. On Malebranche's influence in early America, see Fiering, *Jonathan Edwards's Moral Thought*.

67. Descartes, *Passions of the Soul*, in Haldane and Ross, trans. and eds., *Philosophical Works*, I, 331. For Bacon's remarks see *Advancement of Learning*, ed. Kitchin, 171 *ff*.

68. On Descartes's relation to earlier theorists of the passions, see Levi, *French Moralists, passim*. More's relation to Descartes underwent a sharp reversal in later years. The *Enchiridion Ethicum* was written when More still approved of the "incomparable" French philosopher, but he was already having some doubts. By 1671 he had become a leading opponent of some aspects of Cartesian metaphysics. In that year he wrote to Robert Boyle: "It had been to my great reproach, for me, who have been, from my youth to this very day, so open a stickler for the support of natural religion, and for Christianity itself, in the best mode thereof, to be found of so little judgment, as not to discern, how prejudicial *Des Cartes'* mechanical pretensions are to the belief of a God." Quoted by Colie, *Light and Enlightenment*, 73. Some later editions of his *Enchiridion Ethicum* contain a statement of More's dissent from Descartes.

his reasoning was a concept of natural design into which, he believed, the passions ought properly to fit. In More's treatment the passions take on an extraordinary and momentous moral function. He set about "to interpret the Voice of Nature in them all, as far as we are able," for if we can observe "the end unto which Nature, or rather God, who is the Parent of Nature, has destined each of them," we will know how they are to be used and valued. For unlike thought and speculation, according to More, "Natural and Radical Affections, are not from our selves." They cannot be acquired by "Methods." They are "really in us antecedent to all Notion and Cogitation whatever" and "implanted in us, as early as Life it self" (54–55). In short, the passions and affections carry a certain primitive authority as indexes of God's purposes. "The Intendments of Divine Providence are not less understood by their Use, than by the Structure of those Organs, which compose every animal Body" (34).

More gave dozens of examples to illustrate the purposefulness of human passions. The passions may be consulted for "the rating of things that are laudable and just" (39). The experience of the affection of "devotion," for example, teaches us "by a loud Exhortation of Nature," that there is something which ought to be more dear to us than ourselves. This passion is used chiefly in politics and religion, "neither of which can be without Virtue." From our knowledge of the affection of devotion it follows that "those, who place the highest Wisdom in Self-preservation, and as preferable at all times to all other things, do *sin* against the Light of Nature" (62). The use of the passion of "Commiseration," to take another case, is in "succoring the distressed, and defending him that has right. For to take away the Life of an innocent Man, is so monstrous a Crime, as tears the very Bowels of Nature, and forces sighs from the Breasts of all Men" (70). "Shame and Glory" are another example; both indicate "that we must rather abide by the common Opinion of others, than by our own" (75). Expanded somewhat into a general analysis of human nature, this teleological theory became the absolute foundation of most eighteenth-century ethics, namely, the general conviction that man is a natural creation of God and that from a close investigation of human nature one may deduce God's purposes and ends. This revelation from human nature took on an authority in the eighteenth century that quickly surpassed the Bible or any other souce of moral knowledge and, indeed, had a profound effect on the image of God Himself, who was expected to be at least as humane as man.[69]

69. See Fiering, "Irresistible Compassion," *Jour. Hist. Ideas*, XXXVII (1976), 195–218. The justification of the passions in More's work has a precise parallel in the justifications and apologies then current for other seeming or apparent defects in the natural order or in man. In the course of the 17th century, physico-theological speculation engaged in controversy over whether the natural universe should be viewed as the defective consequence of sin and punishment—for

The most general revelation that was derived from the study of the passions was the principle that goods and evils truly do exist in nature and not, as Hobbes declared, simply in man's transient appetites or aversions. Those objects that our inward propensities and strong inclinations, "antecedent to all Choice or Deliberation . . . dictate as Good and Just [are] really Good and Just." Yet it is true that the law of nature that "bears sway in the animal Region" is only "a sort of confused Muttering, or Whisper of a Divine Law," and that the voice of nature is "more clear and audible in the intellectual State." We are obliged therefore to appeal frequently to the "Tribunal of Reason, and to consult [it] about Time, Place, and Proportion." Reason judges more distinctly and more "*abstractedly*, than what the Animal Light, or any Law of the Passions, can pretend to" (79). The passions respond only to particular cases without clear motive but rather by impulse. More thus made clear that he meant for "reason" to be the higher authority, and he attacked those who claimed that "*every thing* [is] *lawful, that passions* [do] *persuade*" (80). But he could still say what had hardly been heard by New England college students before, that the passions are "little less than Divine" and that we can safely follow their dictates unless reason admonishes us "that something may be done, that is better and more advantageous" (82). The typical Augustinian distinction commonly found earlier, between the passions of the regenerate, which are in God's service, and the passions of the concupiscent soul, which serve only self, was more or less being blurred.[70] Also lost in this transformation of religious ideas into secular counterparts was the rigor of written scriptural law, which served as a rudder in the high seas of antinomian piety.

Much of the moral authority attributed to the passions was an outgrowth of Descartes's insight that of all our perceptions, only those of things that we feel are necessarily free of possible deception. Everything else may not in fact be what the representation we have of it suggests it to be. This flaw is especially true of external sensations. But one cannot imagine feeling anger or joy and then learning later that the feeling was nonexistent, like a delusion. A feeling represents nothing but itself. Of our passions, "it were impossible to

---

example, the craters on the moon discovered by Galileo—or whether it should be understood as the product of God's wisdom, all parts being perfect in themselves. Did the universe exemplify, as Macklem puts it, the disorder famously described by Donne in 1611, "Tis all in pieces, all coherence gone; / All just supply, and all Relation," or the order described by Pope in 1733: "The gen'ral Order, since the whole began, / Is kept in Nature, and is kept in Man." In More's case, the parallel between nature and man holds, for he defended the orderliness of rugged mountains as well as of rugged emotions. See Michael Macklem, *The Anatomy of the World: Relations between Natural and Moral Law from Donne to Pope* (Minneapolis, Minn., 1958), 26.

70. Harvard theses in 1689 and 1710, to mention the earliest, maintained that the passions were in themselves good by nature.

feel them, if they were not" (39). Even in a dream one's feelings are real at the time they are experienced.[71] It was in connection with this axiom that the self-approving joy took on its great significance first in More and then among many British moralists. If we indeed have a special "sense of virtue," or a unique feeling of the moral good when we are either virtuous ourselves or perceive virtue in others, such a sense must excel over "all Opinions and Philosophical Speculations whatsoever" (39). Both Descartes and More spoke of the "sweetness" of this feeling. It is a passion, Descartes said, that follows only upon our having just done some good action and is "the sweetest of all joys."[72] The alleged merit of this test of virtue is that there can be no doubt about its results, for it is "Passion, and not Opinion," as More put it (39). More was himself so imbued with the substance of his religious and moral heritage that he was perhaps less than adequately critical of the reliability of all such internal touchstones when used by persons inferior to him in learning and piety.

There is confusion in More's ethics, possibly not entirely ingenuous, between pleasure, sensation, passion, and something called "interior emotion." An ethics based on the pleasure of the self-approving joy, for example, has been characterized by some modern commentators as pure hedonism and little different from Hobbism in its formal nature.[73] Such a charge, surely unjust to More's intentions, is possible because of the inherent vagueness of his terms and his use of metaphors. Under Descartes's influence More thought of "interior emotions," it would seem, as something quite different from the sensory gratifications that follow upon the fulfillment of bodily appetite. For Descartes, the *"émotions intérieures"* are independent of the body and, unlike the regular passions, respond to the true worth of an object rather than to its attractiveness. In contrast to the passions, which always depend on some movement of animal spirits, interior emotions are excited in the soul by the soul itself. One of Descartes's examples of interior emotion—namely the pleasure, or the "secret joy," that people take in experiencing strong feelings

71. Jonathan Edwards occasionally speculated about the consequences of this principle, which he was probably introduced to by his reading of Malebranche. Since sensations of internal events are representative only of themselves, they cannot be delusions as external sensations may be. Edwards argued that those "ideas" that can be known only through internal experience, such as love, joy, thought, pain, etc., cannot be conceived of without some degree of internal re-creation of the sensation itself. There is no abstract image of them.

72. Descartes, *Passions of the Soul*, in Haldane and Ross, trans. and eds., *Philosophical Works*, I, 417.

73. See Sidgwick, *Outlines of Ethics*, 173. According to Dolson, "Ethical System of More," *Philosophical Rev.*, VI (1897), 593–607, More argues that moral good is to be judged by the boniform faculty, which judges right and wrong on the basis of their power to give pleasure or pain to this faculty. "Virtue is referred to pleasure, and pleasure to virtue." In the 18th century, Hutcheson was often attacked for the same reasons.

of almost any kind, such as at the theater or in reading—was probably the ultimate source of Hutcheson's later argument that the exercise of moral judgments in response to purely fictional situations proves the existence of a detached and disinterested moral sense, exclusive of all personal or self-regarding goals. Descartes himself cited the paradox of a person feeling secret joy in the course of being passionately overcome with sadness.[74] More's boniform faculty and Hutcheson's moral sense may both have derived partly from Descartes's idea of interior emotions that respond to moral situations in conjunction with passions but at a higher level and in accordance with an internal absolute standard. Measuring moral value on the basis of ordinary pleasure conferred by an action or sensation was certainly not part of More's ethical system.

It would be an error, however, to carry too far the differentiation between passions and bodiless emotions, for More was unusual in his day for his integral view of human nature. "I am very prone to think," he wrote, "that the Soul is never destitute of some *Vehicle* or other, though Plotinus be of another minde, and conceives that the Soul at the height is joyned with God and nothing else, nakedly lodged in his arms." In this opinion that the soul cannot, nor ought to try to, dissolve its connection to the body, More differed from some other Platonists to such a degree that one recent author considers the issue "a deep opposition between the members of the Cambridge school."[75] Following Descartes, More used the term "passion" in the widest possible sense, as including any and every "corporeal Impression." "Passion" could refer to a passing sensation or a distinct and prolonged inclination as well as to a whole range of pleasures from the most physical in origin to the most rarified.

Yet the coexisting psychological theory of angelic beings and of God's nature posed a real challenge to theorists of human passions. Although the Stoic ideal of acts of mercy without feelings of pity and compassion and acts of love without desire was widely condemned as a superhuman standard with no applicability to this life; and although it was generally granted that as human beings are constituted, they need their passions in order to function virtuously and well; it was also true that even severe critics of Stoicism, including Augustine, were perfectly ready to adopt the Stoic ideal as the model for non-corporeal beings. It was universal opinion that the angels and God experienced something like human emotions, which Scripture itself indicated; but these

74. On Descartes's theory of interior emotions, see Levi, *French Moralists*, 274–277, 288, and Descartes, *Passions of the Soul*, in Haldane and Ross, trans. and eds., *Philosophical Works*, I, 398.

75. See J. E. Saveson, "Differing Reactions to Descartes among the Cambridge Platonists," *Jour. Hist. Ideas*, XXI (1960), 560–567. The quotation from More is from his *Conjectura Cabbalistica . . .* (London, 1653), as quoted by Saveson. See also, Saveson, "Descartes' Influence on John Smith, Cambridge Platonist," *Jour. Hist. Ideas*, XX (1959), 258–263.

heavenly emotions, it was believed, could not be identified with human passions, since the latter always had a basis in the body or in "animal spirits."
Despite this important distinction, few theologians or psychologists wanted to
let the traditional analogy between the human and the divine mind be completely destroyed. Moreover, a great deal of sound theoretical psychology had
been learned from the contemplation of angels. Hence there was introduced
into human psychology a form of emotion that was not connected to the body
and that was assumed to be common to men and angels. "Passions" such as
intellectual love, "interior emotions," and other similar phenomena were adduced that served as bridges to the noncorporeal emotions of heaven, passions
that men are capable of, too, because men are the closest of earth's creatures
to the angelic. These rarified passions of the mind were noted by Thomas
Wright and by Bishop Reynolds as well as by More. And Descartes defined
them quite precisely in relation to other passions.[76] More's passions, which
can love, sense, give pleasure, create peace and tranquility in the soul, urge
us on to virtue, whisper the divine law, judge and rate the good, and perform
several other tasks, were, like the boniform faculty in which intellectual love
moves, confused but fertile compounds of body and soul, will and intellect,
appetite and sensation. The confluence was symptomatic of the transitional
state of moral psychology in the last half of the seventeenth century.

In More's theory of the passions, as in his concept of the boniform faculty,
there is evidence that the special qualities of the regenerate state were generalized into a universal image of human nature. But how, one might ask, does
fallen man fit into this schema? Do his passions, his reason, and his will also
convey whispers and shadows of the divine law? It was, of course, in their
relegation of fallen man to the realm of the exceptional and the unnatural that
More and many other psychological optimists toward the end of the seventeenth century effected a momentous reversal in the image of human nature.
To Hobbesian egoism (and to Calvinist depravity) More opposed an equiva-

76. See Descartes, *Passions of the Soul*, in Haldane and Ross, trans. and eds., *Philosophical
Works*, I, 398; Reynolds, *Treatise of the Passions*, in *Works*, 624: "Mental passions are those
high, pure, and abstracted delights, or other the like agitations of the Supreme part of the understanding, which Aristotle called νοῦς, the Latines, *Mens*, or *Apex animae*, which are the most
simple actions of the mind, wherein is the least intermixion or commerce with inferior and earthly
faculties." But these passions are "beyond the compass of usual industry, here to attain unto."
There are also passions of the mind that are raised in us by *synteresis*, "unto which, the custody
of all *practical truths* being committed, they there hence work in the *Conscience* motions of joy,
love, peace, fear, horrour, despair, and the like spiritual passions." See also, Wright, *Passions of
the Minde*, 31: "I think it cannot be doubted upon, but that there are some affections in the
highest and chiefest part of the soule, not unlike unto the passions of the Minde; for to God the
Scriptures ascribe love, hate, ire, zeale, who cannot be subject to any sensitive operations."
See also, Levi, *French Moralists*, 284.

lent benevolism.[77] Nature itself lost much of the connotation it derived from being contraposed to grace. Virtue became natural. Earlier, some of Whichcote's aphorisms had pointed in this direction: "15. What is Morally Good, is so suitable to the Nature of Man, that Motion in Religion cannot but be with Pleasantness. . . . 42. Man *as Man*, is Averse to what is Evil and Wicked; for Evil is unnatural, and Good is connatural, to Man."[78]

In More's work we see partly exemplified the well-known secularizing process that sanctified nature and then characterized the devil as unnatural. Or, in a stricter sense, it was perhaps the fleeting prelapsarian state of nature that was gloriously expanded while the other two, much more lasting, realms of sin and redemption were somehow ignored or bypassed. In any case, there can be no doubt that psychological theory changed in this period. With this change an attempt was made to speak as much as possible in terms of constant nature without regard to the earlier (and, indeed, continuing) religious interest in the human potentiality for radical shifts in character. That one may be born with the appearance of goodness and salvation and then be revealed to be reprobated by God, or, conversely, spend years as a seemingly condemned sinner and then be reformed and saved, these kinds of psychological problems, which called for theories of change and development more than simply constant nature, began to slip from view, not to be revived until almost the twentieth century. Instead, a great deal of moral psychology from the seventeenth century onward, obsessed with the problems presented by Hobbes and later Bernard Mandeville, struggled to define and characterize human nature in fixed terms, which came down to the question of whether this nature was essentially good or essentially depraved.[79] This concern with timeless nature

77. I use the term "benevolism" as the philosophical opposite of egoism, but with a particular emphasis; "benevolism" is meant to imply a strong affective component in what might otherwise be characterized simply as altruism. Strictly speaking, the term benevolism does not convey any precise standard or criterion of the good, but simply the passional willing of good. Hence it is not the same as "benevolence," which means specifically promoting the common or public good. Benevolence can have either benevolist or egoist motivations behind it; as an example of the latter, consider the egoism implicit in benevolence that springs from enlightened self-interest. "Altruism," as compared to benevolism, though clearly suggesting the disinterested promotion of good, is a little vaguer about the psychological makeup of the action. Note, too, that More's benevolism was not utilitarian, that is, connected to benevolence, as was Hutcheson's, but was connected to loving obedience to divine reason, just as the good inclinations of the regenerate soul are not tied to promotion of public good but rather to obedience to God's will.

78. B[enjamin] Whichcot[e], *Moral and Religious Aphorisms* . . . , ed. S[amuel] Salter (London, 1753 [orig. publ. 1703]).

79. A third option, the neutralist position, was effectively introduced by John Locke's *Thoughts on Education* and can be seen in Benjamin Franklin. See Fiering, "Franklin and Virtue," *Am. Qtly.*, XXX (1978), 199–223. The emphasis among this group was on the possibilities of training and habituation for improving a human nature that is malleable. The original concepts were

was clearly a pagan survival. Any Judaeo-Christian theory of ethics must base itself on the creature's continual openness to God's providential intervention in human life, that is, on the everpresent possibility of the transmission of the spirit from one soul to another, thereby radically altering one's essential disposition.[80] On the other hand, as we have remarked above, the heavy incorporation into ethical speculation in the seventeenth century of affectional will, of heart, of redeemed inclinations and other such more or less camouflaged religious elements had no, or very few, real precedents in pagan thought. In this respect, More's ethics and the entire sentimentalist movement, along with its many ramifications, were in large part a translation into secular terms of key elements in Christian anthropology.[81]

It may be worthwhile to observe in passing some of More's comments on the reprobated soul, though he offered no systematic treatment of this condition and hardly ever spoke of it in religious terms. There are men who simply "disrelish" moral truths and who set up "*animal Appetite*" for a guide (29). To be so captivated is an "error in the Will" in the same way as to resign oneself only to imagination or sense is an error in the intellect. But even when the will lacks in "some seasons that relish of good which it ought to have; this is merely the Will's neglect, in not exciting" the boniform faculty (31). More thus implied a considerable degree of freedom in the sinner to reform. The good man has "no other Will, but the Will of [his] Creator." The wicked man has a "perverse Will" (96–97). In another place, however, More suggested, in line with the Augustinian position, that after all nobody is really free to remake himself:

> As soon as we advance to the Knowing what appertains to Virtue, and become *Masters of the Divine Sense*, there is a certain Power above all that is Human, that associates with us and gets into us. But as, when Men yield themselves to Animal-Complacencies, and are dipt in the Impurities of Nature; they afterwards run headlong to every pernitious thing, and seem fatally ty'd down by some Chains that are Invisible, so as when Remorse prompts them to return, they cannot arise: So,

---

Classical—cf., for example, Plutarch's emphasis on training in virtue in his *Moralia*—but the 18th and 19th centuries, mainly through the theory of association, placed great hope on training. See the excellent survey of the whole sweep of Western thought by John A. Passmore, *The Perfectibility of Man* (London, 1970), and also, Passmore, "Malleability of Man," in Wasserman, ed., *Aspects of the Eighteenth Century*, 21–46.

80. On the importance of timing in human life as a religious factor and otherwise, see the following works by Eugen Rosenstock-Huessy: *Out of Revolution: Autobiography of Western Man* (Norwich, Vt., 1969 [orig. publ. New York, 1938]); *The Christian Future, or the Modern Mind Outrun* (New York, 1966 [orig. publ. 1946]); *I Am an Impure Thinker* (Norwich, Vt., 1970).

81. Jonathan Edwards's difficulties in defining a specifically Christian ethics, as a result of this translation, are discussed in Fiering, *Jonathan Edwards's Moral Thought*.

on the other side, those who, with Sincere Affections, do even pant
and thirst after Virtue, They on the sudden are caught up by *that Intellectual Spirit, which replenishes every Thing*; They are animated and
supported by it, and finally therewith join'd in the strictest association
of Love, . . . and they are easily and spontaneously led on to every
Good Work (197–198).

The influence of Puritanism is evident in this passage. But in relation to
orthodoxy as a whole there are also glaring omissions.

One of the best assessments of the ethics of the Cambridge Platonists from
the orthodox standpoint was made by Anthony Tuckney (1599–1670), master
of Emmanuel from 1645 to 1653.[82] Tuckney was not entirely unsympathetic
to the Cambridge movement, but in a famous correspondence with Benjamin
Whichcote, who is often considered the inspiration of the whole school,
Tuckney pointed to the major failings of the Platonists:

> The power of Nature in morals [is] too much advanced; Reason too much
> given to it in the mysteries of faith; . . . Philosophers . . . and other
> heathens made fairer candidates for Heaven than the Scriptures seem to
> allow of; a kind of moral divinity minted, only with a little tincture
> of Christ added; inherent righteousness so preached, as to slight imputed
> righteousness, and so set forth as to be something perfectly attainable
> in this life; an estate of love exalted above a life of faith.[83]

But Tuckney also accused Whichcote of reading mainly Schoolmen and Arminians, and Whichcote's reply is revealing: "I have not read manie books;
but I have studied a fewe: meditation and invention hath bin rather my life,
than reading: and trulie, I have more read Calvine, and Perkins, and Beza;
than all the bookes, authors, or names you mention."[84]

More believed in a supernatural ethics. The quest for virtue required divine
assistance—"whoever pretends to Virtue," he wrote, "without Imploring it

---

82. Tuckney was a cousin of John Cotton and succeeded Cotton as the vicar of Boston in
England. He corresponded with Cotton after the latter came to America. Tuckney played an
important part in the formulation of the Westminster Catechism.

83. Quoted by Powicke, *Cambridge Platonists*, 57. See Whichcote's *Moral and Religious
Aphorisms*, ed. Salter, to which these letters are appended. The correspondence dates from 1651,
16 years before More's ethics was published, but the similarity between Whichcote and More is
close enough to make Tuckney's remarks appropriate in this context. Whichcote's tolerant spirit
was remarkable for his time. He believed that men may preach Christ even "though they do not
name Christ in every sentence. . . . If men contend for the effects of real goodness and deny
wickedness, *they* do truly and properly preach Christ." Quoted by Powicke, *Cambridge Platonists*, 63.

84. Samuel Salter, ed., *Eight Letters of Dr. A[nthony] Tuckney, and Dr. B[enjamin] Whichcot[e] . . . Written in Sept. and Oct. 1651* (London, 1753), 54.

at God's Hand, will only catch the empty Shadow thereof"—but the redemptive function of Christ was left out (205). This omission would be of little importance for understanding the teaching of moral philosophy at Harvard in *ca.* 1700 if the old segregation of ethics from divinity had been preserved. Christ had also been left out by Aristotle. But More consciously strove to break through such compartmentalization and to teach a Christian ethics without denominational tenets. It was this achievement—for who can doubt of his brilliant success—that was both enormously attractive to Christian scholars and clerics who wanted more than the old pagan ethics, and at the same time deeply undermining to traditional belief.

One further facet of More's ethics must be described. In order to confute Hobbes directly, More felt that he had to demonstrate that even in totally naturalistic terms "Christian" morality could be sustained. There are some men, he observed with Hobbes in mind, who will accept nothing but "intellect" (i.e., reason without connection to the divine mind) as the measure of good, and who reject reason with its theological associations (20). Thus, for apologetic rather than methodological purposes More, like Hobbes, introduced a deductive system. In More's case it was designed to be a supplement to the method of inward sense, not a substitute for it. He presented twenty-three "Noemata" or axioms, which are "immediately and irresistibly true" and "need no proof," as the basis of a whole system of moral philosophy. The penchant for geometrical rigor was one of the distinguishing marks of the new philosophy in the seventeenth century, and one finds it exemplified in Descartes, Hobbes, and Spinoza, in addition to More. It is notable that before More, one of Whichcote's aphorisms (No. 298) proposed that "in Morality, we are as sure as in Mathematics." And later John Locke retained the same faith: "I doubt not but from self-evident propositions by necessary consequences, as incontestible as those in mathematics, the measures of right and wrong might be made out to anyone that will apply himself with the same indifferency and attention to the one as he does to the other of these sciences."[85]

The first twelve noemata, according to More, are sufficient to provide a foundation for those duties we owe to ourselves; noemata XIII to XXIII are the axioms for those duties we owe to others—"to God, to man, and to virtue itself." The first few noemata simply establish that goods and evils may be related to each other in various quantitative ways, as for example noema IV:

85. Locke, *Essay Concerning Human Understanding*, ed. Fraser, Bk. IV, chap. iii. Fontenelle, writing at the end of the 17th century, held that "the geometric spirit is not so exclusively bound to geometry that it could not be separated from it and applied to other fields. A work on ethics, politics, criticism, or even eloquence, other things being equal, is merely so much more beautiful and perfect if it is written in the geometric spirit." Quoted by Ernst Cassirer, *The Philosophy of the Enlightenment*, trans. Fritz C. A. Koelln and James P. Pettegrove (Princeton, N.J., 1951), 16. Grotius had earlier already spoken of a mathematics of politics.

"One Good may excel another in Quality, or Duration, or in both" (22). Computations like this will appear again in the ethics of Francis Hutcheson, though the reader will probably recall the more famous offspring, the "felicific calculus" of Jeremy Bentham.[86] Another typical rule of the first dozen is: *"A present Evil is to be born, if there be a probable future Evil infinitely more dangerous, as to weight and duration, to be avoided thereby: and this is much more strongly incumbent, if the future evil be certain"* (24). Two examples of the later axioms are noemata XIV and XIX: *"The Good, which in any case in question, you would have another man do unto you; the same you are bound in the like case, to do unto him; So far forth as it may be done without prejudice to a Third."* And *" 'Tis better that one may be disabled from living voluptuously, than that another should live in want and calamity"* (25, 26). That some of these "undeniable" axioms of More's are tautologous, that others merely express his social biases, and that still others are utterly fruitless, are all difficulties that he did not reckon with. What apparently mattered to More was that he was meeting Hobbes on his own naturalistic ground.

Gale

No other moral philosophy text at Harvard between about 1690 and 1730 seems to have been as prominent as More's. No other work better exemplifies the departure from Scholastic-Peripatetic ethics that occurred at this time and was so pregnant with future trends in moral thought. There may be some value, however, in looking briefly at one other contribution to ethics that was also anti-Scholastic and anti-Peripatetic, was identified with Platonism, and was widely known among the New England clergy. This is Theophilus Gale's *The Court of the Gentiles* (1669–1677), a massive work which appeared successively in four parts, the last two of which contain a considerable amount of material on ethics. Gale's great work, "applauded as a marvel of erudition" in its time according to the *Dictionary of National Biography*, was principally directed to establishing the *prisca theologia* and demonstrating how it had been corrupted by the ancient pagans. It has been forgotten that this book also addressed some of the central problems of moral philosophy. *The Court of the Gentiles* was widely known and distributed among the Reformed clergy in part for the same reason that Cudworth's *True Intellectual System of the*

86. See Élie Halévy, *The Growth of Philosophic Radicalism*, trans. Mary Morris (Boston, 1955), 5–34. Halévy mentions Hutcheson but not More. Most of More's noemata were reprinted by James Tyrrell in his *Brief Disquisition of the Law of Nature, According to the Principles and Method Laid Down in the Rev. Dr. Cumberland's . . . Latin Treatise on That Subject . . .* (n.p., 1692).

Universe was valued: such vast learning in Classical and Hebraic sources was a bottomless well of information for the average minister. But at the same time, those who knew and used Gale's book would be heavily exposed to his ethics.

Gale's friendships in New England were extensive. In the 1660s he established a dissenting academy near London, in Newington Green, where Charles Morton also became situated at the head of a different academy. When Gale assumed the pastorate of a congregation in the vicinity, his colleague was Samuel Lee, who later came to America with Morton. At his death in 1678 Gale left the major part of his personal library to "the Colledge of or in New England," the "most considerable accession" to the Harvard library in the seventeenth century, according to Cotton Mather.[87]

Gale defined his central purpose as "the reformation of philosophy in order to reform theology." If this could be achieved, it would, in his terms, reverse the process that had led to the corruption of theology by certain Greek fathers (especially Origen) and later by the Scholastics. The ancient Greek philosophers had received from the Old Testament Jews a pure and divine doctrine. But since these philosophers for all their brilliance were men with only "natural understanding" corrupted by sin, they inevitably corrupted the Jewish revelation. Their faults were many—vain curiosity, spiritual pride, erroneous inventiveness—and the Greek fathers and the Scholastics who made the mistake of relying on the products of the Greek philosophical mind assimilated into Christian theology highly damaging material. Gale was a great admirer of Plato, but it must be a Plato freed from errors and the corruptions of later commentators. With this purification accomplished, Plato could well enrich Christian theology with an authority almost comparable to sacred Scripture, since in both cases the ultimate source is divine revelation. Part 4 of *The Court of the Gentiles* has a subtitle that expresses Gale's aim: "Wherein Plato's Moral and Metaphysic or prime Philosophie is reduced to an useful Forme and Method."[88]

87. According to Josiah Quincy, *The History of Harvard University*, I (Cambridge, Mass., 1840), 513, 184–185, Gale's books "constituted for many years more than half of the whole College library." On Gale in New England, see Morison, *Seventeenth-Century Harvard*, 290–291; and Mather, *Magnalia*, II, 8–9. On Gale at Newington Green, see McLachlan, *English Education under the Test Acts*, 49–51, and Smith, *Birth of Modern Education*, 41–46. On Samuel Lee, see Theodore Hornberger, "Samuel Lee (1625–1691), A Clerical Channel for the Flow of New Ideas to Seventeenth-Century New England," *Osiris*, I (1936), 341–355. Gohdes, "Aspects of Idealism," *Philosophical Rev.*, XXXIX (1930), 537–555, calls particular attention to Gale. Gale graduated from Magdalen College, Oxford, in 1649, and after ejection in 1660 spent some time as a tutor to the sons of Lord Wharton at Caen, which accounts for his close knowledge of Jansenist thought. He started his academy at Newington Green in about 1666. Cotton Mather in his *Manuductio* referred to Gale's work very favorably.

88. Gale reserved his sharpest invectives for Origen, whom he considered to be the chief

In the area of moral thought Gale pleaded most earnestly in favor of two points: first, anti-Pelagianism, or the utter rejection of the concept of a morally effective free will; and second, a corollary, the eradication of the distinction between so-called natural virtues and supernatural virtues, or the distinction between natural goodness and goodness by the grace of God. Both of these positions are familiar to us, for they conform to what we have called Augustinian voluntarism, and both were cardinal principles in William Ames's thinking. Gale was familiar with Ames's work, of course, and referred to it on a few occasions. He noted that Ames was one who knew how much "Philosophie corrupted the Fathers," and he also knew that true moral virtue was a product of supernatural grace only.[89] But in terms of influence, Gale clearly owed nothing to Ames and very little to any figures in the English Puritan tradition, including the Cambridge Platonists, other than John Owen (1616–1683), whom he cited with some frequency. By far the dominant figure in the development of Gale's thought was, interestingly, Cornelius Jansen, the famous Dutch Catholic author of the *Augustinus* (Paris, 1641), which had such far-reaching repercussions in seventeenth-century France. So immersed was Gale in Jansenism that he might well be called the English Jansen, as John Norris of Bemerton, for his active propagation in English of Malebranche's thought later in the seventeenth century, has been called the English Malebranche. Any suggestion that Jansenism had no effect on English Protestant thinking is decisively disproved by the case of Gale, who quoted or referred to Jansen's *Augustinus* on almost every page of the last two parts of *The Court of the Gentiles*.[90] In fact, Gale's acquaintance with French Augustinian moral thought was in general remarkably wide, for he seems to have read St. Francis de Sale's *Traité de l'amour de Dieu* (1616), the hardly known *De Libertate Dei et creaturae* (1630) of Guillaume Gibieuf, which was the most significant predecessor of Jansen's *Augustinus*, and *De l'usage des passions* (1641) by J.-F. Senault, "that sober Jansenist."[91]

---

propagator of what came to be known as the heresies of Arianism, universalism, and Pelagianism. Origen's complete works were first translated into Latin in the 16th century.

89. Gale, *Court of the Gentiles*, III, 132; IV, 74.

90. See *ibid.*, III, 147: "It is, or ought to be the great wonder of pious souls, that in this Age, wherein so many Professors of the Reformed Religion have turned their backs on the Doctrine of Free-Grace, and imbibed so many *Pelagian* Infusions, which are the very vital spirits and heart of Antichristianisme, God has raised up, even in the bosome of Antichrist, *Jansenius* and his Sectators, who, in vindication of *Augustin's* Doctrine, have approved themselves such stout Champions and Assertors of Free-Grace, against al Pelagian Dogmes. O! what matter of Admiration wil this be unto al Eternitie?"

91. *Ibid.*, IV, 16, 59, and III, 13. On de Sales, in addition to Levi, *French Moralists*, 112–126, see also, Louis Lavelle's brilliant essay in *Four Saints*, trans. Dorothea O'Sullivan (Notre Dame, Ind., 1963 [orig. publ. Paris, 1951]). Gibieuf is treated at length in Gilson, *Liberté chez Descartes*, 287–396. On Senault, see Levi, *French Moralists*, 213–233.

The worst fault of the pagan philosophers, the Alexandrian fathers, and the Scholastics, according to Gale, was their upholding of the Pelagian spirit. This spirit took various forms: the belief in natural good nature or in the seeds of natural virtue in man; the worship of subjective right reason as the judge of good and evil; and ultimately the heresy of free will. "The Heathen Moralists, both *Romans*, *Pythagoreans*, *Platonists*, *Peripatetics*, and *Stoics*, supposed there was in men a *Good-nature*, disposition, seeds of Virtue, or *Moral Free-Wil*, which if wel improved would raise men to the highest elevation of Virtue." They also made a "Goddesse" out of "right reason," which, as Jansen observed, they believed should govern "as Mistress and Queen." The duties of virtue are considered "honest and desirable, because they are consentaneous to *right reason*." But in this "there lies hid the greatest pride. . . . Whosoever desireth Virtue in this manner adores his own Reason as the Princesse which he serves. . . . Here we may see whence the Schoolmen borrowed their *Recta ratio, right reason*, which they make with the Philosophers to be the *Regula esse moralis*, the *rule of Moral Beings and Actions*." From such teachings came the doctrine of free will that both the ancient philosophers and most of the Scholastics espoused.[92]

All of the Schoolmen should not be condemned, "for *Thomas Aquinas* and his followers the *Thomistes*, who keep more close to *Augustin*, are nothing near so guiltie of this *Pelagian crime* as the *Jesuites*. Yea, many of the *Thomistes*, as *Greg. Ariminensis*, *Alvarez*, and others, have greatly opposed the *Pelagians* and *Jesuites* in the most principal of their Dogmas against Efficacious Grace." But generally speaking the Schoolmen have been the "great brochers and patrons of *Pelagianisme*; . . . neither did *Pelagius's Doctrine* find any considerable favor and acceptation in the Catholic Church til the Scholeman came in play." The source of all of this depraved teaching, Gale wrote, is Classical philosophy. The "apparatus of that whole Heresie" is nothing else but "pure *Pythagoric*, *Stoic*, and *Aristotelic* Philosophie." Again following Jansen as his authority, Gale reduced the Pelagian heresy to two parts, both derived from Greek and Roman ethics: the Stoic and Pythagorean belief in "*Apathie*, or *Impeccance*," a state of perfection in this life that even the Peripatetics rejected; and the opinion of Seneca and others that some things are to be sought from the gods, "but Virtue from a man's self. . . . The only good which is the cause and firmament of a blessed life, is to trust on a man's self. In which words the whole venome of the *Pelagian* impietie is comprehended." All of the Pelagian disputes against Original Sin and its punishment can be understood as carry-overs from the "Ethnic" philosophers, who were themselves ignorant of the doctrine. In the words of Jansen, "if you

92. Gale, *Court of the Gentiles*, III, 38–39.

take away the *garrulitie* or babling of *Philosophie*, the whole [Pelagian] Heresie may be dissipated by one breath."[93]

Gale believed that the opposition to the free will heresy by the remaining true Christians in the Catholic church forced the defenders of natural human virtue and free will to another scandalous belief, namely the establishment of two standards of ethics, a natural and a supernatural. They treated the pagan virtues as true virtues rather than as splendid vices, as Augustine had rightly called them. The Pelagian and semi-Pelagian Scholastics, as Jansen said, "framed a double man in one man, a double Charitie, double Virtues, double Workes; the one Natural, the other Supernatural." But in truth, Gale asserted, "there is no Virtue natural, or truly moral, but what is supernatural."[94]

Gale opposed the same compartmentalization of pagan moral philosophy into an autonomous discipline that we have seen Ames, More, and Cotton Mather protest against. It is clear that a powerful movement was underway in the seventeenth century to destroy the dual establishment in ethics and to replace it with one science of human conduct, but the opponents could not all agree among themselves. Among the philosophers, Descartes and especially Hobbes wanted to reform moral philosophy along naturalistic lines. Inspired by Galileo's great achievements and by the geometric method, they searched for a new materialistic and physiological science of moral order that would be independent of both the ancient pagan and the Christian traditions in ethics. Among the religious, the seventeenth-century descendants of the "devout humanists," who were opposed to Scholastic intellectualization and Neostoicism, looked for a new comprehensive spiritual philosophy that, without sectarian alliances, would incorporate the vital truths of Christianity and Platonism. More and Gale can be included in this group, but they were also influenced by the philosophers and by a third group, the pietists, such as Ames, for whom theology was either a matter of living a holy life (rather than just disputing about it) or nothing. The pietists, among whom the Jansenists may be included, hoped to erect a viable practical theology that would displace all rival ethical systems.

Thus far we have concentrated on Gale's critique of the philosophical heritage. But he also undertook to construct his own theory of ethics. As predecessors in this task Gale listed Wyclif, Huss, Wesselus, Savonarola (who "reduced Philosophie to a more natural Forme and Method, rendring it subservient to Theologie, so far as the Darknesse and Iniquitie of those times would permit"), Pico della Mirandola, Vives, Melanchthon, Stapulensis (Lefevre d'Etaples), and Ramus (who "followed the steps" of d'Etaples).

93. *Ibid.*, 158–161.
94. *Ibid.*, 40–41.

The basic elements in Gale's reform are easily summarized. He reconstructed, first of all, the notions of conscience and prudence so as to give them a clear objective reference. He attempted to prove that the true end of all things, the good toward which all things are directed and which they innately desire, is God. In the Augustinian manner he reduced virtue to a form of love and joy. And following Gibieuf he redefined liberty as totally passive servitude to God's will. The substance that Gale reworked and clung to was Plato's thought, but as in More's explication of Aristotle, many of the textual translations and interpretations are disputable and sprang as much from Gale's desire to hold on to this admired ancient authority as from anything inherent in Plato's texts. How true Gale was to Plato is a subject we will not enter into. Among modern authorities, Jansen continued to play the most prominent role. It is also notable that Gale frequently referred to Suarez for the subtle resolution of a point. Suarez for him was not an authority to be followed in all cases, but when the Spanish master was on his side, Gale was quick to notice it. Gale cited no other Scholastic philosopher besides Thomas himself more often than he cited Suarez.

Gale believed that moral philosophy properly concerns the exercise of prudence, or practical moral wisdom, as opposed to contemplative wisdom. The end of prudence is to make men happy. In fact, it is the virtue that "of it self [is] effective of human Happinesse." Prudence consists of several qualities, such as foresight, dexterity of judgment, "*Sagacitie* or *perspicacitie* of finding out things," and experience. Prudence is seated in the soul and moves and influences the soul. Specifically, its seat is in the conscience, "which is a petty God, or God's Vice-gerent, and Vicar in the Soul, to command and threaten; to accuse, or excuse; to justifie, or condemne."[95] Conscience itself Gale, like Ames, divided into the two functions of *synteresis* and *syneidesis*. The former is comparable to a habit of the conscience, its "habitual Light"; the latter is not a habit but a particular act of the conscience "whereby we apply our Science to what we undertake." *Syneidesis* is like "self-reflexion" and is followed by the accusation or excusation, which Ames had called the *crisis*. All of this was fairly standard from the Middle Ages.

Gale also implied that there is a sensory dimension to conscience, although he did not develop the idea to the same extent that More did. "The life of the new Creature, as well as of the *old*," he wrote (presumably referring to the regenerate and the natural man), "consistes in these self-reflexive Acts of Conscience, which each spring from inward sense and feeling."[96] Since

95. *Ibid.*, IV, 2–6.

96. *Ibid.*, 6–7. On the importance of the ideas of "*sens intérieurs*" and "*sentimens intérieurs*" (interior senses and interior emotions) for Descartes, see Levi, *French Moralists*, 274–278. The complicated history of the idea of internal senses up through the 14th century has been studied by Harry Austryn Wolfson, "The Internal Senses in Latin, Arabic, and Hebrew Philosophic Texts,"

syneidesis is a reflexive mental act, it could be classified, using Aristotle's terms, as an inward or "internal" sense. The hypothesis of internal senses was needed to account for certain kinds of self-knowledge, such as internal awareness of external sense experience—knowing when we are seeing or hearing, for example—and for certain kinds of synthetic mental abilities, such as the mind's capacity to unify the disparate elements of external sense experience into intelligible wholes. Conscience, as both an inward judge of interior events and a synthetic, supra-sensory faculty, was gradually assimilated into the notion of internal sense. Although the internal senses as first conceived of in Aristotelian thought seem to have had little to do with taste and feeling, the concept of "sense" gradually diverged into this broader meaning, which was exactly the path that Shaftesbury would follow in positing an internal moral sense. In Gale's case, his primary interest in preserving the most objective possible standard of morality kept him from further experimentation with the notion of conscience as a sense.

Synteresis is the same as right reason in the human soul and is representative of the law or light of nature. As indicated in Romans 2:14–15, "these common seeds of natural light are a private Law, which God has deeply engraven on mens Consciences, and is universally extensive unto al, though with a latitude of degrees; it being in some more, in some lesse"; but, Gale added, it is "in al in great measure obliterated, and defaced since the Fall." This subjective measure thus cannot be the rule of morality, and treating the right reason of men's consciences as the rule of morality is a grave error. The only right reason that may be elevated to the standard of good and evil is the "objective Light of Nature comprised in the Moral Law." If the Scholastic principle "Right Reason gives the *esse morale* to moral Beings" is to have any proper meaning, Gale believed, then right reason must refer unambiguously to something beyond a man's subjective light or law of conscience.[97] It is true that every human act, moral or immoral, fundamentally depends upon natural principles in the sense that the reason and will and body of a man are in nature, and they are the seat of the action. But this relation does not define morality. The essence of a moral act is its conformity to the perfect measure of morals, and this measure is the law of God. In Adam before the Fall, the subjective and objective laws were the same. Now the subjective law is only "fragments or broken notices." God in his goodness gave us the sacred Scrip-

---

in *Studies in the History of Philosophy and Religion,* I (1973), 250–314. Wolfson reviews the 17th and 18th centuries only very cursorily in this piece. An investigation of the background of the third earl of Shaftesbury's use of the term "sensus communis" is needed. This "common sense" was considered one of the internal senses in the Aristotelian formulation and was often used to mean consciousness. William Hamilton gives a sketch of the history of the notion of a "common sense" in his notes to *The Works of Thomas Reid,* II (Edinburgh, 1868), 742–803.

97. Gale, *Court of the Gentiles,* IV, 8.

tures to replace the lost objectivity. According to Gale, writers like Samuel Parker (1640–1688), the English author of several well-known works in defense of Natural Law, Amyraldus (Moise Amyraut), "and other Divines, who make . . . *right reason* the Criterion or Rule of moral Virtue," should be understood as referring to the scriptural measure, though some writers are guilty of maintaining the personal or subjective criterion.[98]

As God's law is the measure of all moral action, so God is the proper end of all action. All men desire some good, and God is the prime cause of all the goodness in every good. He is also the cause of every end that men can conceive of. God is the first in order of causes and the last in order of ends. These and other related propositions in Gale follow the traditional Augustinian procedure (found first in Plato) of progressing from the things of this world to God as the ultimate end. All of Gale's lengthy proofs cannot be touched on here, but his concluding remarks in this section deserve notice. "Adherence to God as our last End" means not only "subjection and dependence, but also the best Constitution, Complexion, and Perfection of a rational Creature." Adherence to the "Divine Bonitie," that is, the highest goodness, or God, is man's "supreme perfection." And "what more natural than for a rational Creature to adhere to its last end. . . . To be drawn by God as our last end, is to be drawn by our most noble, perfect, and best self." The last end and the highest good is not only "Bonitie" but also "Beautie." God's "bonitie" attracts the will; His "beautie," the eye and understanding. Plato made beauty consist in symmetry and proportion, which are found in God to the highest degree. The terms harmony, agreement, and "convenance" also apply. As in beautiful music, so in God's Creation is there "a discordant Accord," or an "accordant Discord." Hence, *"Al Beautie* ariseth from *Perfection* and *Integritie* of parts."[99]

With the priorities established, Gale could then define morality in terms of the ordering of personal loves and attachments. Do we put God, the last end, first and make all other ends subservient to Him? Or do we confuse means and ends, which Gale, like Augustine, called "uses" and "fruitions"? For virtue is "nothing else but the order of Love." "To use or enjoy any inferior good for it self is to abuse it. This lower Universe and each part thereof was not made for mans *Fruition*, but *Use.*" Such perversion of the proper order of

98. *Ibid.*, 45–54. It is a mistake, I think, to assume that Gale was reacting here to a problem such as that posed by 19th- and 20th-century philosophical subjectivism and relativism, or for that matter, to Hobbesianism in his own day. Except for the libertines and the Hobbesians, nearly everybody in Gale's day agreed that an absolute standard did exist. Gale opposed those who attributed too much authority to conscience, which was subject to corruption. Above all, it was almost universally agreed that there were no discrepancies between God's moral law as revealed in Scripture and Natural Law, when interpreted correctly.

99. *Ibid.*, 14, 16.

love had been complained of by Augustine, that men "use what they should enjoy, and enjoy what they should use."[100]

Human virtue depends upon actually intending the last end, not simply having a velleity toward it, "which is only a conditionate, faint, imperfect volition of an end, without regard to means." To intend anything, is to "*tend towards it* powerfully." And intention rules the will, for it is the bending of the will. "Where the intention is right, God is the predominant end." As intention directs the will, "so Faith directs the Intention: . . . it is the Intention that regulates the qualitie of the action in the use of things; and it is divine Faith and love that regulate the Intention." All of this pertains to the proper *uses* of things. The action of the will also includes fruition, or the enjoyment of and loving adherence to something for its own sake. The will, or love, in fruition ought to terminate nowhere but in God. Love may be defined as the will tending to fruition, for we can truly love something only for itself. Love and fruition must be understood together, as both Augustine and Jansen have shown. "What is Love, but a secret Fountain streaming towards Fruition? And what is Fruition, but an Ocean of Satisfaction, in which Love is immersed and swallowed up?"[101]

Gale's mention of virtue as a fruition is reminiscent of More. As part of his discussion of the several goods that fruition brings, Gale also spoke of the delectation and joy that follow from it. The "transport of divine Joy is proper to no act but the Fruition of our last end." This joy consists of the possession of "a sweet Good" and of actions consequent to that possession. And "nothing is so sweet as by virtuouse acts to adhere to, and enjoy the sweetest and best good." Sensual pleasures, on the other hand, are "jarring and repugnant" to human nature. "There is no solid substantial joy, but what flows from, and some way refers to the fruition of the sweetest good: all other pleasures are only *opinionative*, and grounded on false imagination."

> What acts of the Soul have more of true pleasure and delight attending of them, than virtuouse exercises? O! what sweet inspirations, what divine suavities are infused into the Soul upon virtuouse actings? . . . Doth not every act of Virtue carry some degree of pleasure? . . . And by how much the more pure and spiritual any virtuouse act is, by so much the more pure is that joy which attends it. . . . The purest and strongest pleasures are such as attend the Souls actual adhesion to its first cause and last end.[102]

This rapturous morality, the most "enthusiastic" state of virtue-devotion, was common also to More and Shaftesbury. It captures perfectly the inter-

100. *Ibid.*, 20–22.
101. *Ibid.*, 22–27.
102. *Ibid.*, 32–33, 38, 36, 101.

mediate stage in English thought between early Puritan piety and the Shaftesburian ethics of taste and feeling. But in the course of the eighteenth century,
the base in enthusiasm became more and more pallid among the secular moralists, and cooler affectional states prevailed. Jonathan Edwards's attempt to
vivify moral philosophy with religious enthusiasm, as it had been vivified for
a time in the seventeenth century, was an exception.

Finally, Gale offered a theory of the will and addressed the problem of
liberty. We have discussed his concept of the *matter* of moral good, both in
terms of its measure or rule and in terms of man's proper relation to God.
There remains the question of the efficient cause or principle of a good act.
For Gale, this principle is

> the Wil, or rather the Soul clothed with supernatural Habits of Virtue
> or Grace. . . . Such therefore as the disposition of the Wil is, such wil
> the action prove as to its goodness or pravitie. The bent of the Wil is
> as a Pondus that carries the whole Soul either to good or bad: when the
> deliberation and intention of a bended Wil concurs in a good mater for
> a good end, the action is good: And what bends the Wil in this manner,
> but virtuous habits? So many degrees as there are of a sanctified Wil
> in any Act, so many degrees there are of moral Good therein.[103]

The habit that Gale had in mind is an infused habit, not the Aristotelian concept. Virtue is a habit in the sense that by its nature it falls somewhere between a power or faculty of the soul and a mere act. In logical order, powers
come before habits and habits before acts. Habits make the soul more facile
and capable in action. "Virtue is a supernatural Habitude, Habit, or active
Forme, whereby the Soul is elevated to supernatural acts." Supernaturality
"is a Mode intrinsically and essentially included in al virtuous Habits . . .
because human Nature, specially as now corrupted, cannot reach an end or act
supernatural."[104] Gale also used heart-language: All "spiritual life and moral
good issueth from the heart rightly disposed and qualified with virtuouse
graciose Principles: where the heart thus qualified is not the Spring, there no
Act is morally or spiritually alive towards God, but dead."[105] Consequently,
all the heroic deeds of the pagans and others whose minds were not "sanctified by Faith and Love, [so] as to act by force received from God," are only

103. *Ibid.*, 60.
104. *Ibid.*, 74–76. See also, *ibid.*, 105: "It's a trite saying in the Scholes, *Cessation from acts diminish habits, but continuance therein emproves the same*. It's true, there is a difference in this regard between acquired habits, and virtuose, which come by infusion; because acquired habits are the natural products of their acts, but virtuose habits are not naturally produced by virtuose acts, but given by God of mere Grace. God rewards virtuose exercises with farther degrees and advances of Virtue, or Grace, and that of mere Grace."
105. *Ibid.*, 61.

splendid sins. In short, all virtue must be the product of a will directly imbued with the Holy Spirit.

At this point we come to the most striking paradox in Gale's ethics, for which he was undoubtedly greatly indebted to Gibieuf and Jansen. Moral liberty, Gale maintained, arises from nearness to God. There is such a thing as natural liberty, too, by which Gale seems to have meant nothing more than freedom from constraint. But in the case of moral liberty, one is governed by necessity in the same way that God's actions are both most necessary and most free. The more the soul is like God, and the more it is one with him, the more it is free. "*Moral Libertie as to state* consistes in virtuose dispositions of Soul, whereby it is capacitated for and made like to God." The connection between "pietie and Libertie is so intimate, as that indeed they have one and the same beginning, progresse, and consummation." Like More, Gale wanted to unite virtue and grace. Only through union with God is the soul free to "understand, embrace and adhere to what is good." When we depart from God we are subject to "a miserable necessitie, and coarctation of sin." [106]

In addition to moral liberty as a state or condition, Gale spoke of moral liberty in exercise or act, which consists in virtuous acts. The soul clothed with virtuous habits and in a state of moral liberty will perform virtuous acts. Herein lies the supreme liberty of the virtuous soul.

> And O! what an high piece of moral Libertie is this, intimately and inviolably to adhere to God, as our last End and chiefest Good. Is the heart ever more free, than when it doth most strongly, by al manner of affectionate exercises, adhere to its chiefest Good? So many grains as there are of a bended wil for God, so much moral Libertie. A tenacious, resolute, invincible adherence unto our last end, by acts of love, desire, and other affections, makes the soul exceding free in al its motions. [107]

Liberty does not consist, then, in the freedom to choose from a variety of possibilities. The power to sin is a diminution of liberty. "Impeccabilitie or an utter impossibilitie of sinning is so far from destroying libertie, as that it is perfect thereby. The sweetest and highest libertie is to have no power to sin." [108]

Gale pressed home the paradox by emphasizing the passivity of the will in its virtuous exercise. The human will cannot act of itself in the pursuit of virtue, he affirmed. It is a "mere passive, though vital, instrument as to the reception of divine influences, albeit it be *active* as to its own operation." The

106. *Ibid.*, 76–78, 81.
107. *Ibid.*, 88.
108. *Ibid.*, 90.

moral divine life in relation to the first cause, that is, God, is nothing but "continual effusions and infusions into the Soul. . . . True moral Virtue is a celestial Plant, fed by some invisible root in the celestial World; from which it derives its influences; . . . al divine and moral *Respirations* towards the celestial world, are from sweet *Inspirations* of divine Concurse." Yet because this rule by necessity is also rule by love, it is free. The service of love, Gale concluded, is most free.[109]

The reader may see in this discussion by Gale simply an elaboration of Luther's famous treatise on Christian liberty. The true Christian is freed from the constraints of the divine law and yet obeys it more fully through love. He is a servant to others, but his service is freely given out of love.[110] The doctrine is also akin to the Platonic principle that only the conquest of the appetites, to which we are ordinarily slaves, can make us free. Virtue is rational or spiritual control over one's life, and this self-rule by intelligence or by spirit is true freedom. Without it we are dominated by blind inner forces. As Gale said, sin is the true servitude of man, whereas moral liberty is a "blessed necessity" to adhere to the best.[111]

Gale, in sum, was a vigorous Augustinian voluntarist as well as a Platonist. How does his thinking on freedom square with Henry More's? We have already suggested that More has perhaps been wrongly categorized as an outright opponent of Calvinist predestinarianism. It is true that on several occasions he directly expressed his rejection of the harsh doctrine of reproba-

---

109. *Ibid.*, 92–93. See also, *ibid.*, 151–153: "He that is not acted by divine Grace, is necessarily acted by carnal lust." There is a parallel of sorts between the discussion in ethics about infused and natural habits and the origin of virtue, and the discussion in theology concerning preparation for salvation. We should not be surprised that Gale wrote: "Should we suppose corrupt Nature to have any moral power for the production of Virtue, would not this subvert the whole Oeconomic and Dispensation of efficacious Grace? . . . That there can be no disposition, though never so remote, unto true moral Virtue from the alone facultie of Nature, is evident; because nothing can dispose it self to a condition above its nature, by its own force, unless it be influenced by a superior Agent." Even if "men should improve their natural forces to the utmost, what obligation is there on God to give . . . supernatural Grace? . . . Doth it not implie a contradiction . . . that man should make a right use of his natural abilities, or prepare himself for the reception of supernatural Grace? . . . Corrupt nature wants not only an active power to do good, but also an immediate passive power to receive good: thence it can't dispose itself to virtue, which is above its natural capacitie."

110. Gilson, *Liberté chez Descartes*, 311–316, argues that Descartes's conception of liberty was a transformation of the teaching of Gibieuf. Descartes made perfect obedience to clear and distinct ideas the highest freedom. Perfect knowledge, psychologically speaking, entails action without any deliberation, choice, or indifference, and this is complete liberty, that is, when the will is irresistibly guided by the intellect. Thus, in place of grace and spirit, Descartes substituted knowledge; and in place of sin and carnal appetite, Descartes substituted error and ignorance.

111. Gale, *Court of the Gentiles*, IV, 139.

tion. Nevertheless, like Gale, he doubted that it was a true "derogation from Humane Nature, to make Men . . . necessarily Good, and to deprive them of all *Free-Will*." For in that case it would follow that "God, who is Good, should be the less Adorable, because he cannot be Naught." Whoever is good, according to More, whether by nature or "Divine Fate, is also endowed with so true and efficacious a Sense of Honesty, that he can no more go against this Sense, than that a sober Man should stab himself with a Dagger."[112]

More's primary difference from Gale was that his concern lay not with those who are happily blessed with necessary virtue, the regenerate or the elect, but with those other mortals whose imperfection is precisely their freedom to incline their wills toward either God or the devil. More did not reject belief in the irresistible power of the spirit, but he did question the notion that those who are without the spirit are unalterably condemned. These men must be told of the "Divine Pre-eminence," which as human beings they enjoy, and that with "the help of Heaven" they may be able to shake off ill desires and "assert that Liberty, which is most suitable to a Creature made by God's Image."[113] Some of More's protestations in favor of free will must be understood in the context of his strong opposition to Hobbesian determinism, which he opposed not because it was determinist but because it left no place for the inner divine principle. More seems to have cared above all about preserving the openness of man's situation with respect to the transcendent. Whatever the degree of predetermination to which humankind is subject—which in practice makes little difference anyway—the important matter, for More, was the very existence of a real alternative to fatality, even though free choice may be limited.

One kind of determinism that More explicitly rejected was the intellectualist proposition that "No Man is willingly wicked," that the simple knowledge of what is good and virtuous will "force him to imbrace it." For it is within the power of our wills "either to acquire . . . a clearer and more extended Knowledg . . . , or else to let that by degrees extinguish which already [we] have." In this sense, men may willingly be wicked. And even in this case, for some the will is not free, for More admitted that there may be men so lacking in "*Natural Aptitude*," or the "Sense of all Good Things," that unless they "be awak'ned by Stripes and Force, or . . . reform'd by something of a Miracle from Above," they will lack the power to pursue virtue.[114]

The intellectualist theory that the will is "perpetually determin'd to what is

112. More, *Account of Virtue*, 173. More's example is similar to one used later by Samuel Clarke, the Boyle lecturer, to illustrate so-called "moral necessity," as opposed to "physical necessity." On theories of the will from More to Edwards, see Fiering, *Jonathan Edwards's Moral Thought*, chap. 6.

113. More, *Account of Virtue*, 175.

114. *Ibid.*, 184, 186.

the most apparent Good" is applicable, More held, only to those men who are like animals. "They enjoy no more Liberty than Brutes, whose Appetite is necessarily ty'd down to the greater Good." But in the "greatest Part of Mankind" there is a double principle, "the one *Divine*, and the other *Animal*." The divine principle always tends toward that which is simply and absolutely the best and proposes to conform to the eternal and immutable law of reason. "The *Animal* Principle dictates nothing to Man, but what to himself is either good, pleasing, or advantageous." More's final comment in his brief treatment of free will is significantly inconclusive with regard to how much power ultimately resides with the individual in moral affairs: "I say, that from the Conflict and Opposition of these two Principles, we have a clear Prospect, what is the Condition, and what the Nature, of that Free-Will whereof we treat."[115]

The idea of the double principle in man, which More called the "animal" and the "divine," was perhaps a successor to Augustine's two loves. In the eighteenth century, after Shaftesbury's remodeling of it into the natural dispositions of self-love and social love, it was destined for a great career. Sidgwick has noted that "in Platonism and Stoicism, and in Greek moral philosophy generally," only "one regulative and governing faculty" was recognized, namely reason, however that term was understood. But the modern ethical view, "when it [had] worked itself clear," recognized two: universal reason and egoistic reason, or rational conscience, based on a principle of obligation to universal good (benevolence), and self-love. Sidgwick argues that this duality, which he called "the most fundamental difference between the ethical thought of modern England and that of the old Greco-Roman world," was first introduced by Shaftesbury but not fully articulated prior to the publication of Bishop Joseph Butler's sermons.[116] Actually, the entire

---

115. *Ibid.*, 187–188. The best insight into More's theory of the will is gained from his exchange of letters between 1684 and 1686 with the young John Norris of Bemerton, who was a great admirer of the aging More. The letters were printed by Norris as an appendix to his *The Theory and Regulation of Love* (Oxford, 1688). More wrote to Norris on Jan. 16, 1685/1686: "You run your self into an unnecessary Nooze of Fatality, by granting the Soul necessarily wills as she understands; you know that of the Poet, *Video meliora proboque, Deteriora sequor*. And for my Part, I suspect there are very few Men, if they will speak out, but they have experienced that Truth. Else they would be in the state of *Sincerity*, which over-few are." "Our being redeemed into an ability or freedom of chusing what is best, is not from mere attention to the Object, but from Purification, Illumination, and real Regeneration into the Divine Image." And on Feb. 22, 1685/1686, More wrote that virtue and holiness are the result not of "notional knowledge" but of a new "inward sense," a "sensibility of Spirit . . . in the New Birth." "It is the *Purity* of the Soul, through *Regeneration*, that enables her to behold the Beauty of Holiness. . . . If this Principle of Life be not sufficiently awakened in us, no Attention is sufficient to make us rightly discern the Beauty of Holiness, but only a *shadowy Notion* or *Meager Monogrammical Picture* thereof."

116. Sidgwick, *Outlines of Ethics*, 197–198.

conception of two legitimate and necessary regulatory principles was stated by Malebranche a generation before Shaftesbury, and the idea is also in More to some degree. Once Descartes had insisted that the passions be interpreted teleologically, that is, in terms of their usefulness to effective human conduct, there was a rapid development, seen in More as well as in others, toward justifying all of the passions, even those formerly considered to be antithetical to virtue. In his *Divine Dialogues* (1668) More anticipated one of the typical eighteenth-century responses to the inescapable presence of self-love in human affairs. Although many vices are "the spawn of self-love," if we view it narrowly, he said, we shall find self-love to be

> very useful, nay, a very necessary mother in society. Self-love is abso-
> lutely necessary: nay, it is no more than the desire of pleasure and
> happiness, without which a sensitive being cannot subsist. . . . If
> rightly conducted, it would lead us to the pursuit of virtue as our in-
> terest. Yet wrath, envy, pride, lust, and the like evil passions are but
> the branches and modifications of this fundamental necessary disposi-
> tion towards good and happiness; for what is wrath, but self-love
> edged and strengthened for sending off the assaults of evil.[117]

To summarize, notwithstanding important differences between them, both More and Gale were moved by the crisis in ethics of the late seventeenth century to attempt to integrate the best of the pagan inheritance with Judaeo-Christian divinity. Both turned to Platonism as the natural medium for such a synthesis, and both were inspired by the Augustinian conception of will and passions. Certainly the core of the virtuous life for both men was not found in Aristotelian reason, but in a regenerate heart. It is significant, too, that both More and Gale were decisively influenced by French thought—More by Descartes and Gale by Jansen. (If one were to add also the great impact that Malebranche had on English thought in the last quarter of the seventeenth century, with two separate translations of *The Search after Truth* published in London in 1694, it might be fair to speak of these years as the "French period" in English and American ethical thought, for More and Gale with their French inspiration, in addition to Malebranche, Rohault, LeGrand, and Arnauld, were certainly as influential in New England as they were in old England.)

That the intellectual authorities at Harvard in the late 1680s allowed, invited, or tolerated—it does not matter which—the teaching of More's ethics is indicative of the progressiveness of the institution at this time, at least in the area of moral philosophy, and showed remarkable sagacity. More's writing

117. More, *Divine Dialogues*, 140. On self-love in the 18th century, see Fiering, *Jonathan Edwards's Moral Thought*, chap. 4.

was an aperture to some of the most significant currents in Continental and English ideas. More important, no other writer in England, including Ralph Cudworth, had an influence equal to More's on future developments in ethical thought. Both the new intellectualist school, represented by Samuel Clarke, and the sentimentalist school, initiated by Shaftesbury, owed much to More. Thus, by its fortuitous adherence to Henry More, Harvard was ideally prepared for sympathetically receiving and understanding eighteenth-century moral philosophy.

7

Conclusion

If we were to continue to trace forward for another fifty years the history of the study and teaching of philosophical ethics in early America, the most visible change would be the complete emergence by the 1730s of the "new moral philosophy," a discipline that was neither an exposition of Aristotle, as the old academic moral philosophy had been for four hundred years, nor an overt presentation of practical theology, such as many Protestants in the seventeenth century had hoped would succeed the old Aristotelian ethics. The new moral philosophy was a Christian ethics of sorts, as I have tried to indicate, but it was not Christ-centered or dogmatic. One might call it a post-theological, but not a post-Christian, morals.[1] The lines of intellectual development to this stage of maturity were complex, with influences from many different directions, but the main outline can be briefly sketched.

The groundwork for an autonomous, naturalistic, and introspective science of human nature, a science with the declared goal of providing firm and unchallengeable foundations for moral virtue, was laid in the seventeenth century, primarily with the work of the Cambridge Platonists. We have called attention to Henry More in this regard, but if the story were continued, Ralph Cudworth would also have to be mentioned. In addition, the extremely fecund, yet recently somewhat neglected, moral thought of Richard Cumberland would have to be taken into consideration, along with the influence of Nicolas Malebranche and his young English disciple, John Norris. This group composed a subfoundation, as it were. Neither Cumberland nor Cudworth seem to have been well known in early America, but Norris and Malebranche were. Indirectly, the ideas of all four of these writers had an impact. Cumberland was one of the first moralists to base his work squarely on the naturalistic principle that Hobbes forced upon Christian apologists: "Human nature suggests certain Rules of Life." To illustrate this belief Cumberland investigated not only what could be deduced from the properties of reason but also what the passions and affections revealed and what could be derived from a study of human faculties and even physiology. Somewhat later Leibniz spoke of the social

---

1. The concept of a post-theological age, when Christian ideas and beliefs themselves become inseparable from the secular order, was first suggested to me by Eugen Rosenstock-Huessy.

instincts as "indices of the plan of nature," a phrase that aptly summarized the new form of moral reasoning.[2]

After referring to these earlier seventeenth-century figures, an account of the development of moral philosophy in the eighteenth century would have to discuss the effect on moral theory of John Locke's *Essay Concerning Human Understanding* (1690). Locke's work was originally written in the context of his engagement with certain questions in ethics and contains many comments and analyses directly relevant to moral philosophy. Nevertheless, the main effect of the *Essay* was not positive. Like Hobbes's work, and Bernard Mandeville's *Fable of the Bees* later, the *Essay* was a prod and stimulus to the reformulation and strengthening of the most vulnerable traditional assumptions about the foundations of morality.[3] Locke reinforced the challenge to tradition implicit in Hobbes's work: How were the false doctrines of hedonism, materialism, radical nominalism, and relativism to be refuted? One of Shaftesbury's main concerns, certainly, and also one of Hutcheson's, was to devise an approach to ethics that could accept at least a modified Lockean empiricism without adopting Locke's own views on ethics.

In the late 1720s Locke's *Essay* began to be used in American colleges, but always as a work in logic, that is, as a propaedeutic for the acquisition and organization of truth. Educators must have realized that Locke's comments on ethics in the *Essay* were inadequate. Moreover, Locke had nothing to contribute on the theory of the passions and affections, which was assuming a vital place in moral psychology, as we have seen.

Immediately following Locke, and to some extent in response to his writing, eighteenth-century moral philosophy may be said to have come into its own with the seminal work of two tremendously influential writers who were nearly exact contemporaries—Samuel Clarke, whose Boyle lectures on natural religion were published in 1705 and 1706, and the third earl of Shaftesbury, whose *Inquiry Concerning Virtue or Merit* first appeared in 1699 and was then incorporated into *Characteristics of Men, Manners, Opinions, Times*, published in 1711. Both of these men were so widely read in America as well as in Britain that it would have been much more of a curiosity to learn of an educated American in the first half of the eighteenth century who was not familiar with the writings of Clarke and Shaftesbury than to learn of one who was. Both authors were consciously engaged in the establishment of the new discipline of moral philosophy and gave it an impetus so powerful that

2. Cumberland, *A Treatise of the Laws of Nature*, trans. John Maxwell (London, 1727), 97, 113; Gottfried W. Leibniz, *New Essays Concerning Human Understanding*, ed. and trans. A. G. Langley (New York, 1896), 91.

3. John W. Yolton, *John Locke and the Way of Ideas* (London, 1956), 21–22: "Those who had the keenest interest in [the *Essay*] were theologians and moralists concerned with seeing what good or harm its principles would involve for their values."

the effects continued throughout most of the century. Yet each gave a quite individual character to the subject.

Clarke is generally recognized as the founder of the eighteenth-century intellectualist/rationalist school, which had significant exponents in British thought for the next fifty years and was also popular in the theorizing of American students of ethics. With regard to the teaching of moral philosophy in America, Clarke may in some respects be seen as a successor to Alexander Richardson and also, in some respects, as a follower of the Cambridge Platonists. Clarke believed that the created world, in which differences of nature and differences in relations between things are manifest, reveals inherent moral truths directly to man. In other words, the divine moral order is implicit in all of nature, and this order is so logically fixed that God himself cannot but act and command in accordance with it. Clarke described these moral relations by using such terms as "agreement" and "disagreement," "fitting" and "unfitting," "suitable" and "unsuitable," concepts that easily slid over into moral categories. A short sample of Clarke's contagious form of reasoning will suffice here:

> There is therefore such a Thing as Fitness and Unfitness, eternally, necessarily and unchangeably in the Nature and Reason of Things. These Relations of Things absolutely and Necessarily *Are* in Themselves; . . . also they Appear to be [so] to the Understandings of all Intelligent Beings; except Those only, who Understand Things to be what they are not, that is, whose Understandings are either very imperfect or much depraved. And by this Understanding or Knowledge of the Natural and Necessary Relations of Things, the Actions likewise of all Intelligent Beings are constantly directed; (which . . . is the true Ground and Foundation of all Morality:) unless their Will be corrupted by particular Interest or Affection, or swayed by some unreasonable and prevailing Lust.[4]

The elicitation of the alleged implicit moral truth in nature and the demonstration of the obligation upon everyone to shape their lives in accordance with it were the two goals of supreme importance to Clarke. Thus, he is one of the earliest exemplars of the virtue-devotion characteristic of the eighteenth century. "Moral Virtue," he wrote, "is the Foundation and the Summ, the Essence and the Life of all true Religion; For the Security whereof, all positive Institution was only designed; For the Restoration whereof, all revealed Religion was ultimately intended."[5]

4. Clarke, *Demonstration of the Being and Attributes of God*, 2d ed. (London, 1706), 183.
5. Clarke, *A Discourse Concerning the Unchangeable Obligations of Natural Religion, and the Truth and Certainty of the Christian Revelation*, 2d ed. (London, 1708), 141.

If Clarke's work connects neatly to the Platonic rationalism that was pervasive in New England philosophical theology, Shaftesbury's may be seen as a secular continuation of the affectional piety, the religious zeal and enthusiasm, that we have described in earlier chapters.[6] Like Clarke, Shaftesbury considered growth in moral virtue to be life's most important endeavor, which in consequence made the science of morals the pre-eminent concern of man. But in contrast to Clarke, Shaftesbury believed that the core of this science must be the exploration of the higher passions and affections, not the study of immanent reason. "By examining the various turns, inflections, declensions, and inward revolutions of the passions, I must undoubtedly come the better to understand a human breast," Shaftesbury wrote, "and judge the better both of others and myself."[7] For as the passions "veer, my interest veers, my steerage varies; and I make alternately, now this, now that, to be my course and harbour." The examination of the "humours" and passions, therefore, "must necessarily draw along with it the search and scrutiny of my opinions, and the sincere consideration of my scope and end. And thus the study of human affection cannot fail of leading me towards the knowledge of human nature and of myself."[8]

The study of human nature, giving particular attention to the affections, was for Shaftesbury "superior to all other speculations," the science that was to preside "over all other sciences and occupations, teaching the measure of each, and assigning the just value of everything in life." "This is the philosophy which by Nature has the pre-eminence above all other science or knowledge. . . . By this science religion itself is judged, spirits are searched, prophecies proved, miracles distinguished: the sole measure and standard being taken from moral rectitude, and from the discernment of what is sound and just in the affections."[9] Since Shaftesbury believed that all judgments, even the most ostensibly rational, were influenced by transient emotional states, he assumed that no real progress could be made in morals without first understanding clearly the human nature that operates independently of rational judgments. The most solid foundation for virtue, then, must be rectified sentiments, not intellect alone.

After the work of Clarke and Shaftesbury, the elements were all on hand for the remarkable explosion of publication in the field that in a period of about seventy-five years established the foundations of nearly all modern speculation on ethics and, indeed, the basis of most of the humanitarian and demo-

6. Clarke's and Shaftesbury's thought overlap more than is sometimes recognized. Clarke often sounds like Shaftesbury, and vice versa, even in their most characteristic modes of reasoning, but their emphases were clearly different.

7. *Advice to an Author*, in *Characteristics*, ed. Robertson, I, 191.

8. *Ibid.*, 192–193.

9. *Ibid.*, 193.

cratic social and political values that are still adhered to in the West. This achievement was as spectacular and important as the extraordinary burgeoning of modern science in the roughly seventy-five years between the publication of Galileo's *Sidereus nuncius* and Newton's *Principia mathematica*. Both Clarke and Shaftesbury were fortunate to have devoted followers who sustained their individual emphases in ethical theory while at the same time expanding and systematizing the new moral philosophy to suit it for presentation in the college classroom. The work of Clarke's most influential disciple, William Wollaston's *The Religion of Nature Delineated* (1724), was in use at Yale College by 1740, and Francis Hutcheson's *Inquiry into the Original of Our Ideas of Beauty and Virtue* (1725), inspired by Shaftesbury, was already taught at Harvard in the 1730s. In 1746 the first American ethics text appeared, Samuel Johnson's *New System of Morality*. Even before Samuel Johnson's effort, the polymath Philadelphia Quaker James Logan had begun work on a "Treatise of the Duties of Man as founded in Nature," which borrowed heavily from both Hutcheson and Wollaston but was never published.[10] It is impossible to recount accurately the intellectual history of colonial America in the eighteenth century without prominently featuring the teaching of moral philosophy, since it engaged the best minds of the time: Benjamin Franklin, Jonathan Edwards, Thomas Jefferson, and others.[11]

As always in this period, the American involvement was mostly a reflex of the intense intellectual excitement in Britain, although the indigenous circumstances on this side of the Atlantic were propitious for the development of moral philosophy. The most superficial survey of publication overseas during the decade following the appearance of Wollaston's *Religion of Nature* and Hutcheson's *Inquiry* reveals what an unusual period this was for original work in moral philosophy: in 1726 Joseph Butler brought out his *Fifteen Sermons*, one of the truly masterly productions in ethics of the last three hundred years, a work that influenced every writer on the subject thereafter; in 1727 John Maxwell's massive English-language edition of Cumberland's *De Legibus naturae* came out, a major event; in 1728 Hutcheson reinforced his earlier *Inquiry* with his *Essay on the Nature and Conduct of the Passions, with Illustrations on the Moral Sense*, a landmark in the theory of the passions, as indicated in chapter 4; in 1731 John Gay published a brief essay "Concerning the Fundamental Principle of Virtue or Morality," which is commonly regarded as the most influential early statement of theological utilitarianism—the happiness of mankind is the criterion of the will of God

10. I am presently preparing for publication an edition of Logan's treatise.
11. On Jefferson's moral thought, see William Parks, "The Influence of Scottish Sentimentalist Ethical Theory on Thomas Jefferson's Philosophy of Human Nature" (Ph.D. diss., College of William and Mary, 1975).

and should be the criterion of all human morality as well—and as the first instance when associationist doctrine was used to prove the implicit universality of this criterion;[12] and in 1732 George Berkeley published *Alciphron: or the Minute Philosopher*, which included valuable discussions of both Shaftesbury and Mandeville. Within the next quarter of a century Hume, Lord Kames, and Adam Smith would enter the field, as would Richard Price, Thomas Reid, and Jonathan Edwards. Edwards's dissertation on *The Nature of True Virtue* was undoubtedly the best work in moral philosophy written by an American in the eighteenth century. Its appearance was not an anomaly but an altogether expectable event in an era dominated by the special concerns of moral philosophy.[13]

That the new moral philosophy moved onto center stage in the college curriculum in the eighteenth century can hardly be disputed. In some respects moral philosophy may also rightly be considered the essential component of the nonscientific American Enlightenment. But to explain, in other than the most general terms, why moral philosophy assumed such high status as a discipline is not easy. Certain answers are immediately obvious. As the subject was taught in the eighteenth century it was uniquely suited to the needs of an era still strongly committed to traditional religious values and yet searching for alternative modes of justification for those values. The new moral philosophy retained comforting metaphysical attributes from the theological era while at the same time being a new science of man. It was introspective and inductive (in a casual way) but not rigorously empirical; it was teleological rather than behaviorist; it was a spirited critical science, but, in America and Britain at least, it eschewed positivism and materialism; it was open-minded, but not relativist; it incorporated diverse schools of thought, yet none could be taken seriously that smacked of nihilism or atheism.

Moral philosophy in eighteenth-century America was not concerned with the most ultimate questions of value, those that start with no moral or religious axioms, but only with the question of how best to prove and strengthen what nearly everybody already believed. Clarke and Shaftesbury disagreed on problems of psychology, metaphysics, and epistemology, but not about moral ends. Both defined immorality in the light of traditional standards and regarded transgressors as perverse and unnatural. It was a safe and constructive science, but one that had freed itself from clerical domination and theological dogmas. The special character of the rise of the new moral philosophy, as

12. Gay's 22-page essay was published as a "Preliminary Dissertation" to William King, *An Essay on the Origin of Evil*, trans. Edmund Law (London, 1731 [orig. publ. Dublin, 1702]).

13. See, e.g., Ernest Campbell Mossner, *Bishop Butler and the Age of Reason* (New York, 1936), 105: "Ethical theory, by and large, was the chief intellectual pursuit of the eighteenth century, coloring even its historiography and its science."

contrasted with later revolutions in thought, has been accurately described by the modern theologian Gerhard Ebeling:

> The fact is, that life does go on even when religion has shrunk to a *quantité négligeable*. Life is in mortal danger, however, if it disintegrates where morals are concerned. That is the difference between the two historical turning points of the modern age:—The *emancipation of ethics* at the beginning of the modern age went hand in hand with optimism, progress, and undeniable advancement of life. The loss of religious tradition might be painful—yet the moral foundations were still preserved. On the other hand, the aspect of the moral crisis of today which conveys the impression of *emancipation from ethics* is incomparably more menacing because it touches the most elementary foundations of life and threatens to rob all mankind of all hope.[14]

It is certain that institutional clerical influence and literalist scriptural authority were declining in the early eighteenth century and that religiosity was assuming new forms. Yet, as Jack Hexter has warned, it must not be assumed that an increase in the secular direction is of itself sufficient evidence of a decrease in the religious direction. The particular advantage of the new moral philosophy was that it seemed to be able to absorb both religious and secular interests in a common blend. Although the pious might still proclaim that morals could not get one to heaven, it became increasingly crankish to denounce secular zeal for virtue or to condemn the promotion of benevolence, compassion, moral sensibility, right reason, and public happiness, simply because these goods were not expressly rooted in churchliness. In a companion work to this book, I have tried to describe Jonathan Edwards's painstaking efforts to construct for religious authority a moral role that was not already expropriated by the new moral philosophy. The world view of orthodox Calvinist theology was in decline, but not necessarily the civilizing and redemptive function of religion. The prominent place assumed by moral philosophy in the eighteenth century need not be viewed negatively as an apostasy from the true faith of an earlier age, or as a degeneration of exalted piety into mere moralism.

The era of moral philosophy, which began in the second half of the seventeenth century, was a relatively short-lived period in the philosophical history of the West, a brief time when it was believed that the traditional moral axioms, the tenets of justice, the standards of goodness, the measure of virtue could be certified by the deductions of natural reason and the examination of

14. Gerhard Ebeling, "Theology and the Evidentness of the Ethical," trans. James W. Leitch, *Journal for Theology and the Church*, II, 102.

humanity in its conscious and purposive functions. Divine endorsement of the enterprise was always tacitly present, and it was assumed that the conclusions were those that would please God. As in the preceding theological era, God's will was the final source of moral truth and obligation, but in the era of moral philosophy His will was to be uncovered indirectly, through the book of nature. The superhuman standpoint no longer overtly predominated, although it was constantly implicit.

The era of materialistic science, which followed the earlier periods, attempted to derive moral principles from the subhuman: from biology, from the demands of the unconscious, from unwitting cultural mores, from the blind forces of history, or from the marketplace. To some extent this third enterprise continues to this day, yet it is highly questionable that it has succeeded. We find ourselves, then, hoping to retrace steps back to the time when ethics emancipated itself from its theological moorings and from the domination of Classicism, and wondering if a knowledge of the beginnings of modern moral philosophy cannot be helpful in undertaking anew the task of establishing lasting foundations for an ethics of humanity, nothing more and nothing less.

APPENDIX

A Note on the Problem of Will
in the Twentieth Century

There are few philosophical debates from long ago, no matter how remote their concerns may appear to be, that do not have modern relevance, although sometimes the relevance is hard to discover. The debate over the nature of the will can never fully subside because, at bottom, it has to do with alternative postures in life, both of which have validity and both of which are also subject to dangerous extremes—excessive passivity, on the one hand, like seventeenth-century Quietism, or excessive activity, on the other, like nineteenth-century "will-power" ("I am the master of my fate; I am the captain of my soul"). Freud, for example, may seem to be in a world altogether distant from the seventeenth-century issues, but the distinction between the Ego and the Id is actually closely related to the moral question of whether man lives properly by rational self-assertion or by giving way to inner forces that make his Ego, or his "I," passive. Freud restored some respect for the passive elements in experience after the Victorian orgy with intellectualized will.

> When Freud wants to describe goings-on of which it is appropriate to say that a man is acting, that he has a *reason* for what he does, and so on, he talks about the Ego; when on the other hand, he wants to say that a person suffers something, or is made or driven to do something, he speaks of the Id. . . . Freud used the model of the Ego and the Id to bring out that sometimes we take account of facts, act deliberately, plan means to ends, and impose rules of prudence on our conduct, whereas at other times we take no account of facts, act impulsively, and are driven, obsessed, and possessed.[1]

Another psychoanalyst, Leslie Farber, using no jargon and drawing from his own clinical experience, has resuscitated unknowingly the essential ele-

---

1. R[ichard] S. Peters, *The Concept of Motivation*, 2d ed. (London, 1960), 69–70. Cf. William James's essay, "The Gospel of Relaxation," which deals mainly with the importance of passivity as the paradoxical way to reach certain vital ends.

ments of the seventeenth-century debate. Farber distinguishes "two realms" of will. The first realm is unconscious in the sense that our will in this realm "is not a matter of experience," although we may retrospectively infer its existence or operation. In this first realm of will, we recognize only later what was in fact our real tendency or will. This first kind of will moves in a general direction "rather than toward a particular object." The second realm of will, on the contrary, is conscious and is "*experienced during* the event" rather than inferred "after." Our awareness of "willing" is quite present to us in this realm, and we usually have a consciously held objective.[2]

When we are moving in the first realm of will, we are sufferers, as it were; in the second realm, we are self-conscious agents. As a therapist Farber's concern is for the proper balance of these two modes of experience—the will beyond personal control, characteristic of the first realm, and the rational will of the second. The predominant temptation in the present day, according to Farber, is "to apply the will of the second realm to those portions of life that not only will not comply, but that will become distorted under such coercion." His list of examples of areas of confusion reveals a profound similarity between seventeenth-century psychological theory and the perspicacity of a modern student of the soul:

> I can will knowledge, but not wisdom; going to bed, but not sleeping; eating, but not hunger; meekness, but not humility; scrupulosity, but not virtue; self-assertion or bravado, but not courage; lust, but not love; commiseration, but not sympathy; congratulations, but not admiration; religiosity, but not faith; reading, but not understanding.

Wisdom, humility, virtue, courage, love, sympathy, and faith all rest on forces, however they may be understood, that no person can bring into being merely by dint of rational deliberation and effortful conscious willing.[3] In the seventeenth century this realm of passively won qualities of the soul was called the realm of spirit or the realm of grace.

The parallel can be carried a step further. What happens, Farber asks, to the man "who turns for help to his will to achieve those qualities of being that

2. Farber, *Ways of the Will*, 1–25, quotations on pp. 7, 9, 11.

3. *Ibid.*, 15. See the similar conclusions in May, *Love and Will*, 194–245, 278–286. Farber's excellent list can be extended, of course. In the 17th century Thomas Shepard used strikingly similar rhetorical style to describe the condition of a man without divine assistance: "Look upon a man quite forsaken of God in Hell, there you may see as in a lively looking-glass what every man living is when the Lord leaves him: he can blaspheme him, he cannot love him, he can contemn God, he cannot esteem him: he can wish there were no God to punish him: he cannot submit unto God, though he leaves the most heavy load upon him, and you see not your selves untill you see your selves here, and see your selves thus." Cf. also the important discussion of the fallacies of Pelagianism in Passmore, *Perfectibility of Man*, 287–289.

cannot be achieved, or even approached, by means of [conscious] will?" The answer is that "eventually it is will itself that increasingly becomes his experience, until the private voice of subjectivity and the public occasions from life that might raise this voice are almost stifled, if not silenced. . . . *What is* in his experience gives way to *what should be,* as decreed by his [conscious] will." And those other powers "that cannot or should not be willed" become gradually atrophied.[4] But it must not be forgotten that these two realms—of will as rational appetite on the one hand, and will as "heart" on the other—are interdependent, so that it can be an equal danger to betray "the objectifications" that the rational will is capable of. It was the past achievements and the real promise of such objectifications of conscious will that the intellectualists rightly were most concerned to protect and emphasize.

4. It is perhaps a symptom of our present straits and a validation of Farber's thesis about the pathology of the will, that all of the good words formerly available to describe happy and healthy passivity—such as patience, sufferance, passion—have subtly changed meanings, so that there is no longer a traditional vocabulary of spiritual waiting. Yet there are many signs in the past quarter-century of American life that a swing in the other direction is under way.

Some Suggestions for
Further Research

There are two things that any sane author of a history book knows better than an outsider can possibly know: the deficiencies of his own work when measured by all the tasks, all the research and reading, that he did not do but might have done; and second, his utter dependence on the preceding work of other historians for most of his information and for most of his understanding of his subject. One way that these two truths may be made more explicit is through a bibliography, where the author exposes his debts to the scholarship and ideas of others. Such a bibliography may also serve to highlight, perhaps inadvertently, much of what has been left undone.

I know all too acutely what I have left undone in this study and what I owe to the books and articles of other historians. Most of the documentation for this volume is recorded in the footnotes, however, and it would be pointless as well as onerous to repeat the same titles in a bibliography. In addition, my dissertation, "Moral Philosophy in America, 1700 to 1750, and Its British Context" (Ph.D. diss., Columbia University, 1969), contains a list of some of the more general titles pertaining to philosophy in early America that may not have been mentioned in the footnotes to this book. Other titles are listed in the bibliography to my forthcoming volume, *Jonathan Edwards's Moral Thought and Its British Context*. I intend to use this space, then, only to make a few remarks about research methods and opportunities in areas related to the present work. Several of the suggestions presented here I have developed more fully in an earlier article, "Early American Philosophy vs. Philosophy in Early America," which appeared in the *Transactions of the Charles S. Peirce Society*, XIII (1977), 216–237.

The single most important advance that could occur in studies of seventeenth-century theology and philosophy is also the one least likely to occur: namely, that all of the major Latin works of the period be translated into English. Given the hopelessness of such an undertaking, one could wish for dozens of reliable secondary studies based squarely on the huge Latin literature of the age. At present, only a small piece of the continent of early modern Scholastic writing has been explored. Even in the case of the Puritans, who would seem to have been analyzed to death, the Latin background of their philosophical theology—in effect, their reading in the Latin works of their time—has not been adequately examined. The Puritan mind, therefore, is perhaps not known quite so well in its esoteric reaches as is usually supposed.

A second desideratum if there is to be growth in the study of early American intellectual history is that the context of the subject be considerably broadened. An underlying premise of the present book has been that nearly everything philosophical and theological that New Englanders said was derived from teaching that originated overseas, either in Britain or on the Continent. Even if one chooses to assume that the character of "American" thought in this period is distinctive in its selectivity—which I do not really assume—the substance is still entirely derivative. All that the historian can do is to trace the progress or the dialectic of essentially borrowed ideas. By taking a single commencement thesis or several that are related, one can reconstruct the elements of a contemporary philosophical argument. These elements will not be found, however, in anything indigenous to the American scene but rather in the wider European literature. In the realm of ideas uniqueness or origi- nality is generally rare, and it was particularly rare in colonial America. But even to appreciate these rarities and to know them precisely, it is necessary to begin with a broad context. Historians of ideas in early America should thus be striving to get a better grasp of the background of their subject by reading more widely.

The present volume can hardly be said to have exhausted the possibilities for the study of seventeenth-century moral philosophy, and more could un- doubtedly be done also even with theology to achieve better understanding of the thought of the time as manifested in America. But two other disciplines, certainly as central to the intellectual life of seventeenth-century New England as moral philosophy and theology, remain by contrast almost virgin territory, namely logic and rhetoric. Because these disciplines in the twentieth century are mere splinters on the borders of the typical curriculum, there is a tendency to assume that they were equally peripheral and dessicated in the seventeenth or eighteenth century. And given their apparent barrenness—everyone has heard of the supposed sterility of Scholastic logic and of the alleged vacuous- ness, pomposity, insincerity, and terminological exuberance of early modern rhetoric—it might be believed that historians of colonial America have wisely skirted these wastelands. Yet logic and rhetoric were far broader subjects in the seventeenth century than they are conceived to be today, and both were deeply enmeshed in virtually every intellectual activity of the time, reli- gious and secular. Intensive investigation of their study and teaching in early America could not help but produce important results. Moreover, because these subjects were so fundamental, the systematic tracing of the evolution of logic and rhetoric can serve as a sensitive gauge of intellectual change in the seventeenth and eighteenth centuries, providing more precise determinations of developments in the realm of thought and understanding than most of the other measures that historians rely on.

The close investigation of the study and teaching of logic and rhetoric in early America would require the researcher to make use of manuscript and archival sources similar to those used in this book on moral philosophy: commencement broadsides, lecture notes, student commonplace books, antiquated textbooks or the student cribs taken from them, academic orations, the minutes of student societies, library lists, and so on. There is not a lot of this material left from colonial America, but enough has survived in most cases to provide the basis of a story. So the fourth research opportunity I want to call attention to concerns the usefulness of the records of college teaching as sources for a better understanding of colonial intellectual life. Student notebooks may be elementary in content, but they are often immediately reflective of major trends in thought. It is one of the strangest anomalies of current historiography that the surviving documents representative of reading, learning, and discussion at eighteenth-century Harvard have hardly been touched by historians of ideas. Since it is a safe assumption that much of what one learns in college remains with one for life, the close study of the substance of college training is a useful guide to more than the minds of youths. Furthermore, since educators until the twentieth century tended to see their task as essentially conservative, the investigation of teaching in any given subject is a good corrective to the tendency of historians to overvalue the contemporary impact of "major" writers, that is, those authors who only in long retrospect come to be regarded as the leading luminaries of an age.

In summary, the canons I have tried to follow in this work and those I would recommend as fruitful guides for others interested in studying early American intellectual history are: 1) the greater use of Latin sources; 2) a definition of the subject that automatically includes the European and British context; 3) the directing of more attention to the internal history of academic disciplines, as they were interpreted at the time (not as they are interpreted now); and 4) the fuller exploitation of the resources of college archives or other repositories that contain materials indicative of collegiate intellectual life.

Index

Abbadie, Jacques, 196

Abelard, Peter: on moral philosophy, 22; on intention in ethics, 94; on intention as moral criterion, 192

Adam, Antoine: on Stoicism, 153

Adam and Eve: affections in, 163

Adams, Eliphalet: on ethics and theology, 38n

Addison, Joseph: on man as religious animal, 221n

Aesthetic sense: as distinct from desire, 202; nature of, 202

Affection: as attribute of something, 164

Affections: and temperament, 90; distinguished from passions, 90, 90n, 171, 233n; different in beasts and men, 91; and will, 117; in pietist religiosity, 158; types of, according to William Fenner, 160; benefit of mutability of, 162; carnal versus regenerate, 162; role of, in moral life, 162, in Puritan self-scrutiny, 188–189; corruption of, 163; and divine grace, 164–165; and preaching, 169; as source of action, 171; divine origin of, 171; balance of, 171–172; and reason, 173; in religion, 175; as substitute for Spirit, 178; in moral judgment, 180; distinguished from sensations, 200; equated with desires, 202; Charles Morton on, 227. *See also* Passions; Sensitive appetite

Alsted, Johann Heinrich: on organization of the disciplines, 22n; on moral philosophy, 28

Altruism: meaning of, 275n

Ames, William: on St. Thomas Aquinas, 23; opposed to Aristotle's ethics, 24; and William Perkins, 24n, 59; on Plato, 25; on theology and ethics, 25; Karl Reuter on, 25n; attacks secular ethics, 25–26, 25n; John Eusden on, 27; Cotton Mather on, 28; influence of, in 17th century, 28; *Marrow of Theology* read at Harvard and Yale, 28n; in

relation to Alexander Richardson and Peter Ramus, 43n; on the arts and theology, 48; on *prisca theologia*, 48n; on practical theology, 48, 239; and example of Socrates, 50n; on conscience, 55, 120; and Scholasticism, 59, 125; on natural goodness, 61; on Original Sin, 61; on synteresis, 61; on virtue as habit, 61n, 93; on will, 61n, 104, 110n, 128; defense of, in New England, 63; on happiness, 76; and Franco Burgersdyck, 86n; and Adrian Heereboord, 87n; on inward versus outward virtue, 94; on will and goodness, 94; on will and intellect, 108, 120–125; Perry Miller on, 121; and Augustinian voluntarism, 138; and Petrus van Mastricht, 140; on pneumatology, 211; and Theophilus Gale, 281

Amyraldism: in New England, 126

Amyraut, Moise: as intellectualist, 112n; influence of, in New England, 126n; on right reason, 286

Analysis: defined, 45n

Andrewes, Lancelot: on natural moral understanding, 13–14

Angelology: Charles Morton on, 218

Angels: Eustache on, 80; and pneumatology, 213–214; study of, defended, 215n; passions in, 273; and psychological theory, 274

Anger: as basic passion, 179

Animals: souls in, 221–222

Anselm, St.: as Augustinian, 117

Appetite. *See* Sensitive appetite; Rational appetite

Apprehension: as stage in analysis of moral action, 229

Aquinas, St. Thomas: on natural moral understanding, 13; William Ames on, 23; on synteresis, 53; as guide to Puritan thought, 66; on happiness, 75; and Eustache, 80; on passions, 83, 199; on love in God, 84; on